WHO HATH OUR RE

**A BIBLICAL AND HISTORICAL
DEFENSE OF THE ANGLO-ISRAEL
MESSAGE THROUGH THE LIVES,
TESTIMONIES AND MINISTRIES OF
MANY OUTSTANDING MEN OF GOD!
*IN TRUTH THEY CAN SAY:***

***"I WAS NOT DISOBEDIENT UNTO THE
HEAVENLY VISION"***
Acts 26:19

Charles A. Jennings

Editor of **TRUTH IN HISTORY** *Magazine*

Printed in the United States of America

ISBN 13: 978-0-9829817-1-9
ISBN 10: 0-9829817-1-9

*The chapters in this book outlining the lives and testimonies
of the various ministers and their belief in the Anglo-Israel
message were originally written as individual booklets.   This
accounts for some repetition in the text and the format of the
book.*
*The sentence structure, spelling and grammar of each
respective author were retained as it was in their original treatise.*

Published by
TRUTH IN HISTORY

An Outreach of
KINGDOM TREASURE MINISTRIES
P.O. Box 808
Owasso, Oklahoma 74055-0808

www.truthinhistory.org

This book is dedicated to the thousands of saints who have faithfully proclaimed the Gospel of the Kingdom of God unto their generation, as *"a witness unto all* [Israel] *nations."*

And to

My father, Clarence G. Jennings whose love for the Kingdom of God and his dedication to God's Word, is his richest legacy to his children. He was my greatest mentor.

And to

Pastor George W. Southwick whose long life and ministry was one *"who followed the Lamb whithersoever He goest."* His treasured friendship of 25 years still serves as an inspiration to me. The theme of his ministry was the Words of Jesus; *"my doctrine is not mine, but His that sent me."* John 7:16

~~~~~~~~~~~

"A life of learning is not lost . . . For we take with us the gathering of His eternal Word for the furtherance of His Coming."
George W. Southwick

CONTENTS

PENTECOST - ITS TRUE
BIBLICAL CALLING
By Charles A. Jennings

THE SNARE

Has the traditional Pentecostal movement failed to fulfill its God given mission? Has modern Pentecost been side tracked from the beginning by the previous religious affiliations of its leaders?

Did the stronger personalities present in the early 20th century outpouring capitalize on this new wave of glory to promote themselves into a position of ecclesiastical power? Did the newly formed denominations with their respective doctrinal boundaries actually usurp the headship of Jesus Christ over His church?

As the administrator of the Body of Christ; was the Holy Ghost restricted by human personalities in the revelation of truth? Was the Spirit of God limited in its operation mainly just to the visible, audible and emotional manifestations that satisfied the hunger of the human heart and the curiosity of the mind?

Why has the 20th century Pentecostal phenomenon fallen far short of the first Pentecostal experience as recorded in the Book of Acts? Has it been because of the many religious differences resulting in the various factions within the greater movement, or has it been high-jacked by self-seeking men who saw their opportunity to ride the religious wave to power and popularity?

No doubt these questions and many other factors have played a major rule in hampering the growth of the Pentecostal movement into full maturity and thus failing to fulfill the God-given purpose for which the Holy Ghost was poured out at this time in history.

Much confusion has resulted over the constant emphasis on so-called Bible prophecy in the modern church today. Walking the aisles of your average Christian Book store, one can get the impression that 'Bible' prophecy is now a very lucrative market. The popularity of prophecy is at an all-time high. There are hundreds of prophecy books, television and radio programs, prophecy clubs, conferences and a wide variety of other publications dealing with what they consider important end-time events. Some national media ministries are constantly promoting their latest 'must have' videos dealing with their favorite and most marketable prophecy subjects. This fad is nothing new in the American church world, but we certainly can say it is now at an all-time high with profit$

to match. No doubt, the modern church has more *"prophets for profit"* than any previous time in history.

A popular prophecy fiction series brought multiplied millions of dollars into the pockets of both the authors and publishers. The marketing schemes for these pseudo-prophecy books were overwhelming. The story plot in these and many other so-called end-time prophecy books are built on an entirely false premise of Bible interpretation. Yet millions of Christians in the Western World continue to support with their presence and their pocket book, the purveyors of prophetic falsehood. The advertisers in the secular market discovered a long time ago that *sex sells*. Well, the advertisers in the religious market have discovered that *fear of the future* coupled with 'Christian blood and guts' also sells.

The prophetic interpretation known as *Futurism* is not only popular and profitable, but holds millions of sincere Christians in abject ignorance of the true prophetic message of Scripture. Their minds are locked into thought patterns such as; 1) the modern Israeli Zionist state is the center of all prophetic events, 2) the 175 year old secret rapture of the church doctrine, 3) the hideous events of the coming 'great tribulation' of Daniel's 70th week (which was completely fulfilled 2000 years ago), 4) the one man antichrist who is going to rule the world, and other man made ideas with roots going back to the 16th and 17th century Counter-Reformation conducted by the Jesuit Order of the Roman Catholic Church.

Most prophecy teachers have discovered that *'current events'* type prophecy is more lucrative and appealing to the masses than the great verities of the real plan of God that are found in the Old Testament. The 2000 years of church history since Pentecost are also relegated to the 'cold case file' never to be considered as relevant to what is transpiring in our world today. Even political correctness now dictates what some church leaders can or cannot talk about in a public setting. *Sensitivity preaching* has finally reached the modern pulpit which controls the men who once committed themselves to preach the Word of God without fear or favor.

There are some real serious questions that the modern church has for to long completely ignored. What does the last 2000 years of Christian History prove to us concerning the workings of God in the earth? Are the people of Western Europe, Canada and America mentioned in the Bible? Should Christians be looking for a 'hole in the sky' whereby to escape this present evil world and shirk their God-given responsibility in proclaiming the Lordship of Jesus Christ over all the kingdoms of this world? Where is the location of the kingdom of heaven, New Jerusalem and the throne of David? Are they on some planet a million miles from here or on this renovated and perfected earth?

Unfortunately, the early Pentecostal forefathers of the 20th century fell prey to the interpretational errors of Dispensationalism. The vast number of God's Pentecostal sheep people has been snared by the devouring wolf of the false prophetic system of John Nelson Darby and C. I. Scofield. This fresh outpouring of the Spirit of God, at the most crucial time in history, could have brought the greatest revelation of spiritual understanding, had it not been for the snare of Dispensational theology.

Over one hundred years later the Pentecostal movement still has not received the full truth of the manifestation of who Jesus Christ is according to I Timothy 3:16. The Apostle Paul said that *"God was manifested in the flesh."* This clearly proves the Old Testament teaching of monotheism that Jesus was God in the flesh. Yet, still most Pentecostal teachers take serious issue with the revelation that Jesus Christ was the fulness of God in His flesh (Col. 2:9) and in His multiple and timeless manifestations is the totality of the Godhead in His deity.

Modern Pentecost still has not accepted the revelation of the true identification of the House of Israel and the House of Judah. Its theological authorities have convinced the masses of the sheep that the Jewish people comprise all twelve tribes of Israel. This unproven supposition has led Pentecostalism down the dark path of theological confusion, abdication of spiritual authority, vast ignorance of Biblical knowledge and has helped in creating cultural and political chaos.

The Apostle John tells us that the true *Spirit of Prophecy* is the testimony of Jesus Christ (Rev.19:10). The major emphasis of the ancient Hebrew prophets was rebuking the people because of their sins, calling the nation of Israel back to the terms of the covenant, the proclamation of the coming Kingdom of God on earth and the promise of a coming Redeemer for the people of Israel (Luke 1:67-79).

The Spirit filled prophetic office for this new covenant age should be **1)** the message of Peter when he declared *"Therefore let all the house of Israel know assuredly, that God hath made that same Jesus, whom ye have crucified, both Lord and Christ"* (Acts 2:36) **2)** the message of the angel that *"He [Jesus] shall be great, and shall be called the Son of the Highest: and the Lord God shall give unto him the throne of his father David: And he shall reign over the house of Jacob for ever; and of his kingdom there shall be no end"* (Luke 1:32-33) and **3)** the message of James that *"After this I will return, and will build again the tabernacle*

3

of David, which is fallen down; and I will build again the ruins thereof, and I will set it up" (Acts 15:16).

True prophetic voices have and are now declaring **1)** the supreme Lordship of Jesus Christ; **2)** the true identification of the House of Jacob and the Throne of David; **3)** the work of the Holy Ghost in rebuilding the Tabernacle of David and **4)** the soon return of Jesus Christ in power and glory to possess His eternal kingdom on this earth.

THE PROMISE - Isaiah 44:1-5

One of the most gracious gifts that the Lord ever promised to give His people Israel is found in the Book of Isaiah. By divine inspiration this prophet saw beyond the captivities into an age of hope and comfort, when he declared; *"Yet now hear, O Jacob my servant; and Israel, whom I have chosen: Thus saith the LORD that made thee, and formed thee from the womb, which will help thee; Fear not, O Jacob, my servant; and thou, Jesurun, whom I have chosen. For I will pour water upon him that is thirsty, and floods upon the dry ground: I will pour my spirit upon thy seed, and my blessing upon thine offspring: And they shall spring up as among the grass, as willows by the water courses. One shall say, I am the LORD'S; and another shall call himself by the name of Jacob; and another shall subscribe with his hand unto the LORD, and surname himself by the name of Israel"* (Isa. 44:1-5).

The Lord continued His pleasant speech unto the family of Jacob by renumerating His peculiar relationship with them. The Lord proclaimed to be *"the King of Israel and his redeemer."* The Lord then reinforces His promise *to* Israel and His relationship *with* Israel by identifying Himself as; *"I am the first, and I am the last; and beside me there is no God"* (Isa. 44:6). By this declarative statement, it was reminding Israel of their peculiar marriage bond with their husband YHWH which was established at the foot of Mt. Sinai some 700 years before as recorded in Exodus chapters19-24.

Therefore, the outpouring of God's Spirit upon the House of Jacob/Israel would take place under the authority of the kingship of their God. It would also be an expression of the redemptive nature of their husband to bring them back to a relationship that Israel

4

once had with Him in her youth. Yet, it would be absolutely imperative for two major events to take place before Israel as a national body of people could or would return to her God and once again enjoy the relationship as a Bride to her Husband. The bill of divorcement that God issued to His covenant nation of Israel brought about an irreparable separation for over 700 years that was impossible for man to restore. Only by the divine initiative of God Himself could his condition of spiritual separation be healed.

THE FEAST OF PASSOVER

The first required event in order to reconcile national Israel back to her husband in a covenant marriage relationship was the Passover. The Passover lamb was the purchase price that was paid for Israel's deliverance out of Egypt and the crossing of the Red Sea. The Lord told Israel that *"the blood shall be to you for a token upon the houses where ye are"* (Ex. 12:13). The blood was a 'token' over the household, but the act of deliverance and the crossing of the Red Sea was purely a supernatural act of God. Based on this act of deliverance, the Lord then had legal right to initiate a Master/servant and a husband/wife relationship with Israel. This was the principle upon which the Lord based the Ten Commandments when He stated; *"I am the LORD thy God, which have brought thee out of the land of Egypt, out of the house of bondage. Thou shalt have no other gods before me"* (Ex. 20:2-3).

Without the Passover in Egypt there never would have been a Pentecost at Mt. Sinai. Passover and Pentecost were inseparable and interlocking events in Old Testament history and theology. In establishing a covenantal relationship with the national family of Israel, the deliverance of Passover would have been incomplete and served no purpose without the marriage of Pentecost at Mt. Sinai. The covenantal marriage of Pentecost would have never occurred without first the divine act of Passover.

God's relationship with either an individual or His people Israel is always predicated first upon the offering of a sacrifice involving the shedding of blood. The writer of Hebrews plainly states; *"Whereupon neither the first testament was dedicated without blood. For when Moses had spoken every precept to all the people according to the law, he took the blood of calves and of goats, with water, and scarlet wool, and hyssop, and sprinkled both the book, and all the people, Saying, This is the blood of the testament which God hath enjoined unto you.*

Moreover he sprinkled with blood both the tabernacle, and all the vessels of the ministry. And almost all things are by the law purged with blood; and without shedding of blood is no remission" (Heb. 9:18-22). The series of Assyrian captivities which took place between 745 B.C. and 721 B.C. were the means whereby the Lord, Israel's husband, divorced and sent her away because of her unfaithfulness. The weeping prophet proclaimed: *"The LORD said also unto me in the days of Josiah the king, Hast thou seen that which backsliding Israel hath done? She is gone up upon every high mountain and under every green tree, and there hath played the harlot. And I said after she had done all these things, Turn thou unto me. But she returned not. And her treacherous sister Judah saw it. And I saw, when for all the causes whereby backsliding Israel committed adultery I had put her away, and given her a bill of divorce; yet her treacherous sister Judah feared not, but went and played the harlot also"* (Jer. 3:6-8).

This was the destruction of the kingdom that the prophet referred to when he declared: *"Behold, the eyes of the Lord GOD are upon the sinful kingdom, and I will destroy it from off the face of the earth; saving that I will not utterly destroy the house of Jacob, saith the LORD"* (Amos 9:8). The 'Kingdom' referred to the national political, economic and social structure, yet the House of Jacob; referring to Jacob's physical offspring would not be destroyed. The Lord made Himself very clear concerning His preservation of the 'House of Israel' by saying, *"For, lo, I will command, and I will sift the house of Israel among all nations, like as corn is sifted in a sieve, yet shall not the least grain fall upon the earth"* (Amos 9:9).

This prophecy definitely referred to the Northern Kingdom of Israel and not the Southern Kingdom of Judah. (Read Amos 7:10-15). The prophet Amos lived long before the Assyrian captivities took place, yet he predicted their future occurrence. The destruction of the kingdom had to take place in order to scatter the people 'among all nations'. This corresponds with the prophecy of Hosea in the naming of his first son Jezreel, which means to scatter. When seed is scattered, it is sown, therefore increases in its production in bringing forth a harvest. This is what happened in the sowing of the children of Israel in the West when they migrated throughout the European continent, the British Isles and the North American continent. During the 775 years between the first captivity and the death of their Redeemer, they were *"the lost sheep of the House of Israel"* (Matt. 10:6; 15:24).

This 'House of Jacob/Israel' that had been scattered became paganized or gentilized while in their wayward condition. In their rebellion and lawlessness, while in their dispersion, they lost their identity which they had as the chosen family of God which they once knew while living in the land of Canaan. The prophet Amos told the people that their punishment from the Lord was actually based on the fact that they were the only family God had known. The Lord said to Israel; *"You only have I known of all the families of the earth: therefore I will punish you for all your iniquities"* (Amos 3:2). The Apostle Paul aptly described them in the following terms. *"Wherefore remember, that ye being in time past Gentiles in the flesh, who are called Uncircumcision by that which is called the Circumcision in the flesh made by hands; That at that time ye were without Christ, being aliens from the commonwealth of Israel, and strangers from the covenants of promise, having no hope, and without God in the world:"* (Eph. 2:11-12).

This lost condition necessitated a redeemer to restore unfaithful Israel back to her husband. It was to these same Israelites that were once 'aliens' that Paul said; *"But now in Christ Jesus ye who sometimes were far off are made nigh by the blood of Christ"* (Eph. 2:13).

The Biblical concept of redemption involves mainly two parties; the redeemed and the redeemer. Paul the Apostle was referring strictly to the family of Jacob/Israel when he wrote to the Galatians and declared; *"But when the fulness of the time was come, God sent forth his Son, made of a woman, made under the law, To redeem them that were under the law, that we might receive the adoption of sons"* (Gal. 4:4-5). Jesus came to redeem a people that were once under the Law. Only Israel had been under the Law. The word 'redeem' means "to buy back, recover as by paying a fee." A person cannot redeem something that was not previously theirs. Jesus Christ 'paid the fee' by the sacrifice of His own blood to buy back the wife that He had once known in her youth.

The Lord first married Israel at Mt. Sinai which was the first Pentecost, then divorced her because of her adultery, but at Calvary paid the price for her redemption. Jesus Christ, who as Kinsman Redeemer then had the legal right to remarry Israel at the New Testament Feast of Pentecost fifty days after paying the supreme price on Calvary.

The first of these two events to reconcile Israel back to God would be the sacrificial death of Jesus Christ at Calvary. The two fold purpose of the death of our Lord Jesus (Israel's God) would be for **1)** *the atonement of sin* and **2)** *the ratification of the New Covenant*. While at the communion table with His disciples, Matthew records that Jesus *"took the cup, and gave thanks, and gave it to them, saying, Drink ye all of it; For this is my blood of the new testament, which is shed for many for the remission of sins"* (Matt. 26:27-28). The death of Jesus for the

7

atonement of sin is often emphasized in Gospel preaching, but the ratification of the New Covenant is largely ignored. When Jesus paid the full redemptive price by the sacrifice of Himself at Calvary, He satisfied the demands of the Mosaic Law which gave Him the legal right to remarry His wayward wife, Israel. Even though at Calvary the price was fully paid, that relationship with Israel was not yet restored. There yet had to be a reunion and reconciliation between the two estranged parties.

THE FEAST OF PENTECOST

The second of these two required events would be the outpouring of the Holy Ghost on the day of Pentecost as recorded in Acts chapter two. This event was fifty days after Passover when Jesus died, thus fulfilling the Old Testament pattern as seen in the book of Exodus. The high water mark of Israel's history in the Old Testament was the Exodus out of Egypt and the giving of the Law at Mt. Sinai fifty days later. Several Hebrew prophets reflected on these two events in their rebuke of Israel and her sins. The grievous complaint of the Lord against Israel throughout her history was that she had transgressed the terms of the marriage covenant that she had made after accepting the marriage vows with YHWH, her husband. The Scripture records; *"And Moses came and told the people all the words of the LORD, and all the judgments: and all the people answered with one voice, and said, All the words which the LORD hath said will we do. And Moses wrote all the words of the LORD, and rose up early in the morning, and builded an altar under the hill, and twelve pillars, according to the twelve tribes of Israel"* (Ex. 24:3-4).

This was a part of the marriage ceremony when Israel as a chosen nation was betrothed to her husband. Israel vowed a vow that she would perform all the words that the Lord had spoken. This betrothal vow and promise of obedience to the Law of God was legally binding not only on the generation that heard God's voice and saw the burning of Mt. Sinai, but on every succeeding generation of Israelites. A personal vow made between an individual and the Lord is binding only on that individual, but not on his or her succeeding generations. When a nation makes an official covenantal vow unto God, not only the present, but the succeeding generations are also held responsible for the terms of that covenant.

At the first Pentecost, there were ten elements involved in the making of the first marriage covenant between Israel and the Lord God her husband as seen in Exodus 24:

8

1. Worship   24:1-2
2. Vow of betrothal   24:3, 7
3. Inscription of Law   24:7,12
4. The people   24:2,3
5. An Altar   24:4
6. Shedding of blood   24:4,7,12
7. Feasting   24:9-11
8. The mediator – Moses   24:1, 2, 3
9. Ministers – Witnesses   24:9
10. A display of God's Glory   24:12-18

There was only one Exodus and one original Passover in the Old Testament. Each subsequent Passover commemoration was a reflection of and a reminder of the first Passover. The same holds true for that first Pentecost held at the foot of Mt. Sinai. Each subsequent Pentecost was only a reflection of the first. That first Passover delivered Israel from Egypt, but it was the Pentecost experience that created the marriage relationship between Israel and her Husband. When the Lord delivered His people from Egypt, He made the demand that they make a one time application of the blood of the Passover lamb to the door of their houses. Once this deliverance took place, this was a one time event that could not be undone once it was performed by the sovereign, miraculous design and power of God. This event became the high water mark of all Old Testament history.

Pentecost was different in that it was here the people were made a bilateral partner in the whole ceremony in acknowledgement and acceptance of the Law. This was in essence the national constitution whereby Israel was legally obligated to live by. The Assyrian and Babylonian captivities were not the result of violating any Passover agreement, but violation of the Feast of Pentecost with its binding covenantal agreements.

In showing that this covenant was binding on all succeeding generations, about 800 years after the first Pentecost, Jeremiah spoke the words of God to the people saying ; *"Hear ye the words of this covenant, and speak unto the men of Judah, and to the inhabitants of Jerusalem;   And say thou unto them, Thus saith the LORD God of Israel; Cursed be the man that obeyeth not the words of this covenant,*

9

Which I commanded your fathers in the day that I brought them forth out of the land of Egypt, from the iron furnace, saying, Obey my voice, and do them, according to all which I command you: so shall ye be my people, and I will be your God: That I may perform the oath which I have sworn unto your fathers, to give them a land flowing with milk and honey, as it is this day. Then answered I, and said, So be it, O LORD.

Then the LORD said unto me, Proclaim all these words in the cities of Judah, and in the streets of Jerusalem, saying, Hear ye the words of this covenant, and do them. For I earnestly protested unto your fathers in the day that I brought them up out of the land of Egypt, even unto this day, rising early and protesting, saying, Obey my voice. Yet they obeyed not, nor inclined their ear, but walked every one in the imagination of their evil heart: therefore I will bring upon them all the words of this covenant, which I commanded them to do; but they did them not" (Jer. 11:2-8).

CALVARY AND THE OUTPOURING OF THE HOLY GHOST

The high water mark of New Testament history was the incarnation of God in flesh, in the person of Jesus Christ. In fact the focal point of all world history was the death and resurrection of Jesus. The second most important and influential supernatural event into the affairs of men was the outpouring of the Holy Ghost as recorded in Acts chapter 2.

What was the purpose of this Spirit outpouring? What actually happened in the furtherance of the fulfillment of God's overall plan in the earth? Both John the Baptist and Jesus came preaching the same message of repentance. Their call to the people was for 'repentance', because the kingdom of heaven; literally the Kingdom of Israel was now going to be restored. They preached, *"Repent ye: For the Kingdom of Heaven is at hand"* (Matt. 3:2; 4:17).

Why was this such a pertinent message of the hour? The reason was because the kingdom that God had established with the Jacob/Israel family in the Old Testament had fallen into disrepair. God's kingdom, at the time of Jesus' first coming, was in shambles, because of utter transgression from within and fierce enemies from without. It was in serious need of restoration.

In Abraham, the embryonic stage of God's kingdom started with just one man. Then it grew into a family with Isaac and Jacob. As time progressed it expanded into twelve tribal families and took on **nation status** under Moses. With Moses as mediator and under the

10

administration of the Aaronic priesthood, it was given a binding constitution of Laws. The words of the Lord to Israel were; *"And ye shall be unto me a kingdom of priests, and an holy nation. These are the words which thou shalt speak unto the children of Israel"* (Ex. 19:6). It was under King David when the nation of Israel took on official **kingdom status**. Through the prophet Nathan, the Lord spoke to David and said, *"And thine house and thy kingdom shall be established for ever before thee: thy throne shall be established for ever"* (II Sam. 7:16).

God's plan for restoration of His Israelite kingdom would now be under the terms of the New Covenant, with Jesus Christ as the new mediator and the Holy Ghost as the administrator. At the first Pentecost, it was the giving of the Law, but at the New Covenant Pentecost it was the giving of the Holy Ghost. Once it was Moses, now it is Jesus. Once it was Law and now it is Spirit.

Generally, within the wide range of belief concerning the identification of Israel during this New Testament dispensation, there are three proposed options.

1. *The Jews are Israel* – Overall, the people of the Jews have not accepted the atonement of Calvary, nor have they been the recipients of the Pentecostal outpouring of God's Spirit. The writer of Hebrews made it clear that the New Covenant has already been made with the House of Israel and the House of Judah (Heb. 8:7-13). There is no Biblical or historical evidence that this New Covenant has been made with the Jews.

2. *The Church is Israel* – Taking into consideration the many spiritual and material blessings promised to natural Israel, it would be completely illogical that the church would fulfill all the Old Testament promises given to Israel. Jesus told the Pharisees that the kingdom would be taken from them and *"given to a nation* [not the church] *bringing forth the fruits thereof"* (Matt. 21:43).

3. *The Anglo-Saxon people are Israel* – Historically, it has been the Anglo-Saxon and related people located in the western world that have accepted both the provisions of the supreme Passover sacrifice of Calvary and the outpouring of the Holy Ghost. It is obvious to any serious and honest student of Scripture and history that the Gospel came west in its expansion from Jerusalem. Then from these same people of the west, the Gospel has been taken to *"all the families of the earth."*

11

With the distracting influence of Dispensationalism and Futurism which were being strongly promoted in the early twentieth century, most Pentecostal leaders failed to be fully open to the revelation of *"all things"* (John 14:26). Instead of accepting this genuine outpouring as a fresh awakening into an era of further revelation knowledge, they soon became occupied with defending their former sectarian views and forming religious denominations. Centuries of time have proven that denominations are the graveyards of fresh revelations of spiritual truth.

In this book are the testimonies of many men of God who were willing to throw off the restraints of former religious affiliations when confronted with a living truth from the Word of God. They had an ear to hear what the Spirit was saying to the churches. These were common men who faced the carnal struggles of life; some endured severe rejection from ministerial peers, yet accepted and believed an unpopular truth, regardless of the price they had to pay.

I am convinced that the Anglo-Israel message, in its purity, is a Bible based truth that will yet impact the Body of Christ and the secular world with the spiritual force exceeding that of the Protestant Reformation. This truth has been rejected and maligned by modern ecclesiasticalism, but it is yet to break forth as the dawning of a new day. This great understanding will be an integral part of the future *"manifestation of the sons of God"* when *"the whole creation,"* including both Israel and all races of mankind will *"be delivered from the bondage of corruption"* (Rom. 8:19-23).

~~~~~~~~~~~~~~~~~~~~~

It would be impossible to list all the men and women, ministers and laymen who have believed and taught the message of the Kingdom of God, which incorporates the Anglo-Israel truth of Scripture. The people mentioned in this book are only a small percentage of those who dedicated their lives to this truth. They represent many religious backgrounds and experiences from all persuasions of the Christian faith, yet united together in one common belief: their discovery that the 'lost' House of Israel has been found. Unfortunately, in spite of the volumes of favorable evidence, modern church historians completely ignore this Biblical truth in preference to their popular traditions of men.

12

THE FUTURE OF ISRAEL AND JUDAH

Joseph Wild, D.D

INTRODUCTION

By Charles A. Jennings

In keeping with His faithfulness, the Lord raises up stalwart servants in each age that are willing to resist the spiritual apathy taking place around them, to fulfill their calling to present the truth without fear or favor. During the nineteenth century, Satan and his emissaries were putting forth a concerted effort to destroy this nation and its Christian foundations. Notwithstanding, the Lord was watching over His Covenant Word to guard it from being totally silenced by the sinister forces at work. As a prophetic voice to our nation concerning its marriage covenant with our God based upon Exodus 19:1-8; 24:1-8, many anointed men of God were proclaiming the truth of the national message of Scripture as a witness to our people.

One such anointed servant of God was Dr. Joseph Wild. A native of England, he was born on November 16, 1834 at Summit, Littleborough, in Lancashire. As a young man, he first entered the ministry with the **Primitive Methodist Church** at the early age of sixteen years old, where he served as an itinerant preacher. At the age of twenty-one, he emigrated from his native land to the United States, where he traveled throughout the South and West holding religious meetings as a preacher and lecturer. After this two year phase of his ministry, he accepted the

13

pastorate of a **Methodist Episcopal Church** located at Hamilton, Ontario, where he remained for one year.

Feeling his need for further Biblical education, Joseph Wild enrolled in a three year course of theology at the **Biblical Institute** of Concord, New Hampshire. Returning to Canada, he ministered at Goderich, Ontario, and after one year went to Orono, Maine. Following a two year stay in Maine, he returned to Canada to accept another Methodist pastorate in Belleville, Ontario. While there, he also served as professor of Oriental languages and secretary of the treasury at Albert University.

In 1870, Joseph Wild received his Doctorate of Divinity degree from Wesleyan University in Ohio. In 1872, he accepted the pastoral charge of another Methodist church in Brooklyn, New York, remaining there for three years. In order to avoid the itinerant system, he accepted the position as pastor of **Union Congregational Church** in Brooklyn for about six years. Returning to Canada in 1881, he was called to serve as pastor of the **Bond Street Congregational Church** of Toronto, Ontario remaining there for many years. Dr. Wild became a very popular preacher of God's Word and was known throughout Ontario. The church increased in attendance where it became the largest regular Congregation in the whole of Canada. His Sunday sermons were published in the *"Canadian Advance"* and were circulated in Great Britain, Australia, as well as in Canada.

Dr. Wild was a personal friend of Dr. John Alexander Dowie of Zion, Illinois. By invitation of Dr. Wild, Dowie conducted an evangelistic healing service in the Toronto church. Dr. Wild was a strong believer in the doctrine of the new birth, divine healing and the Anglo-Israel message of the Bible as well as all the other great truths of God's Word. Being a well known and eloquent preacher of the Gospel, he spoke the profound truths of Holy Writ with passion and conviction to capacity crowds of over 3,000 people each week. His sermons were often printed in the *"Toronto Evening News."*

In his effort to present the full counsel of God to the people of the Western World, Dr. Wild expounded the national message of Scripture along with the Anglo-Israel truth in an effort to awaken the people to their national origin and destiny. Being a prolific writer, he authored *"The Lost Ten Tribes"* (1878); *"How and When the World Will End"* (1879); *"The Future of Israel and Judah"* (1879); *"Talks For The Times"* (1886) and *"Songs of the Sanctuary"* (1886).

The following text is from excerpts of Dr. Wild's book, ***"The Lost Ten Tribes."*** In his book, he so adequately presents the truth of Scripture that the Anglo-Saxon, Germanic and related people are the true genetic descendants of Jacob/Israel of ancient Hebrew history.

The Lost Ten Tribes

When I first entered the ministry, I made up my mind that I would try and thoroughly understand the Scriptures. I soon found that a large portion was of a prophetic nature. I set to work according to the usual method, but to my sorrow I soon discovered that the method and rules in general use for Scripture exegesis, among what they called orthodox authors, were very defective and unsatisfactory. The fact was forced upon me that the true method, or key of interpretation, was not in use. I was always persuaded that the Bible was a unit, and that the principles contained in such a unit were beautifully related; and because of such a faith, I wondered more and more as I grew older why we had not a better key of interpretation. Men spiritualized at random, without any kind of rule, except their own fancy. In this manner they expounded the material history of the Old Testament. The whole arrangement was a Babel.

I had faintly discerned that the Scriptures made a distinction between the House of Israel and the House of Judah, and that the prophecies belonging to one could not, in fairness, be applied to the other; and that some prophecies applied to both. It always seemed strange to me, that the people which God said He has chosen for Himself should not be known. The Jews were always known, but where was "Israel, His inheritance?" Again, I could see no point in the Lord swearing so positively about David's seed and throne lasting to the end of time. Taking them in a typical sense, they were about the poorest types that could have been selected, because of the shortness of their existence, according to the general mode of interpretation.

Some three years ago I began to give a series of sermons on the Ten Lost Tribes. I soon found my own congregation, as well as the public, were interested and profited with the same, as was manifest from the large and constant attendance thereon. By personal interviews and letters, I have been gratified to learn that many have been savingly and truly converted to God through these Discourses. Especially has this been the case with those who were infidel in faith and action towards God and His Word. I have received hundreds of letters thanking me that the key of interpretation presented had made the Bible an interesting and easily understood book. The interest created gave rise to numerous requests for copies of my sermons. The notice by the public press now and again intensified the interest and increased the demand. To meet this desire I made arrangements with the editor and proprietor of a weekly paper called the *Champion* to publish my evening Discourses. At once the arrangement was found to be profitable to him, agreeable to me, and admirably suited to the public. So for more than a year the *Champion* has been my faithful messenger on this line. It is a weekly paper, published at New York. I am not personally interested more than this. With its politics and other matter I have nothing to do; but for the sermonic matter I hold myself responsible. I feel free to express my pleasure in the wonderful increase of its circulation. I am glad it goes all over the States, the Dominion of Canada, and is in goodly demand in Great Britain.

What is here made a matter of supposition, has been a solemn fact on the line of human experience. Men have studied the Bible and Providence in this ignorant and confused way. Theologians have thrown away all restraints, and well defined limitations and distinctions of the Bible in their assumed liberty of expounding and spiritualizing the same. No matter to them that there is a God-revealed distinction between Judah and Israel, Manasseh and Ephraim, Samaritans and Gentiles, and the throne of David and the throne of the heathen. Writers and speakers are guilty of using the words Judah and Israel in a synonymous sense, though the words stand for different people, history, and prophecies, soon after the descendants of Jacob settled in Palestine. To aid you in seeing this historical confusion and folly, let me call your attention to them separately.

JUDAH

What does this word stand for in the Bible? In the first place it is the name of the fourth son of Jacob. In the second place it was the name of his direct descendants or Tribe. In the third place it became the name of the portion of the country occupied by this Tribe in the Promised Land. In the fourth place it became the name of a kingdom and government; this fourth name included the Tribe of Benjamin and their territory. In the fifth place it became the name of the whole country of Palestine, and is now often so used.

On the death of Solomon the country and Tribes finally separated into two Houses, kingdoms, and governments. Nine Tribes went with Jeroboam and three with Rehoboam-namely, Judah, Levi and Benjamin. The Nine Tribed House was called Israel, and the Three Tribed House Judah. This separation was about 975 BC (I Kings 12). From that day until this these two houses have never been united; but they are to be, as scores of statements to that effect are in the good Book (Hosea 1:11). About 580 BC the House of Judah was taken captive into Babylon, remaining 70 years, then they returned to their own land, and remained until the year of our Lord 70, when Jerusalem was destroyed and they were scattered.

ISRAEL

1. A name given to Jacob after wrestling with the Angel.
2. A term applied sometimes to all the descendants of Jacob.
3. In a spiritual sense, those who believe in Christ.
4. A name that covered and included the Nine Tribes which went with Jeroboam and formed the kingdom of Israel. They remained a distinct kingdom, and til now a nationality. From 975 to 725 BC they had some nineteen kings. They were finally carried captive into Assyria by Shalmanezer (II Kings 17). From that captivity they have never returned; as a body they never can, only representatives as stated in Jeremiah 3:14, "One of a city, and two of a family".

Now prophecy points out that it was Israel that was to be lost for a while, and come to light in the latter day. They are known in the Scriptures in contradistinction from others by such terms as the following: *"All Israel," "All the House of Israel wholly," "The House of Israel," "Men of Israel,"* and God calls them His *"Servants, Witnesses, Chosen People, Inheritance, and Seed."* The lot, course, and providential portion of this people are very marked from any other, especially from the Jew, with whom they are so often confounded. The histories of the two peoples have been wide apart and as different as they well could be.

1. They were to be *lost*. 2. They were to be *divorced* from the Mosaic Law. 3. They were to lose their *name*. 4. They were to lose their *language*. 5. They were to *possess* the Isles of the sea, coasts of the earth, waste and desolate places, to inherit the portion of the Gentiles, their seed, land, and cities. 6. They are to be great and successful *colonisers*. 7. Before them other people are to *die out*. 8. They are to be a *head* nation. 9. To be a *company* of nations. 10. To be *great* in war on land or sea. 11. To be *lenders* of money. 12. To have a *monarchy*. 13. To be *keepers* of the Sabbath. 14. To have David's *Throne* and seed ruling over them. And thus I might repeat some 60 positive marks and distinctions setting forth Israel; and yet men willfully persist in confounding them with the Jews.

17

BENJAMIN

The Tribe of Benjamin has a singular and special place in the history of Israel and Judah. Neither the Old nor the New Testament can be well understood unless one understands the place of this Tribe in Providence. They were always counted one of the Ten Tribes and reckoned with them in the prophetic visions. They were only loaned to Judah about 800 years. Read I Kings 11. They were to be a light for David in Jerusalem. God, foreseeing that the Jews would reject Christ, kept back this One Tribe to be in readiness to receive Him, and so they did. At the destruction of Jerusalem they escaped, and after centuries of wanderings turned up as the proud and haughty Normans. Finally they unite with the other Tribes under William the Conqueror. A proper insight into the work and mission of Benjamin will greatly aid one in interpreting the New Testament. He was set apart as a missionary Tribe, and at once set to work to spread the Gospel of Jesus. Most of the disciples were Benjamites. Then, after 800 years of fellowship with Judah, they were cut loose and sent after their brethren of the House of Israel. It was needful that the Lion and Unicorn should unite.

EPHRAIM

This word is not only the name of Joseph's son and the Tribe, but it is used quite frequently in a generic sense and stands for the Ten Tribes and Manasseh. To Reuben by birthright was the lead politically, but it was taken from him and given to Joseph, and so to Ephraim. From Judah came the Chief Ruler- that is, Christ; but the birthright was Joseph's (I Chron. 5:1).

To the Ten Tribes the special promises of fruitfulness were given. To the Ten Tribes belongs a greater portion of prophecy; and in the history of the world more is allotted to Israel than to Judah. Indeed, the world's history pivots on the Ten Lost Tribes. I believe you know the God-revealed distinction between the words Israel and Judah. You know that they have a distinct history. Their place and work, promises and blessings, chastisements and rebukes, are as distinct and different as silver and gold.

18

THRONE OF DAVID

To this throne God pledged under oath a perpetuity. Also He pledged that someone of David's Seed should always be on it. The throne and seed are pledged an unconditional existence. This being so, it follows that they must now be in existence, and that finally all thrones will be swallowed up by this one. Queen Victoria is of David, and the English throne is David's. Hence all the promises and prophecies referring to David's throne may be found on this line. For prophecy not being of private interpretation such facts may be proven.

That in blessing I will bless thee, and in multiplying I will multiply thy seed as the stars of the heaven, and as the sand which is upon the sea shore; and thy seed shall possess the gate of his enemies;" Genesis 22:17 Under a divine oath was this prophetic promise made to Abraham. At the time it was given Abraham had, by command, offered his only son Isaac, which offering, to all human appearance, would leave the old patriarch again childless; but his faith staggered not, for human incompetence does not circumscribe the bounds of divine sufficiency. The God who commanded Abraham to offer, recalled the command at a certain stage of fulfillment, counting the faith of Abraham as righteousness. In Abraham's faith Isaac was really sacrificed; hence the divine approval: *"By myself have I sworn, saith the Lord; for because thou hath done this thing, and hast not withheld thy son, thine only son, that in blessing I will bless thee and in multiplying I will multiply thy seed as the stars of the heaven and as the sand which is upon the sea-shore; and thy seed shall possess the gate of his enemies."* Genesis 22:16-17. An oath with men in this day does not mean much in the way of confirmation, but not so with God's oath. An oath ought to be sacred, and should be the end of doubt and strife. God made a promise to Abraham, and because he could swear by no greater, He swear by Himself. And Abraham lived to see the promise begin to fulfil, and today the heirs of Abraham may look and see the same promise fulfilling, for, as Paul says in Hebrews 6:17; *"Wherein God, willing more abundantly to shew unto the heirs of promise the immutability of his counsel, confirmed it by an oath:"*

Who are the heirs of promise? For to them belong many and precious promises, both spiritual and temporal. Spiritually, they are to lead and be responsible for the evangelization of the world. Temporally, they are to be a numerous seed, a powerful people. They are to occupy the ends of the earth, the uttermost parts of the earth, the coasts of the earth, the waste and the desolate places of the earth, the isles of the sea, the heathen, as an inheritance. They are to inherit the Gentiles, and make the desolate cities to be inhabited; they are to be the chief of nations; they are to be a company of nations; they are to be a great people; they are to possess the gates of their enemies. Surely such a people should be found, for all these things make it impossible for them to be hid in a corner. One cannot help saying with the Psalmist: *"Blessed is the nation whose God is the Lord: and the people whom He hath chosen for His own inheritance."*

In the English Court of Chancery are vast sums of money, large fortunes waiting for heirs. The court frequently advertises for them, and many in every land respond and are eager to prove their claims; they are anxious to be known and accepted as the descendants and lawful heirs of certain testators. It is often times difficult to establish their claims and prove satisfactorily their identity. The court demands that the evidences of heirship be very evident. In this they are right. But we venture to say that even the English Court of Chancery would not turn away a claimant who had all the distinct marks and abounding evidence of identity that mark and characterize the children of Abraham, especially so in the latter day, for then these characteristics are to be clearer and fuller.

But who are the seed of Abraham according to the flesh? We answer, the descendants of the Twelve Tribes. Now to the natural seed the Bible assigns a distinct work and place. This natural seed is divided in the Bible, the word Israel standing generally for the Ten Tribes and Judah for Two Tribes. These divisions have separate paths appointed them to walk in through the centuries. "All of the House of Israel wholly," "the whole House of Israel," "all the House of Israel," have a special work. The Ten Tribes are especially called in the Scriptures the seed of Abraham. Sometimes "My chosen;" and again, "Mine inheritance," and "My servant." God, in referring to them in their scattered state, as of His gathering them together, says (Isaiah 41:8) *"But thou, Israel, art my servant, Jacob whom I have chosen, the seed of Abraham my friend. Thou whom I have taken from the ends of the earth, and called thee from the chief men thereof, and said unto thee, Thou art my servant; I have chosen thee, and not cast thee away."* The Ten Tribes are sometimes designated by the word Jacob. If we once get a clear idea who the seed are, then we can search among the people of the earth to find them, because in the latter day they were to be so different from other people, and distinctly marked, we will have no great difficulty finding them. Of the special marks, one was they were to possess the gates of their enemies.

20

"Enlarge the place of thy tent, and let them stretch forth the curtains of thine habitations: spare not, lengthen thy cords, and strengthen thy stakes; For thou shalt break forth on the right hand and on the left; and thy seed shall inherit the Gentiles, and make the desolate cities to be inhabited." Isaiah 54:2-3

In the writings of the prophets the feminine gender is often used when speaking of the House of Israel. Quite frequently Israel is spoken of as a divorced woman, as being cast off, and as being barren. Judah remaining faithful to the throne of David and the temple service, and abiding in the land much longer than Israel, is presented as one married. So you will understand Jeremiah 3:8, when he says, *"And I saw, when for all the causes whereby backsliding Israel committed adultery I had put her away, and given her a bill of divorce;"* Again, Isaiah 50:1 *"Thus saith the LORD, Where is the bill of your mother's divorcement, whom I have put away? ..."* Yet, though Israel was divorced, forsaken, cast off, and desolate, she was to have more children than married Judah. So the verse preceding the text says, *"Sing, O barren, thou that didst not bear; break forth into singing, and cry aloud, thou that didst not travail with child: for more are the children of the desolate than the children of the married wife, saith the LORD."* Then came the words of the text bidding her enlarge the place of her tent, or dwelling place, to stretch forth her curtains so as to cover over the new-gotten habitations. To spare not - that is, to be not tardy, or slow - in lengthening out her cords - that is, her influence - and strengthen her stakes - that is, her authority: but to break forth on every hand where there is an opening, and inherit the seed of the Gentiles, and make the languishing and poverty-stricken cities of the nations to be inhabited; in this conquest to go on and fear not. These exhortations are given, and promises are made to Israel after she had left Palestine. No one can say truthfully that they have yet been fulfilled in no degree or sense, unless they find such fulfillment in the conquest of the Saxon race. These predictions cannot apply to the Jews, for they are few.

We have been blind and guilty in the past, unconscious of our origin, and, as a natural consequence, ignorant of our place and special work. In interpreting the Word of God we have been lavish in spiritualizing, and greedy in materializing, over looking the fact that nine tenths of the Old Testament is a material history about one people, and that through them God's special providence was to flow to all other nations; and the New Testament plants the life and prosperity of the Gentile world upon the course and progress of Israel. God said to Abraham, *"In thee shall all the families of the earth be blessed;"* and more, *"And in thy seed shall*

21

all the nations of the earth be blessed." Israel, being scattered and cast off, became a blessing to the world. They gave to the surrounding nations the only true idea of God, for in their lowest condition and idolatry they preserved the name and knowledge of Jehovah, and Christ sent His disciples after them through one of their own Tribe - namely, Benjamin - telling them not to go into the way of the Gentiles, nor into the cities of the Samaritans, *"But go rather to the lost sheep of the house of Israel."* To these sheep Christ declares He was sent. Where were these sheep? They were scattered about in Central Asia - in Scriptural language in Cappadocia, Galatia, Pamphylia, Lydia, Bithynia, and round about Illyricum. From these very regions came the Saxons: From here they spread abroad North and West, being the most Christian of any people on the face of the earth then, as well as now. Their reception of the Gospel gave them power over the surrounding nations, to whom they were, as it had been foretold, witnesses for Jesus and Providence in a very special manner.

By the same rule and for the very same reason that Israel conquered Palestine, does England go on from conquest to conquest? And because God remembered to perform His promises made to the patriarchs upon their seed, America was opened for the Puritans, who are without doubt, the descendants and representatives of Manasseh of whom God said, *"He should be a people, a great people."* Of course, both in England's rule and America's there are many defects; but taking all in all; the good will out-way the bad; and more so as the years roll on.

The Saxon people, England and America, stand in a new light to the world by the teachings of the Bible. Being Israel or the Ten Lost Tribes they become at once the chosen agents of God for the glorious purpose of evangelizing the whole world, and finally, by reducing the whole earth to the plane of universal liberty and peace. No hand nor power, nor combination of powers, can stop the onward march of Israel to her God-ordained goal. Her future is to spread on the right hand and on the left. This purpose is strongly set forth by Isaiah 44:7,

"And who, as I, shall call, and shall declare it, and set it in order for me, since I appointed the ancient people? and the things that are coming, and shall come." This same sturdy fact is taught by Paul when speaking to the Athenians, telling them that God *"hath made of one blood all nations of men to dwell on the face of the earth, and hath determined the times before appointed, and the bounds of their habitations."* National destinies are not so much things of chance, or prizes for the sword, as many think. God promised to David, when both Israel and Judah were prosperously settled in Palestine under David's

reign, that He would appoint a place for His people Israel, and plant them there, and they should not be moved, neither should the wicked afflict them, as aforetime. (II Samuel 7:10) This promise God has kept. He has given them the British Isles, where none can afflict them, as they were wont to do when Israel was scattered in Asia and Europe. God has found Manasseh a home in this land of blessings and rich acres.

To this end God is overturning, and will overturn until the whole world shall be federated around one throne, and that throne is David's - the only throne God ever directly established, and the only one He has promised perpetuity to. He has a people - Israel. He has a throne - David's, and for that throne He has a seed, just as the seed of Levi was selected for Temple service. Turn your attention to the founding of this throne of David. You will find the throne and seed unconditionally confederated, the place and measure of prosperity conditioned on the obedience of the people and throne to God. *"The Lord hath sworn in truth unto David; He will not turn from it; of the fruit of thy body will I set upon thy throne."* (Psalm 132:11) Again, *"I have sworn unto David, thy seed I will establish forever, and build up thy throne to all generations."* (Psalm 89:3-4) This promise is to all generations - not a part, nor simply for sixty years. For the kingdom was rent in twain when Rehoboam, the grandson of David, began to reign. The throne of David would be about the poorest type of Christ's throne and rule, and reign, if we can only see it in Palestine. There it was soon divided, very corrupt. *"Thus saith the LORD; If my covenant be not with day and night, and if I have not appointed the ordinances of heaven and earth; Then will I cast away the seed of Jacob, and David my servant, so that I will not take any of his seed to be rulers over the seed of Abraham, Isaac, and Jacob: for I will cause their captivity to return, and have mercy on them."* (Jeremiah 33:25-26) Let anybody with the same mind read the seventh chapter of the second book of Samuel, and they will see that God promised to David that his house and kingdom should be established forever, and that God would set up the seed of David after him. Well might David exclaim when he said before the Lord, *"Who am I, Oh Lord God, and what is my house, that thou hath brought me hitherto? And this was yet a small thing in thy sight, Oh Lord God; but thou hath spoken also of thy servant's house for a great while yet to come."* It is a pity men will not take and interpret the Bible by the rules of common sense.

David at this time was king over all the Tribes and was at peace, and settled and prospered. But God told him that *"He would appoint a place for my people Israel, and will plant them that they may dwell in a place of their own and move no more."* This promise was to Israel. If the promises of the multitudinous seed were to be fulfilled in Israel, then it would be necessary to find them another place, for Palestine would not hold them. So God has planted them. When Nebuchadnezzar carried the Jews captive, he took the king, Zedekiah, with him, and destroyed all his family, and all the real royal seed of David. Now all of this is plain if we keep in mind that Zedekiah was the last prince of the House of David that ever reigned in Palestine. God removed the Diadem. But in the course of time a lawful heir of the seed of David shall appear, and the throne and the seed will be established in Jerusalem. But where is this seed royal? Answer: It is on the English throne. Listen carefully to the following: Jeremiah tells us that with him he had the daughters of Zedekiah, who had by some means escaped the destroying edits of Nebuchadnezzar (Jeremiah 43:6). And from Jeremiah 44:14, we learn that they visited Egypt and from Jeremiah 44:28, we learn that a small number escaped.

Now Jeremiah, being the only prophet in Judah at that time, had a right to take charge of the royal seed. He could not stay in Egypt, nor in Palestine, nor would be go to Babylon. Where then, did the prophet go? He no doubt took ship with the Danites, and sailed for Cornwall, in England for this place was called Tarshish. We learn from Ezekiel the ships of Dan traded in tin, and other things. History and tradition both agree that there landed on the coast of Ireland in the North, a divine man and a princess. God had promised to Jeremiah, his life wherever he went. *"But thy life will I give thee for a prey in all places whither thou goest."* Jeremiah 45:5

The North of Ireland had been settled with the Tribe of Dan; they at once understood who their visitor was. They called him Olam Folla meaning a divine man or teacher. The princess they call Tea Tephi, the beautiful one from the East. This princess was married to Heremon, of Ulster, the king of Lothair Croffin, for such was the name of the city of Tara. This word Tara is Arat spelled backward. The Hebrew reads from right to left; English left to right. Lothair Croffin was changed in Tara at the time of the wedding. Tara means law. Thus began the seed of David to take root, and from there it spread all over Ireland, then to Scotland, thence to England, and Jacob's Stone in Westminster Abbey marks the journey of David's throne, and has always kept with the seed, and they have been always crowned on it. Ezekiel's riddle is at once solved. The tender twigs were Zedekiah's daughters. One of these twigs was planted by the great waters in a land of traffic.

24

The main idea I wish to convey in this book, is that God is conducting His Providence through His ancient chosen people, Israel, whom I believe are found in the Saxon race. And His throne on earth, through which flow the purposes of Providence, is David's throne, which I believe to be at present the English throne. Queen Victoria (and God bless her) I believe to be of David's seed. The United States fulfills the role of the Tribe of Manasseh. Therefore, to understand the prophecies, Providence, and the present movements of nations, as well as the future lot and destiny of each, we must read the Scriptures in this light. God has made the children of Israel and throne of David His executive, in time, on earth. They are his executive for civilization, evangelization, order, and conquest. Through them God will conquer the world to a universal peace. As Moses was to God, so is Israel. Moses being a divine executor, was to the people a god - so is Israel to all mankind. Spiritual Israel will come through literal Israel.

I have expressed myself freely, and shall cheerfully grant reviewers, critics and readers the same privilege. I send forth this book with a pure desire that it may do good. Amen, so be it.

Joseph Wild
Brooklyn, New York
May 1, 1879

The Anglo-American Alliance in Prophecy
or
The Promises to the Fathers

Martin Lyman Streator, M.A.
Researcher, Author, Christian Church Minister,
State Evangelist and Home Missionary

A PRAYER FOR AMERICA
By Pastor George W. Southwick, D.D.

Our Father, which art in heaven, we have not hallowed thy name, we are in a storm, thy mournful remnant is in anguish. LORD, in wrath remember mercy.

Gather America under the shadow of thy wing. Look upon us who have eaten the fruit of lies. Turn us, we pray, to seek thy face and thy way. We confess now our sins, for vain and fruitless is mortal strength. Evil and wickedness now fills our land and cities. We know not where to turn in this dark hour, but unto Thee.

Look down upon our unemployed, the widow and the orphan. Visit the sick and the wounded, the afflicted with wounds and putrefying sores. Pity the poor, the downtrodden, and the debt ridden. Oh God, our help in ages past, be thou now our hope. Have regard in us. Send forth now thy saving health.

God, in whom we trust, guide our ship of state - which is now drifting helplessly upon jagged rocks. Let thy grace and glory shine forth like a beacon light. Are we to be devoured, swallowed up in the belly of the beast from out of the sea?

LORD, take thou the helm of our nation. Bring us to safe harbor, "home." Give unto our leaders wisdom with right understanding. Remove far from us, wicked and greedy politicians. Sweep them all away with the besom of thy destruction. Drive out the money changers from the 'temple.' Curse now, with thy cursings, the "almighty dollar." Dethrone mammon from all hearts. Teach unto our judges the meaning of justice from now on, upon ungodly lawyers and unrighteous judgments.

Deliver us from preachers and false prophets who feed themselves, and not the flock of God. Make our nation free from the gangster's yoke. Deliver us from all crime and hate - this demonic frenzy! Bundle for burning all noxious tares - injurious tumble weeds. Cause the noise from the beast to cease from our environment. Make our land a Beulah, safe for our children.

Send forth Thy light and Thy truth. Be thou our salvation, for we are perishing!

In Jesus Name. Amen

INTRODUCTION
By George W. Southwick, D.D.

One of the most remarkable things about the sovereignty and faithfulness of our God is that He always prepares a man for each age and locale to proclaim the message of His Word that is missing from most pulpits of the day. One of those men for America in the late nineteenth and early twentieth centuries was Martin Lyman Streator. He was born into the home of a *Disciples of Christ* minister on November 12, 1843 in Martinsburg, Washington County, Pennsylvania. His father, Lyman P. Streator was the founder and operator of an academy in Washington County when Martin, the oldest of five sons and one daughter was born. Each son excelled in his respective career; one as a lawyer, another as a medical doctor and two as ministers of the Gospel.

28

In fulfilling his call to Christian ministry, Martin L. Streator attended Bethany College in West Virginia which was founded by Alexander Campbell. Martin graduated in 1866. As a minister he served at *Disciples of Christ* Churches located in Connellsville and Bethel, PA. On June 2, 1868 he married Anne Rebecca Bugher. The Disciples of Christ organization was co-founded by Alexander Campbell in 1832, which was also known as the *Christian Church* and for all practical purposes was the same as the *Church of Christ* until 1906.

Martin L. Streator filled the position as the *State Evangelist* for Pennsylvania for five and a half years before becoming the minister at Youngstown and Ravenna, Ohio. He then accepted the charge as a missionary pioneer to the State of Montana under the auspices of the *Christian Women's Board of Missions*. While serving the congregation at the Helena Christian Church, he was asked to assist in the forming of a new congregation in the frontier town of Bozeman, Montana. In about 1888 this new congregation was formed largely from pioneer settlers from Missouri, Kentucky and other eastern states.

After a long, productive and faithful life for his Lord and Savior, Martin L. Streator passed away in Helena, Lewis and Clark County, Montana in 1926. He was an eloquent speaker and prolific writer. Among his most noted literary works were *"The Anglo-American Alliance in Prophecy,"* published in 1900 and *"The Hope of Israel,"* in 1903. In his first book, he sets forth a profound and convincing exegesis from Scripture in favor of the Israelitish origins of the Anglo-Saxon, Germanic and related peoples.

A quote from Martin Streator's book so aptly shows the depth of understanding that he was taught by Professor Campbell concerning the permanency of God's chosen people Israel as a national entity. Concerning this, Streator remarks; "Alexander Campbell, who was a profound investigator of the development of the divine purpose in its unity and simplicity, has some notable sayings in the "Millennial Harbinger," which are worthy of reproduction at this crisis in the affairs of the world, when the manifestation of the divine purpose is beginning to dawn on the minds of men. Writing of the "permanency of Israel as an everlasting nation, or people," as foretold in Jeremiah 31:35-37, Mr. Campbell says:

"They were from their origin, and they will be to the close of the earthly drama of humanity, a standing monument and miracle of the special providence, and special moral government of Jehovah, as the God of Abraham, Isaac and Jacob...

29

"There is one oracle of our Apostle Paul that commands much thought, and which furnishes a very safe sign post, at a very difficult angle, in our pathway along the lines of the prophetic chart. It is laconic in a superlative degree. It reads thus: 'The gifts and callings of God are without change of purpose' or 'repentance,' on his part. He has a scheme, a purpose, a plan in creation, providence, moral government, and in redemption, from which He never departs.

"Our highest wisdom is expressed, and our most profound devotion developed, when we sincerely, humbly, and prayerfully ask - What saith the Spirit of Inspiration in His holy oracles?"

Alexander Campbell was very instrumental in the "Restoration Movement" that influenced a large portion of American Churches in the nineteenth century. To this present day the effects of that religious movement are still felt throughout many denominations and independent churches. It determined the informal way of worship as opposed to the ceremonial and traditional service of the historical European churches of the American Colonial period. It was an effort to return to the original Apostolic form of worship.

After reading the profound and eloquent exposition of the Abrahamic Covenant, the fulfillment of the work of Christ in redeeming His people and the role that the Anglo-Saxon and related people have played in fulfilling Bible prophecy, one can not help but feel that Streator's listeners were privileged to hear such Biblical teaching. Is it possible that this teaching was not only widely known, but was a mainstream belief in the late nineteenth century?

In 1903, three years after his book was published, Streator commented on its wide spread public acceptance and quoted several literary reviews. He said; "The author wishes to express his gratitude for the various notices and reviews of the book which have appeared in the public Press, and for the strong words of approbation of it from all parts of the Anglo-Saxon world. The people and the Press have recognized that 'the chief purpose of the book is to ascertain the true philosophy and the sure consummation of history as revealed in the Bible.'

"An Ohio editor gives this estimate of the author and his book: 'Being spiritually enlightened, and of sufficient mental grasp to apprehend the great world-movements of today, he has so well succeeded in connecting prophetic truth with the living national and international issues of our times that no editor, no minister, no statesman, no man who cares to keep abreast of the times, can afford to do without this book.'

"The *British Californian* says: 'He shows wherein it is foretold in the prophecies in the Bible that the Anglo-Saxon race shall dominate the world.' The Baltimore *Sun* admits that, according to the teaching of the book in its unfolding of the ethnical covenant of promise, 'The Anglo-Saxon race is the heir to all the prophetic greatness of the Lost Ten Tribes of Israel.' The *Christian Standard* of Cincinnati, one of the greatest religious weeklies of America, characterizes it as 'a timely book, with a world of thought that should receive the careful attention of all students of the times who are believers of the Bible.' *Past and Future*, a London journal says; 'The truths which it contains are of much worth to Christians at the present crisis of the world's history.'

"A popular religious journal said concerning the work devoted to their investigation: 'This is the most fascinating book on the prophecies that has appeared.' A busy author wrote in the midst of hard work: 'The reading of it fascinated me more than a volume of the best romance.' If it is romantic, the reason thereof is simply that it deals with the divine romance of the ages, in which Jehovah, while executing justice and righteousness in the earth, manifests his loving kindness towards Israel, to whom He makes this precious declaration:

"Yea, I have loved thee with an everlasting love: Therefore with loving kindness have I drawn thee." Jer. 31:3

"S.H. Barlett says in *The Ohio Work:* 'The third chapter, on the planting of Israel in Britain, begins to fix one's faith. It develops the tie that binds the old Israelites to the Anglo-Saxon of today. The work is splendidly done, and with convincing force.' Professor Dimbleby said in his monthly journal, *Past and Future,* published in London, and circulating in every English speaking country in the world: 'Approaching next is the planting of Israel in Britain, the Islands of the West. Whatever strength he obtained from Scripture in the former part of his subject, he now seems to move with a consciousness of the artillery of power.' Concerning this distinction in the covenants of promise given to the fathers, *The Christian Evangelist* of St. Louis says: 'the author sights many prophecies concerning Israel which he claims have never had any fulfillment unless in the history of the Anglo-Saxon people."

Commenting on the faithfulness of God toward His people Israel, Streator said: "Jehovah is faithful to His covenant in fulfilling every promise concerning His chosen people. Now we can see how He is performing His pleasure and accomplishing His purpose, even that which, foretold from olden time to the Hebrew patriarchs, has never been done till fulfilled by the Anglo-Saxons in our own days. So it was to be according to the prophecy. The great deeds in their modern history, marvelous in themselves, become more wonderful when seen to be the literal fulfillment of the promises given to the fathers, which manifests 'coercion that belongs to the decrees of God,' in giving to His chosen people 'the heritage of the nations' (Psalm 111:6). He says to them with the assurance of omniscience:

"Ye are my witnesses that I am God." Isaiah 43:12
"The God of truth does not confirm a lie in fulfilling promises that are false."

"They are the living and the life giving centre of the patriarchal history which radiates from Him. Far more than this is true, for they are the theocratic center of the whole history of the elect race with it's promised 'company of peoples' in the great Republic of the United States, and its promised 'company of nations' in the Empire of Great Britain."

"The covenants of promise are cyclical. The course of the development of the chosen seed is this: A son, a family, twelve tribes, a nation, two nations, a race of many nations, a company of peoples and a company of nations, an alliance of all the families and nations of Israel, the fullness of the nations promised to Israel that fill the face of the world with fruit, and the inheritance and the dominion of the inhabited earth by the holy seed of the stock of Israel. This is the divine scheme as declared expressly in the Holy Scriptures."

"Through the manifestations of His judgments all the nations will come worship before Him. Trusting in Him we can rest in perfect peace in this comforting assurance of the God of the covenants of promise given to our fathers: - 'I Yahweh, thy God, am firmly grasping thy right hand, who am saying unto thee: Do not fear! I have become thy Helper, do not fear! Thou worm Jacob, ye men of Israel, I have become thy Helper, declareth Yahweh, and thy Redeemer, the Holy One of Israel." Isa. 41:13-14 (Rotherham's translation)

"With his presence, and help, and blessing, we will not fear, but will triumph through the might of the God of our Salvation, to whom we will ascribe through the ages to come the glory, and the honour, and the power."

Blessed be Jehovah God, the God of Israel, who only doeth wondrous things: And blessed be His glorious name forever: and let the whole earth be filled with His glory. Psalm 72:18-19

In the second volume of Streator's book entitled, *"The Anglo-American Alliance in Prophecy -or- The Promises to the Fathers"* he lists the following table of contents:

32

The following article is composed of excerpts taken from Martin Streator's book,

"The Anglo-American Alliance in Prophecy."

A firm and deliberate conviction that the origin and destiny of the Anglo-Saxon race, with its "assembly of peoples" in the United States of America, and its "company of nations" in the Empire of Great Britain, were foreseen and foretold by the Hebrew prophets, and that these nations, favored of God, are the natural descendants of the beautiful Joseph and the Egyptian princess Asenath, according to the ethnical covenant of promise given in the ancient days to our fathers, and which is now approaching the culmination of its marvelous development in the era of crisis into which the world has entered, has impelled with a force that no longer could be suppressed, the author to write and publish this book. Having been taught from childhood the distinction between Israel and Judah, he has entertained for a quarter of a century the idea of our Israelitish origin and destiny. But he has never held the idea that we are Jews, or that we are of Jewish descent. The patriarch Jacob had twelve sons, of whom Judah was only one son among twelve brothers. The nation of Israel had twelve tribes, of which Judah was only one tribe among the twelve.

The searchers for truth on this subject are exploring every realm of information, seeking for it as for hidden treasures in archaeology, mythology, chronology, and history. They are finding pearls of great price buried in the rubbish of ages. While appreciating the evidence from all of these sources, I have searched the Scriptures diligently to find out what they taught on the topic in promises, prophecies, and recorded facts.

These ideas are the thoughts of God flashing forth in these modern times from the ancient divine revelation. They were the inspiration of the chosen people of God in the olden days. They are not an invention of human genius, but a discovery of divine thoughts that were hidden for

33

ages in a mystery. The finding of our Identity with Israel has restored to their original power the promises given to the fathers, and has revealed for our admiration and delight the significance of great and mysterious prophecies that were written for the fuller development of the racial covenant of promise. These thoughts of God are becoming living realities, embodied in the words and actions of His chosen people. They are giving direction to the international policy of the two greatest nations on the earth. They are to be accomplished by the stupendous and magnificent facts of history fulfilling on a world-wide scale the unfailing promises of the Almighty to His elect race. They are the ideas which make heroes of God for the impending war of Armageddon.

The three covenants of promise, national, Christian, and racial, which were given to the patriarchs, Abraham, Isaac, and Jacob, pervade in their development the entire divine revelation from the call of "the friend of God" and "the father of the faithful." They determine the course of events throughout the ages, they reveal the mystery of the Providential government of the world, they explain the true philosophy of history, they exhibit the order of the great dispensations of religion, they announce the divine plan of the ages, they show the sacred origin of the most vigorous race the world has ever seen, they foretell in words of patriotic delight its glorious destiny, they indicate what will be the final outcome of the eminent war of races for which the nations of the world already are arming themselves to the upmost, and they demonstrate in their fulfillment the plenary inspiration of the Bible and the truthfulness and the faithfulness of God. These things justify the most thorough investigation of the covenants of promise given to the fathers, and confirmed by the mission and work of the Messiah.

Secular history generally is written from the standpoint of Rome. It is a suitable center for studying the world empires of the Gentiles. But it is not at all adapted to studying the prophecy and history of Israel. We need to take our stand at Jerusalem and Samaria, follow the elect race and its wanderings among the nations, and study history in its relation to the chosen people as the center and finally as the circumference of the whole historic movement. The world empires of the Gentiles however stable and mighty they may appear are standing on fragile feet of iron and clay, destined to totter and fall into irretrievable ruin, and to be swept away by the wild winds of anarchistic revolution into utter extinction. But the nation of Israel, according to the sure promises of the God of the covenants, is as firmly established and as permanent as the laws of nature, and will continue to be a nation while the sun endureth.

This Israel we find in modern times in the Anglo-Saxon race, the people which God hath blessed. We can now see that they with their many nations are the people of chief importance in the world. God saw that always, and has prepared the way for it. This is one of the great mountains of God that arrested the gaze of the inspired seers as they looked out across the ages. They could not ignore the vision of this grand epochal mountain. We will not ignore the preeminence of the Anglo-Saxon race in this era of crisis. Epochs are the beacon lights on the mountain tops of prophecy and history. Their light shines out into the darkness far into the past and the future.

CHRONOLOGY IS THE BACKBONE
OF PROPHECY AND HISTORY

The eternal Jehovah, the God of the covenants of promise, according to the good pleasure of His will, which he purposed in Himself, saw fit for reasons satisfactory to infinite omniscience to give the ethnical covenant with its manifold blessings of a multitudinous race developing into "a company of peoples" and "a company of nations" to the pure and beloved Joseph and his two sons, Ephraim and Manasseh. Tracing the essential elements of these promises through the Bible, and watching their gradual fulfillment in history, we find the promised 'company of peoples' in the peoples of many states united in "a strong nation," constituting the great Republic of the United States of America. The most notable events of our history were foretold in the Bible.

As Palestine was the land of promise for the nation of promise so Britain is the land of the covenant for "the many nations" promised in the racial covenant. It is the place appointed of God for the planting of His people Israel; it is "a place prepared of God" for the refuge of Mother Israel beyond the dominions of Rome, into which she fled for safety from the face of the serpent; it is the place into which the "wanderers among the nations' called from "the corners" of the earth, gathered together for a new national and racial development; it is the place where it was said to them, *"ye are not my people"* and where through their conversion to Christ they became *"the sons of the living God"*; it is the place in which under the divine planting they took root; the place where they blossomed and budded, increased and multiplied until the place became too narrow for them; the place from which they sent forth their swarming colonies into "the desolate heritages" of the earth; the place which fondly is regarded as the mother land of the free nations of the Anglo-Saxon race around the world: – this place the Almighty guaranteed in His sure covenant of promise to protect by the might of His omnipotence from the assaults of foreign invasions. Since the settlement of the tribes of Israel in the Islands of the West no armed forces have been able to land on their shores. Phillip of Spain with his "Invincible Armada" tried it. *"The Lord sent His wind and scattered them."* Napoleon Bonaparte gathered his flotilla for the purpose, but did not dare to attempt it. The children who went forth from that island home have not forgotten their mother. They are growing into many nations, and are found in all quarters of the globe.

In the solemn warnings which God gave to Israel through Moses, he said concerning their long racial chastisement for willful and persistent disobedience: *"I will smite you, even I, seven times for your sins... I also will chastise you seven times for your sins."* Lev. 26:24, 28

This repeated warning intensifies its solemnity, and assures the elect race of the certainty of the divine chastisement for their sins. This did not involve their rejection, but their correction and reformation, and their final restoration. In taking a comprehensive view of the chosen people in relation to the Seven Times of Israel's chastisement as foretold by Moses, and the corresponding Times of the Gentiles in their dominion over the promised land, we find three great things foretold by the Hebrew prophets concerning the elect race:

1st The *scattering* of the chosen people (Lev. 26:31-33), and the *sifting* of them "like as grain is sifted in a sieve" (Amos 9:9) in their wandering among the nations (Hosea 9:17) during the first half of the Times of the Gentiles. (Daniel 2:37-40).

2nd The *planting* of the chosen seed in the land of the covenant according to the promise given to King David (II Sam. 7:10-11), and the *sowing* them for God in the earth (Hosea 2:23), even in far countries (Zech. 10:9), which takes place during the second half of the Times of the Gentiles. *"There were given to the woman (Israel) the two wings of the great eagle, that she might fly into the wilderness unto her place, where she is nourished for time, and times, and half a time, from the face of the serpent."* (Rev. 12:14). This is three and a half times, the half of the Seven Times of chastisement foretold by Moses, the 1260 year-days of John. (Rev. 12:6).

3rd The *gathering* of the scattered people of the elect race into a compact ethnical union in the era of crisis at the end of the Times of the Gentiles.

"Thou shalt arise, and have mercy upon Zion: for the time to favour her, yea, the set time, is come. For thy servants take

36

pleasure in her stones, and favour the dust thereof. So the heathen shall fear the name of the LORD, and all the kings of the earth thy glory. When the LORD shall build up Zion, he shall appear in his glory. He will regard the prayer of the destitute, and not despise their prayer. This shall be written for the generation to come: and the people which shall be created shall praise the LORD."
Psalm 102-13-18

And their seed shall be known among the Gentiles, and their offspring among the people: all that see them shall acknowledge them, that they are the seed which the LORD hath blessed.
Isa. 61:9

Inspired seers that looked afar, and heroic statesmen that grappled with the vital principles of national and racial prosperity were the Hebrew prophets. They were taught of God to discern the real course of the life of their race, and to foretell its development unto the remotest ages. Their warnings and instructions and policies were based on the world-wide expansion of their race, and its final triumph over all opposing forces. The world idea originated in the promises given to the fathers which related to "many nations" of both the natural and the spiritual seed, and the blessing through them of *"all the nations of the earth."* We need not think it strange that the prophets of Israel deal with world-wide issues, for these were the things guaranteed in the ancient promises given to Abraham, Isaac, Jacob, and Joseph. They inaugurated policies of national and ethnical development that were to extend over the earth, widening in their influence through the ages, and reach their consummation only in the millennial reign of righteousness and peace throughout the world. In spite of all divisions, in the midst of all disasters, these sagacious and prescient statesmen of God looking forward to the unity and universal expansion of their race as the means chosen of God according to His promises for the consummation of His work in the world. Many men have been deceived concerning the scope of the Bible by some of the later manifestations of narrow Jewish exclusiveness. The purpose of God in choosing an elect race was not limited to the confines of little Palestine. God promised, and reiterated the promise over and over again, that in the seed of Abraham all the nations of the earth should be blessed. But in order to bless all nations He especially blesses one nation. To bless all races He peculiarly blesses one race in order to fit them as a means of blessing for all people. This was fully recognized in ancient Israel as evinced in their sacred prayer-

37

song in which they sang as the chosen servants of God for the blessing of the world. This was its burden:

"God be merciful unto us, and bless us;
And cause his face to shine upon us;
That thy way may be known upon earth,
Thy saving health among all nations." Psalm 67:1-2

The divine work is accomplished through the Messiah, the Holy One of Israel as the personal servant of Jehovah. But His work is carried on through ages and throughout the world by Israel as the ethnical servant of Jehovah.

Jeremiah . . .in the third chapter he repeatedly contrasts "backsliding Israel" with "treacherous Judah," and addresses Israel in exile beyond the confines of Palestine. He declares: *"And the LORD said unto me, The backsliding Israel hath justified herself more than treacherous Judah. Go and proclaim these words toward the north, and say, Return, thou backsliding Israel, saith the LORD;"* (Jer. 3:11-12). This language of Jeremiah is conclusive evidence that "backsliding Israel" had left the land of promise and was dwelling at the time of Jeremiah's writing in the land of the North. Although God had cast out His people, He did not cast them off. The Psalmist says: *"Jehovah will not cast off His people, neither will He forsake His inheritance."* (Psalm 94:14).

In the same chapter in which Jeremiah foretells the new Covenant, and in immediate connection with the great prophecy concerning it, God declares that the nation of Israel, which then had been in exile over a century, shall be as enduring as the ordinances of nature, that it is as permanent as the stars. Note the force and decisiveness of his language concerning the exiled race of Israel of the Ten Tribes.

"Thus saith the LORD, which giveth the sun for a light by day, and the ordinances of the moon and of the stars for a light by night, which divideth the sea when the waves thereof roar; The LORD of hosts is his name: If those ordinances depart from before me, saith the LORD, then the seed of Israel also shall cease from being a nation before me for ever. Thus saith the LORD; If heaven above can be measured, and the foundations of the earth searched out beneath, I will also cast off all the seed of Israel for all that they have done, saith the LORD." Jeremiah 31:35-37

If there be any such a thing as veritable prophecy, we find it here under the repeated affirmation of Jehovah. The Apostle Paul was familiar with this prophecy, and when he recalled it and the promises to the fathers on which it is based, he could not do otherwise than write, when treating of the rejection and the final restoration of Israel, what should be a delight to every Israelite in the world. *"God did not cast off His people whom he foreknew."* (Romans 11:2). The divine scheme of the ages involves that they shall never cease from being a nation before Him. According to the fiat of the eternal Jehovah the laws of moon and stars will perish when the seed of Israel ceases to be a nation. Why not take God at His word, and believe what He says? It is of little importance that men lost sight of this nation and race for a time, and that when they appeared again in the arena of history as its chief actors, the men of Greece and Rome did not at all know who they were, and characterized them as Northern Barbarians. God never lost sight of them. Before Him they constitute a nation forever. He has a plan of the ages involving their destiny and the dominion of the world from which He never departs. Nature itself will sink into decay and ruin when the race of Israel ceases to be a nation before Jehovah. This language of the prophet cannot possibly refer to the House of Judah, for the Jews ceased to be a nation when Titus destroyed Jerusalem, since which time they never have had a national existence. But throughout all this period the race of Israel has maintained itself as a nation, and has finally developed into many nations.

PLANTING OF ISRAEL IN BRITAIN

The Israelites did not return to Jerusalem with the Jews. But they cherished the hope of Israel in looking forward to the restoration and dominion of the chosen people. While many of the Jews returned to Palestine, the Israelites did not return. Josephus says expressly:
"Many of them took their effects with them and came to Babylon, as very desirous of going down to Jerusalem; but then the entire body of the people of Israel remained in the country wherefore there are but two tribes in Asia and Europe subject to the Romans, while the Ten Tribes are beyond Euphrates till now, and are an immense multitude, and not to be estimated by numbers." (Antiquities, B. XI, Ch. V, sec.2)
When God cast out the Ten Tribes He did not cast them away, but even then renewed to them the promise of multiplicity given to their fathers saying to them in Hosea:
"Yet the number of the children of Israel shall be as the sand of the sea, which can not be measured or numbered." Hosea 1:10

This declaration of the prophet confirms the accuracy of the statement of Josephus that the Ten Tribes were "an immense multitude, and not to be estimated by numbers." This is a fulfillment of the promises given to the fathers. These things refute the hypothesis that they were absorbed and assimilated by other nations. They retained their identity and distinct nationality, and became the heroes of earth's history. The race of Israel was transplanted from Palestine to the Islands of the West, and became the great maritime people of the world. they occupied the end of the earth in the old continent.

Jehovah addresses them in these words adapted to islanders and mariners.

"Sing unto Jehovah a new song, and His praise from the end of the earth; Ye that go down to the sea, and all that is therein, the isles and the inhabitants thereof. Let them give glory unto Jehovah, and declare His praise in the islands." Isa. 42:10, 12

God made a covenant with David, ordered in all things and sure. There was nothing haphazard about this covenant. It was all ordered of God. Every promise in it is sure, that is, it is certain of accomplishment in its appointed place and at its appointed time. One of the chief things in this covenant was the land of the covenant, the place appointed by the God of the covenant for the planting of His people Israel, the children of the covenant. Now the Hebrew word for covenant is BRIT or BRET, and the word for island in Hebrew is AI, whence comes our English word Is-land. Hence BRIT-AI or Brit-ain, according to its Hebrew etymology, means covenant-island, or the island of the covenant. Paul B. Du Chaillu says in *"The Viking Age"*; "In the Sagas . . . Britain itself was called Bretland, and the people Bretar." Now Bret-land means literally covenant-land, or the land of the covenant, as Britain means the island of the covenant. Here are two witnesses in the ancient names of this land indicating that it is the land of the covenant promised for the planting of Israel in the covenant which God made with David, and the island of the covenant according to the descriptions of the islands in the west at the ends of the earth as given by Isaiah. But, in addition to this, consider the following truths: The Hebrew word for man is ISH. Hence BRIT-ISH means literally covenant-man, or man of the covenant. The islands to the northwest of Britain are called Hebrides to this day. Why? How did they get that name? The simple and rational explanation is that they were settled and named by the Hebrews.

ISRAEL AND CHRIST

The blessings guaranteed to the elect race in the promises to the fathers will not be exhausted for a thousand generations. When God remembers the promises which He made in ancient days for us we in these modern times should never forget them. The Virgin Mary cherished the memory of the theocratic government and referred to it in the climax of her magnificent song of praise, saying in the fullness of faith and hope:

"He hath holpen Israel His servant, that He might remember mercy (as He spake unto our fathers) toward Abraham and his seed forever." Luke 1:54-55

The birth of Christ was for the purpose of helping Israel, the servant of God, and was in remembrance of His mercy, toward Abraham and his race forever: all of which was according to the promises which he spake in the covenants given to our fathers Abraham, Isaac, and Jacob. The events attending the birth of the Messiah and his harbinger, John the Baptist, had reference to the fulfillment of things promised to our fathers in the covenants given to them by Jehovah. This was recognized by Zacharias, the father of John, when filled with the Holy Spirit. He said regarding the covenants of promise:

"Blessed be the Lord, the God of Israel; For He hath visited and wrought redemption for His people, And hath raised up a horn of salvation for us in the house of His servant David. . . to show mercy towards our fathers, and to remember His holy covenant; the oath which He sware unto Abraham our father." Luke 2:68-73

The whole Gospel of Christ is but one of the developments of the theocratic covenants of promise given long ages before in the times of the patriarchs. As Christ is the personal servant of Jehovah, so Israel is His ethnical servant, through whose multitudinous seed, consisting of the many nations of promise, the triumphs of Christ among all nations throughout the world are consummated. This is the divine order, revealed of God, indicated in the covenants of promise, and expressly declared in His Holy Word. In the Psalm of the Cross, after depicting in vivid terms the passion of the Redeemer when they pierced His hands and His Feet, Jehovah, the omniscient One, said: *"All ye seed of Jacob, glorify Him; and stand in awe of Him, all ye seed of Israel."* Psalm 2:23

The people of the multitudinous race of Israel become submissive to Christ, the Holy One of Israel. The Lord declared through the evangelical prophet Isaiah: *"In Jehovah shall all the seed of Israel be justified and shall glory."* Isaiah 45:25.

This shows that the race of Israel becomes a Christian people. It is folly to look for lost Israel among heathen tribes. The people of Israel trust in the Messiah are justified in Jehovah, and glory in the Cross of our Lord Jesus Christ. If you wish to find the lost Tribes of Israel search for them with the lamp of divine truth in your hand, which will give you the needed light, in the most thorough going Christian race in the world.

The work of Christ, and the proclamation of the Gospel among all nations, is a condition for the conversion and the development of the "many nations" of the Anglo-Saxon race and their expansion under Christian influence *"unto the utmost bound of the everlasting hills."* Genesis 49:26. Judaism was not the cause of Christianity; but it was a favorable condition for its revelation and progressive development. The Gospel of Christ is not the cause of the "many nations" of promise springing from Isaac but it is the indispensable condition for the Christian civilization and the world development of the Saxons. Israel is the heir of the world. Jehovah, the God of the covenants of promise, made this sure pledge:

"I will be as the dew unto Israel; He shall blossom as the lily, and cast forth His roots as Lebanon. His branches shall spread, and His beauty shall be as the olive tree, and His fragrance as Lebanon." Hosea 14:5-6

The spreading branches of the elect race of Israel could not be confined to ancient Palestine. The Messiah blesses them with His gospel and liberty, His righteousness and peace,

"That they might be called trees of righteousness, the planting of Jehovah, that He might be glorified." Isa. 61:3

This was according to the patriarchal blessing which Jacob gave to Joseph. He said of the race of his favorite son:

"Joseph is the son of a fruitful tree, a fruitful tree by a fountain: His branches run over the wall." Genesis 49:22

One of the most vigorous influential writers of our times is Dr. Josiah Strong, the General Secretary of the Evangelical Alliance for the United States. He says: "Evidently it is chiefly to the Anglo-Saxon race that we must look for the evangelization of the world. And to show that this is preeminently the missionary race is to show that it is the most Christian race, for the missionary spirit is the essential spirit of Christianity. As the Hebrew carried his pure monotheism around the Mediterranean, so the Anglo-Saxon is carrying a spiritual Christianity around the world."

To one versed in the Hebrew prophets these notable characteristics of the Anglo-Saxon race are theocratic marks of the elect race of Israel. Dr. Strong says truly: "It is the most Christian race." A Christian is characterized by faith in Christ. The Apostle Paul says: *"We believed on Christ Jesus that we might be justified by faith in Christ."* Galatians 2:16 The prophet Isaiah says,: *"In Jehovah shall all the seed of Israel be justified, and shall glory."* Isa. 45:25. The race of Israel is justified in Jehovah by faith in Christ. They become the chief Christian race of the world. Compare these Scriptures: *"Israel shall be saved by Jehovah by an everlasting salvation."* Isa. 45:17

"I said not unto the seed of Jacob, seek ye me in vain. Isa. 45:19 *"I will pour my spirit upon thy seed, and my blessing upon thine offspring."* Isa. 4:3.

"Jehovah hath redeemed Jacob, and will glorify Himself in Israel." Isa. 44:23

"Thou shalt rejoice in Jehovah, thou shalt glory in the Holy One of Israel." Isa. 41:16

"I will make a new covenant with the house of Israel." Jer. 31:31 *"It shall be said unto them, ye are the sons of the living God"* Hos. 1:10

"And so all Israel shall be saved: Even as it is written, there shall come out of Zion the deliverer; He shall turn away ungodliness from Jacob." Rom. 11:26

Anyone of these declarations in the Word of God is sufficient to show to any candid mind that Israel becomes a Christian people. Taken together they indicate the preeminence of Israel as a Christian race. In this respect the Anglo-Saxon race, and it alone, fulfills the prophetic destiny of Israel.

The logic of events fulfilling for ages the promises of God is the most stupendous evidence in the world. It binds the mind with the golden chain of truth, yet at the same time, setting it free from the delusions of error and falsehood. It gives it the largest possible freedom. Real freedom comes through the hearty acceptance of truth. The Messiah said, *"Ye shall know the truth and the truth shall make you free."* John 8:32

43

Anything short of truth enslaves as far as its influence extends. Truth unites thought to reality and wings it for its flight to the stars.

The history of the mightiest race in the world in the most enlightened age, fulfilling the promises and prophecies in the Bible concerning the destiny of the chosen people, demonstrates that it is the living word of the living God. The skeptical "higher criticism" will succumb to the disclosures of "the highest criticism," which exhibits to the people the thoughts of God in their reality, in their significance, in their truthfulness, and in their full accomplishment. No infidel can say of this long chain of promise and prophecy that it was "forged" after the events. These things were foretold long ages ago and they are being wrought out through the ages by the chosen people just as they were foretold in that order, as the prophet Isaiah declared, *"They may see, and know, and consider, and understand together, that the hand of Jehovah hath done this, and the Holy One of Israel hath created it. Produce your cause, saith Jehovah; bring forth your strong reasons, saith the King of Jacob."* Isaiah 41:20-21

This is the challenge of the Eternal to the men of reason in this skeptical age. Will they dare to accept it? Will they dare to see and question these things? No, they ignore them, for they cannot see and know them and still hold fast to their skepticism. Will they at all consider them? Not yet, but they will be compelled in the end to consider them, however much they may dislike to do so. The stupendous facts of the history of our race in our own times, fulfilling the ancient promises to our fathers, will force intelligent men of all shades of opinion to consider them. The meaning of the promises is plain. Their fulfillment is manifest when you compare the promises with the accomplished facts. The atheist denies the existence of God, and the possibility of any divine revelation. The infidel critics belie the promises, and tear into tatters the sacred prophecies, and prate of their learning and their wisdom. The most intense and bitter bigots in the world are the scientific skeptics who flout at divine revelation. False teachers and erratic preachers are retailing their strong delusions as an evidence of their superior wisdom. As it was in the days of the prophet Jeremiah, in the closing cycle of Judah's dominion, so it is now in the closing cycle of the Times of the Gentiles.

The Need of the Anglo Israel Truth

By: Dr. Mordecai F. Ham
1877-1961

INTRODUCTION
by Charles A. Jennings

During times of national turmoil, God always raises up men of equal strength and courage to meet the demands of the time. One such time was the first half of the 20th century and one such man was Mordecai Fowler Ham. He was born on April 2, 1877 in Scottsville, Kentucky, into the home of a seventh generation Baptist preacher. He attended Ogden College in Bowling Green and took private tutoring lessons in law, but was too young to take the bar exam. After college he worked as a traveling salesman for a grocery company and a Chicago photo enlarging firm.

Even as a young boy, he always had a consciousness of and a firm belief in the Lord Jesus Christ. While in business, he began to feel the call of God to preach the Gospel. In July 1900, just before he gave up his secular career and entered the ministry, he married Bessie Simmons. He preached his first sermon one week later. From his first revival at the Mt. Gilead Baptist Church in 1901, he entered an evangelistic ministry that would impact the lives of millions of Americans.

Rev. Ham held revival meetings across the nations, which were attended by thousands. He was well known for his boldness in the pulpit when preaching against both individual sins and public corruption. He would single out the most well known sinners in town for his personal evangelism. Throughout his preaching career he endured much opposition, receiving threats, bodily assaults and police arrests.

In December 1905 his wife died of cerebral meningitis. For several months he took an overseas tour to help him recover from his grief. In June 1908 he married Annie Laurie Smith and they were blessed with three daughters. He served as pastor of the First Baptist Church of Oklahoma City from 1927-1929 and then returned to full time evangelism. From 1929 to 1941 he held sixty-one meetings in fifteen states. He claimed that there were 168,550 converts to Christ throughout his ministry. Many prominent and later influential people were converted during his ministry, such as; Wyatt Larimore, 'king' of the local Chattanooga underworld in the 1932 crusade; Otto Sutton, a wild and wicked heavyweight fighter from Little Rock, AR in the January 1933 Crusade; and Billy Graham, the internationally known evangelist, with his friend Grady Wilson in the November 1935 Charlotte, North Carolina crusade. It is reported that following the Macon, GA crusade that thirteen brothels closed because all the prostitutes were converted to Christ.

In 1935, Bob Jones University conferred upon him an Honorary Doctorate of Divinity degree and in 1936 he was elected the president of the International Association of Christian Evangelists. In 1940, Dr. Ham started a radio ministry on the Mutual Broadcasting Network of fifty stations and made personal appearances in over 600 American cities. In June 1947, he published a paper known as "The Old Kentucky Home Revivalist" and later authored several books which included; The Second Coming of Christ, Believing a Lie, The Sabbath Question and The Jews. After a long outstanding ministry of Christian evangelism, Dr. Ham passed away on November 1, 1961 in Louisville, Kentucky.

Even though Dr. Ham is still remembered and revered as one of America's most prominent and greatest evangelists, his stand against Communism and Zionism is quietly ignored. In 1925, he, along with one hundred other fundamentalists answered the call of Dr. Gerald B. Winrod to meet in Salina, Kansas and to establish the Defenders of the Christian Faith organization. Among the official speakers for the organization were, Mordecai Ham, Paul Rader and Charles E. Fuller. They tenaciously defended the historical Christian faith and fought against the schemes of the Communists and Zionists. As a result, this earned them the label of being 'antisemitic' and controversial.

Dr. Ham also took a stand in favor of the Christian Anglo-Israel message of the Bible. The following article is an address given by him at the Seventh Annual Conference of the British Israel World Federation on October 4, 1926. This is a reprint from the August 7, 1954 edition of The National Message magazine.

When Dr. Ham mentions "this message" or "this truth" in the following article, he is referring to the Christian Anglo-Israel message which the British Israel World Federation so strongly advocates.

THE NEED OF ANGLO ISRAEL TRUTH

I am going to give you some of the reasons why I believe that the world is in need of this message.

Carrying Out A Divine Purpose

I am going to quote from the first chapter of Deuteronomy, verses 6-8: "The Lord our God spake unto us in Horeb, saying, Ye have dwelt long enough in this mount: turn you, and take your journey, and go to the mount of the Amorites, and unto all the places nigh there unto, in the plain, in the hills, and in the vale, and in the south, and by the sea side, to the land of the Canaanites, and unto Lebanon, unto the great river, the river Euphrates. Behold, I have set the land before you: go in and possess the land which the Lord sware unto your fathers, Abraham, Isaac, and Jacob, to give unto them and to their seed after them."

These words were spoken to a people who had just been emancipated from slavery, who had never known anything but the brick kilns of Egypt, and the rigours of bondage; who at this time sat under the shades of Horeb, enjoying, not only the shade, but the sweet cool water that flowed in from that mountain; and who were fed with manna from the hand of God. Free from all terror, they sat there enjoying their freedom. Then God said, "Ye have dwelt long enough in this mount". God did not save Israel out of Egypt just to make pets of them, and to lavish His love upon them, to the exclusion of the rest of the world. Of course, He had a divine purpose, and that purpose down through the ages He has been carrying out. And based upon that, we might study four things that God had in view:

He saved this people, He emancipated them, first of all, to reveal to them the great truth: *"Hear, O Israel; The Lord our God is one Lord." He wanted to give to the world a knowledge of the one and only true God."*

The next thing He wanted to show to the world was the beauty of the divine government, *"Happy is that people, whose God is Jehovah"*.

Then He wanted, through them, as the custodians of His divine oracles, to carry the truth to all the world.

And, last of all, to give to the world the promised Savior, the King of Kings, and Lord of Lords.

The World Needs This Truth

Now with this I wish to say, first of all, that the world needs the Truth that you are now putting out, in order that it might have restored to it confidence in governments. The foundations of governments are trembling everywhere. People, because of subtle propaganda, have lost faith in the powers that be, and especially in America we are suffering at this time from the loss of confidence in rulers, in established governments. Everywhere we hear that governments must all be destroyed, and that we must bring in a new order; that everything now existing is wrong.

Suppose, for instance, that all people become obsessed with that idea, that all established authority and all government are wrong, then the result would be that there would be no appeal to patriotism, there would be no enlisting in the hour of trouble, as you had in your last great war. There would be nothing but a chaotic state of society, and such distress and misery as we have never had on this earth before would be the result. The moment that everyone was convinced that the present governments are all of Satan, and of his rule and dominion, and that they are under his power, the only result would be chaos and war and sorrow. We need somehow to restore the confidence of the people of this world in the fact that government is of God. And, as I understand it, I do not see anything that can better serve in this respect than the Anglo Israel gospel, and the Truth that you are presenting.

Then the world needs this truth to enlighten the intelligencer. What do I mean by intelligencer? It is that agitated man without intelligence. We are told that we have come from a lower order of animal life, and the child of today is traced back through some inferior creature down into the cave or to the scum of a drake pond, or somewhere else; and the consciousness of God is being wiped out. Recently a poll was taken of our college boys and girls in the States, and it was found that only one out of ten had not forgotten to go to church when they returned home. The creation of everything is accounted for without God. They will give

48

the theory of evolution, or something of that kind. We need something that is definite.

Divine Plan Behind History

Our histories have assumed that which is not true; they have begun with a falsehood. And it certainly would appeal to any man's intelligence if he could discover that back of all history is the divine programme and plan. You can trace back practically everything today. If men were but enlightened they would find that God, the great Builder, had a well-defined programme when He started colonizing in this world. Just as there is the architect, then someone to excavate, another to put the foundation, and another to build up the structure, so in God's great plan. When God laid His hand upon Abraham, and called him out of the land, He had His divine programme, and once you see it, history is interpreted for you, and the great mysteries which our scholars today are trying to account for by speculation and uncertainties will become well-defined, intelligent programmes behind which we can read the words, "In the beginning God". Read and see how God planned that the sons of Isaac should each give to the world certain things.

Needed Unity of our Christian Nations

Then, again, the world needs the Anglo Israel Truth in order that it may ensure the amity and the unity of the great Anglo-Saxon or Christian nations. I was impressed with this fact when, a few weeks ago, I visited the territory where the men who first came from this country came with the idea that, under God, they were doing something. And, as Benjamin Franklin said, when they had wrangled for several days, trying to formulate a constitution without coming to any agreement, "It seems strange that such intelligent men as you are should ever have undertaken such a tremendous task without calling upon the Supreme Being". So they knelt and prayed, and immediately order and harmony were restored. They like you, felt it was under God they were working.

And everywhere you go in Anglo-Saxondom today, you can see the order, the programme, the laws, the institutions; from the circuit judge, on through our entire governmental institutions, you can see that they are based upon the great foundation that God Himself laid down. For what we have with us today, we are bound to give credit to God and His Book.

49

Britain and America Inseparable

But there is mischief abroad today. There is an effort being made to destroy the amity and the unity between Britain and America. Let me say this to you: Britain and America have never been separated. It is the work of the enemy that is seeking to bring about embarrassing conditions between the two countries. And I know of no truth today that can so restore confidence as this Anglo Israel Truth. Because in my country, in the South land of America, you find the old Anglo-Saxon Puritan blood in the ascendancy. We still believe this Book, in spite of all the attacks that are being made upon it.

This Truth Stimulates Missionary Zeal

We also need this Truth to stimulate missionary zeal. Study God's Word and note the order. First possession; then practice. God never gives an exhortation, and never outlines for us a practice, or gives us a task to do, until He has told us what we are, and who we are. Read that Ephesian Epistle: "In Him" appears thirty times, perhaps, in the first chapter. Then He comes down and tells us who we are, and where we are, and then He tells us how we are. When we are made to feel that we have been appointed of God to carry to the world His Truth, it brings with it a feeling of tremendous responsibility, and also such a sense of power that we cannot resist.

How we have in a measure fulfilled our task can be seen when we know that out of 23,000 missionaries that have gone out into this world, over 19,000 of them have gone from Britain and America. The execution of that noble work in obedience to Christ's commission has had a wholesome effect upon us. I could better illustrate it than I could establish its truth by argument:

A few years ago, on the shores of Lake Michigan, a steamer was sighted battling with the storms. It was foundering, and it seemed that death was almost certain. Efforts had been made by the little life-saving crew, but they had been a failure. After a while there came down to the shore a little woman, and walking up to her big son, she said 'remember when you accepted this position, I told you of its responsibility. Have you done your level best? Go, and mother will pray for you'. And, against the persuasion and the advice of his fellows, he leapt into the boat, and battled with the storm. After a while they saw his boat coming back, and when he got near enough to the shore he began to shout, 'I have saved my brother'.

To the storm-distressed nations we have brought salvation, and have brought blessing to our own people.

This Truth Restores Faith In The Bible

Last of all, the world needs this Truth, and we need it to give us back our Bible. For years I have seen the Book going from us, taken gradually from us by people who profess to believe it. In that subtle way they have interpreted this passage and that, until finally we have concluded that the Book, after all, is only a bit of ancient literature. How different it is when once we see that, from the first, not one single promise that God made to our fathers has failed, and not one single prophecy.

God knows the future, and this is God's Book, and we need this Book given back to us, and this Truth which rejects none of it, can show the fulfillment of each promise and each prophecy. And let me say without any fear of being misunderstood that, busy in the work as I have been, I have read my Bible more since this Truth got hold of me than I ever did in the same length of time before.

Anglo Israel Stands The Great Test Of Truth

Are these men who cast doubt on the Bible men of experience, of learning, or are they ignorant men? Let me say this: there is one test by which to try them, I John 4:3:

"And every spirit that confesseth not that Jesus Christ is come in the flesh is not of God: and this is that spirit of antichrist, whereof ye have heard that it should come; and even now already is it in the world".

And again in the Second Epistle:

"For many deceivers are entered into the world, who confess not that Jesus Christ is come in the flesh. This is a deceiver and an antichrist" (v. 7).

Everyone that does not admit that Christ has come in the flesh is of the antichrist. That is a double test. When people would have me believe that anything is from the antichrist, I put that test, and it settles the question for me. Now I hold in my hand the Bible containing some of the most ancient, and the most modern, of all utterances that men have ever come in possession of, written by different men, under different civilizations, at different times, in different environments, from the king's palace to the shepherd's tent. There are no contradictions; each is complementary to the other. I made this statement once, and have made it again and again in the university chapels of our land:

51

"I challenge you to show one single historical mistake, one single scientific blunder in this great Book–a magnificent temple of Truth, containing the utterances of the noblest characters that this old world has ever heard of."
And as President Wilson said when our boys left for the Front: "Boys, read the Bible; the world's greatest heroes and characters are there. Get acquainted with them."

'Isaiah Who Talks Of Israel In The Isles'

I pass through the Judges, and into the Psalms. I step down awhile, and hear King David playing with his harp, and listen to the sacred music and the precious words that express the deepest secrets of my soul. I not only listen to the loftiest music and the rarest poetry, but I pass on to listen to the wisdom of Solomon; and then I pass on to hearken to the glorious strains of Isaiah, who talks of Israel in the isles; then to the minor tones of Jeremiah.

'Hail The Power Of Jesus Name'

I not only listen to this grand orchestra, but I pass on and sit down in the observatory there with Daniel. I see the rise and fall of kings and empires and kingdoms. Then through each of the Minor Prophets who with their telescopes, search the heavens for the star of Bethlehem. I travel on through the New Testament, carried, as it were, into the heavenlies, until in the end I see the King of kings and Lord of lords; whether it be what Ezekiel saw, or that which is pictured in the four Gospels. He is ever the same. And in the final Book of Revelation I see the capstone. There we see the redeemed hosts, singing, "All hail the power of Jesus' Name". And some day you and I, the one great flock of King Jesus, will march into our full inheritance.

JERUSALEM
(The Glastonbury Hymn)

And did those feet in ancient time
Walk upon England's mountain green?
And was the Holy Lamb of God
On England's pleasant pasture seen?
And did the Countenance Divine
Shine forth upon our clouded hills?
And was Jerusalem builded here
Among those dark Satanic mills?
Bring me my bow of burning gold!
Bring me my arrows of desire!
Bring me my spear! O clouds unfold!
Bring me my chariot of fire!
I will not cease from mental fight,
Nor shall my sword sleep in my hand,
Til we have built Jerusalem
In England's green and pleasant land.
By William Blake
1757-1827

****

"God hath not cast away His people which He foreknew."
Romans 11:2

"The Apostles passed beyond the ocean to the Isles called the Britannic Isles." Eusebius (265-340 A.D.) Church Historian

"We certainly know that Christ the true son afforded His light, the knowledge of His precepts, to our Island in the last year of the reign of Tiberius Caesar." Gildas (516-570 A.D.) British Historian

THE LOST KEY TO THE OLD TESTAMENT... FOUND

LUKE M. RADER

INTRODUCTION
By Charles A. Jennings

Luke Rader was born into the home of a pastor of the Methodist Episcopal Church in 1890. Early in life he had a strong faith in the Lord Jesus Christ as his Savior and an understanding of true spiritual realities. Though he was raised in an age of religious skepticism, his faith was seriously challenged yet not shaken in the Bible as the Word of God. By the providence of God through the work of the Holy Spirit, Luke Rader, dedicated his life to the Lord and Christian service.

As a young man Luke Rader entered Christian ministry and later became associated with his famous brother Paul Rader. After his brother founded the big *Chicago Gospel Tabernacle* in the early 1920's, Luke Rader became one of ten members of the Board of Managers. One of the major outreach ministries of the church was foreign missions and the evangelization of the world.

In the month of May 1928 a small group of business men invited Luke Rader to come in Minneapolis, Minnesota. He accepted their invitation and conducted an evangelistic campaign in the Minneapolis Curling Rink. The campaign began in July that same year and continued without interruption for nineteen weeks. It was very obvious to all involved that the divine blessing of the Lord was upon the campaign. Therefore, they decided to build a permanent tabernacle building in order to continue the Gospel outreach in the city. Within a short period of time a fine brick and tile building was constructed at 4610 East Lake Street in which the first public service was held on Sunday, November 18, 1928. The *River Lake Gospel Tabernacle* was located on the main thoroughfare between St. Paul and Minneapolis on the western approach of the bridge over the Mississippi River. It could be reached by one trolley transfer from anywhere in the Twin Cities. A ten by twelve foot neon sign was installed on the building in sight of the passing motorists on the adjacent busy thoroughfare. The sign read, *Jesus the Light of the World* and was surmounted by a star.

The letters of the sign were red and blue while the four foot star was a Nile green which made a very attractive sign by which the Gospel was proclaimed day and night.

In 1930, Pastor Rader commented concerning the vision and purpose of the founding of the Tabernacle in an article entitled, *"The Reason."*

"Since it is true that man can only find outlet for his great throbbing heart passions, either in God, or achievement, or the lusts of the flesh, and since we as Christians have the only message that leads men to God, we today face the most tremendous challenge the world has ever given. The issues are so far-reaching and pregnant, and the challenge so urgent, we must face it immediately. Which road shall America's unprecedented prosperity and power take? The materialistic, pleasure mad path of Rome's, Greece's and Babylon's downfall or the path our glorious beginning promised? Which way shall the impounded floods of Japan and China flow? Destructive or constructive? What answer to Bolshevism's threatening knock at the world's door? Mussolini's marvelous achievements? Shall they lead to great advancement or blighting ruin?

"The answer to all of these is wrapped up in the question whether they find God, or no. We must get men to God. God's method of bringing others to Himself is men – supernaturally born again and baptized with the Holy Ghost - going out to testify to others about the resurrected Christ. This is the world's need; this is the only answer to the challenge of the hour. Either this, or war that will annihilate Western civilization.

"Upon this vision then, and to help meet this need the River Lake Gospel Tabernacle was built."

By November 1958, after thirty years of ministry, this church which became known as *The Evangelistic Center of the Upper Midwest* had influenced the lives of tens of thousands of people for Jesus Christ. It stood for:

1. Preaching of the Word of God not only by the local pastors, but by some of the most prominent and greatest evangelists and Bible teachers of the day. The list included Mrs. Billy "Ma" Sunday, Paul Rader, Gerald B. Winrod, Mordecai Ham, Oswald J. Smith, Raymond T. Richey, A. P. Gouthey, Harry D. Clarke (successor of Billy Sunday), George Bennard (author of the song, *"The Old Rugged Cross"*), Wm. Pascoe Goard, A.C. Gabelein, Wm. Biederwolf, Kathryn Kuhlman, Phil Kerr (famous for his music and hymn writing), Charles F. Weigle, who was famous both as an evangelist and the author of the song *'No One Ever Cared for Me Like Jesus'* and many others.
2. That men and women might be born again. More than 67,000 souls made a confession in Jesus as their Savior.
3. That bodies might be strengthened. Thousands testified of being helped in Jesus name.
4. That Christians might grow spiritually. Hundreds were touched by the Holy Spirit and called into full time Christian service.
5. That the Word of God might be taught. More than 7800 Bible classes were held and about 400,000 Bible lessons were distributed.

The church had a regular attendance of hundreds of people and over the years was attended by multiplied thousands. Its outreach touched additional thousands by means of its radio ministry. For years Pastor Rader held church services every night of the week except Saturday and had three services each Sunday. The various departmental ministries of the church ministered to each member of the family and the community. Music and singing were a big part of each service, which included a choir, a band, quartets, trios and family ensembles.

Luke Rader became known throughout the nation as a stalwart defender of the Christian faith and was invited as a guest speaker in many large churches, including Angeles Temple in Los Angeles, pastored by Aimee Semple McPherson in 1937. He also produced a weekly publication entitled *"Sunshine News."* As a pastor who loved his flock, he made visitation to homes and hospitals. He prayed for the sick both privately and publicly.

Pastor Luke Rader was widely known for his uncompromising defense of the infallible Word of God and the supremacy of Jesus Christ both in the life of the individual and the nation. He took a public stand against the political liberalism and religious skepticism of his day in spite of the reproach that he had to endure. He was also very outspoken against the local mafia of the city that had control of racketeering, prostitution, the liquor trade and other forms of vice. The local mob boss, Isador Blumenthal, commonly known as Kid Cann, put out a contract for the assassination of Luke Rader. During church service one evening, while Rader was preaching, a man in the congregation stood up and fired a gun at him in an attempt to kill him. The shot missed and the perpetrator was subdued while Rader continued preaching. In his proclamation of God's Word to the masses, he was a strong advocate of the Gospel of the Kingdom of God. Luke Rader, A.P.Gouthey, and F.F. Bosworth, all able ministers of the Gospel and believers in the Anglo-Israel truth held successful evangelistic campaigns for Dr. Oswald J. Smith, pastor of the *People's Church* in Toronto. Dr. Smith commented to Luke Rader, "that Evangelist Bosworth's meeting did more to build up his work than all other meetings put together."

From the writings of Luke Rader contained in his various articles and publications including the article entitled, *"The Lost Key to the Old Testament Found,"* Rader clearly sets forth his conviction as to the identification of God's true Israel people today. He gives "a presentation of the dilemma faced by those who believe that the Jews are all Israel; and a short concise treatise on the Biblical and Historical proofs that the Anglo-Saxons are fulfilling the prophesied destiny of Israel." He spent eight years in careful research on this subject before he began to publicly preach it.

THE TESTIMONY OF LUKE RADER

In an article printed in the *Sunshine News* of July 16, 1936, Pastor Luke Rader is showing from the Scriptures that Israel and Judah were divided and became two separate nations. He also points out that Israel, also known as Joseph, Ephraim or the Northern Kingdom was not absorbed into the Judah nation, therefore, debunking the amalgamation theory. He writes:
"How could this be possible when both the blessing and the birthright of Abraham's Covenant belong to Ephraim? I Chron. 5:1; Gen. 49:22-26; 48:17-20. How could Ephraim be absorbed and God's Unfailing Covenant fail? But it does fail, if Ephraim is absorbed.

By God's own order, the Jews were separated from the Northern Ten Tribes, called Israel in distinction from Jews. (Incidentally the word

58

"Jew" is not in the original text. It is the Judahite's nickname used by the translators.) I Kings 11:1-43; 12:1-24.

In 721 to 719 BC, some twenty million of the Northern Ten Tribes were deported to the headwaters of the Euphrates River. II Kings 17:6.

In 606-584 BC, a hundred and twenty years later, some four million Judahites or Jews were deported to Babylon, six hundred miles or thirty days journey southeast from the Israelites. II Chron. 26:15-21.

In 536-445 BC, under Ezra and Nehemiah, less than a mere 50,000 Judahites or Jews returned to Palestine; leaving at least, thirty million Israelites and seven million Jews still in exile. Nehemiah 7:66-67.

Isaiah, writing eight years after Northern Israel's exile, says Israel and Judah will be separated until Christ sets up His kingdom. Isa. 11:10-12.

Jeremiah, writing one hundred and ten years after Northern Israel's exile, said Israel and Judah would be separated until Jerusalem became the throne of the Lord. Jeremiah 3:17-18; 30:-3; 50:4.

Ezekiel living in exile, writing twenty years after the Judahites or Jews were taken into exile, said Israel and Judah would be separated until God once more dwelt with them. Ezekiel 37:19-27.

Zechariah, the prophet to the remnant who returned with Ezra and Nehemiah, writing fifty years after the Judahites or Jews returned to Palestine, said: *"And I will strengthen the house of Judah, and I will save the house of Joseph, and I will bring them again to place them; for I have mercy upon them: and they shall be as though I had not cast them off: for I am the LORD their God, and will hear them."* Zechariah 10:6.

Josephus says they were still separate in his day, 80 AD. "There are but two tribes in Asia and Europe subject to the Romans, while the ten tribes are beyond the Euphrates until now, and are an immense multitude and not to be estimated by numbers."

The Jewish Encyclopedia says they are still separated today. "If the ten tribes had disappeared, the literal fulfillment of the prophecies would be impossible. If they have not disappeared they must exist under a different name."

Isaac Leiser, the famous Jew, says they are still separate. "By this return of the captives from Babylon, the Israelitish nation was not restored, since the ten tribes were yet left in banishment; and to this day the researches of travelers and wise men have not been able to trace their fate."

The Jewish Chronicle says they are still separate. "The Israelites, who were subjugated by the Assyrian power, disappeared from the page of history as suddenly and as completely as though the land of their

59

captivity had swallowed them up. . . . The Scriptures speak of a future restoration of Israel which is clearly to include both Judah and Ephraim. The problem then is reduced to its simplest form. The ten tribes are certainly in existence. All that has to be done is to discover which people represent them."

Rabbi Gershom says they are still separated. "We are longing to find our lost brethren who for two thousand years have baffled all our efforts to discover their whereabouts, and are at this day a riddle even to the greatest of our illustrious Rabbis."

Professor A. Neubauer, the Jewish savant says they are still separated. "The hope of the return of the ten tribes has never ceased among the Jews."

Therefore, "Israel" and "Jews" are still separated. It would seem apparent then, that the Jews are not Israel.

Now let us ask ten questions.

1. Where is the Stone Kingdom prophesied to be set up in the days of the kings of Babylon, Medio-Persia, Greece and Rome, as recorded in Daniel 2:31-44? *"In the days of these kings shall the God of heaven set up a kingdom, which shall never be destroyed. . . and it shall stand forever."* Remember there is no mention of the ten toes being kings, so *"In the days of these kings,"* must refer to the four kingdoms noted.

2. Where are the saints who shall possess this kingdom forever? *"But the saints of the most High shall take the kingdom, and possess the kingdom forever, even forever and ever."* Daniel 7:18-27. It cannot be the Jews for the Kingdom was taken away from them. *"Therefore say I unto you, the Kingdom of God shall be taken from you and given to a nation bringing forth the fruits thereof."* Matt. 21:43

3. Where among the Jews are God's battle-ax and weapons of war? Jeremiah 51:19-20; Isaiah 41:15-16

4. Where among the Jews is the *Company of Nations* promised to Jacob and Ephraim? It will not be in the Millennium, then they will be one nation.

5. What Jews possess the gate of their enemies? It will not be in the Millennium as then there will be no enemies. "Thy (Abraham's) seed shall possess the gate of his enemies." Gen. 22:17.

6. Where among the Jews is Ephraim the first born of God to whom, as Joseph's son, went the birthright and blessing? Jeremiah 31:9; I Chron. 5:1-2.

7. Where among the Jews is the stick of Joseph which is to be united with Judah, remembering none of Ezekiel 37:16-25 was fulfilled under Ezra and Nehemiah?

8. Where was Judah's never departing sceptre for the six hundred years between Zedekiah and Jesus Christ? Gen.49:10.

9. Where is David's Throne which shall be established forever? II Sam. 7:16

10. Where among the Jews are "the Lo-Ammi," "not God's people," "Gentiles," who were later to be called the Sons of God, by being brought under the rod and into the covenant? Hosea 1:6-11; Ezekiel 20:35-37.

If the Jews are all Israel, then the Bible is untrue. Since this is unthinkable, Israel is somewhere on earth. As believers in the Bible, it is of the utmost importance that we locate Israel. The Anglo-Saxon people are fulfilling Israel's prophesied tasks and occupying Israel's positions. The end of time, when Israel is to be manifested, is here. No other people can possibly fulfill Israel's prophesied task and position. The Anglo-Saxons do. It is self evident then that the Anglo-Saxons are Israel.

In another article written by Luke Rader, he points out how some Bible students:

"forget to explain how it transpires that the Anglo-Saxons are the only people to exhibit the identifying badge of a faith like Abraham's, being the only people ever to have nationwide revivals. They might ask themselves how it comes that with a few exceptions all missionaries are Anglo-Saxon Celtic people.

Then perhaps they might have an answer to why the "merchants of Tarshish and the young lions thereof" are not the Jews, are the principal opponents of Gog and Agog in the Battle of Armageddon, as Ezekiel's thirty-eighth chapter relates.

Also, just where among the Jews are those "company of nations" from Jacob and "multitude of nations" from Ephraim, as promised in Genesis? *And God said unto him, Thy name is Jacob: thy name shall not be called any more Jacob, but Israel shall be thy name: and he called his name Israel. And God said unto him, I am God Almighty: be fruitful and multiply; a nation and a company of nations shall be of thee, and kings shall come out of thy loins; Gen. 35-10-11.*

And his father (Joseph's father, Jacob) *refused, and said, I know it, my son, I know it: he* (Manasseh) *also shall become a people, and he also shall be great: but truly his younger brother* (Ephraim) *shall be greater than he, and his seed shall become a multitude of nations.* Gen. 48:19.

Further, it would be interesting to know where the "stick of Joseph" is to be found among the Jews, spoken of by Ezekiel.

61

"The word of the LORD came again unto me, saying, Moreover, thou son of man, take thee one stick, and write upon it, For Judah, and for the children of Israel his companions: then take another stick, and write upon it, For Joseph, the stick of Ephraim, and for all the house of Israel his companions: And join them one to another into one stick; and they shall become one in thine hand. And when the children of thy people shall speak unto thee, saying, Wilt thou not shew us what thou meanest by these? Say unto them Thus saith the Lord GOD; Behold, I will take the stick of Joseph, which is in the hand of Ephraim, and the tribes of Israel his fellows, and will put them with him, even with the stick of Judah, and make them one stick, and they shall be one in mine hand. And the sticks whereon thou writest shall be in thine hand before their eyes. And say unto them, Thus saith the Lord GOD; Behold, I will take the children of Israel from among the heathen, whither they be gone, and will gather them on every side, and bring them into their own land: And I will make them one nation in the land upon the mountains of Israel; and one king shall be king to them all: and they shall be no more two nations, neither shall they be divided into two kingdoms any more at all: Neither shall they defile themselves any more with their idols, nor with their detestable things, nor with any of their transgressions: but I will save them out of all their dwellingplaces, wherein they have sinned, and will cleanse them: so shall they be my people, and I will be their God. And David my servant shall be king over them; and they all shall have one shepherd: they shall also walk in my judgments, and observe my statutes, and do them. And they shall dwell in the land that I have given unto Jacob my servant, wherein your fathers have dwelt; and they shall dwell therein, even they, and their children, and their children's children for ever: and my servant David shall be their prince for ever. Moreover I will make a covenant of peace with them; it shall be an everlasting covenant with them: and I will place them, and multiply them, and will set my sanctuary in the midst of them for evermore. My tabernacle also shall be with them: yea, I will be their God, and they shall be my people. And the heathen shall know that I the LORD do sanctify Israel, when my sanctuary shall be in the midst of them for evermore." Ezekiel 37:15-28

THE TREASURES OF JOSEPH

ROGER RUSK

INTRODUCTION
By Charles A. Jennings

Roger Rusk was born in Atlanta, Georgia into a Christian home in 1906. He first joined the church under the preaching of Evangelist Billy Sunday around World War I.

He grew up in a middle income neighborhood as an average teenager. His mother was a school teacher and taught him to read and write before he went to school. He left school at the end of the sixth grade to work in industry. He entered school again in the seventh grade and then attended Atlanta Tech High School. He graduated from a four year program in just three years. It was at this time that he started reading material that created doubt concerning his Christian faith. Upon graduation he went to work at Western Electric Company. He started living an undisciplined life and made things miserable for his family.

He then attended an institute run by the Presbyterian Board of Missions located in North Georgia. While there he earned additional credits in preparation for college. One night while returning from a basketball game a group of students started sing the song *"I'm Praying For You."* This song reminded him that his mother was praying for him, but he didn't realize that others were also praying for him. He arrived at his dormitory in a state of emotional upheaval that he didn't understand. He looked up Ed Ross and older advisor to the boys and asked him to go with him out in the woods to pray for him. Ed Ross prayed and was in a great agony of spirit for him. Roger had a million questions in his mind, but soon realized that his own agony of soul was a personal conflict with the person of the Lord Jesus Christ. He finally gave in and began to cry. He cried for a great long while. He completely surrendered to the Lord Jesus Christ with no resistance left. A great peace came over him. In his own words, Roger recalls his Christian conversion experience.

"Then I saw Him. Jesus appeared to me standing with an overwhelming view of His love, patience and compassion. He was just standing there. I couldn't see His face or where His feet touched the ground. His presence was so overwhelming, I just couldn't resist. After a while the vision passed. I found myself lying on the ground with the dirt and leaves from the forest floor in my mouth. He literally knocked me down and made me eat dirt that night. How long I lay there, I don't know. I had this unusual experience of coming back to my body after this ecstatic experience with the Lord. After lying there so peaceful for so long, I got up and shook myself off. I then returned to the boys dormitory."

The boys in the room woke up and Roger shared the good news of his new found salvation. All 25-30 boys were awaked. They all gathered in a meeting room and had a prayer meeting rejoicing over Roger's experience. Soon the whole school was aware of what had happened. Everyone rejoiced and sang songs at the breakfast table the next morning over the good news of Roger's conversion to Christ. Soon a preacher was called in and a week of meetings was held for more rejoicing over the fact that *"Roger Rusk had become a Christian."* He had a new found life in Christ. There were also physical consequences such as his hair turning from red and kinky to straight and black; a mole on his lip disappeared and his eyes improved so that he did not require eyeglasses for the next 15 years. Roger recalled; "The Lord Jesus marked my body so that I would never forget what He did for me. This was the crowning experience of my life to meet the Lord Jesus the way I did."

Roger Rusk went on to become a public school teacher for thirteen years. He then became a professor of physics at the University of Tennessee for twenty eight years, where he held the distinguished position of Emeritus Professor of Physics. He was also a member of many professional associations such as the *American Physical Society* and the *Tennessee Academy of Science*. In his commitment to his Lord and Savior, he was a life-long student of the Holy Scriptures and wrote extensively on Biblical subjects. Some of his writings have appeared in

Christianity Today including the article *"Seven Guidelines to a Christian Interpretation of History."*

Roger was the brother of Dean Rusk who served as Secretary of State in the administrations of Presidents John F. Kennedy and Lyndon B. Johnson.

After a sincere and in-depth study of history and the Bible, Roger Rusk was convinced of the true identification of ancient Israel's modern descendants as being the Anglo-Saxon, Germanic and related peoples. The following testimony is taken from chapters twelve and thirteen, *"The Treasures of Joseph"* and *"Oh Rachel, Don't You Weep"* contained in his book entitled, *"The Other End of the World."*

THE TREASURES OF JOSEPH
by Roger Rusk

Joseph is one of the most remarkable men in all of Holy Scripture. His character is unimpeachable. He lived from humble beginnings to become the second in office to the ruler of a powerful nation. His wisdom averted a great national catastrophe. He is remembered as a great provided of the people.

The story of Joseph really begins with the courtship of his father, Jacob. When Jacob went back into the East country to obtain a wife from among his own kind of people, he saw and fell in love with Rachel, the daughter of his uncle Laban. Jacob worked seven years for his uncle in order to obtain Rachel for a bride. However, when the expected moment came Laban provided Leah, the elder sister of Rachel, with the excuse that it was the custom that the elder sister should marry first. When Jacob returned to the land of Canaan, Rachel died when she gave birth to Benjamin as they came to Bethlehem. Thus Jacob had twelve sons, only two of which were Rachel's.

Jacob loved Joseph more than any of his other children and his preferential treatment of Joseph provoked the other sons to jealousy. There are several significant events in the life of Joseph. He developed an ability to interpret dreams. His brothers sold him as a slave in Egypt. Joseph was elevated in position and became second only to Pharaoh in all of Egypt. In the place of Joseph, Jacob adopted the two sons of Joseph into the family as full-fledged sons. This was a private affair, between Jacob and Joseph, and we read the account of this transaction in Chapter 48 of Genesis. It was not necessary that the boys be present. In this act of adoption, Jacob made mention of the promises of the land and the multiplicity of descendants. Also, by this act of adoption, Jacob had thirteen sons, counting Ephraim and Manasseh, as full sons in the place of Joseph.

In the latter half of this same chapter, a wonderful ceremony is recorded. Joseph presented his two sons to Jacob who proceeded to bless them. This is a very special blessing, and it is to be noted that the name Israel is used on this occasion for Joseph's father. Therefore, this blessing is of covenant significance. The blessing was in two parts. First, there was a blessing pronounced on Ephraim and Manasseh together, with a mention of Abraham and Isaac and the promise of a multitude of children. Then there was a blessing pronounced on Ephraim and Manasseh separately, with the pre-eminence given to Ephraim the younger brother. To Ephraim, Israel gave the blessing of a multitude of nations and to Manasseh the blessing of a great nation. How can these blessings ever be realized by a small group of people in the land of Palestine today?

Jacob, knowing that he was about to die, called all his sons together and orally gave his last will and testament. The most prominent of these blessings is that given to Joseph in verses 22-26 [Genesis 49:22-26]. We read, *"Joseph is a fruitful bough, even a fruitful bough by a well; whose branches run over the wall."* The blessing of Joseph thus begins with the blessing of a multitude of children; which had already been passed on to Ephraim and Manasseh the sons of Joseph in the previous chapter. The blessing of Joseph continues in verse 23, *"The archers have sorely grieved him, and shot at him, and hated him: But his bow abode in strength, and the arms of his hands were made strong by the hands of the mighty God of Jacob; (from thence is the shepherd, the stone of Israel:) Even by the God of thy father, who shall help thee;"* This portion of the blessing speaks of conflict or military activity in which the people of Joseph would be aided by the Almighty. Continuing in verse 25, we read, *"and by the Almighty, who shall bless thee with blessings of heaven above, blessings of the deep that lieth under, blessings of the breasts, and of the womb:"* This certainly speaks of a favorable environment of land and sea in which the people would flourish and produce many offspring, fulfilling the promise of a multitude of seed.

The birthright passed from Reuben, the first born of Leah, to Joseph, the firstborn of Rachel, Jacob's favorite wife. The passage in I Chronicles five continues: *"The genealogy is not to be reckoned after the birthright. For Judah prevailed above his brethren, and of him came the chief ruler; but the birthright was Joseph's."* Let it be repeated and emphasized that Jacob's blessings upon his sons and his grandsons took place several centuries before the old covenant at Mt. Sinai and a

66

thousand years before there was a Jew. We encounter a similar situation again in Deuteronomy 33, when Moses blessed the tribes of Israel when they were ready to enter the Promised land after their wilderness years. Again, as in Genesis 49, Joseph is prominent. In Deuteronomy 33:13 we begin to read, *"And of Joseph he said, Blessed of the LORD be his land, for the precious things of heaven, for the dew, and for the deep that coucheth beneath, And for the precious fruits brought forth by the sun, and for the precious things put forth by the moon, And for the chief things of the ancient mountains, and for the precious things of the lasting hills, And for the precious things of the earth and fulness thereof."* All these are promises of great material abundance, involving wealth from sea, sky and land. Great agricultural wealth and great mineral wealth are here promised.

The blessing of Moses continues in verse 16. *"and for the good will of him that dwelt in the bush."* This may refer to good relationship with less fortunate peoples in distant lands. We read on in verse 16, *" let the blessing come upon the head of Joseph, and upon the top of the head of him that was separated from his brethren."* This repeats the words in the blessing pronounced upon Joseph by his father Jacob, showing the favored position of Joseph of the distribution of the promised blessings. In verse 17, we read, *"His glory is like the firstling of his bullock, and his horns are like the horns of unicorns: with them he shall push the people together to the ends of the earth."* The word for "unicorn" is RAME, which is a very large wild bull, second only to the elephant in size, which became extinct in parts of Asia Minor long ago. It was noted for its ferocity and strength. The word does not refer to the unicorn of mythology. This passage symbolizes an aggressive, expanding, military power which subdues many weaker people throughout the earth. Finally, in verse 17, we read, *"and they are the ten thousands of Ephraim, and they are the thousands of Manasseh."* This much repeats the blessing of the multitude of seed which was transferred to Joseph and through him to his sons as mentioned before in Genesis 48.

These two mainstreams of covenant blessings provided the natural cleavage in later years which became the basis of the division of the kingdom following the death of Solomon into the House of Israel and the House of Judah. These two groups have different histories, different promises, different functions, and different destinies. *"But the birthright was Joseph's,"* we read. Not only the birthright, but great and wonderful promises of blessings were given to Joseph. Promises of greatness and wealth. Promises of strength and power. Promises of abundance and treasure. Since the people of Joseph are never called Jews in the Bible,

67

then how can we expect that these promises can ever be fulfilled by a people to whom they were never given? The last verse in the book of Genesis reads, *"So Joseph died, being an hundred and ten years old: and they embalmed him, and he was put in a coffin in Egypt."* This is where the majority of Christians leave him: dead, in a coffin in Egypt. We shall see.

The Bible frequently uses the name Joseph and Ephraim when it speaks about the northern people; not on every page nor on every breath, but enough to show they are synonymous. All of Hosea is a message addressed to the people of the northern tribes under the name "Ephraim." How did God "sow them in the earth"? He scattered them among the nations. He covered them as seed is covered. He sowed them where they would remain undetected until the coming forth of the green leaf. Although Israel disappeared from the pages of history, Israel was never lost. God hid them. They were lost to public view, but always known to God. To the world, "they were not." In many Old Testament passages it can be seen that Joseph-Israel or Ephraim-Israel came into the blessings made to the fathers, but usually in some limited way.

Just as emphatic as were the prophets in denouncing the people for their sins, so were they emphatic in their message of redemption and restoration. Not only emphatic, but exultant in their proclamation of God's final consummation of His purpose in Israel and Israel's glorious restoration. Paul tells us in Galatians 3:17, *"And this I say, that the covenant, that was confirmed before of God in Christ, the law, which was four hundred and thirty years after, cannot disannul, that it should make the promise of none effect."* Although the Law would not hinder or set aside the fulfillment of the promises, it is the Cross that makes fulfillment possible.

Jesus came to confirm the promises according to New Testament scripture. Romans 15:8 says, *"Now I say that Jesus Christ was a minister of the circumcision for the truth of God, to confirm the promises made unto the fathers."* In Luke 1:54-55 we read, *"He hath holpen his servant Israel, in remembrance of his mercy; As he spake to our fathers, to Abraham, and to his seed for ever."* Also, Zacharias exclaimed, in Luke 1:72, *"To perform the mercy promised to our fathers, and to remember his holy covenant; The oath which he sware to our father Abraham."* The coming of Jesus Christ, the "one seed" of Genesis 22:18 and Galatians 3:16, is the most essential part of the promises which God gave to Abraham. The entire program of redemption hinges upon the Cross.

During the period of history when Israel was entering the long-term punishment for their sins, the prophets, in additions to their indictment to the sinful people, almost in the same breath, proclaimed a bright future in which the promises would be realized. In Hosea 1:10, we read, *"Yet the number of the children of Israel shall be as the sand of the sea, which cannot be measured nor numbered; and it shall come to pass, that in the place where it was said unto them, Ye are not my people, there it shall be said unto them, Ye are the sons of the living God."*

In Isaiah 54:2-3, we read, *"Enlarge the place of thy tent, and let them stretch forth the curtains of thine habitations: spare not, lengthen thy cords, and strengthen thy stakes; For thou shalt break forth on the right hand and on the left; and thy seed shall inherit the Gentiles, and make the desolate cities to be inhabited."* In Deuteronomy 32:8, we are told, *"When the most High divided to the nations their inheritance, when he separated the sons of Adam, he set the bounds of the people according to the number of the children of Israel."* And remember, this promise of the multiplicity of seed was given to Joseph and his sons Ephraim and Manasseh. Since the prophets speak of it as yet future, then in no way can we say this promise was fulfilled in Old Testament times.

When shall these promised blessing fall upon Israel, and upon the people of Joseph in particular? When are the "latter days" and the "last days"? The term "last days" is used in II Timothy 3:1, Hebrews 1:2, and I Peter 1:20, all referring to the time Christ was made manifest. The terms "last days" and "last time" are used in II Peter 3:3-4, I John 2:18 and Jude 18 to refer to still future events of the time of writing. Then the "latter days" or "last days" must refer to this present days between the two advents of Christ. The people of Israel are to be called the Sons of God. Christians today are called the Sons of God. Then is Israel to be found among Christians? Why not? What is there to hinder? The promised blessing of material well-being and power do not pertain to a millennial age of bliss and peace. We should see some fulfillment of them, therefore, in this present age. Neither are we to look for their fulfillment in the life of the people known as Jews in the world today. There is a vast difference between what Jewish scholars write and what Jewish politicians say about these matters. Beginning with Ezra and Nehemiah, then Josephus, and including the scholars who wrote the Jewish Encyclopedia, all agree that the Jews did not include the ten tribes of the House of Joseph.

Joseph, in terms of his own life and in terms of the wonderful promises given to him, is a type or foreshadowing of what the people of Joseph are to be, are to do, and are to have. We should expect to find

69

the people of Joseph in this right relationship to God, in a position of authority and power among the nations of the world, with surpluses and plenty, rich in natural resources, strong in military power, expanding about the earth, having appeared from out of a wilderness, with an obscure history and without traceable parentage, establishing themselves in a land of their own, an "appointed place", as God told David. There are the things that we might expect on the basis of our Bible study to characterize the people of Joseph in the "latter days."

Now there is such a people. There is a people in the world today whose past history is lost in considerable obscurity. There is a people who have such great agricultural wealth that the rest of the world is in poverty by comparison. There is a people that well-nigh have a monopoly on the mineral wealth of North America, South America, Europe and Africa, leaving only Asia and the Far East to others. There is a people whose military might is greater than that of all other armies of all other nations in all of recorded history. There is such a people. There is a people who are Christian and are known to the rest of the world as Christian. There is a people whose destiny has been to bear witness of the Christian faith to the rest of the world. There is a people blessed of God above all measure, more than all other people upon the face of the earth. Blessed with natural resources, blessed with wealth, blessed with power and blessed with faith.

Did you ever wonder who these people are? Well, did you ever look in the mirror? To show the relationship of scripture to history, what better hypothesis can we set forth to defend than that we are that people? We have been involved in a westward movement for centuries and centuries, starting in Media the place where Israel was taken into captivity, sweeping across the northern shores of the Black Sea, up the Danube Valley, through the forest of Eastern Europe, skirting the fringes of the Roman Empire, converging on one little island in wave after wave, and later moving out from that spot to the rest of the world. We have spied out a vast new land, established a great civilization in what had been a wilderness. We have established in this land the greatest agricultural prosperity the world has ever known, and this great abundance is being produced by only three percent of our population. We have taken from the ground more mineral wealth in coal, oil, metals and other valuable materials than all other peoples in all of history put together. These things were promised to the people of Joseph. If we are not these people, then why do we have these blessings?

We are a people who have unimaginable military might. Twice in this century we have rescued the world from evil men. Even in this

70

generation we are pushing at the heathen in the ends of the earth in order that some men might have freedom. In none of our efforts have we sought territorial gain or the punishment of conquered people. The benign treatment we have given our enemies following military victory is unheard of in the annals of history. Our effort has been in behalf of freedom.

We are a people in whose heart is the law of God. It is built into our national life because it was in the hearts of those men who founded our nation. It has set the standards of our private and corporate behavior. This law of God is the touchstone by which we judge the increasing evil and lawlessness of our times. This law of God is the mortar which holds the stones of our social structure together. It is our public philosophy.

We are a people whose land is filled with churches. It has been so from the beginning. We are a church-going people. We are known the world around as the people of the Book. The Bible does say that in the latter days the people of Israel shall return and seek the Lord. In the providence of God it has been our destiny to be a witness to the world, to proclaim that the Lord God is God, and that His mighty work through Jesus Christ is the way whereby men must be saved and live as children of God. It has been said that 98% of all Christian literature and 95% of all Christian missionaries, outside the Roman church, have come from this one particular group of people, namely, the English speaking people and their kinsmen in northern Europe. We have witnessed to the world, and this witness has gone to every nation. Some governmental representative of every soul on the face of this earth in this generation has heard the Gospel message. Not every individual, but the political and social leaders who represent every person in the world have heard it. Why this drive to evangelize the world? It just comes with us; it has been our burning desire since Reformation days, and God has provided the material means in the form of transportation, communication and printing to enable us to carry out the Great Commission.

We are a people whose history is consonant with the fortunes of the people of Israel as told in the Bible. We have returned to God, and God has blessed us mightily. Do you realize just what it means that we as a people have practically encircled the whole world since the time we first began our westward trek? We have gone nearly all the way around the world; westward, westward, always westward. *Why did Paul go west?* Why did God call him to Macedonia? Why did he not go into Africa, or India or China? Did you ever consider what fortunes of history were involved in the selection of a direction for the main thrust of the Gospel? There must have been a purpose in it, for in God's history, nothing is left

71

to chance. Could it be that the people whom God intended should receive the Gospel were already in northern Europe? These are the promises, and these are the facts. We have looked in the mirror of history. What is the explanation? Who are we? Make no mistake, we need to be explained. There is just a tremendous amount to be explained to account for our place in history. Whatever scheme of interpretation of scripture that we adopt must include an explanation of our own people in the world today. What are the alternatives? If we are not literally, historically and corporately the people of the Book, then just who are we? It might be said that all these blessings have come upon us because as any other Christian people we enjoy the blessings in which God showers upon His children in any age. This is contrary to the teachings of Scripture to the effect that as Christians in this age we are to expect suffering. The blessings we enjoy are of the specific kind given to the House of Joseph as the descendants of Abraham, not to Christian gentiles, although the condition for the restoration to the place of blessing is contingent upon the people of Joseph becoming Christian.

Many people have been led to believe that the people we know in the world today as the Jews are to fulfill all the prophecies relating to Israel and enjoy the blessings promised to the fathers. But the Jews do not qualify. They cannot qualify. They cannot qualify because they are not the whole of Israel. The Bible says much about the separation of the people of Abraham into distinctive groups each with its own part to play in the story; and the Jews are only one part. If we think that at some time the Jews are to fulfill the promises made to the fathers, why not more rightly think that the people to whom the promises were made would fulfill them? The Jews are not that people. They say so. Yet Christian people go on assigning to them this role without question. For too long we have ascribed the fulfillment of many promises to the wrong group of people, promises specifically assigned to the people of Joseph and Ephraim. The Jews nowhere have ever admitted that they are those people; in fact, they themselves disclaim it, completely and explicitly, in the statements of their scholars and by their prayers for the future restoration of their brethren of the House of Joseph.

Now this is not a doctrinal matter. It is a primarily a question of who we are. Christians who were brought up to believe that all these wonderful things in some far off future time would happen to the people that we know as the Jews, should reexamine their understanding. If the Jews are a real people who are to do real things in a real time, then why not Israel? Why should a question of this importance be swept off into some dark corner as if it were sacrilegious or unworthy of consideration?

The time is come in the history of the world when God's people are going to know who they are. *Well, just who do you think they are?* The churches have traditionally taught that the church in a spiritual sense has inherited all the promises made to the Old Testament people, and that in a spiritual sense the church today is the Israel of God. If this were true, then why, after nineteen hundred years, is there still a people identified as the Jews? And if Judah is still here, then why not Israel? A lot of straining is being done today to make this Jewish venture in Palestine fit prophecy, and it just will not fit.

This proposition explains our history as a people, our present position in the world, and our entire missionary witness. We are known corporately as a Christian people; whether we think we are or not, to the outside world, we are. And we are in the land to which multitudes wish to come. What better rationale of history can we find?

O Rachel, don't you weep! Joseph is alive!

73

EVANGELICAL WITNESSES TO THE ANGLO-ISRAEL TRUTH
By Charles A. Jennings

Clem Davies   J.C. Kellogg   L.McConnell   H. Stough   W. Groom

TWENTIETH CENTURY PIONEERS OF TRUTH

During the second half of the nineteenth century, the forces of political, social, educational and religious liberalism intensified throughout every fiber of American life. The military victory of Union forces over the South's effort to secede and the utter desecration of our once Christian culture resulted in a cataclysmic change that has determined the national moral standard to this very day. As a whole, the widespread traditional influence of Biblical Christianity of the South and the remaining embers of it in the North had been crushed under the brutal heel of the self-appointed radical social reformers. The venomous philosophies that had made havoc of the by-gone nations were now tearing at the very framework of the once Christian American way of life. Before long, the once forbidden principles and acts of unrighteousness would be publicly flaunted as the expression of moral and social freedom as the restraints of the Victorian age were being broken.

Religious denominations would also join the ranks of those who cast aside their traditional Biblical beliefs and adopted the tenets of 'higher criticism.' Instead of total depravity, it was the sanctity of man; instead of true repentance it was a change of environment as the means of man's salvation. Instead of the altar, it was now a soup line as the way to express the love of modernism's 'god' and the new 'social gospel.' It was apostate religious leaders who were leading the people away from personal and national righteousness. As a counter attack, God began to raise up 'preachers of righteousness' to call the nation back to Him and to preach the ***Gospel of the Kingdom of God***. This powerful restorative message would include the knowledge of the Biblical Israelitish origins of the Anglo-Saxon and related peoples of western civilization.

FORGOTTEN PREACHERS OF RIGHTEOUSNESS

It was not by coincidence at this time in American history, that the Holy Spirit began to reveal to many pastors and evangelists this great truth. Without the knowledge of this Biblical understanding of the correct identification of God's covenant people, the principles of covenant law cannot be properly applied. The Holy Spirit, in His faithfulness raised up many prophetic voices to warn the American nation of the consequences of its national iniquities. Yet at the same time provided a message of hope, if we would acknowledge our family and covenant connection with our ancient forefathers, Abraham, Isaac and Jacob; truly repent and turn from our wicked ways. The promise of our Lord to *"heal their land"* as recorded in II Chronicles 7:14 was addressed to *"my people."* Through decades of neglect and ignorance of this Anglo-Israel truth the vast majority of God's Israel people have lost or given away their Biblical heritage. It's past time that we return to the God of our patriarchal fathers.

For every truth contained in the Holy Scriptures, the Lord has been faithful to reveal it to at least one of His servants. That revelation of truth may be in obscurity even for years, but God will not leave Himself without witness (Acts 14:17). Even though the light of a Biblical truth may burn dimly at times, the Holy Spirit maintains that flicker for succeeding generations. Sometimes that light is dim for a period of time, because it is not the right time to reveal it to the masses. God's truths are precious and He ever guards them for revelation to His prepared servants to be proclaimed when the spiritual and cultural conditions are right.

The true identification of God's people Israel is one of those precious truths. This truth God has chosen to reveal in His sovereign plan to certain of His saints among different bodies of believers as a witness of His faithfulness. This He does in preparation for a wider and more public revelation in His future timing of events.

The true Biblical perspective of the Kingdom of God must include an accurate description of the three-fold realms of the Kingdom, which are physical, moral and spiritual. The greatest physical extent of the Kingdom of God would include the universe itself and everything contained therein. Ever since the Protestant Reformation there has been a strong emphasis upon the institution of the Church, which is only one

76

element of the greater and larger institution of the Kingdom. Many Bible teachers have attempted to equate them as one and the same. They are definitely organically related to each other, yet they are not synonymous. The true Church is the genuine spiritual body of Christ within the Kingdom, but it is not the totality of the Kingdom.

One of the most confusing things in the minds of many Christians is the difference between the Kingdom of God and the Kingdom of Heaven. As it is obviously taught in the Old Testament, and reinforced by the teachings of our Lord, the Kingdom of Heaven is that national entity that is Israelitish in nature. The Kingdom of Heaven is within the greater and larger universal realm of the Kingdom of God. The Kingdom of Heaven, sometimes referred to as the Kingdom of God in the Gospel accounts, which denotes ownership, was the main topic of our Lord's teaching and preaching, Matt. 4:17 and 23. The thirteenth chapter of Matthew is totally devoted to our Lord's teaching and explanation of His Kingdom that He came to possess, redeem and purify. The Israelitish Kingdom established by God in the Old Testament furnishes the structural framework for the whole context of Scripture. This Kingdom was established within the loins of Abraham, began as a physical reality in Isaac and his descendants and finally came to mature fulfillment in King David. There are five component parts to any earthly kingdom which is also true of God's Kingdom. Those component parts are: people, land, law, throne and king.

Traditionally, the Christian Church has been extremely negligent in teaching and defining the Kingdom of Heaven in its doctrinal tenets of faith. In the mid nineteenth century when the Holy Spirit began to reveal the mystery of the Kingdom to many servants of God, they were misunderstood and sometimes even maligned. Still the Spirit was faithful to reveal this truth to many back then and has continued to reveal it to many in this present day. If the full truth be known, the men listed in this booklet is only a small portion of the multiplied thousands who believed that the true physical descendants of ancient Israel are the Anglo-Saxon, Germanic and related peoples of today. This revelation knows no denominational boundaries. This truth was known and proclaimed by Baptists, Congregational, Christian Church, Methodist, Presbyterian, Church of the Brethren, Pentecostal and Independent ministers and laymen. No doubt many ministers of the past who believed this message left no written record for posterity to read. The biographical information concerning some ministers has been difficult to obtain, so about them, we know very little, yet they have left a written record about their belief. For other ministers, we have much biographical information, yet very little record of their belief. For some, we are fortunate to have both.

Many opponents have unfairly accused the adherents of this truth of being members of a 'cult.' Upon proper examination, this body of Christian believers, neither believes, practices or displays any typical signs which are definitive of a cult. The faith and lifestyle of a true Christian believer who accepts the Anglo-Israel message is based solely upon the infallible Word of God, acknowledges Jesus Christ as the only begotten Son of God, His sacrifice as the only means of man's salvation and all the verities of New Testament Apostolic faith. The purpose of this booklet is not to set forth the tenets of the Anglo-Israel truth, sometimes referred to as the Gospel of the Kingdom, but to inform the reader of the variety and high caliber of some of the men of God who believed it.

The following is by no means an exhaustive list of ministers who believed and taught the Gospel of the Kingdom, which included the Christian Anglo-Israel message of Scripture. If the full truth be known, the list would consist of multiplied thousands of both ministers and laymen of many different denominations and Christian persuasions who had knowledge of and believed this great truth.

MATTHEW M. ESHELMAN

INTRODUCTION
By Charles A. Jennings

One of God's servants who had an ear to hear what the Spirit was saying about the identification of true Israel was Matthew M. Eshelman. He was raised on a farm in the state of Pennsylvania where he was born. After receiving his preliminary education, he pursued his career as a school teacher. After teaching school for a while he became a co-editor of a religious paper called *"The Brethren At Work."* This was published for seven years under the auspices of the Dunkard Church at Lanark, Illinois. The paper was previously known as *Der Bruderbote*, a German language paper. Then it became an English and German paper with the English version called the *Brethren's Messenger*. The paper was later moved to Mount Morris, Illinois. Eshelman, with the other two editors continued to edit both the English and German version until 1883. He joined the Cherry Grove Congregation at Virden, Illinois in June, 1873. Soon afterward, he became clerk of the church in 1874. He soon moved his family to Jewell County, Kansas, where they resided for about five

78

years.   In the autumn of 1884 Elder Eshelman took charge of the Belleville Church until the end of 1887.   During this time, membership greatly increased and a house of worship was built.

He and his family then moved to Republic County, Kansas where he was instrumental in founding a Dunkard College. Eshelman was the secretary of the McPherson College Building Association, whose purpose was to construct and equip the buildings for the McPherson College and Industrial Institute.   The charter stated that their purpose was to develop and maintain facilities for the attainment of higher Christian education in keeping with the principles of the **Church of the Brethren**. Eshelman served as a member of the Board of Trustees for many years.

In 1891, M.M. Eshelman along with George McDonagh, purchased the empty Lord's Hotel and one hundred city lots in Lordsburg, California for $15,000.   In this facility, Lordsburg College which was associated with the Church of the Brethren got its start with 135 students. Attendance greatly increased in subsequent years.   The name was eventually changed to the University of La Verne.

M.M. Eshelman was a prominent member and highly respected Elder in the Church of the Brethren until his passing at the age of seventy-six years.   He was the father of seven children.   He passed away in Los Angeles County after a life of devoted work in the vineyard of the Lord. The Church of the Brethren also included the Dunkards and the German Baptist Church. McPherson College which is still connected with the Church of the Brethren and the University of La Verne are still in existence and have grown to be highly accredited institutions of higher learning.

In 1887 while associated with McPherson College, Elder M. M. Eshelman wrote and published his book, *"Two Sticks or the Lost Tribes of Israel Discovered"* identifying the Anglo-Saxon and related people as the descendants of the ancient Israelites of the Bible. It was published by the Brethren's Publishing Company of Mount Morris, Illinois.   The following article is an excerpt from his 265 page book which affirms his belief.

"Two Sticks or the Lost Tribes of Israel Discovered"

During the year 1886 I had the pleasure of becoming acquainted with an octogenarian, by the name of William Montgomery, by birth an Englishman. He called my attention to the Biblical distinction between the "house of Judah" and the "house of Israel," that the Jews were one class and the Israelites another. This awakened a pleasurable interest in me and immediately I began an investigation of the subject. The deeper I dug, the greater number of precious prophetical gems were cast up; and, being somewhat unselfish, I resolved to scatter them abroad, through the Gospel Messenger, published at Mount Morris, Illinois. This done, an interest was aroused, requiring the remarkable prophetic chambers to be further explored, and the results given in book form.

In accordance with this unselfish desire, I am before you with this volume. It aims to regard the Bible as the Divine unit of the revealed will of God to man, with all of its principles harmoniously related to each other.

That the Anglo-Saxons possess a large number of the qualities ascribed to Israel in her preparatory state, prior to entering the Holy Land, cannot be successfully denied. So numerous are these identities that the mind is unwilling to reject them, or to ascribe them to mere chance. Many of them are here given, with the hope that an increased interest in prophecy may result, to the glory of God and of Him who hath redeemed us. Abstract spiritualism doth blind the sight and blunt the understanding.

In adventure, enterprise and daring, Dan occupies the pre-eminent position among all the tribes of Israel. He was the son of Jacob, by one of his concubines and the first adopted child of Rachel. She named him Dan because she believed that God had judged her. Thus the name *Dan* and the word *judge* are synonymous in juridical parlance. In the Gothic, Anglo-Saxon and English languages, the word Dan, under the forms of Don, Dun, Din, has ever carried with it the sense of judge or ruler.

About eighty-five years after the tribes of Israel had settled in Canaan, Dan began to bestir himself; for "in those days the tribe of the Danites sought them an inheritance to dwell in."–Judges 23:1. The plain reason of this was, that "*all their* inheritance had not fallen unto them among the tribes of Israel." At this time they lived along the shores of the Great Sea.

Now Dan, on the old homestead along the sea-coast early took to the sea and became a mariner–Judges 5:17. It is but natural to conclude that, in a period embracing hundreds of years, Dan being well-skilled in nautical affairs, would, when sorely pressed by the kings of Moab, Canaan and Mesopotamia, seek a more genial habitation. Eldad, a Jewish writer, when writing to the Jews in Spain, says: "In Jereboam's time (B.C. 975), the tribe of Dan, being unwilling to shed their brethren's blood, took a resolution of leaving their country."

80

The increase and perpetuity of Dan have ever asserted themselves wherever they planted their habitations. The histories of the Greeks, the Irish, the English and the Scandinavians are mines of information concerning the characteristics of the Danites, for the impress of their peculiarities are everywhere manifest.

The purport of this lesson is, to teach that the people of Dan along the sea-coast became adventurers in new countries, opened them to settlement and prepared the way for the rise and progress of the other eleven tribes in these latter days. They visited the countries now known as Greece, Italy, Spain, France, Ireland, Denmark and portions of Germany. On the other hand, Dan in Bashan went into captivity with the other tribes of Israel, and when they began their migrations out of Asia into Europe, Dan took the lead.

With the word *Dan* in its variations and other strong evidence of his pioneering, what shall be the conclusion? In view of God's promises to Abraham and this array of evidence of Dan's explorations by the sea and by land, there can be but one conclusion. Long time have historians been stumbling over these evidences, clear as the unclouded skies. Why has this mine of information been so long undiscovered? "Even so, Father for so it seemed good in thy sight."

The "veil has been kept on all eyes" until the day of Israel's hiding should be taken away. As Christ's coming was heralded by many prophets, these all became clearer and more easily understood by the faithful as the day approached, but "the wise" and "the prudent" of this world knew it not.

We have seen that the Ten Tribes, of Israel, went into captivity to Assyria B.C. 725. About 140 years later, Judah was taken captive. During this time the Assyrian empire had gone down, and the Babylonian realm had arisen in its glory. The Israelites were taken to Nineveh and located along the river Gozan. I Chron.5:26.

He said, *"the house of Israel rebelled against me,"* Ezekiel 20:13. And again, *"Son of man, the house of Israel is to me become dross: a ll they are brass, and tin, and iron, and lead in the midst of the furnace; they are even the dross of silver."*–Ezekiel 22:18. Now, what are brass and tin and iron and lead put into the furnace for? Is it not that the *dross* may be separated from the pure metal? God Himself gives an answer: *"Because ye are all become dross, behold, therefore I will gather you into the midst of Jerusalem. As they gather silver, and brass and iron, and lead, and tin, into the midst of the furnace, to blow the fire upon it, to melt it; so will I gather you in mine anger and in my fury, and I will leave you there, and melt you."* Ezekiel 22:19, 20. Thus He gave Israel over unto the heathen, that she might be melted, purified, cleansed of her dross, to be molded for the Master's use. They were to be disciplined into submissiveness. Scores of times in their own country, He endeavored to bring them into the enjoyment of unalloyed and unending bliss by the hand of affliction, and frequently turned their feet into the holy way; but, alas! They soon again wandered after "strange gods." Now He turned them over into the refiner's pot for a long season to be scourged, smitten, subdued and made sensible of the exalted state by relationship with Abraham. Israel was then among the heathen in Assyria, and Judah was on her way to serve under the same nation.

These prophetical passages cannot be opened with a denominational key, nor with badly-mixed presumptions. We must use the Divine Record and the events as they come to pass, to obtain the true answer. The movements of God in providence and grace are always with wisdom. Hosea proclaimed coming events sixty years before Israel's captivity. *"And God said unto him, Call her name Lo-ruhamah:"* that is, *"not having obtained mercy;"* but I will utterly take them away. *"But I will have mercy upon the house of Judah."* Hosea 1:6-7

The other child of Hosea was called Lo-ammi, that is, *"not my people;"* for *"ye are not my people,"* yet the number of the children of Israel shall be as the 'sand of the sea, which cannot be measured nor numbered." In this first chapter of Hosea we see Israel heathenized under a very tangible and practicable figure, their name, religion and nationality completely wiped out, except the gracious promise made to Abraham, Isaac and Jacob. Having shown the thoroughness of Israel's punishment for their idolatry, the prophet next enters the field of their resuscitation and says:'

"It shall be at that day, saith the Lord, that thou shalt call me Ishi [my husband]*; and shall no more call me Baal, that is my Lord."*–Hosea 2:16

The children of Israel shall abide many days without a king and without a prince, and without a sacrifice, and without an image, and without an ephod and without teraphim. Afterward shall the children of Israel return and seek the Lord their God, and David their king; and shall fear the Lord and his goodness in the latter days.–Hosea 3: 4, 5.

Did not the children of Israel, in their wanderings in Media and Persia and through Europe, abide many days without a king, without an ephod, pillar, sacrifice and teraphim? And in the latter days they are to fear the Lord and His goodness.–Hosea 11:10; 13:14; 14:4-9.

Israel having lost her identity by the removal of the Urim and Thummim, the sacrifice, the ephod, and pillar, she was like the Gentiles;

82

and Paul may have referred to this class in Romans eleven when he says: "Blindness in part has happened to Israel, until the fulness of the Gentiles be come in. And so all Israel shall be saved." He expressly states that "you (gentiles) in times past have not believed God, yet have now obtained mercy through their (Israel's) unbelief: even so have these (Israelites) also now not believed, that through your mercy they also may obtain mercy." Again he says: "For if the casting away of them be the reconciling of the world, what shall the receiving of them be, but life from the dead" Romans 10:13-16. Just now Israel is emerging from the dead; for the time or period of the Gentiles is nearly completed.

Viewing Romans eleven as referring to Gentile fulness, and lost Israel's relationship, all becomes clear, and the fogs and mists of unbelief vanish as before the noonday sun.

Behold the awful state of Israel in Assyria! "A rebellious nation," "impudent children and stiff-necked nation," and "a waste and a reproach among the nations." Upon them the Lord sent famine and blood and pestilence and evil beasts and the sword for their iniquity; after which they shall arise in favor and goodwill. *"Yet will I leave a remnant, that ye may have some that shall escape the sword among the nations, when ye shall be scattered through the countries"*–Ezekiel. 6:8.

Undoubtedly this blessing of Joseph's two sons and the circumstances attending it, were controlled by a divinely directed hand. Manasseh was to become a great people, and the United States, in our judgment, contains this 'great people" and the British nation the "multitude of nations"–the modern Ephraim.

It will be noticed that Jacob *crossed* his arms in blessing Ephraim and Manasseh. This is the sign by which the British conquer – The Union Jack–emblazoned on her national banner. Jacob said, "Let my name (Israel) *be named on them*, and *the name of my fathers, Abraham and Isaac.*"

That Ephraim is now arising out of his obscurity, and Manasseh coming forth as a great people, shall now engage much of our attention. The interest in "the lost tribes of Israel" is increasing, and many recognize the American and British nations as these tribes; and if this be correct, then no one can estimate its importance. It would verify the divine Scriptures in seven hundred different ways, and so completely establish the truthfulness of the Bible that unbelief must needs seek shelter among the caves and dens of despair.

"In Isaac shall thy seed be called."–Gen. 21:12. It is admitted by the most learned Hebrew scholars in the world, that the word "Saxon" means

sons of Isaac." They follow the old rule of the Hebrew "by dropping the prefix and adding the affix "ones" or "sons of."

Ephraim was to become a multitude of nations (Gen. 48:17), or *a nation and company of nations*–Gen. 35:11. Now Israel must possess these characteristics with many others; and if we can find a nation, or two nations answering to all the requirements of the divine prophecies, then we shall have found "lost Israel." We must find a people who were taken captive B.C. 725, and transported to Assyria–a people who emerged from that country, from the very spot where Israel was planted, and journey through Europe to the British Isles. If we can find a people from that particular locality in Asia, who have left marks and monuments of their migrations and evidences of their ancestry, moving out into the present world with all the identities of Ancient Israel, then we shall have found the people who were long lost to the intelligence and records of the world.

Again, we must find a people who are great in the Islands, possessing many colonies, immensely wealthy, controlling the strongholds of the sea, a mighty maritime nation, and we shall have found Ephraim or the Ten Tribes of Israel. Then, if we can find "a great people" who have left Ephraim, possessing wealth, liberty, fruitfulness, on an immense continent, making the desert blossom like the rose, joining Ephraim in commerce, in teaching liberty and in giving lessons on arbitration, we shall have found Manasseh.

With this picture upon the wall of intelligence, much of the past becomes clear and luminous, and the future opens up with a grandeur which can only emanate from the regions of unfading glory.

HENRY WELLINGTON STOUGH, D.D.

He was born in Williams County, Ohio on August 15, 1870. This is where Henry Stough spent most of his early life and received his primary education. He received his name, Henry, from his mother's father and his middle name, Wellington, in honor of the Duke of Wellington. When Henry was a young boy, his family moved to Bryan, Ohio and became affiliated with the Presbyterian Church. His son, Henry W. Stough, Jr, in the biography of his father wrote, "There were protracted meetings, or revivals in the churches during those days, and one night, as William and his son 'Wellie' were bedding down the cow for the night, and had finished milking the cow, that the son said to his father, "Father, I'm going to stand tonight and ask for prayer." In those days, that was all that was expected of one in the Presbyterian Church-just to stand and so

84

confess to the world that one was giving his life to Christ. When 'Wellie' said this, the father was overjoyed, and putting his arm around his son, he said, "Let us kneel and pray together." So there in that old farm barn was began a ministry that would take him into most of the states of the Union, and even to foreign lands."

He attended Oberlin College from 1888-1891. While there he was very active in rescue mission work with drunkards and derelicts leading many of them to Christ. He then became the General Secretary of the Young Men's Christian Association in East Liverpool, Ohio, which was a full time position. He then transferred to Moody Bible Institute and was there from 1891-1893.

As a young minister Henry Stough was chosen by Dwight L. Moody to preach in the revival tents erected during the World's Columbian Exposition of 1893 in Chicago. Afterward he attended the Moody Theological Seminary from 1893-1896. He also held the pastorate of the Third Congregational Church of Oak Park, Illinois from 1894-1901. In 1911 Defiance College in Ohio conferred upon him an honorary Doctorate of Divinity degree.

Henry W. Stough married Helen A. Russ on June 23, 1898 in Hyde Park, Illinois and they were blessed with eight children. Three of their five sons became ministers who also believed the Christian Anglo-Israel message of the Bible. His son, **Henry W. Stough, Jr.** was a very prominent Baptist minister in Knoxville, Tennessee who wrote several books advocating this Biblical point of view. He was the director of two Baptist Associations. Dr. Stough's other son, **Harold E. Stough** was for many years associated with the British Israel World Federation in London.

In 1901 he began his full-time evangelistic work with Dr. J. Wilbur Chapman. Dr. Chapman was a prominent Presbyterian minister known as "The Prince of Preachers." He was instrumental in leading Billy Sunday to Christ. Stough remained in evangelistic work until his death in Savannah, Georgia on October 27, 1939. His body was transported to Illinois and buried in the Wheaton Cemetery.

During his life he held crusades throughout the United States sponsored by groups of churches. Many cities lacking adequate facilities, huge tabernacles were built to accommodate the crowds. The meetings would often last from six to eight weeks. He conducted powerful city wide campaigns in Altoona and Lancaster, Pennsylvania that impacted those cities for God and righteousness. His revival campaign in Evansville, Indiana lasted for seven weeks. In his sixty-two sermons preached during this revival, he openly took a stand against both personal and public sins which made the local liquor traffickers angry. In one city they even brought a lawsuit against him. At one time he had fourteen members in his evangelistic party, which included the well known song leader, D.L. Spooner.

He boldly proclaimed the message of the saving power of Jesus Christ with scores responding to the Gospel call. At Harrisburg, Pennsylvania, where the shops of the Pennsylvania Railroad were located, Dr. Stough received a $500.00 check from the company. The reason was that so many workers had been converted to Christ and had returned thousands of dollars worth of tools that they had previously stolen. Many saloons were closed, gambling and immorality had greatly decreased and the whole city was made aware of the transforming power of Jesus Christ. He even conducted a campaign in Atlantic City, New Jersey with over 6,000 in attendance.

Rev. Stough was highly respected among his ministerial peers and was elected Secretary/Treasurer of the Interdenominational Association of Evangelists. He held this position from 1906 to 1912. The members of the association included Billy Sunday, Milford H. Lyon, W.E. Biederwolf, Bob Jones, Mel Trotter and other prominent evangelists of the day. Among his ministerial acquaintances were such prominent men as Dr. James Gray of the Moody Bible Institute and William Jennings Bryan.

Dr. Stough moved his family to Wheaton, Illinois, the location of the Association. He was trustee of Wheaton College for several years and members of his family attended there. Due to a severe accident of his son Philip in 1922 and his son Harold having double pneumonia, Dr. Stough entered an extended and deep study into the doctrine of divine healing. After his own healing, he began preaching the Gospel of *'The Healing Christ'* in his meetings. He also began to preach many sermons on the prophetic events of the time. It was not long until he became friends with F. F. and B.B. Bosworth. Many people testified to being divinely healed and even delivered from demonic possession.

More and more the matter of prophecy and prophecy- fulfilled was studied which led Dr. Stough to believe in the Anglo-Israel message which identifies the Anglo-Saxon-Celtic- Scandinavian people as the literal descendants of ancient Israel. He was a very strong advocate of that truth and the Gospel of the Kingdom of God. In 1932, in Knoxville, Tennessee, he held a sixteen week meeting proclaiming this message and establishing a permanent Gospel work in the city. He authored several books on various religious subjects which include: *Faith and Prayer in*

86

Their Conflicts With Unbelief, The Three-fold Resurrection, The Great Seal of the United States and many more.

WARREN BRUCE (W.B.) RECORD - 1886-1971 (circa)

W.B. Record received his ministerial training at Northwestern Bible College in Seattle, Washington and was affiliated with the Presbyterian Church. He was the founder of the National Message Ministry. He had a radio program on a Los Angeles, California radio station on which he preached the Christian Anglo-Israel message. His radio career began in 1938 and continued until shortly before his death. His son, **ROBERT RECORD** (1910-2005) was ordained into the ministry in the First Baptist Church of Rochester, Minnesota in 1936. For many years Robert Record shared the responsibilities of the radio ministry with his father and continued for many years after his father's death. Between the father and son, they had a continuous radio ministry proclaiming the Kingdom/Covenant message of the Bible for sixty-one years.

During his residence and ministry in the Minneapolis, Minnesota area in the 1940's, W. B. Record became friends with Evangelist Grady Wilson. Grady Wilson has been a close associate with Evangelist Billy Graham since their younger years in Charlotte, North Carolina. Both Wilson and Graham made their profession of faith in Christ under the ministry of Dr. M.F. Ham during the Charlotte Crusade in 1935. W.B. Record told Pastor Robert Woodworth that he had several conversations with Grady Wilson concerning Zionism and the Anglo-Israel message. Wilson confessed that both he and Evangelist Graham were aware of the Zionist movement and also believed the Anglo-Israel message, but felt that they could not afford to preach it because of their world-wide evangelistic efforts. Through the efforts of W.B. Record and other ministers was founded the National Association of Kingdom Evangelicals which was headquartered in Minneapolis, Minnesota.

CLEM DAVIES, D.D.

He was born in 1890 of Welsh ancestry. As a young man he was the pastor of Centennial Methodist Church in Victoria, Vancouver Island, B.C., Canada. While there, he had a very aggressive outreach ministry by utilizing every possible means including a 500 watt Marconi radio transmitter in order to spread the Gospel. In 1925 he resigned this pastorate and moved to southern California. There he continued his ministry by public preaching, radio and by printed publications. For many years he held weekly meetings in the Shrine Auditorium in Los Angeles. In his book, *The Racial Streams of Mankind* (1946), he clearly sets forth the Biblical foundation for his belief in the fact that the Anglo-Saxon and related peoples are the literal descendants of the ancient Israelites. For many years he published a paper called, *"Timely Topics"* in which he dealt with prophetic and current events until his death in 1951. Below is the conclusion of one of his radio sermons.

"Hence it is in this great group of nations having the name of Isaac that we must look for the fulfillment of the prophecies of the Bible at the time of the end – the great striking utterances concerning Israel. That is the value of this Anglo-Israel teaching – and you will have seventy-five per cent more Bible if you understand this message- and thus do not confine 'Israel' to one small part of it, the 'remnant' (as the Bible puts it) of the tribe of Judah that have survived the persecutions of the Jews throughout the centuries – numbering today only about 9 millions throughout the world – and certainly not numerous enough to fulfill the prophecies concerning **Israel**. If you will just have patience you will eventually see this wonderful truth – as many of us have already seen it. It was one of the greatest joys of my life when I saw the light of this truth, and it has stimulated my ministry – helped me to be a winner of souls for Christ. It has stimulated my desire to win souls to the Lord Jesus Christ that they may be saved. It has given me a great love for America and Britain–not only from the standpoint of patriotism, but dignifying that patriotism in a deeper spiritual sense, because I know that these nations are of the seed of Israel, and as such are being used by the Almighty to work out His purposes on the earth. I've always recognized that salvation was free to all, regardless of nationality, and we do not preach salvation by race but salvation by grace, the grace of God through Christ's atonement on the Cross of Calvary, but I find it much easier to understand my Bible when I realize that God's purposes for the world are being wrought out through the instrumentality and the destiny of the Anglo-Isaac-Israel people, with their kith and kin throughout the world."

LINCOLN McCONNELL, D.D. LL.D.

Among many characteristics of Lincoln McConnell, he possessed a very influential and charismatic personality. He grew up with a leadership ability that he expressed throughout his life. He was born the son of a Tennessee lawyer and was trained early in the study of Law. After spending some time out west after college he moved to Atlanta, Georgia. He became a member of the Atlanta police force, then he became a detective and later served as assistant to the solicitor in criminal court. While a member of the Atlanta police force he was converted to Christ and immediately began to get involved in ministry to the down and out of the city. He was influential in starting a rescue mission in Atlanta. He also served as pastor of the downtown *People's Church* of Atlanta and attracted an audience of 2,000 people which came to hear him. From April 1927 to February 1929 he was the pastor of First Baptist Church of St. Petersburg, Florida. This 4,000 seat capacity church was full each Sunday as the people of the city were anxious to hear this powerful man of God. He then pastored the First Baptist Church of Jacksonville, Florida from 1929-1930. At the time this church had a membership of 2,162. Many of his Sunday sermons were broadcast on radio and heard by millions of Americans. He was also a popular speaker in large conferences throughout the country.

In a twelve year period, he made over 8,000 public speeches and was considered to be one of the most humorous, dynamic and effective speakers of his day. As an avid believer in the Anglo-Israel message he responded in a letter to an inquiry by saying; ". . .I must say that if you really want to know your Bible you will have to get the books on "Anglo-Israel"...you will never know the real truth the book is teaching without this key." The following article is a part of his speech that he gave before an annual meeting of the British Israel World Federation in London, England in 1928.

"I am exceedingly glad that I have had the opportunity of staying these two days at this Congress, and I greatly regret that the pressure of my engagements, and the calls for my presence in Florida, my home, make it virtually impossible for me to delay sailing after tomorrow. I am a speaker at several Conventions in the States, and I cannot possibly defer my departure longer. If it had been a personal matter merely, or a matter concerning my own congregation–though I have been away for three months, and they are extremely loving folk–at the same time I might have put off my departure for another week. But before I say what I want to say, I want to express my high appreciation of the splendid spirit I have found among you beloved folk. Naturally I expected to find cordial people in England. I have known a great many of your illustrious platform and ministerial men, as well as quite a good many other public men who have come to the States in my long platform experience, and I naturally have met a great many of them. But I have been more than delighted to find the heart and the brain and the faith of these British-Israel leaders at Headquarters are so nearly balanced that I hardly know which the better is.

I have been thinking a great deal, and naturally lately, as I have thought for many years in a cursory manner, of the marvelous providence of God in directing the affairs of our twin nations. No one can look at the British-Israel teaching without taking a long view of the plan of God for the race of man. It has been a matter of great interest to me to read British history. You have had so many kings, and we folks have to remember which did that and which did this. Therefore I do not claim to be very well versed in English history, only in just a very casual way. But I know something of your struggles. And some of us in America believe that it was the providence of God that kept the United States, our American Continent, from being colonized. It was not until this Bible was permitted to do its work that God permitted the people to successfully colonize in the United States. And God selected families who went there to found that new Republic that He had in His mind.

Now we who understand something of the American Constitutional law know this, that there are three great ideas underlying our Constitution. I was asked by several Bar Associations a few years ago to address them on something appertaining to the Constitution and I chose for my subject, "Back to the Constitution." A good many people wondered why our fathers could get together and in a few weeks and months formulate doctrines that the greatest economists of England, and that means of the world, describe as one of the greatest documents from the hand of uninspired man. That has been the pronouncement of several of your greatest Englishmen in regard to that document known as the Constitution of the United States, that a people so primitive, without the background of a long Governmental history, could formulate a document like that, a structure that could be as abiding, and as well qualified as it has proved itself to be, of sustaining the weight of the gigantic United States, that has been built upon the foundation first laid for an infant nation. For when the Constitution was born there was only a population of 3 million; now there are 110 million, and it supports it today quite as well as it did then.

You have been developed because you had the germ of the thing back yonder in the Common Law. Our forefathers believed that the highest intelligence possessed by people would be found in the majority of that people, and therefore, the best laws that might be evolved would be those laws that emanated from the best brains selected from all sections of the country, and that would represent the highest intelligence of the democracy. There was a complete submission to the reign of law. Where did we get that idea? We got it from the grandest nation under God's sun, the nation that was born a people under the Common Law of

Almighty God, the Law of Israel. That is how it happened. A good many of our younger men do not understand our kinship, but admire and appreciate the old English Common Law, and they know the draw and pull, and how to proceed to get their case somehow.

When men leave God out, when men leave part of God's plan out, when men try to build the structure of a Church, or a great civilization, cutting out the major part of the plans of the Architect of the building, they need not complain if the building that they erect is not as beautiful and as abiding as they would have hoped it to be. God Almighty had a plan for the building of Great Britain and America, and just in proportion as we folk harmonize with God's plan will the building be erected speedily, soundly, firmly and beautifully. There is no getting away from that. And the British-Israel Movement and its teaching is nothing more or less than the flooding of Biblical light penetrating into the dark recesses of social and political and industrial conditions in both our countries, which will be a marvelous luminant, explaining these things to the people of our twin nations, if they will only be willing to see them as such.

If you good folk are not going as deeply into British-Israel Truth as you might go, then let me urge you to go as deeply as you can go. Do not allow yourselves to be repelled. It is true, and your disbelieving of it will not affect its operation; it is going straight on. I want to be with God on this matter. I would rather believe too much about God's power than believe too little. It gives me a great deal of joy and comfort in my soul to believe in a personal God, One who is personally interested in Lincoln McConnell.

I thank God for the revelation of One Who cares, and not only a God Who cares for us individually, but a God Who had planned a mighty movement, not only of the planets, but of mankind on this planet. I thank God that there are a God-loving and a Bible believing and a consecrated body of people in this great throbbing heart of the world who dare to teach that, and to preach that.

GEORGE B. PECK, M.D.

In his book entitled, *"All Israel Restored"* Frank S. Murray comments concerning Dr. Peck's belief in the Anglo-Israel Truth.

"In God's providence one good and godly man did appear at about this time to reinforce Mr. Sanford's feelings about Anglo-Israel. His name was Rev. George B. Peck, who was also a medical doctor, a friend of A. B. Simpson and one of Mr. Sanford's enthusiastic co-operators in the first years of his work. Dr. Peck not only assisted Mrs. Sandford on the occasion of her first confinement for childbirth, but was instrumental in many instances of anointing for healing in the early Shiloh conventions. He was also an intent student of the Bible, and had found a divine fitness in the Anglo-Israel explanation of the otherwise mystifying promises made to the covenant fathers. When Mr. Sandford had listened to this man, who had no connection whatever with Totten, it was clear to him that God had provided two witnesses to this line of truth."

Dr. Peck (1833-1906) was a personal friend with A.B. Simpson who was the founder and president of the Christian and Missionary Alliance Church which is still in existence today. They even traveled together in ministry, conducting evangelistic campaigns and praying for the sick and suffering. While in attendance during the 1906 annual Christian and Missionary Alliance Convention held in the Berkeley Temple in Boston, Dr. Peck passed away. His funeral service was held in the Clarendon Street Baptist Church with several distinguished ministers eulogizing his life of faith and service to the Lord and his fellow man. As a prominent member of the Christian Missionary and Alliance, an article of his death appeared in the church's official paper.

J.O. SCHAAP

According to Ernestine Young, a personal friend of Pastor J.O. Schaap, he and his wife Grace, moved from Minnesota to Idaho in the early 1940's. While in Minnesota, it is believed that he was connected with Luke Rader of Minneapolis. While holding ministerial credentials with the Church of the Nazarene, he began to preach the Anglo-Israel message and as a result was excommunicated from the denomination. He was the founder of Five Mile Community Church located on the west side of Boise, which still remains after more than fifty years. Pastor and Mrs. Schaap are remembered as gracious and loving servants of the Lord who encouraged family prayer and a life of strong commitment to the cause of Christ. He passed away in 1959 due to a severe heart condition. His wife, Grace, who died in 1988, was inspired to write over one hundred choruses of worship and consecration such as:

Oh Israel, come back to Jesus; Your Bridegroom now is calling thee Repent of all thy vast transgressions; And you will find your nation free.

It is also reported that in 1934 two laymen of the Nampa, Idaho Nazarene Church taught the Anglo-Israel message. Mr. Hillborn and Mr. Milligan taught this message for six months in the church until a new

District Superintendent took office. According to Esther Young, the mother of Ernestine, Howard Rand, the director of the Anglo-Saxon Federation of America spoke in the Nazarene College of Nampa, Idaho in 1935 with two thousand people in attendance.

JAY C. KELLOGG

One of the most illustrious characters in the history of American evangelism was J. C. Kellogg. He was known as "The Cowboy Evangelist." He often dressed in western style clothing, including his hat, during his evangelistic meetings. His ministry was known as the *Whole Gospel Crusaders of America*. He ministered in some of the largest churches of America including the Chicago Gospel Tabernacle, pastored by Paul D. Rader. He authored several books including; *The Brand of Hell - 666, The Midnight Cry, The Mark of Cain, The United States of Europe and Is Capitalism Doomed?* The following article is an excerpt from his book copyrighted in 1932 entitled, *The United States in Prophecy*. In this book, he shows from Scripture the part he believes that America and the Anglo-Saxon people play in Bible prophecy.

Isaiah's Vision of America

There is clear and infallible proof that the Holy Spirit gave to the prophet Isaiah a vision of America as existing and playing a conspicuous part in the providence of God among the nations of the earth in the last days. In the very nature of things it is reasonable to suppose that a nation of the magnitude and power and service of the United States should occupy a place in divine prophecy. When we consider the origin of this nation, and the fact of its being born of religious principle, the work it has done in the providence of God, and the work it has yet to perform, we need not be surprised to find that these things were foretold by the Holy Spirit in connection with this prophecy.

Nations in the Last Days Prophecy

The prophet Isaiah was led to deliver a series of prophecies concerning various nations as to events that would transpire in the last days. In chapter 13 he delivers a prophecy concerning Babylon on the east; in chapter 15 a prophecy concerning Moab on the southeast of Jerusalem; then in chapter 17 he delivers a prophecy concerning Egypt; in chapter 21 a prophecy about Media, and in chapter 23 a prophecy concerning Tyre, making, as it were a circle of nations; and right in the midst of this circle, in chapter 18, he delivers a prophecy concerning a country which at that time had no name. Now it is evident that this prophecy in chapter 18 forms a part of this great message concerning the nations of the earth in the last days. Let me call your attention to the marvelous items mentioned in this chapter and see how infallibly they refer to our American nation.

The United States in Prophecy

In the prophet's vision he saw a nation arise far in the west, of wonderful power and service, but which had no name. He called it, *"The land of outstretched wings,"* which is a more correct translation than in the Authorized Version. It was by divine providence that the eagle was selected as the emblem of the United Sates as a nation, but there was a deeper truth hidden under the emblem, and that was that America, in the providence of God, should be a land that would serve as a refuge to all other nations of the earth. Since the world began there never had been any other country that from its beginning offered a welcome and hospitality to all other people for the purpose of giving them religious and civil liberty except America.

The Anglo-Saxon and Saxon Nations

Who are the Anglo-Saxon people? From whence do they come? Surely God's hand has been with the Saxon people in a remarkable way, especially the Anglo-Saxon. The Anglo-Saxon and the Saxon nations are a branch of the Caucasian race-the white race. The Anglo-Saxons have always embraced Christianity more generally than any other people. Have always believed in law and order in government and have contributed more to society. Now it seems that God has His hand with the Anglo-Saxon people in a peculiar way. The Anglo-Saxon believe in religious liberty and freedom and, as a whole, are Protestant. It is a known fact that down through history ninety-five per cent of all foreign missionaries have been Anglo-Saxon, and how do you account for that except that God has His hand upon the Anglo-Saxon people in a peculiar way?

The Origin of the Anglo-Saxon People

From whence came the original Anglo-Saxon people? There is much evidence that the two great Anglo-Saxon peoples, Great Britain and the United States of America, are descendants of the two sons of Joseph, Manasseh and Ephraim. That is, the fulfillment of many prophecies and promises that were given to these two tribes, Manasseh and Ephraim, are falling upon America and Britain today. Many prophecies have a three and four fold application; they are given to the people at the time and have to do directly with them. There is the spiritual application down through the ages, a dispensational application and often a national application to the different nations as they walk with God.

WILLIAM MARION GROOM D.D.

Other than the date and the place of his birth, nothing else is known of the life of William Groom before he emigrated to America. He was born in Erith, Kent, England in 1884. There he received his elementary secular education. It is believed that he first went to Canada for a brief period of time before moving to Texas. In 1912 he entered Southwestern Baptist Theological Seminary in Fort Worth where he earned a Master of Theology degree. During his time in Seminary, he was connected with several Baptist churches in the area. Not long after graduation from Seminary in 1915 he married Lorena M. Ford from Arkansas. Two children were born to this union.

William Groom's first pastorate was the First Baptist Church of Haskell, Texas from April 7, 1915 to October 9, 1917. By September 1915 the attendance had increased to the extent that it was necessary to construct a new building. The new church sanctuary would seat 400 people. He also served as pastor at the First Baptist Church in Corpus Christi, August 15, 1920 to November 30, 1924; Ross Avenue Baptist Church in Dallas, December 1, 1925 to January 1, 1931. He also served Central Baptist and Oak Lawn Baptist Churches in Dallas.

While pastoring in Corpus Christi, William Groom was very instrumental for the Southern Baptist Convention in advocating the Baptist Hospital to be constructed in the Texas Valley. Due to Mrs. Groom's sickness, the family was forced to move to Minneapolis where he became engaged in the hotel business. In 1941, Mrs. Groom accepted employment at the Northern Baptist Theological Seminary and eventually became Dean of Women until the early 1950's. For the last several years of his life William Groom lived in the Los Angeles, California area until his death on April 6, 1957.

He was the author of several books which include: *The Genesis to Revelation Bible Course; Bible Men and Things with their Gospel Meanings;* and *Greatest Bible Doctrines Explained.* In 1934 he published a book entitled **Bible Proof That America is God's Chosen Nation** in which he clearly advocated the Anglo-Israel message of Scripture. The texts below are excerpts from William Groom's statements concerning the promises of God fulfilled in the British and American nations.

Bible Proof That America is God's Chosen Nation

In almost every country of the civilized world multitudes have come to believe that the Anglo-Saxon peoples are descended from the Ten Lost Tribes of Israel. Theologians and ministers, statesmen and educators, army officers and business men, are all awaking to the thrilling fact that America and the British Commonwealth of Nations are God's chosen people. Of course, this mighty truth is stirring up opposition in some quarters, for the blindness that is upon Israel as to her identity will not be removed by miracles, but only by the earnest study of receptive minds.

God said to Abraham in Gen. 21:12, "In Isaac shall thy seed be called." Not in Ishmael, not in the sons of Keturah, but the chosen people should be of the line of Isaac only. What revelations, miracles and training God gave to His elect race in the wilderness! There they received the Moral, Ceremonial and Civil Laws, upon which the life of Israel and the entire Anglo-Saxon world has been based. There the Tabernacle was erected, public worship was instituted, and the Sabbath was made a sign of the covenant. Contrast Israel at the time with the miserable autocracy, slavery, and heathenism of other nations like Egypt and Assyria. This vivid contrast holds good today between God-fearing, law-keeping, Sabbath-observing modern Israel, and the atheistic, oppressing Gentile nations.

About 1799 A.D. the Seven Times or 2520 years of national discipline and blindness meted out to Israel, as spoken of in Lev. 26:34, expired, and then began the most wonderful era for the Anglo-Saxon race that any race has ever seen. At the beginning of the nineteenth century, the United States had a population of four millions which has now grown to 132 million, until we with Britain comprise one-third of the population of the world, and one-fourth of all the earth's surface.

96

The development of this country is one of the miracles of all history. When you look at the nation's wide-spreading farms and ranches, her gigantic industries, her colossal cities and sky-scrapers, her magnificent institutions of learning, art and of science, her multiplied number of majestic churches and benevolent philanthropic agencies, we are led gratefully to exclaim with our great forefathers in Deut. 33:29, "Happy art thou, O Israel, who is like unto thee, O people saved by the Lord."

Christ twice referred to the "lost sheep of the House of Israel" (Matt. 10:6, 15:24). He does not mean lost spiritually, but lost nationally, otherwise the conclusion would be that Israel only was lost in sin while the Jews and the Gentiles are not. On the contrary it is true that only Israel was lost to her national identity while the Jews and the Gentiles were not. Many of the Epistles were addressed to Israel. Not but the Israelite, Jew, and Gentile are all one in Christ and in the Church, but the Israel nations, as nations have birthright blessings and are elected to certain privileges and service.

In Rom. 9:31 Israel under the law, which was Judah, is contrasted with the children of the living God, in Rom. 9:26, which is a quotation from Hosea 1:10 and shows that the Ten-tribed Kingdom is in view. The Galatians were part of Israel in dispersion and were not converted from Judaism, but from heathenism, into which the stock had lapsed. There is strong evidence that Hebrews was written to Israel, and James wrote to the Twelve Tribes, and not to the Two Tribes into which the others had been absorbed as some suppose. Peter in 2:9, 10 has the divorced Israel of Hosea in mind as having now become again the people of God. Much more New Testament evidence might be given to show that although Israel was very much dispersed yet it did not pass off the stage of history, and the birthright was not taken from them.

When, after teaching and training the twelve disciples, Jesus sent them forth to their labors, He commanded them, *"Preach the Kingdom of God"* (Luke 9:60), and when the Twelve returned, and multitudes had gathered about Him, He spoke to them of the Kingdom of God. When He sent out the Seventy evangelists He instructed them to say to the people, *"The Kingdom of God is come nigh unto you"* (Luke 10:9-11). After Jesus had risen from the dead, He spoke to them the things concerning the Kingdom of God (Acts 1:3). When the apostles asked him, *"Dost thou at this time restore again the Kingdom of Israel?"* (Acts 1:6). He did not rebuke them for wanting the Davidic Kingdom restored to Palestine, but only told them it was not for them to know the times and seasons of such restoration.

97

Not only did our Lord not discourage Kingdom preaching and hopes, but He made them the main subjects of His preaching, and taught us to definitely pray, *"thy Kingdom come"* (Matt. 6:10). In the very last picture that we have of the Apostle Paul, he was a prisoner in Rome, and he was not using the popular themes so common today, but he, *"Expounded and testified, and preached the Kingdom of God"* (Acts 28:23, 31). Surely it is time for us to awaken to the fact that nine-tenths of the New Testament preaching was about the setting upon the earth of a kingdom of peace, prosperity, and righteousness.

It is a well known fact that every great doctrine presents some difficulties to those who would accept it. For instance there are the doctrines of the Trinity, election, and the eternal punishment of the wicked, etc.; and some of the most devout Christians have seen insurmountable difficulties in accepting the orthodox teachings on these profound subjects. It therefore will be readily understood that there will be many sincere objections raised to the thesis that the Anglo-Saxons are the lost Ten Tribes of Israel. Earnest seekers after truth have carefully and prayerfully examined these spectres of the mind and laid them low, until today, not only some of the most scholarly preachers, but great thinkers in every walk of life, have unreservedly accepted Israel truth. This world-wide galaxy of adherents, ten million strong, includes college professors, statesmen, authors, army and navy officers, lawyers and business men, so there is no need for anyone to think that this is just a hole-in-the-corner fad, but rather with assurance we should be ready always to give an answer to everyone that asketh a reason for the hope that is in us.

It is perfectly legitimate to ask what is the good of the Anglo-Israel doctrine, and what does it matter whether we are Abraham's seed or not. Since, we are assured, Christ is the Savior of all who believe, therefore He is our Savior, what more should we want? Now we gladly concede that this is true and more. That salvation is not only offered to all mankind, but that a kind Heavenly Father makes the sun to shine on the just and the unjust, and yet it can be proved that it is an assuredly blessed thing to be the children of Abraham by race as well as by grace!

1. It proves the truth and inspiration of the Scriptures.
2. It teaches us to look to God for bodily necessities.
3. It will be the cure for international unrest.
4. It will do away with Social injustice.
5. It would solve the crime problem.
6. It will give assurance as to our nation's future security.

7. It will lead to great revivals all over the land.

Since one fourth of the Bible is prophetic and five sixths of it is addressed to God's nation, Israel, any system of Bible teaching that ignores prophecy and kingdom truth, or spiritualizes it is incomplete and misleading. While many think it is fanatical to really try to understand prophecy, yet it is much better to be such a crank than an ignoramus and a coward. No one would wish to be operated on by a doctor who knows as little about surgery as the average preacher knows about prophecy. That the world today is awakening to a sense of its obligation to Israel, is seen from the amazing output of literature on the subject, and from the fact that in every civilized country large numbers are accepting the Israel message. If the question were asked, what was the greatest discovery of the last century, there would be varied answers. Yet the day will come when all will agree that the crowning glory of the twentieth century was the discovery that the Anglo-Saxons are the Ten Lost Tribes of Israel, and of what has gone with it, the re-discovery of the Old Testament.

It is an amazing thing that God has in this world a lost people, and a lost Testament, and that most of the seers do not even know that they have been lost. Yet most preachers neither preach nor teach the Old Testament as a whole, and those who do usually spiritualize its real teachings away. The Old Testament actually represents 1500 years of divinely given laws, worship and prophecies, that were to make Israel an ideally righteous nation for all other nations to emulate. What then must be the incalculable loss that it has been so grossly neglected or misunderstood!

DETROIT BELIEVERS

Taken from the book entitled, *"Lives Of The Saints" - Early History of Christian-Israel Belief in Detroit* by J.S. Brooks
DANIEL J. SMITH - Evangelist Daniel J. Smith was not an ordained minister, but wherever he went, the Gospel of the Kingdom and National message of the Bible went with him. He faithfully proclaimed Bible truths to all who would listen; so that he was known to neighbors as, "the local preacher."

Daniel led a fascinating, varied life. In 1871 he opened up a dry goods shop with an associate as "Smith and Tenney," at #453 - 7th Street in Detroit, Michigan. Six years later, in 1878, he opened a larger dry goods store himself at 433 - 435 Grand River Avenue, one of the major thoroughfares through the city. In those days, most food stuffs were sold in a semi raw state, bagged in large burlap sacks and called, "dry goods." Not satisfied with that career, however, in late 1880 he moved to 122 Cass Avenue in downtown Detroit and briefly tried his hand at real estate; and then five years later opened shop as a photographer at 212 Woodward Avenue. Daniel was tremendously fascinated with new technology, and photography was a rapidly expanding invention. His photography studio was one of the first companies in Detroit to have telephone service, and the business grew with two partners in 1890 to become the firm of "Galloway, Butterfield and Smith."

But God's Word was his main interest. In 1881, the book, *"Anglo-Israel in Nine Lectures"* by Dr. W. H. Poole, reprinted a letter by Daniel Smith. The letter told how Smith had first learned the great and little known truths of Scripture several years earlier from Dr. Poole, and said in part, *"When our people come into a full realization of the worth of this...and the truth it reveals, it will be like a flood of light from on high, for I consider in value it stands in close proximity to that of the gift of the Bible itself, for it is in the direct line of an explanation and corroboration of the revealed truth; and without it, there cannot be a correct and, consequently, an intelligent understanding or a proper interpretation of the sacred books; but with it, the difficulties of prophecy and of many historical allusions vanish like dew in the sunshine."*

"I am aware that many men, in other things wise men, have said these things were not, could not be, true; but I have thus far in every case found that, like myself (before I had given the matter the thought it demands) they had spoken unadvisedly with their lips. And I find, too, that in every case when men of intelligence and candor open their minds and hearts to the truth, and obtain a clear conception of its value, and of the beauty of the Divine plan, they must and do acknowledge themselves convinced; even though, as one good brother said to me, 'If I teach this thing I will be obliged to rearrange most of my sermons.'

"All hail the glad day when the Christian world, enlightened and convinced by the truth, shall arise and give light that shall lighten the Gentiles, and fill the world with the knowledge and the glory of God, and when this world shall know that Israel, whom God hath exalted chief among the nations, is the seed that the Lord hath blessed...I believe that when these truths are fully known and accepted, that infidelity, with its last proof swept away, will slink away before the light and hide its deformity forever, and the millennial glory will

speedily spread its joy and gladness over all the earth to the glory of our God and His Christ."

DR. JOHN WELLINGTON HOAG   One of the leading churches in Detroit for many years was Woodward Avenue Baptist Church. It was founded in 1860 as an offshoot of the oldest Baptist congregation in the city, and was the first Detroit church to have electric lighting installed in 1890. The authoritative *"History of Detroit"* by Silas Farmer states, "The church, which is built of Ionia stone, is deemed the handsomest in the city." (p. 608)

In 1915, the church called the noted Dr. John Wellington Hoag to pastor. During his leadership, at the time of the First World War, the church became the largest congregation in the state of Michigan, with 3,500 members. Hoag was pastor for a total of 32 years until his death in 1947, and often had Anglo-Israel leaders such as Dr. Howard B. Rand and William J. Cameron as his guest in the pulpit. Cameron was vice president of the Ford Motor Company, and a close friend of the inventor, Henry Ford. How and when Dr. Hoag came to knowledge of the Christian Israel truth has not survived, but his belief is believed to have dated back to at least the World War I era.

Dr. Hoag was one of the most respected leaders in the City of Detroit. In 1926, an anthology was published, "entitled, *"Preachers and Preaching in Detroit,"* which gave him a prominent place.   His biography states in part, "Dr. Hoag was born in Canada, but has spent most of his life in the United States.   Lansing, Michigan, was his boyhood home, and Kalamazoo College his Alma Mater, being graduated there in 1900.   His theological training was received at the Divinity School of Chicago University. Opening his ministry in the First Baptist Church in Trenton, New Jersey and the Calvary Baptist Church of New Haven, Connecticut. Woodward Avenue Baptist Church where Dr. Hoag is now located is one of the great preaching centers of America.   The church membership is approximately 3,500, and the constituency of the church is exceedingly large.   It is an evangelistic center with one of the largest Sunday night congregations in the city; and the sane, challenging, and uplifting sermons of this genial prophet of God has made this possible...such conspicuous service in the heart of Detroit is a record upon which we all look with admiration and respect. Many affirm that Dr. Hoag and his associate, Samuel Meyers, formed the best evangelistic team now in the active pastorate." Yes, Dr. Hoag's emphasis was on evangelism reaching others with the Word of God and its message for today. He stated, *"Men are called to be saved – and to be saviors. What can the master say if we fail of our very reason for being saved, and we come home at the end of our season of harvesting without any sheaves for the heavenly garner? Jesus was constantly calling. He preached to the vast multitude; He talked with the individual; He went into the temple and synagogue; He went out to the streets, the markets, the lanes calling men to come after Him...we are stewards of the mystery of God. Take my voice and let me speak ever only for my King."*

Dr. Hoag died suddenly of a heart attack in 1947 after a long ministry of 32 years at Woodward Baptist Church. He was succeeded finally by Pastor William J. Washer, who also proclaimed the Israel truth from the pulpit for another quarter of a century.

HOWARD B. RAND

Without question, the most fertile writer on the Anglo-Israel truth was the great lawyer and theologian, Dr. Howard Benjamin Rand. This man of God was born in Haverhill, Massachusetts, June 13, 1889. He married Hazel Gertrude Smith in 1913. He died on August 17, 1991 at the very advanced age of 102 years, and was in Christian service up to the very last. Rand graduated from the University of Maine in 1912, where he received the LL.B degree and was a member of Phi Alpha Delta. He passed the bar in Maine and Massachusetts, and served in the Maine National Guard during the great Bangor fire. He was an avid outdoor horseman in his youth and a gifted artist. An inventor, he held many patents, including the electric incandescent lamp in 1916, and the automobile headlamp socket. He held patents in the United States, Great Britain, Australia and France.

Rand, for several years maintained an office in London, England and loved to relate how his window overlooked Buckingham Palace, where he would see the present Queen Elizabeth II as a child playing outdoors. He authored many theological studies, including *Digest of Divine Law*, *Primogenesis, Study in Revelation, Study in Hosea, Study in Daniel*, as well as many other books and pamphlets. In July 1997, *"Bibliotheca Sacra"* magazine published by Dallas Theological Seminary, gave a favorable review of Rand's teaching concerning the two witnesses of the Book of Revelation.

During the 1930's, Rand moved to Detroit, opening an office on the sixth floor of the Fox building. This was located nearly across the street from Woodward Baptist Church, where Dr. Hoag was pastoring, and in the neighborhood of several other historic churches as well. Because of these famous churches in the area, it became known as the "Piety Hill"

102

section of Detroit. During this time he toured the United States, Canada and Great Britain lecturing before thousands of people concerning the Anglo-Israel truth. He was the publisher of *__Destiny Magazine__* from 1937 to 1968, but continued to write his *Destiny Editorial Letter Service* until shortly before his death.

OTHER DETROIT CHURCHES

Other historic Detroit churches where the Anglo-Israel truth was heard in the past include old *Trinity Reformed Episcopal Church,* where Dr. William Henry Poole also pastored. *Mariner's Church*, a beautiful English Gothic cathedral, downtown near the City-County building, was pastored during the 1930's by Rev. Robert Randall, who was active in the Anglo Saxon Federation of America. Well known downtown landmark, *Fort Street Presbyterian Church*, where famous theologian Dr. Edward Hart Pence pastored between the years 1900-1938, had frequent Anglo-Israel guests in the pulpit. Early downtown landmark, *Central Presbyterian Church*, now torn down and replaced by a bank building, had been pastored by Hugh Jack, a frequent early feature writer for Destiny Magazine. Detroit's *First Church of the Nazarene,* known as 'The Big Nazarene Tabernacle,' hosted the Anglo Saxon Federation of America National Convention in 1930. These are just a few of the many churches of many denominations, whose pulpits were filled by men with an understanding of the Bible Covenants and their fulfillment in the world today.

HONEST CONFESSIONS

There have been wonderful men of God that were not believers in the Anglo-Israel truth, but were not hostile to it or those that did believe it. Throughout the years some of these men were personal friends with prominent proponents of this truth. Some even worked together in ministry or shared their church pulpit. The following are just a few examples of honest confessions of reputable ministers concerning the Anglo-Israel truth and those who believed it.

THOMAS T. SHIELDS, D.D. Dr. Shields was pastor of the well known historic *Jarvis Street Church* in Toronto, Ontario. His sermons were published in the *Gospel Witness and Protestant Advocate*, a weekly paper that was circulated throughout the world. During his sixty year ministry, he held pastorates in historic churches in London, was Vice-

Chairman of the Home Missions Board of the Baptist Convention of Ontario and Quebec, President of the Baptist Union of North America and Vice-President of the International Council of Christian Churches. In his sermon *"Who and Where are the Ten Lost Tribes of Israel?"* published posthumously in the December 10, 1959 issue of the Church paper, he made the following statement. "Where are the Ten Tribes now? Are they in Britain? Is Manasseh in the United States? I will not quarrel with my British Israelite friends. I am not a British Israelite, but, as an interpretation of British history, I have no quarrel with it. I know some of you ardent premillennialists hold up your hands in horror, and cry, "Heresy." Not at all. Some of the noblest and soundest preachers in this earth today accept that. The great Dr. Dinsdale T. Young, than whom there is none truer to the great verities of evangelical faith, accepts that theory. He insists upon regeneration in order to have salvation, upon the blood atonement. He preached very much as Spurgeon himself preached. I would judge of a man's orthodoxy by his attitude toward the central truth of the deity of Christ, His atoning sacrifice, the necessity of the new birth, the resurrection from the dead. . . . I rather suspect that some of you are part of the Ten Tribes."

CHRISTIAN AND MISSIONARY ALLIANCE

In the official paper of the Christian and Missionary Alliance Church dated September 7, 1894, the editor gives this congenial answer to a reader's question.

"**Query:** Do you believe in the Anglo-Israel theory, or is it accepted by the Christian Alliance? **Answer:** We do not believe the theory, but some excellent members of the Christian Alliance, we believe, do hold to it. It is not a matter essential to fellowship in the Fourfold Gospel, and while we do not deem it profitable to discuss these side issues in the Alliance, yet we do not deem it of sufficient importance to interrupt our perfect communion with those who hold these views."

In the November 13, 1891 issue of the *Christian Alliance* was the following entry entitled: **Professor Totten**. "We have published a few selections from the writings of this remarkable man. We do not endorse all of his views; but we regard them as of a very providential character. A scientific man enjoying the confidence of the class he represents, he feels himself to be specially called to emphasize in these last days the prophetic testimony of God's holy word and the second coming of the Lord Jesus, and he certainly, has brought to bear upon these questions a very remarkable degree of freshness, force, Scriptural knowledge, and scientific accuracy."

JOHN HARDEN ALLEN
1847-1930

As far as can be ascertained concerning J.H. Allen's early life, very little is known. Assuming his early years were spent in Illinois, he came to Missouri in 1879 as a licensed Wesleyan Methodist minister. He became one of the founders of the Church of God (Holiness) which began in 1883. He conducted evangelistic meetings in Louisiana, Missouri and throughout the Midwest preaching the message of holiness and sanctification.

As a student of the Scriptures, he authored at least four books dealing with the Abrahamic Covenant and its relation to Western European civilization. He authored: *Fact and Fiction Concerning Israel and Judah; The National Number and Heraldry of the United States of America* (1919); *A National Rebirth of Judah* (1920); and his most popular book, *Judah's Sceptre and Joseph's Birthright* (1902). In review of his latter mentioned book the **Baptist Messenger** said,

"This is one of the most interesting volumes we have read in many a day and we confess that the arguments produced by Mr. Allen seem to be unanswerable. It is more thrilling than Western fiction. The description of the scarlet thread, the royal remnant, and the part played by Jeremiah in the preservation of the ruler for David's throne, will cause you to lose sleep rather than to go to bed without knowing the outcome."

By 1917 Bishop Allen published a periodical entitled *"The Stone Kingdom Herald"*, referring to the Stone of Scone under the British coronation chair. In his research identifying the modern Western European nations as the House of Joseph, he visited the British Royal Library of the King's Palace and viewed a chart showing the Royal family's descent from King David. In London he spoke at a meeting where several members of the Royal Family were present.

Bishop Allen was personal friends for over thirty years with the Pentecostal pioneer, Charles F. Parham. After Parham's death on January 29, 1929, Allen wrote the following letter of condolence to Parham's widow.

"I first met our Brother Parham, when he was a young preacher and unmarried. He then being pastor of the Methodist Episcopal Church at Eudora, Kan., at which time I was holding the Blue Mound Holiness Camp Meeting. Bro. Parham came into the service a little late, his congregation having come to the Camp Meeting. I had announced previously that I would preach on our Anglo-Saxon identity with the

105

House of Joseph of "the ten lost tribes of Israel." The theme was new to him as it was also to the entire congregation. The inspiration of the Holy Spirit was upon me, and I preached for two hours and a half, and no one left or thought of dinner. After looking at my watch, I told the people to get some dinner and that I would continue the subject at the afternoon service. I did and preached for one hour and a half.

During that morning service, I was especially drawn to that young boyish looking brother who came in late and sat in the rear of the tabernacle, and I went to him. After the introduction and first meetings were over I said, "Brother, do you know that these are the last days, and that Jesus is coming soon?" His reply was, "Every sanctified man knows that."

That melted our dawning fellowship and brotherhood, which remained unbroken and which, I am sure will now remain unbroken throughout the eternity of God. Yours in that marvelous love and inheritance of the saints. " (Signed) Bishop J. H. Allen, Pasadena, CA
Source: *The Life of Charles F. Parham - Founder of the Apostolic Faith Movement, by His Wife, 1930.*

Bishop Allen died on May 14, 1930 in Pasadena, California, but his influence will ever live in the hearts of God's people.

DR. CLARENCE TRUE WILSON

It is little known that the great Methodist divine, Dr. Clarence True Wilson, a household name with Methodists and the evangelical world, collaborated with and advised Bishop Allen as he wrote his book, *Judah's Sceptre and Joseph's Birthright*" in 1902. Dr. Wilson's book on *The United States in Prophecy*, is an exposition of Isaiah 18 and its application to the United States.
(Covenant People's Advocates, Curtis Claire Ewing)

DR. JAMES S. McGAW

Dr. McGaw was a Scottish Covenanter and a lifelong member of the Reformed Presbyterian Church. For over 17 years he represented the National Reform Association, which took him into 46 states on speaking engagements. It was his interest in Christian civil government which laid the foundation for a ready acceptance of the national message of the Bible. He wrote a book entitled, *Suppose We are Israel, What Difference Does it Make?* He was thoroughly convinced of the Anglo-Israel message after reading Bishop J.H. Allen's book.

106

WILLIAM H. POOLE   LL.D

Rev. William H. Poole was born on April 3, 1820 in the County of Kilkenny, Ireland.   In 1831 his father and family emigrated to Canada, and settled in the village of Carlton Place, Lanark.   In that village his father, William Poole, taught school for thirteen years, until 1844, when he was removed by death, loved and esteemed by all who knew him.   Our subject is descended of a very ancient and prominent English family.   The Pooles sprung originally from the County of Derby, England; and for many generations members of the family have been prominent as authors, as divines, and as military officers.   When sixteen years of age, William Henry was offered a situation as school teacher, and strongly urged to accept it.   After passing a creditable examination before the county board of examiners, and receiving the highest class certificate, he yielded to the solicitation of friends and accepted the situation.   That school-house was four miles from his father's residence and yet, for three years, he returned every evening to his studies.   Never, even for one night did he allow storm or bad roads to keep him from his books.   After several years of study and teaching, he worked his way to Victoria College, where the first term of eleven weeks, he paid his way by teaching two hours a day.   On his father's death he left college and took the latter's place and taught until 1846, when he was called to engage in the work of the Christian ministry, in connection with the Wesleyan Methodist Church.   That love of learning which distinguished his ancestors for several generations, especially the Rev. Matthew Poole, the annotator, found in our Canadian minister a healthy body and a vigorous mind, which led him to pursue his studies in various fields of knowledge.   His studies in college were the usual course of classics, mathematics, philosophy and divinity.   In later years, philology and ethnology, with the history of races and nations engrossed his attention.   On the 17th of June, 1850 he was united in marriage to Mary Ann.   In the year 1879, after thirty-three years of close reading and faithful service as a minister, our subject received the title of LL.D.   Of the thirty-three years of ministerial labor, twenty-seven were spent in the large towns and   cities of Ontario.   In the fall of 1879, Mr. Poole received an invitation to the Simpson Methodist Episcopal Church in Detroit, Michigan.   He has written a great deal in the religious press of Canada and in the United States.   The subjects of our educational institutions, of temperance and of prohibition, of the different phases of religions life and work, have often interested his pen. Several sermons of his have been published, and he has sent out a number of tractates, pamphlets and lectures. He has published a volume on "The Fruits of the Spirit", which was highly commended by the press; and others are in the hands of the publishers. Few men have a warmer heart, or a lighter step, than our Canadian friend, Dr. Poole.

EXTRACTED FROM: Cyclopedia of Canadian Biography, Edited by Geo. MacLean Rose, Toronto: Rose Publishing Company, 188?

Dr. Poole died on August 7, 1896 at the age of 76 years old.

WHERE IS ISRAEL?
Author Unknown

Men don't believe in the Bible now, as they really ought to do
They've locked the door on the "chosen race" and won't let "my nation" through
There isn't a print of Israel's foot or a dart from Joseph's bow
To be found in earth or in air today, for "the church" has voted it so.

But who owns "the gates" of the world today? Who is it rules the waves?
Who dwells alone in the "appointed place," while the enemy hates and raves?
Who stands today in the thick of the fight, oppression and sin to quell?
If it isn't the hosts of the living God; won't somebody rise and tell?

Who sends God's Word to the world, to prepare the path for our Savior's feet?
Who frees the captives and plants the rose, who is reigning from David's seat?
So Israel is voted not to be, of course this is untrue
For who is doing the kind of work, Israel alone can do?

We're told the church takes Israel's place; but the Bible plainly says
A kingdom of stone that's cut out for His own, shall stand till the end of days
Who owns and carries the flags that wave, to the earth's remotest bounds?
If Israel by a unanimous vote, is nowhere to be found?

Won't somebody step to the front, forthwith and make his bow and show
Where the chief of the nations is today? We very much want to know.
For Israel is blindly voted out; and Israel 'tis said is gone
But the Anglo Saxons would like to know, who carries God's business on.

JOSEPH'S BIRTHRIGHT
AND
MODERN AMERICA

Robert B. Record

*Pastor, Author and Host of the National Message
Radio Ministry*

About the Author
By Charles A. Jennings

In writing to the Corinthian Church, the Apostle Paul stated that "moreover it is required in stewards, that a man be found faithful" (I Cor. 4:2). In reviewing the life of Robert Bruce Record, one would have to say that he was faithful as a steward of his Lord for the work that he was given to do.

Robert Record was a tireless worker in the vineyard of the Lord and spent the majority of his life in Christian ministry. In preparation for his life work he attended Northwestern Bible College in Seattle, Washington and graduated in 1933. After several months of ministry he was ordained by the First Baptist Church of Rochester, Minnesota. He then preached in Baptist affiliated churches in the Midwest for about five years.

His father, Pastor Warren Bruce Record, was the founder of the National Message Ministry and in 1938 he began a long career in radio broadcasting. His National Message Radio Ministry was launched on December 25, 1938 on KMTR in Hollywood, California. In 1940 his son, Robert Record became associated with him and together their combined radio ministry lasted for over sixty-one years.

Robert Record was one who valued the knowledge of Biblical truth of far greater worth than religious tradition or ecclesiastical acceptance. As a result of sincere and intense Bible study, he said he became convinced "that there had to be an Israel people other than the Jew, for they had fulfilled none of the prophetic history of National Israel." Being thoroughly convinced of this truth, he resigned from his Baptist Association in 1940 and joined with his father in radio broadcasting. He then moved to Portland, Oregon and began broadcasting on radio station KWJJ. In 1947, he became associated with the Kingdom Gospel Institute of Chicago, Illinois. With other pastors in this fellowship, he made yearly trips to visit members of Congress in Washington, D.C. to share with them the national message of the Scriptures. While in Chicago, Robert Record preached the message of salvation through Jesus Christ and the Gospel of the Kingdom of God on radio stations WGN and WJJD. He later broadcasted in the greater Los Angeles area for many years until shortly before his death.

Until his death in October 2005, Pastor Robert B. Record was faithful to his Lord and Savior Jesus Christ who saved him and changed his life while yet a young man. He endeavored to remain true to his Master in studying God's Word in order to proclaim God's message without fear or favor. In his acceptance of the knowledge of the true identification of God's covenant people Israel as being the Anglo-Saxon, Celtic, Scandinavian, Germanic and kindred people, he endured the rejection of some ministerial acquaintances, but remained true to his convictions. The message contained in the following pages is a small sample of his heartfelt passion for God's Word and desire to reach his fellowman with the Gospel of the Kingdom of God. The following chapters contained in this book are a series of messages delivered by Pastor Record and therefore accounts for some repetition in thoughts and style of writing.

America, The Ephraim "Fulness of Nations"

Here in America, as history testifies, the Anglo-Saxon, Celtic, Nordic and English-speaking people migrated from Britain and Europe to found and build what was destined to become the greatest single nation of all time. We are the Land of Israel's regathering – not little Palestine. No other land in the entire world can be found which has been so blessed of God by the dew of heaven and the richness of the earth. In contrast to other nations, we need not look to other countries for the supply of our need. We are the breadbasket and the feeders of the world. This was the role of Joseph in Egypt, and it is the role of America today. We are a people and nation of destiny, and are proven by every Biblical mark of identification to be the literal descendants of ancient Israel. This is our birthright!

Israel's Westward Migration

When we realize from Deuteronomy 32:8 that almost from the very beginning the boundaries of the nations were set by God according to the number of the children of Israel, thus, only *one people* would have been found migrating. Only one people would be leaving their prescribed national boundaries to go someplace else. Deuteronomy 32:8 says, *"When the Most High divided the nations their inheritance, when He separated the sons of Adam, He set the bounds of the nations according to the number of the children of Israel."* Therefore, we would expect only one people, of all the peoples of the earth to be moving, to be migrating.

What most people seem not to realize is, that while civilization moved from the East to the West, it actually followed in the wake of the Westward migration of the Israel people. When Israel left some of these lands which they had helped to build, like Greece – when our fathers left those lands, then they reverted to a lesser stature. During this time our Israel forefathers were not known as Israel. They were called by other names, just as God said they would be. They were to be "swallowed up," or lost among the Gentiles. In earlier times, they were known as the Scythians, the Sache, etc., and later they were called the Caucasian people. Later still they became known as the Goths, Visigoths and the Ostrogoths; and finally they became the nations of Western Europe. It was from here that God once again allured His people; it was from here that they took ship for the New World.

To Not See God's Hand

To not see the hand of God in all this, to not see that this was God fulfilling His promise to Israel: that in the last days He would establish them in the "top of the mountains," or "chief among the nations," is not to see America correctly, historically.

America Is God's Country

We are the land of regathered Israel. The word Gentile means heathen or nations, as taken from the Greek: *ethnos*. That is exactly what it means, and it doesn't mean anything else. I know we have given it a meaning. Popular usage has given it a meaning that the Bible doesn't give to it. Let's discover the real America by discovering what God has wrought here in fulfillment of His promise to His people, which people we are, and it's marvelous in our eyes.

WILLIAM PASCOE GOARD

Introduction by Charles A. Jennings

In His merciful plan, our God so favors His people in choosing His servants and giving them as 'gifts' unto the Body of Christ. This is what our Lord did when He chose a young English lad named, William Pascoe Goard.

He was born in Cornwall, England in1863. He was miraculously converted to Christ while still a young boy. At the insistence of his father he studied law, but his first love through a divine call was to preach the Gospel of Jesus Christ. He preached his first sermon at the age of fourteen.

While still a teenager, his family moved to Canada where he soon became involved with The Salvation Army. He was promoted to the rank of Captain at the age of twenty-one.

In order to prepare himself for Christian service, Goard studied theology at Wesley College located in Winnipeg, Manitoba and was ordained in the Methodist Church. He later pastored the Grandview Congregational Church in Vancouver, British Columbia.

In the early1890's, he was introduced to the Christian Anglo-Israel message of the Bible by Victoria University Professor Edward F. Odlum. He soon launched his own intensive research on the subject and became thoroughly convinced of its validity both by the Scriptures and secular history.

William P. Goard went on to distinguish himself as editor of the NATIONAL MESSAGE magazine, helped to establish the Harrow Weald Park College, and was an international lecturer and prolific author. His life-long love was the study and proclamation of God's Holy Word.

In the following article entitled IN THE COOL OF THE DAY, Goard relates his warm heartfelt testimony of how his Blessed Savior revealed Himself to him while still a young lad. There the Lord placed within him that divine call that stayed with him until he was called home on February 9, 1937.

In the second article entitled FROM ISRAELITE TO SAXON, Goard so adequately – yet so briefly – presents to the reader his knowledge and commitment to the Christian Anglo-Israel message of the Bible.

IN THE COOL OF THE DAY

"The LORD God walking in the garden in the cool of the day . . ." (Genesis 3:8)

"And the Lord appeared unto him . . . in the heat of the day." (Genesis 18:1)

"And behold the word of the LORD came unto him . . . and he brought him forth abroad, and said, Look now toward heaven and tell the stars . . ." (Genesis 15:4-5)

Is there a God? Thus cries the class which takes its pleasure in negations.

How do you prove that there is a God? is the question of the class which delights in the acrobatics of philosophical debate.

Such questions as these could never be entertained by the writer and by the many millions of the class to which he belongs, for the simple reason that God is a well-known Personality to them, having joined them at the cool of the evening, in the heat of the day, or when the stars march forth in their stately progress across the sky.

It has seemed to the writer that many questions might be relegated to the scrap-heap of unnecessary things by simply telling of some of the times when God has spoken to ME.

This is a case when only the first person singular may be used. I cannot tell when God has joined you as you have walked abroad, or come to you when you have been in receptive mood at home.   That would be hearsay evidence on my part, and would not be admitted in a court of law. But my personal testimony in the first person singular would be entertained and classed as evidence of the first order, that is to say, evidence by direct testimony.

This evidence was voiced by former generations who sang:

"What we have felt and seen, with confidence we tell- And publish to the sons of men, the signs infallible." That is to say, personal experience published by direct personal testimony. It is a long time ago now that the first experience of a conscious personal meeting with God came to me.

I had gone to a little church to hear a preacher, not very noted perhaps as far as the great general public was concerned, but known and beloved as an annual visitor in our community.

He preached a sermon—as usual—and the text was: "Having slain the enmity thereby . . . nailing it to His Cross."

I am not quite sure that I should at this time phrase things just as he did. But he caused me to see that those transgressions and sins which separated me from both my fellow-men and from God had been taken away and nailed to the Cross of our Lord Jesus Christ.

* * *

Perhaps the next day, at all events before the week was far gone, I was walking in one of the beautiful Cornish lanes in the heat of the day. A glorious sun shone overhead. Fleecy clouds sailed across a vividly blue sky. The hedge-rows and ditches were filled with ragged robins and other midsummer flowers, the meadow-sweet contributed their perfume, the red clover filled the air with sweetness, there was the hum of busy insects and the midday twitter of the birds. It was all so perfect.

Suddenly the thought of what I had heard and what I had meditated upon on the Sabbath came back •to me. Withall, there suddenly came a new brightness to the sun, a new sweetness to the perfume, a new tone to bird and insect notes, A NEW PERSONALITY WALKING WITH ME UNSEEN, but manifest by new brightness in what I saw, and new sweetness in the tones I heard.

Startled, I halted for a moment, and in that moment's halt seemed to hear a Voice around me and within, thrilling my whole being:

"My son, give Me thy heart."

The beauties which I have described, of eye and ear, are a general impression such as a great painter creates by a landscape masterpiece. I may or may not have got the details exactly as they were. The impression which remained I have.

But there was startling clearness in this Voice, which seemed to fill the surrounding space and at the same time to fill my inner being. I knew it for what indeed it was, THE VOICE OF GOD CALLING TO ME IN THE HEAT OF THE DAY.

I did not want to share this experience with any living soul. Looking about for a retired place, I noticed that I was near a well-known "gap" in the hedge which gave access to a well-known field. I mean that "gap" and field were well known to me, for this was my birthplace – and I had rambled over every field, and was well acquainted with the surroundings.

So I passed through the "gap," as entering into a sanctuary where God was. I remember the waving wheat just headed out. I remember the triangular little patch of red clover in the corner of the field. I can smell the perfume, and hear the bird and insect voices still. But under, and over, and through it all was the insistent Voice: "My son, give Me thy heart."

I knelt there in the Presence of my God and gave to Him my heart. Then the brightness and the lightness which flooded everything and inspired even my feet to walk in the midst of the glories of that midday

115

was an experience the memory of which is vivid after a half-century of travel and activity has passed away.

This might have been looked upon as the dreaming, the vivid dreaming, of a twelve-year-old boy, and nothing more, but for the fact that in many lands, and under many circumstances, for fifty years and more, that meeting has held its place and power in my life. As surely as the life of Saul of Tarsus was changed into that of St. Paul the Apostle to the Gentiles, from Jewry, in its most intense form, to Christianity as manifested in his life and writings, so surely was my life changed and given a set direction in that meeting with God. The place was in a Cornish lane, but the meeting place was at the Cross.

* * *

"Again the word of the Lord came unto me, saying . . ." This would have been the form of expression in Old Testament days. In faint measure the experience was the same for me.

This time it was a Sunday afternoon, and the place was the deep window-seat of my bedroom. The outlook from my window was beautiful. "Just the place to breed a poet," said a visitor friend of my youth when he caught the outlook from my window.

Well-kept gardens, with treasures of bloom and shrub, were under my window. The River Strat murmured by outside the garden wall, to be met by a tributary which, on occasion, could flood the lower part of the village and form "land waters" over orchard and field; but which usually murmured its way by the end of the garden.

Just where the two met at the angle of the garden was a weir over which all the water, but such as passed into a mill "leat" or "lead," fell with a musical song, the tone of which varied according to the volume of the stream. Beyond opened out a valley, with orchard and meadow, and swelling hillsides, filled with the wild life which makes such landscapes vivid and vocal.

The question in my mind that afternoon was: "Lord, what wilt Thou have me to do?"

Three openings were before me at that particular time. An opening into a business house on good terms, openings into mechanical pursuits, and an opening into a law office.

What age? About fourteen.

I was musing over this. It had been a matter of conversation between my parents and myself at the midday meal.

The feeling of the Presence led me to take a course somewhat like the enquiry of our forefathers by Urim and Thummim in order to obtain direction from the Lord. I relate the facts. They include the course taken by a boy. I might not take the same course now.

Yet I do not know, granted the same sense of the Presence.

I knelt in the window and prayed after the manner of Gideon's prayer. I asked that direction might be afforded me through the words of the Book. Closing my eyes, I placed the Book upright between my two hands. Withdrawing my hands, I allowed the Book to fall open, and placed my finger on the words. How they shone. I am not aware that I had ever noticed them before, but now they seemed to be written in letters which glowed: "Son of man, eat that thou findest; eat this roll, and go speak unto the House of Israel."

I examined the passage, and found that the roll was the roll of a Book. I understood that the eating of the roll meant the mastering of the Book. I had not heard of Anglo-Israel in those days, but I never doubted for a moment then nor later that the House of Israel were my own British people. Not "a people of a strange language," as the passage goes on to say.

I was startled, but not convinced that here was more than coincidence. I prayed again and followed again the same course. My finger lit on the same words: "Son of man, eat that thou findest; eat this roll, and go speak unto the House of Israel."

But, my mind seemed to say, this Book has been so used that it falls open that way, and the repetition is therefore an accident.

Turning to my dressing-table, I took a Bible which had been given to me the preceding Christmas as a "reward" from the Sunday-school. It was a leather-covered, brass-bound, brass-clasped Book, which had not been in use at all. I prayed yet once more as Gideon did regarding the fleece. Then I stood the Book between my hands with my eyes closed. It fell open, and I placed my finger. Opening my eyes I read: "Son of man, eat that thou findest; eat this☐ roll, and go speak unto the House of Israel."

And I said, "I will, Lord."

It was an intense moment. It seemed to me then and seems to me still that there and then the Lord gave to me my commission and my marching orders.

* * *

Later in life the hands of a distinguished Bishop were laid upon my head, a Bible was placed in my hands, and the voice of Bishop Carman said: "Take thou authority to preach the Word of God..."

I took the Bible, but I had received the authority before. Never when thinking of my ordination does my mind halt at that service of

117

ordination. My mind goes back to that Sabbath afternoon when I was caused to read, "Son of man, eat that thou findest; eat this roll, and go speak unto the House of Israel."

Can one wonder that the authorities of the Church called upon me almost at once, before that year had ended, to begin that long period of service in preaching, "speaking unto the House of Israel"?

My father had received no such impression. Therefore an arrangement was made by him whereby I should continue to attend school in the morning and go into a law office for the afternoon. My employer, the lawyer, set me the task of reading law, and held me to it. He □ rained me like a veritable martinet in the reading of documents and in the preparation of cases, and in the various things which it is necessary for the legal man to know. But underneath it all was the urge, "Eat this roll, and go speak unto the House of Israel." Preaching and teaching on Sundays and week evenings, school and office, books and documents on weekdays, filled in my time, and I did not know how matters would be arranged.

* * *

Then suddenly came the consciousness of the Presence. The Voice this time seemed to be saying, "Get thee out from thy country, and from thy kindred, and from thy father's house, to a land which I will shew thee."

At first we talked of Australia and of all going together. A broken bank rendered that move out of the question.

Then the United States of America, and conjunction with my mother's brother, came up for discussion. I wrote to my uncle. He thought it wise to write and state the difficulties of the new land. I read into it a reluctance to take the responsibility of my coming to him. This I later found to be entirely a wrong reading of a very wise letter, but it turned me aside.

One day I came home to my father's house with the ticket in my pocket to Ontario, Canada, and so the die was cast.

The Presence had again guided my footsteps. A hundred proofs of that have come to me since that time.

So on a Sabbath in June,1880, I found myself standing on the deck of the Polynesian in mid-ocean, preaching the Word to the company from the British Isles who were on the way to make the great Dominion their home.

A fortnight later, in little Salim Church in Durham County, I began the work of "speaking to the House of Israel" in the Dominion of Canada. I have not finished that task yet.

* * *

Time will fail me to tell of a later occasion when the Presence came to me and sent me forth again, this time from the most comfortable surroundings and the happiest fellowship, conjoined with the most congenial labours, to pioneer life on the great Western plains.

Yes, He was with me there in the heat of the day, in the cool of the day, and when the stars shone in the sky.

Once again He came and sent me still farther West to the great Province of British Columbia. There He caused me to stake down my tent and to make my home.

Again, and the Voice bade me to recross the continent and the ocean and to go to London. But there were physical obstacles in the way I would not bargain. I told the Lord of the physical difficulty and of my willingness to go; but I prayed that the physical difficulty might be removed. It was removed. To His glory be it spoken.

And so there has been the long route. Vancouver in the West, London in the East, and the yearly migration between them. Thus He has staked out my parish, and kept me traveling from end to end of it. Now in Canada, now in the United States, now in Britain, and so it goes.

Then came the call to write the message for the Manifestos and the call to His servant to publish the same. And so the work goes on, and still we hear His Voice walking in the garden in the cool of the day.

He spoke in the "Crossing of the River." He has spoken in many and many a message. He will speak again, bye and bye, and He will say: "It is enough, Come up higher, enter into the joy of thy Lord."

The following article first appeared in THE NATIONAL MESSAGE in Great Britain.

FROM ISRAELITE
TO SAXON

In speaking of the United States and Britain as modern Israel, it is necessary to remember certain things in order to avoid confusion.

First of all, the people of Israel were no more divided into tribes, but had, centuries before, passed into the more advanced stage of national organization. It is the natural progress of any progressive people. First, it is the family, then the tribes, then the nation embracing the tribes. We must think of Israel as a nation and a company of nations, no more called Israel, for the best of reasons, but called by the name, above all others, of sons or House of Isaac, or Saxons, with many other branch names.

119

Secondly, we must remember that they were not the original founders of Israel in the Isles - that is to say, in Britain - but they came in very late in British history, even a thousand years after the House of David had arrived and been established there.

We shall, therefore, approach the subject of the ten-tribed House of Israel as being the consideration of a branch of the Israel people which, late in history, arrived in Britain, and added their strength to those who had preceded them.

We begin with the separation of the House of Israel from the House of Judah. Thereafter there were two nations in Palestine of the Israel stock, and their histories are separately recorded, with their separate lines of kings, in the books of Kings and Chronicles. Read them there, and be sure to read them separately.

Thence we find Israel carried captive to Halah, Habor, and the River Gozan. Professor Odlum says of this deportation: "The distance to which Israel was carried from their own country in about 721 B.C. was not less than seven hundred miles in a north and east direction. The Syrian Desert, the River Euphrates, the Mesopotamian region, the Tigris, and three ranges of the Kurdistan mountains intervened between Samaria and the new home of Israel in captivity. In this district were the cities and regions of Halah, Habor, and the River Gozan, which flowed into the Caspian Sea, as it does today. This new home was the high tablelands of Media and Armenia . . ."

While settled in this district, they aided the Medes and Persians to break the power of their captors, the Assyrians. Afterwards Babylon went down before their arms.

From this time they were on their way to their new European home. They found unoccupied territory in the neighbourhood of Ar-Sareth in southeast Europe.

Here they occupied the Crimea, and spread up the waterways, passing the watershed and down the waterways to the Baltic and the North Seas.

Sharon Turner says: "The migrating Scythians crossed the Araxes, passed out of Asia, and suddenly appeared in Europe in the sixth century B.C."

Esdras in the Apocrypha tells us that the Ten Tribes left their exile and moved away across the Euphrates to a place called Arsareth (City or Hill of Sareth) (2 Esdras 13:39-45). To the northwest of the Black Sea is a river called Sareth to this day.

Herodotus, speaking of the same date as Esdras, says: "The Scythians emerged from beyond the Euphrates across the Armenian river Araxes."

120

Rev. W. M. H. Milner says: "The fugitive host, starting from upper Media, passed the north end of Lake Umri into the mountain valleys of the Kurds; here some dropped off, and their children became in after ages the Nestorian Church. These were for thirteen centuries the missionaries of Asia."

Herodotus says the Persians called the Scythians Sakai, and Sharon Turner identifies these very people as the ancestors of the Anglo-Saxons. The old Greek writers spoke often of the valour and the undaunted spirit of these Scythians. They say "No nation on earth can match them. They are unconquerable."

Professor Odlum continues: "From Josephus, the Jewish historian of the first century, we learn that at A.D. 70 the Ten Tribes were outside the Roman Empire. By other means we learn that they were in the south of Russia in immense multitudes, and known as the Scythians of Herodotus."

The burial places of the Israel people have furnished ample inscriptions to show clearly that the Crimea was a centre of residence for this people for ages and that from it they spread up through Europe and eastward as far as China.

Diodorus says: "The Sacae sprang from people in Media who obtained a vast and glorious empire."

Ptolemy finds the Saxons in "a race of Scythians called Saki, who came from Media."

Pliny says: "The Sakai were among the most distinguished people of Scythia who settled in Armenia, and were called Sacae-Sani."

Albinus says: "The Saxons were descended from the ancient Sacae in Asia."

Prideaux finds that "the Cimbrians (Kumrii) came from the Black and Caspian Seas, and that with them came the Angli."

Sharon Turner, the most painstaking Saxon historian says: 'The Saxons were a Scythian nation, and were called Saca, Sachi, Sach-sen. "

Colonel Gawler, in Our Scythian Ancestors, says: "The word Sacae is fairly and without straining or imagination translated Israelites."

The Bible (Amos, chapter seven) solemnly takes cognizance of the change of the name of the nation and people from Israel to "the House of Isaac" (Saxons).

Thus we see these people settled about the Crimea, along the rivers of Europe from the sixth century B.C.

Their migrations to the Baltic and North Seas are well told by Du Chaillu, a scholar of England with a French name.

The militant progress of the Goths, Gotti, "Men of God," is well known in the history of Europe. The divisional names of Angles, Jutes, and so on, are duplicated today by the names our race now bears as English, Welsh, Scotch, Canadians, Australians, New Zealanders, (Anzacs), Americans, and so on.

From the sixth century B.C. to the time of the landing of Hengist and Horsa, these people had been steadily progressing up through Europe, God's Battle Axe Brigade (see Jer. 51:20). Finally, they came in and occupied the place, which had been made for them in the British Isles by the Roman occupation. Since that time they have been not the least important part of the Israel peoples dwelling in the "appointed place" (the British Isles), and extending to the overseas dominions the strength and energy of their race.

It has been possible only to touch authorities and evidences of the identity of the Anglo-Saxons with ten-tribed Israel. But even so, the array of standard authors who make declarations regarding this matter is startling, and it is clear that the scholar who denies an historic basis to the claim of Saxon identity with Israel speaks rather out of his lack of knowledge of standard literature, than out of his knowledge of the subject.

The identity of the Saxon and Israel is proven, and we are now put in the responsible position of asking what it means in the way of responsibility under God's plan for His nation, and through them for the world. With Paul we ask, "What shall we say then? Hath God cast away His people whom He foreknew? God forbid ... God hath not cast away His people."

WATCHMEN UPON MOUNT EPHRAIM

INTRODUCTION
By Charles Jennings

ISRAEL IN THE ISLES - *Isaiah 42:4, 10-12*

"Blessed is the nation whose God is the LORD; and the people whom he hath chosen for his own inheritance." Psalm 33:12

Of all the gracious favors that our Lord has bestowed upon any people, surely it can be said that the nation of Great Britain has received an abundant supply. The richest blessing that a nation can enjoy is to be a recipient of the Gospel of Jesus Christ. Early in the life of the New Testament church, Britain was blessed with true Apostolic messengers sent from Palestine in the First Century A.D. Eusebius (265-340 A.D.), the church historian said; "The Apostles passed beyond the ocean to the Isles called the Brittanic Isles." Bishop Ussher wrote; "The British national church was founded in 36 A.D., 160 years before Rome confessed Christianity. Britain was officially proclaimed Christian by King Lucius at the National Council at Winchester in 156 A.D."

Ever since those early days the Lord has sent faithful missionaries, numerous waves of spiritual revival, raised up anointed men of vision and passion who established churches and foreign mission societies, protected the islands against attacking armadas and the designs of evil invaders. Great Britain became the strongest naval and military power in the world and the bastion of Christianity. From its shores have flowed the blessings to the rest of the world equal only to the promises given to Abraham and the two sons of his great grandson Joseph (Gen. 12:1-2, 48:1-22, 49:22-26, Deut. 33:13-17).

The renowned Baptist pastor and theologian Charles H. Spurgeon declared; *"English history, from the first day until now, is as full of instruction as the history of Israel from Egypt to Babylon. Our nation has been as much under the special, and peculiar providence of God as were the descendants of Jacob themselves; therefore, God deals with us as He does not with any other nation."*
(The Treasury of the Old Testament - Vol. 2 p. 154)

The words of the great theologian echo the words of the Lord in Deut. 14:2; *"For thou art an holy people unto the LORD thy God, and the*

LORD hath chosen thee to be a peculiar people unto himself, above all the nations that are upon the earth."

Among the richest blessings bestowed upon the nation of Great Britain are men and women God has raised up who have contributed to its greatness in every area of life. Among the most profound have been those that have proclaimed the Word of God and given their lives in calling the nation and individuals to repentance. Many such men of God labored for Christ under the most severe and difficult conditions, yet they remained faithful. There have been scores of the Lord's servants throughout the history of the British church who have made tremendous contributions, but sadly are soon forgotten.

The ministers in this brochure are just a few among hundreds who remained true to their convictions in believing a Biblical truth that has been less than popular. That truth is the Anglo-Israel message of Scripture and the Gospel of the Kingdom of God. All of the men included in this brochure were born and ministered in Britain with the exception of Harry Clarke who was born in Wales, but primarily ministered in the United States. In His divine providence, the Lord has favored this company of nations known as the United Kingdom of Great Britain and Northern Ireland, with some of the greatest ministers that ever graced the sacred desk. Today, that nation stands without excuse for not acknowledging its Biblical identity as being a part of the House of Israel and its election in the plan of God. It has had sufficient witness in the testimonies of the mighty saints listed in this brochure who proclaimed the Gospel of the Kingdom.

Today, Britain and the other Israel nations are in a severe spiritual backslidden condition whom the Lord will punish for their iniquities. Yet the Lord says: *"For I am with thee, saith the LORD, to save thee: though I make a full end of all nations whither I have scattered thee, yet will I not make a full end of thee: but I will correct thee in measure, and will not leave thee altogether unpunished."* Jer. 30:11.

HARRY DUDLEY CLARKE 1888 -1957

Harry D. Clarke was born on January 28, 1888 in Cardiff, Wales. Very little is known of his early life other than he was orphaned at an early age due to the death of his parents. In his dissatisfaction of the orphanage home in which he lived, he ran away and got a job working on a ship. He worked at sea for almost ten years. As a young man and feeling a desire to better himself, he moved to London, England. Still not satisfied, he moved to Canada and then to America.

It is uncertain where Clarke heard the Gospel and gave his heart to Christ, but sincere love for his Savior was the factor that determined his life's work. He attended Moody Bible Institute in Chicago and there served as a professor teaching a course in personal evangelism. He served in evangelistic work while composing Gospel songs and eventually was engaged in music publication. Some of the songs that are known to be composed by Clarke are; *"Awake, O Church of Christ,"* (copyright 1926), *"Fishers of Men," "Into My Heart"* and *"What Must I Do."* Some have even attributed to him the well-known chorus *"Sweep Over My Soul."*

Clarke served as song leader in the evangelistic campaigns of Harry Vom Bruch. For three or four years from 1932 to 1935, he served as song leader in the large campaigns of the famous evangelist Billy Sunday. He also served as business manager for Sunday for eight years. He served as Director of Music for the famous young woman evangelist Uldine Utley. He helped compile her song book entitled *"Songs of the Rose and Word"* which was published by Rodeheaver Company.

Being so greatly influenced and impressed with the ministry of the famous evangelist, Clarke established the ***Billy Sunday Memorial Tabernacle*** in Sioux City, Iowa. He served as pastor from 1935 to 1945 and was succeeded by Dr. Roy Lockwood.

During his ministerial and musical career, Clarke was widely known and was friends with other well-known ministers such as E.J. Rollins of Detroit, Michigan and Luke Rader of Minneapolis, Minnesota. He was a frequent guest speaker in some of the largest evangelistic tabernacles in the country at that time.

Another outstanding fact about Harry Clarke was his unwavering belief in the Anglo-Israel message of the Bible. Dr. Roy Lockwood, who is still living as of this writing, served as pastor of the Billy Sunday Memorial Tabernacle from 1945-1960. He personally affirmed to me that not only Clarke was a believer, but he himself is currently a strong believer in the Anglo-Israel message. This raises the valid question of "How many other prominent evangelists and pastors of the Twentieth Century were believers in the great Anglo-Israel truth of Scripture?

Harry D. Clarke passed away on October 14, 1957 in Lexington, Kentucky and is buried in Sioux City, Iowa.

MAYNARD GORDON JAMES - 1902-1988

If ever there was a saint of God whose passion was totally consumed for the cause of the Gospel and the spiritual welfare of his fellow man, it was Maynard James. Maynard was born in Bargoed, South Wales on

April 17, 1902, the second son of Joseph and Gwen James. He was raised with a strong sense of community spirit in this mining town where his father was a railway signalman. His parents were very godly people who raised their sons in the Hanbury Road Baptist Chapel. As a young boy, Maynard joined the **_Band of Hope_** and other activities of the Chapel. While he was yet a small child the Welsh Revival of 1904 and 1905 had swept Wales and greatly affected his parents which profoundly influenced Maynard's entire life.

After the death of his father in 1914, Maynard and his mother began to attend the Bargoed Holiness Mission. It was there at the age of thirteen, he had a conversion experience at which he wept so much that another boy offered him a handkerchief. There he came into a personal relationship with Jesus Christ. In January 1920 he came under the ministry of Leonard Wain, a leading figure in the International Holiness Mission (I.H.M.). From this time onwards until he died, over 68 years later, he never looked back.

In 1920, he went to London for the annual Easter Holiness Convention at Battersea. He had heard about the experience of entire sanctification at the Mission, but now he wanted it for himself. The following is a description of his experience in his own words.

"Twice in that Convention I went to an altar of prayer, resolved at all costs to obtain the coveted blessing. Relying too much on emotional surges as evidence of the Spirit's indwelling fullness, I almost missed my Pentecost. Then God sent a Manchester business man to deal with me as, in desperation, I knelt at the altar. Gently but firmly he said to me: 'What you need is faith, not in your own faith, but faith in God.' That timely word was a veritable Joshua to lead me into Canaan that Easter Monday. In simple faith I claimed the promised Holy Spirit; and according to Galatians 3:14 ('that we might receive the promise of the Spirit through faith'), the Comforter came into my longing heart.

"I did not hear a sound of a rushing mighty wind. Neither did a cloven tongue of fire rest on my head. Nor was it given to me to break into another language when the Holy Spirit came in. But my Christian life was revolutionized from that hour. Carnal fear was cast out by perfect love. Frustration was exchanged for a life of victory in the Holy Spirit. Prayer became an intense delight and the Bible was my veritable meat and drink.

"More wonderful than all was the unveiling of Christ to my longing heart. He became the loadstone of my affections. His beauty and grace ravished my happy soul. And something happened that I had never

known - the Holy Spirit melted me to tears when praying for needy humanity. Truly the love of God had been shed abroad in my heart by the Holy Spirit."

Maynard became deeply involved in the work of the Cardiff Holiness Mission. In 1925, he became one of the vice-presidents of the I.H.M. and in 1930 was married to Louie Jackson after an eight year engagement. He was associated with the Methodist Cliff College and its principal Samuel Chadwick, which trained men for public evangelism. Principal Chadwick wrote; *"The vision as I see it is to send forth a band of young men full of faith and the Holy Ghost, to preach Christ to multitudes unreached and unsought by the churches. They will receive no salary. They will go as they are led, and they will live by faith.*

No collections will be taken. No subscriptions solicited, no favours begged. They will tramp from place to place, preaching, testifying and singing in the street, market place, village green and pleasure beach; depending upon God for everything, and sleeping wherever a shelter can be found."

This form of evangelism was known as *trekking*. Beginning in 1927 as a student at Cliff College, Maynard became involved in trekking evangelism which he continued during his I.H.M. years which were to follow. Along with his fellow workers, Maynard was a passionate prayer warrior who engaged in many fervent prayer meetings such as the one he describes below.

"Of the many wonderful prayer meetings we had as students of Cliff College, one stands out like a mountain peak. We had commenced to pray in one of the lecture rooms at about 9 P.M. Later we transferred to a large bedroom on the second corridor. For about three hours we waited quietly upon the Lord. There was no attempt to stir up fleshly emotion; we earnestly desired only what the Lord would give us. Then suddenly, about midnight, the heavens opened and the glory of the Lord fell on all in that room. All those present burst into audible prayer, which seemed to increase in volume and yet was not confusing or fanatical. It went on for hours. One of the quietest members of our group, a shy country student, became almost the noisiest that night! The results of that memorable prayer meeting were soon seen. Practically all the students who went forth from the "upper room" to preach in various churches later that day had seekers at the Cross."

Maynard James' calling was mainly in evangelistic type ministry, but served as pastor whenever that ministry door was opened. In 1929 he accepted the pastorate of the Holiness Tabernacle on Brunswick Street in Manchester, England. Those were the days when Stephen and George

127

Jeffreys were holding big revival campaigns in many parts of the country, resulting in many conversions and thousands of miraculous healings. Pastor James admired the ministry of these brothers and incorporated into his own ministry what he had learned from their Pentecostal revivals. Pastors James and Dan Phillips conducted a ten week tent campaign in Bolton, Lancashire with one thousand conversions to Christ. They anointed and prayed for the sick (James 5:14) with definite results of divine healing that generated local and national newspaper coverage.

In the summer of 1932, James and his fellow workers conducted a tent revival in Oldham, England with equal results and the establishment of a large Holiness Tabernacle. This same scene was repeated many times later.

James publicly confessed his belief in the Baptism of the Holy Spirit, but he himself never experienced speaking in tongues. Over the 'Pentecostal issue', James with three of his friends, Clifford Filer, Dr. Jack Ford and Leonard Ravenhill, who authored "Why Revival Tarries" withdrew from the I.H.M. and formed the *Calvary Holiness Church* in 1934. Together they started the magazine called the *Flame* of which James was the editor for nearly fifty years. Through the various outreach ministries, James became the primary leader for the direction of the holiness movement in Great Britain for many years. Among his friends and co-workers were outstanding men of God such as Norman Grubb, director of the Worldwide Evangelisation Crusade and son-in-law of the famous C.T. Studd; Harold Kuhn, Reginal Nash, Leonard Ravenhill, Martyn Lloyd-Jones, Rees Howells, Duncan Campbell, the prophet to the Hebrides and Catherine Booth Clibborn, the eldest daughter of William Booth of the Salvation Army.

In the post World War II years, James' outreach included world missions and preaching in France, Cuba, Colombia, South Africa and in a number of Church of the Nazarene centers in the United States. He was also influential in the founding of *Beech Lawn Bible College* in Yorkshire, England. In 1955 the Calvary Holiness Church along with the I.H.M. merged with the *Church of the Nazarene*.

In his book, *"The Story of Maynard James - A Man on Fire"* his son Paul confirms the fact that his father was a long time and strong believer in the Christian Anglo-Israel message of the Bible. As far back as the thirties, after ardent study of the Scriptures and related material, James became convinced that the British people, that is the English, Welsh, Scots and Irish, are part of the lost tribes of Israel. In January 1945 he wrote in the *Flame*, *"Some of us may believe that Britain is part of*

Israel. " He later clearly identified himself with other Israel believers such as Richard Reader Harris, the founder of the Pentecostal Prayer League and Mrs. George Sharpe, the wife of the founder of the British Church of the Nazarene.

In the March-April 1979 issue of the Flame, James expressed his belief that though he believed Britain to be a part of God's chosen people Israel; he felt it was past time for the nation to repent of its unrighteousness. He wrote:

"Fearful, judgements are now falling upon Britain. They will continue until the nation, from the Queen downwards, sees not only its identity, but in consequence, realizes how great is its sin against the God of Israel. Until certain vile laws are expunged from our statute books and the nation repents in 'sackcloth' and ashes' before a Holy God, then no amount of planning and expediency will save us from the wrath to come."

Paul James wrote the following words concerning his father. "I think if Maynard were alive he would reply: "but we all belong to our race and this carries responsibilities as well as privileges. Christ died for the whole world, and He loves all men. But in His love for them He chooses some to have special responsibilities. To deny this is to deny the whole Biblical drama." In practice, Maynard was most gracious to people of other races, as his visits to Swaziland and India clearly demonstrates, but he simply refused to believe God's purposes were identical for all nations." (Pp. 154-155)

At Maynard James' funeral service in May 1988, Rev. Herbert McGonigle declared: "Truly a great man and Prince in Israel has fallen this day." (p. 181)

All quotations are taken from "The Story of Maynard James - A Man On Fire" by Paul James, Pub. 1993.

MRS. GEORGE (JANE) SHARPE

It is interesting to note that Paul James in the biography of his father stated that Mrs. George Sharpe was also a staunch believer in the Anglo-Israel message.

Jane Sharpe was the wife of Pastor George Sharpe, D.D. who organized the Parkhead Pentecostal Church of Glasgow, Scotland in 1906. In 1915, he founded the Church of the Nazarene in Great Britain. The *Holiness Today* magazine of December 1999 stated that "Jane Sharpe, George's wife, often preached in his absence and was ordained in 1917." Both George and Jane Sharpe were very influential in the holiness movement throughout Great Britain, America and mission churches in Africa, India and the Middle East.

REV. JAMES MOUNTAIN, D.D. 1844-1933

Truly a minister of no small influence, James Mountain was destined to share the Gospel of Salvation and the Kingdom with thousands throughout his lifetime. As a young man in the early days of his ministry he was greatly influenced by German Rationalism. He doubted the authenticity of the Word of God and the fundamental truths of the Gospel. While living in Germany, he was unable to preach for three years due to a serious physical ailment. During this time while studying the Bible and seeking the face of God, he became convinced of the truthfulness of the Anglo-Israel message of the Bible. Following his recovery he attended Heidelberg University for six months while engaging in an in-depth study of Rationalism. He credits the Anglo-Israel truth as being one of the foundational truths of Scripture that prevented his faith from being shaken in the authenticity of God's Word and the faithfulness of God to fulfill His promises.

James Mountain proclaimed this great truth as part of the total message of Scripture while declaring the Gospel of Salvation as found in the Lord Jesus Christ. Throughout his ministry he composed the music for several Gospel hymns including: *Like a River Glorious*; *At the Name of Jesus; I Am His,* and *He Is Mine; Let Your Heart Be Broken and Fill the Earth With Music.* He was also the compiler of a book called "Hymns of Consecration and Faith." (1876) He also authored two books; **British Israel Truth Defended** and **The Triumph of British-Israel.**

The article below is his personal testimony that he gave at an annual conference in London in 1928.

"It is a great pleasure to me to address this grand meeting. And as I look upon your happy faces, indicative of a surpassing intelligence and courage and devotion for the service of the Lord Jesus Christ, I feel that nobody can estimate the spiritual power and influence that may go forth to the ends of the earth, if only each one of us will consecrate himself and herself entirely to the Lord Jesus Christ. All through the Bible from Genesis to Revelation there is one grand theme–The Messiah, and His Chosen People Israel; and I thank God that forty years ago I was led to make the full surrender to the power of the Truth of Israel that has been brought before us in the meeting today. I have been giving my testimony off and on in various parts ever since those forty years began, and if I could broadcast my voice at the close of this day I would utter this invitation to the extreme ends of our Commonwealth, and say, "Come and hear, all ye that fear God, and I will tell you what He hath done for my soul through the British-Israel Truth." It has been to me an untold blessing, though it has brought to me ridicule and sneers and jeers, and though it has closed many a door to usefulness, much to my regret. Prejudice, abuse, and higher criticism are very active at the present time. But let us have patience with one another. Let us exercise charity towards each other. Let us pray, and I have not the faintest doubt but that victory will crown the work in which we are engaged. As I understood, when the invitation was sent to me to address this meeting for about ten minutes, I was requested to speak to you on what the British-Israel Truth has done for me. In other words, how has British-Israel affected my life? Well, I could give you several facts, which, I daresay, might be interesting, but you cannot say much in ten minutes; I could speak to you for an hour on the subject, and then begin all over again! However, I will mention just two things that British-Israel has done for me. I thank God it has strengthened and perfected my faith in the Bible as the Word of God, its full inspiration, its absolute integrity, its Divine authority. In the early days of my ministry, I am sorry to say, I began to suffer from an attack of German Rationalism. I got into Doubting Castle, and I remained in that Doubting Castle for a considerable time. I often feel very thankful to my Heavenly Father that He did not permit me to lead others astray. He laid me aside by a serious illness for three years and three months, and I never preached a sermon during that time. Do you know why? God was saying to me, "My child, I have silenced you that you may sit at My feet, and learn the Truth about which you are now hesitating." And I thank God for the silence, as I thank Him that ever He set me apart for this great work. I was living at that time on the Continent, where I lived about three years, and when I began to recover from my illness, I thought, I have heard a great deal about Heidelberg University, about its learned men, and the Rationalism taught there, and with the permission of my devoted wife, I decided to spend six months at Heidelberg University. I determined that I would see for myself the effect of their teaching upon their students, and I determined also that I would sit at the feet of the professors and hear what they had to say. I was acquainted with German, and had been for some time, and so I gave myself over for six months absolutely to the study of Rationalism as it was taught at the Heidelberg University. Well, when I left I had the pleasure of telling the chief Theological Professor there that I was leaving the University much more Evangelical than I was when I came. Do you know what it was that cured me completely? It

131

was British-Israel. For seventeen years I had been off and on studying it, and wherever I had gone on my tour round the world during seven years I had met with devoted men and women who believed in the British-Israel Truth, and at length by the study of Bishop Titcomb's book and Mr. Aldersmith's book, I was led straight to the foundation–the Bible, and I surrendered completely; and that was the death of my higher criticism and my incipient Modernism. I have been for some time a member of various Bible Unions for the defense of the Bible. There is that Bible League. There is the Wesleyan Bible Union. There is the Bible Witness League. All these Unions, and others I might mention, are doing a splendid work for the Bible; but if you ask me what is the most efficient and the most effective defense of the Bible, I would say it is to be found on this platform, it is in this Federation. We stand upon the Bible, the whole Bible, and nothing but the Bible. We stand upon the great Apostles' Creed, and the Nicene Creed, and all the great fundamentals of the Christian faith. And if any of you have had any hesitation about receiving to your hearts and your intellects the teaching of these meetings, permit me to assure you that if you follow our example the Bible will become stronger, more virile, more powerful in your life, and you will say, as I say, in the second place that this British-Israel Truth has given me, not only a stronger Bible, but it has given to me an illuminated edition of the Bible. The Bible is lit up to me now as it never had been before. I neither understood parts of its history, nor parts of its prophecy. I never could understand how Judah did not mean Judah, and Israel did not mean Israel, but that they both meant the Church in some period of its existence, and I came at last to see what the great Bishop Ryle saw, that Judah means Judah, and Israel means Israel, and that Zion means Zion, and Jerusalem means Jerusalem.

I passed through an experience very similar to that of a Dutch minister who attended the great Oxford Conference in 1874. That was a marvelous Conference. I daresay there are some ladies and gentlemen here today whose hearts warm as I mention the very name. For ten days clergy and ministers and prominent laymen assembled together at Oxford to wait upon God in prayer, and to study the grand old Book. Now this Dutch minister was suffering from German measles–higher criticism. And somehow or other he was invited to the Conference, and the Lord spoke to him day by day. And when the last day came, the day of testimony, he stood up and said, "I go to my Church and my people with an illumined edition of the Bible." And then twelve month afterwards I was Secretary of a Committee in London for another Conference, and we invited this gentleman, and Pastor Monod of Paris, to be two of the speakers. I sat beside this Dutch gentleman while he told us what he did when he arrived at this home from the Oxford Conference. This is what he said, "When I got home, after greeting my wife and four boys, I went into my study, I shut the door behind me and locked it, and then I went to all my drawers and shelves and other places where my old sermons and essays were and I gathered them all together, and I put them into the grate, and I set them on fire. My word, they did burn, for they were so dry. The only heat that ever came from those sermons was that which went up the chimney." Well, something of that experience was mine. I had to put aside a great many of my old sermons. I should call them cold porridge now. Well, they are gone, but I remain–a new man, with new light, new love, new grace, and a new knowledge of this grand old Book, and in my 86th year I have definitely dedicated myself, with whatever energy God may favour me, whether I live long, or whether my career be short, it shall be laid upon that one altar of God and His Truth, Jesus Christ and Him crucified, and His Chosen People, represented by the great Commonwealth of Great Britain."

BISHOP JONATHAN HOLT TITCOMB
Bishop J.H. Titcomb and The Israel Message

The Rt. Rev. Jonathan Holt Titcomb was a strong advocate of the Anglo-Israel teaching and a highly respected clergyman of the Church of England. Writing of him, the Rev. James Mountain, D.D., another Anglican clergyman, said, "He was a learned man of sound judgment, urbane and of a lovable character. He won the affection of all who knew him. He was courageous and fearless in his proclamation of Israel truth."

Bishop Titcomb became a believer in, and a public advocate of, Anglo-Israelism before being elected to the episcopate; and this belief never had negative consequences for his work and ministry because it was considered a perfectly orthodox view within the Anglican Church. Prior to his election as bishop, he had been Vicar of St. Stephen's, South Lambeth. In 1875, he wrote a book called "The Anglo-Israel Post-Bag," in which he explained how he had come to believe that the Anglo-Saxon and kindred peoples were the literal descendants of the ancient Israelites. Two years later, in 1877, he was consecrated to the episcopate by Archbishop Tait of Canterbury as a missionary bishop for Burma. For the next five years he served as the first bishop of Rangoon, Burma. In 1878, a second edition of his book on Anglo-Israelism was published under the title of "Letters to a Friend." In 1882, Bishop Titcomb returned to England for health reasons. After recovering his health he became

Assistant Bishop of London, charged with overseeing the Anglican congregations scattered across the Continent of Europe - a post of great responsibility. During his ministry he also served a period as president of the Metropolitan Anglo-Israel Association, and was a frequent contributor to The Banner of Israel magazine.

Bishop Titcomb passed into eternity on April 2, 1887, but some forty years later his book was published in a third edition, this time titled *"British-Israel: How I Came to Believe It."* The Rev. James Mountain, D.D., editor of the third edition of Bishop Titcomb's book, wrote in the Editor's Preface, "My first perusal of the book took place forty years ago when voyaging from New Zealand to San Francisco, and afterwards when sailing from Montreal to Liverpool. On both occasions I read the treatise with delight and profit on account of the cogency, lucidity and fairness of its arguments. For seventeen years previously I had been interested in the subject through the reading of numerous pamphlets; but when I had given two prolonged prayerful studies to the Bishop's scholarly treatise, I was practically convinced and almost on the point of decision. It was not, however, until a few weeks later that the final decision was made to surrender to the Truth which I have never regretted, and which wider and profounder studies have abundantly confirmed."

In his book, Bishop Titcomb writes, "Some of my friends of late have jokingly said to me that they think I am getting ready for Hanwell, or some other similar retreat, where overheated brains find time for cooling down into a restored condition of common-sense. And why? Because I have, at length, yielded to the belief that the Anglo-Saxons are descended from the Ten Tribes of Israel. I say 'at length yielded'; for, during many years, I argued against and resisted the opinion.

"If I have changed my opinions, therefore, it is not because I have brought to the investigation any views which were predisposed to the reception of that Theory. Still less has it been that my brain has become softened. 'I am not mad, most noble Festus.' I do but now see what I could not before discover; and enjoy, as an inheritance of reason, that which was previously a dark and unsolvable riddle (excerpted from BRITISH-ISRAEL: How I Came To Believe It, pp. 2-3)."

I believe has been the experience of many devout minds in reference to this subject" (p. 5).

Bishop Titcomb was not the first or the last Anglican clergyman to profess belief in Anglo-Israelism. There have been many Anglican bishops and other clergymen, as well as vast numbers of laity that have come to this belief. Another early missionary bishop, the Rt. Rev.

134

Samuel Thornton, first Bishop of Ballarat, Australia, and later Assistant Bishop of Manchester, England, said, "British-Israel truth is most wonderful. I wish I had known it twenty-five years earlier. It makes clear so many things that had been obscure."

Bishop Titcomb believed that understanding the identity of the Anglo-Saxon and kindred peoples was vital for an accurate understanding of the Holy Scriptures. He said, "The inspiration of the Scripture must stand or fall by the discovery of Ephraim [the Ten Tribed House of Israel] as a company of non-Palestine nations restored to the Covenant of God during the last days, that is, the Christian Dispensation. Thousands who have begun by caviling at British Israel Truth have ended with conviction; and, for the most part, those who have not become convinced have failed only because they were without sufficient patience to go through an examination of the subject carefully."

ALEXANDER CRUDEN 1700-1770

From an early age, Alexander Cruden had an instinctive desire for learning and the Christian ministry. He was born in Aberdeen, Scotland on May 31, 1700. He was educated at Marischal College and Aberdeen University. He worked as a private tutor from 1722-1732, moved to London as a bookseller, a printer's proof corrector and then a bookseller to the queen. In 1737 he produced his famous work, *"A Complete Concordance of the Holy Scriptures of the Old and New Testaments,"* which he dedicated to Queen Caroline, the consort of King George II. He later produced two more editions. Cruden felt a divine passion to call Britain to repentance for its moral laxity, and therefore was known as "Alexander the Corrector." He was a well-known figure of his day among the common people, government officials and the monarchy. He also wrote, *"A Scripture Dictionary"* and his autobiography, *"Adventures of Alexander the Corrector."* Cruden was known as a lover of God's Word and spent his life in deep study of its truths. He was also a pious and humble Christian and a devout member of a London Independent Church. In November 1770 he was found dead on his knees with an open Bible before him, while engaged in prayer. (Source: The Wycliffe Biographical Dictionary of the Church, Elgin S. Moyer)

In 1761, Alexander Cruden dedicated his concordance to King George III which included the following statement in his message of salutation. "May the great God be the guide of your life, and direct and prosper you, that it may be said by the present and future ages, that King George the Third hath been an Hezekiah to our British Israel." (Signed) Alexander Cruden, London, June 11, 1761.

DINSDALE THOMAS YOUNG 1861-1938

Early in life while still a young man, it was obvious to Dinsdale Young what his calling and profession was going to be. He was born on November 20, 1861 at Corbridge-on-Tyne, England, received his education in private schools and earned a degree from Headingley Theological College in Leeds, England. At the age of eighteen, he was the youngest minister to be received into the Wesleyan Conference. As a popular preacher, he held pastorates in Birmingham, Edinburgh, London, Manchester and York. From 1906 to 1914, he pastored in John Wesley's historic pulpit at Wesley Chapel, City Road in London. He went on to become the president of the Wesleyan Conference and the pastor of Westminster Central Hall in London where he attracted capacity crowds. Among his many friends were such mighty men of God as F. B. Meyer and G. Campbell Morgan. He authored several books including, *Silver Charms, Neglected People of the Bible, The Enthusiasm of God* and his autobiography. He died on January 21, 1938.

Dinsdale T. Young was a strong believer in the Anglo-Israel truth of Scripture as shown by his following declaration.

"I increasingly believe that the weight of argument is with the British Israel position . . . I am more and more drawn to the great truths which the Federation represents. My heart warms to it, because of its splendid adherence to the Bible . . . The British Israel Federation has lighted a lamp, the golden beauty of which will never be obscured. In the great truth which this Federation holds, you have the explanation of the wonderful British Empire."

(Sources: *The Wycliffe Biographical Dictionary of the Church*, Elgin S. Moyer; *Facets of the Great Story* by H. Robin Tourtel.)

MERTON SMITH

The nineteen century was an era filled with highly charged philosophical and revolutionary change. Into this age of change Merton Smith was born in 1853 in Glasgow, Scotland. Having studied in Scotland and Germany, he got caught up in the agnosticism of the time. During his stay in Chicago, Illinois he was converted to Christ under the ministry of Dwight L. Moody and later became a ministry associate of the famous evangelist. He assumed the pastorate of a church in Vancouver, Canada and then served overseas during World War I. Having moved back to Great Britain after the war, he passed away in 1934.

Pastor Merton Smith was a strong advocate of the Anglo-Israel truth as is evidenced in his book entitled, ***"Israel - Her Racial Divisions and***

Geographic Wanderings" (pub. 1926). In brief summary statements he wrote: "Israel = ruling with God. Easy to write, easy to speak, but difficult to understand, for in this word and in the people it represents, God has hidden His purposes for the re-establishment of His Kingdom on this earth." "...When Christ came in the flesh and was rejected by the Jews, all that was left of Judah in Palestine, He, Jesus, told the Jews (Matt. 21:43) 'Therefore the Kingdom of God shall be taken from you and given to a nation bringing forth the fruits thereof." That nation was and is 'Israel in the Isles": "the servant of Jehovah" of Isaiah 40 to 66. The position taken in this paper is that Israel (twelve tribed Israel) has nationally accepted Christ, and that she has, since the first century of this era, been carrying the message of God into every corner of the earth. This nation Israel is still, as Christ said it would be, in a mixed condition - tares and wheat (Matt. 23:24-30."

The D.L. Moody Connection

Reported in *"The Messenger of the Covenant"* of November 1934 was an article about the death of Merton Smith. It was entitled; *"An Israel Warrior Goes Home"* and reads in part as follows:

"The Roadbuilder mentions in his "Along the Road" the home-going of Captain the Rev. Merton Smith. He was an old war-horse of Israel. Even unto advanced age he kept his vigor and insight nor ever halted in his study of the Word. He was a great missionary of the Israel truth and was privileged to present it to many great men. In earlier life he was for five years one of the most effective of D.L. Moody's assistant, but he was not static enough for that great leader. Merton Smith was always pressing into the regions of truth farther on, and this was disconcerting to a campaign built on but one phase of the truth. The writer of this note distinctly remembers Merton Smith relating his experiences with Moody and his attempts to have Moody come out boldly for the whole truth of Israel's destiny. He declared that Moody–who also was no mean student of the Scriptures–saw the Biblical basis of what we stand for, but was then engaged in those great educational works which required immense sums of money, and was dependent on wealthy donors for the means, which he felt would be jeopardized by any new or sensational enlargement of his preaching. Besides, he saw the economic implications of the truth and knew instinctively that this would result in the alienation of many of the wealthy supporters of his revival and educational work. So he elected to go on as he had always done. In this

137

doubtless, Moody acted wisely. But Merton Smith had no such ties and was free "to sail all the seas with God." Which he did most valiantly.

DR. H. ALDERSMITH

Another scholar of high standing and prominence among his peers was Dr. H. Aldersmith. It's very obvious in his books that he possessed great insight in Biblical studies and logic in setting forth its principles. In his book *'The Fulness of the Nations'* (Pub. London 1889, 1898 & 1945) he builds a magnificent defense for the Anglo-Israel truth. In his first edition preface he writes; "A great many persons put aside the subject of the present whereabouts, and number, of the Lost Ten Tribes, and will not look into it, as they think the view, that they are now a mighty host, to be a 'heresy of the last days' or 'a delusion of a few enthusiasts;' and some do not hesitate to denounce it in   stronger terms, even as 'a device of Satan:' but, if they would only carefully search the Scriptures, they would probably come to a different conclusion."

He then quotes Rev. Robert Douglas in his defense of this truth.

1. *"Our doctrine destroys infidelity* for it shows every word of the Bible to be true. An ancient and mighty nation rises from the dead to attest the faithfulness of Jehovah.

2. It kindles hope for the world which shall be forever blessed in Israel.

3. It shows the necessity for faith and holiness, for the covenant was established on grace through faith, and that a faith which produces obedience as its fruit.

4. It stimulates love and zeal. The mind is overwhelmed by the matchless goodness of God to Israel."

The magazine *Banner of Israel* published an article in the 1920's written by Dr. Aldersmith entitled, *"The Evidence Afforded by the Speaker's Commentary on British-Israel Truth."* The Speakers Commentary was a commentary on the Bible written by bishops and other clergy of the Anglican Church edited by F.C. Cook, M.A., Canon of Exeter, late preacher at Lincoln's Inn and Chaplain- in Ordinary to the Queen.   Dr. Aldersmith points out that the notes in this commentary are in agreement concerning the historical difference between the House of Judah and the House of Israel as a Biblical foundation for Anglo-Israel teaching.   In other words, correct Biblical exegesis supports the veracity of the Anglo-Israel message.

ADDITIONAL WITNESSES

Bishop Samuel Thornton, D.D. - First Bishop of Ballarat and afterwards Assistant Bishop of Manchester – "British-Israel truth is most wonderful. I wish I had known it twenty-five years earlier. It makes clear so many things that had been obscure."

Archbishop Bond - Montreal "I strongly advise a study of the Scripture prophecies upon British-Israel lines."

Mark Guy Pearse - Methodist Minister - "If Britain is Ephraim, i.e., the ten tribes of Israel - then I can see the prophecies of Scripture being fulfilled in our midst. If Britain is not Ephraim, then there are no such people answerable to the prophet's description, nor, as yet, has there been such a people, nor is there any promise of such a people appearing."

J.P. Van Huysteen - Afrikaan Minister - "The British-Israel teachings show clearly that the Lord has chosen and made great His empire, as His servant, to bring His rule over the earth. Having read much about the prophecies, I believe the Lord has chosen this people to be a blessing to the world. I am glad to know that we, the Dutch are part of that empire."

Professor Piazzi Smyth - Astronomer Royal for Scotland - "The effect of the discovery of the identity of the Anglo-Saxons as Israel is twofold. First, it causes us to behold and acknowledge therein the accomplishment of a true miracle, and of the mightiest kind, through the ages consummated in our own days. Second, it causes the Bible to become for us, as it was for the tribes of Israel of old, an infallible book for national guidance in politics, as well as a collection of inspired instruction for each individual soul in religion."

Rt. Hon. W.F. Massey, P.C. - Former Prime Minister of New Zealand. - "British Israel truth is God's truth. It is therefore bound to win; it is winning all along the line."

The United Israel Bulletin, a non-Christian Jewish publication, of New York, April 1951, in its *Declaration of Principles*, declared *inter alia* ". . . We believe that the ten tribes of Israel, hitherto lost in identity, exist within the Anglo-Saxon-Celtic-Scandinavian-American realm of peoples;"

139

A letter appearing in the London *Daily Mail*, 5th May, 1917, headed Mispah, Jerusalem, said "The erudite editor of the German paper *Volkeerzicher*, Dr. Swamer...according to him, when a recension shall be taken of their descendants, it will not be surprising to find Britain is to be identified with Israel...The Anglo-Saxon race, who in all probability are the genuine descendants of the House of Israel."

The above eight entries from *Facets of the Great Story* by H. Robin Tourtel, pp. 138-142.

Dr. Aszkenazy, a prominent Polish Jew, who has recently become a Christian and a British-Israelite, then addressed the meeting, and was interpreted by Rev. D.J. Newgewirtz. He said he was a Jew, but had now become a disciple of the Lord Jesus Christ. He now wished to give expression to his new vision and belief. He has written books in exposition of the Bible. From Mr. Newgewirtz he heard of British-Israel for the first time. At first he was doubtful, but had now settled down to a close study of the subject, and was now absolutely convinced that the British people were Israel."

From: The National Message Nov. 18, 1933, Vol. 12 p.727

By no means do the proponents of the Anglo-Israel truth in Great Britain listed in this booklet exhaust the names that could be added. There have been multiplied thousands of ministers and laity of various denominations, esquires, military personnel and even members of the Royal Family who have added their testimony to the long list of believers.

"Give ear, O Shepherd of Israel, thou that leadest Joseph like a flock; thou that dwellest between the cherubims, shine forth. Before Ephraim and Benjamin and Manasseh stir up thy strength, and come and save us. Turn us again, O God, and cause thy face to shine; and we shall be saved." **Psalm 80:1-3**

The Lost Tribes of Israel

Where Are They?

Richard Reader Harris
1847-1909

Prominent English Barrister, Counselor to Queen Victoria, Methodist
Minister, Founder of the Pentecostal League of Prayer

INTRODUCTION
By Charles A. Jennings

Richard Reader Harris, K.C. (1847-1909) was an eminent British lawyer and a King's Counselor. Early in life he was an atheist but accepted Christ as Savior after realizing the Bible was true as a result of the Anglo-Israel truth. He gave up his lofty and respected secular career and became a Methodist minister, highly respected Christian leader and author who wrote over 34 books. He and his wife, Mary, founded the Pentecostal League of Prayer in 1891 as "an interdenominational union of Christian people who, conscious of their own need, would join in prayer: 1) For the filling of the Holy Spirit for all believers; 2) For revival in the Churches: 3) For the spread of Scriptural holiness." They named their League publication, "Tongues of Fire." He remained a firm believer in the Anglo-Israel message and in 1908 he wrote a book on the topic, entitled, "The Lost Tribes of Israel."

Reader Harris and Oswald Chambers were close mutual friends and were held in very high esteem among their Christian contemporaries. Oswald Chambers is revered as an outstanding mainstream evangelist,

141

missionary, Bible teacher and author. The following is excerpted from the book, Oswald Chambers: Abandoned to God: *The Life Story of the Author of My Utmost for His Highest.*

When Reader Harris, founder of the League, first met Chambers, he took a special interest in the keen young tutor from Dunoon. They talked about Oswald's gift and desires, and where God might be leading him. Harris helped raise Chamber's vision from Britain to the world. And the more Oswald learned about this tall man of dignified grace and decisive action, the more he liked him. Harris was a prominent London barrister and also a King's Counsel, a lifetime appointment recognizing his skill and success in the legal profession. His leadership in the League of Prayer was voluntary and unpaid. From the circles of royalty to the slums of London, Harris moved freely as a fearless but compassionate representative of Christ.

Richard Reader Harris was an unlikely person to establish a religious organization devoted to scriptural holiness and spiritual revival. As a teenager, Harris had sought God, but his conversations with a liberal clergyman left him so disillusioned that he later became a follower of Charles Bradlaugh, the well known London atheist. Bradlaugh often lectured on Bible texts, ridiculing Christians for their weak response to its teachings while he called people to live moral lives and put into practice the ideas in the Sermon on the Mount.

Joining the Puritan Wing of Bradlaugh's Ethical Society, Harris pledged not to smoke or drink. If a man lived more uprightly than most Christians, he thought, why did he need their God? "For ten years," Harris later said, "I remained an honest doubter because no one pointed me to Jesus Christ as the One who saves 'to the uttermost.' I had wanted to know God, but the professing Christians I knew failed to introduce me to Him, because they did not know Him themselves."

His conversion to Christ came through Mary Griffin Bristow, a gifted and cultured young lady whom he married in 1880. Reader and Mary Harris could easily have remained well respected, comfortable members of the upper strata of London society. But Reader could not forget the scathing accusations of Charles Bradlaugh from years past: "If Jesus had been divine," Bradlaugh thundered, "his followers would long ago have claimed the power He offered them, obeyed His command, and evangelized the world."

The Pentecostal League of Prayer whose magazine was named "Tongues of Fire" was immediately associated with the emerging "tongues movement." When Harris founded the League in 1891, the terms *pentecostal* and *tongues of fire* had no connotations beyond the familiar passage in the second chapter of Acts. Within a few years, however, the growth of Pentecostalism as a movement in Britain and the attendant emphasis on speaking in tongues caused confusion about the League's orientation.

Reader Harris distinguished between the gifts of speaking in an unlearned foreign language (Acts 2:6-12) and the ecstatic utterance or glossolalia mentioned in the letters of Paul. Harris had no quarrel with either 'gift' but strenuously opposed those who made "tongues" the litmus test of being filled with the Holy Spirit. In a November 1907 address he said: "There is nothing wrong with speaking in tongues; it was the privilege of the early Church, and it may be the privilege of any believer today"

Oswald knew Reader and Mary Harris as few others did, and he considered them "the Lord's choicest saints." Some looked at Harris and saw only the prominent barrister. Others focused solely on his leadership in the League of Prayer. Chambers saw the man of God whose winsome, yet fearless testimony for Christ extended from the circles of British aristocracy to the poor in the slums of Battersea.

On November 13, 1908, the day of his engagement and imminent departure for Ireland, Chambers wrote: "What I owe to the League of Prayer only our heavenly Father knows. How it exalts me and humbles me when I remember so many hundreds are praying for me all over the country."

Perhaps Oswald might have looked longer at the bearded face of the organization's founder or gripped his hand more tightly if he had known it would be the last time he would see Reader Harris alive.

Chambers was five days into his mission at Lowestoft when the shocking news came on March 26 that Reader Harris had suffered a stroke and lay in a coma at his London home. Four days later, without regaining consciousness Harris died at the age of sixty one.

On Tuesday afternoon, April 6, two thousand people overflowed Speke Hall for the funeral. Hundreds of others stood outside, lining the streets. Chambers gave a brief tribute at the service. Then, along with hundreds of others, he boarded a special train carrying the funeral party to Norwood and interment in the cemetery there high on a hill.

That evening in Queen's Hall, Langham Place, a memorial service paid further honor to Harris. Franklin Chambers came from Perth to preside at the organ and Oswald joined a large party on the platform. His remarks revealed not only his personal relationship to Harris, but his awareness of people's questions regarding the future of the League: "He was a King's Counsellor to me in the very highest sense," Oswald said, "by one of those strange turns of God's providence; Mr. Reader Harris came across me. How, I do not know; God knows, and he began to counsel me, and from that moment the counsel and the prayers and the guidance of Mr. Reader Harris have been to me as those of a commander. "Others of you may have known of his winsomeness, of his beauty and humor. I have known of these also, but to me he had a clarion voice spiritually and he was indeed a man by whom God witnessed to my own heart with these words the first day he shook hands with me, "I have chosen him to be a witness, and a leader and a commander," and God knows he has been that to thousands.

"There is no second Reader Harris, and never will be. There never was a second Moses. God does not repeat His servants.

THE LOST TRIBES OF ISRAEL
(*The following are excerpts from the book written by Reader Harris*)

The subject of the lost tribes of Israel is a study of great interest. Two perplexing questions meet us on the threshold, vis., how is it that so little is known of the ten tribes of Israel, and why has so little enquiry taken place concerning them? This may well be because the devil has succeeded in frustrating any serious research into the matter.

It is remarkable that until the middle of the nineteenth century there was little or no serious enquiry in Protestant countries regarding the fate of the ten tribes; and noteworthy, also, that from that period was awakened in some of God's people a spirit of enquiry as to the fate of the ten tribes with regard to their destiny.

The discovery and the acknowledgment of the lost tribes would revolutionize the whole world, give an impetus to Scriptural study, and encourage men in a wonderful degree to believe the promises of God; while on the other hand, if any nation or aggregate of nations could be proved undoubtedly to represent in large measure the ten tribes of Israel, it would inspire them and encourage them to possess their possessions as nothing else could do.

From the "holiness" standpoint and from what I may call that of the "fifth Kingdom" (Daniel 2), the subject of the history of the lost tribes assumes tremendous importance, and must be of intense interest to every Bible student. The faithfulness of God in regard to promise, covenant and prophecy is herein involved. It is a well known fact that the historian Hume justified his unbelief by what he declared to be the failure of the

Bible promises to Israel. I believe that if we study this subject under the light of God's Spirit, resting in the revelation of God's Word, God will give to us, and to others through us, a new interest and confidence in the Bible, a further impetus to religious experience and to prophetic study; and perhaps a clearer apprehension of the political future of the world, and of the signs which foretell the return of our Lord.

First and foremost let us understand that difference between the Jews and the lost tribes of Israel, between the kingdom of Judah and the kingdom of Israel. This distinction between the two nations is never lost sight of in the Bible, and until it is understood we cannot follow the Scriptural truth on this subject. The majority of Christian people at the present day have never seen this distinction. They confuse the Jews with the Israelites in various ways. Some, in reading of Israel, apply the passage to the Jews, while others think it refers to the Church. Some people apply the curses of the Bible to the Jews, and its promises to the Church. The Bible, however, is perfectly plain. When it speaks of Israel, in ninety-nine cases out of a hundred the ten tribes are meant. There are some few passages where the word "Israel" undoubtedly refers, as it did originally, to the twelve tribes of Israel; but generally speaking there is a marked and definite distinction between Judah and Israel, and unless we realise that distinction we cannot understand the prophecies concerning this wonderful people.

That the missing tribes exist, no serious person can doubt. If, under persecution such as the world has never before seen, after massacre upon massacre, torture upon torture, the remnant of part of the tribe of Judah, Levi and Benjamin, can have multiplied until they reach something like twelve millions of people, what must be the number of the ten tribes? Then tribes equally virile; ten tribes of the same stock; ten tribes that have lived their lives and spread their race without persecution, massacre and torture! What a multitude must they now have become! *Where are they?*

Let us begin with their earliest history. God chose Abraham, and made an unconditional covenant with his lineal seed (Genesis 22:15-18). That covenant was repeated by God to Jacob when He called him Israel, as you will see in Genesis 35:11:*"GOD SAID UNTO HIM, I AM GOD ALMIGHTY. BE FRUITFUL AND MULTIPLY. A NATION AND A COMPANY OF NATIONS SHALL BE OF THEE, AND KINGS SHALL COME OUT OF THY LOINS."*

Jacob before his death blessed the sons of Joseph, Ephraim and Manasseh, giving the birthright to Ephraim, although Ephraim was not the elder of the two. If you will look at Genesis 48, you will see that the

145

blessing which ought to have been Reuben's was taken from him because of his sin and given to Ephraim. Judah received the emblem of the Lion, and obtained the promises of kingship, and that from him should spring the Messiah. Moses before his death blessed the sons of Joseph, Ephraim and Manasseh and gave to them the emblem of the Unicorn (Deut. 33:17). It is remarkable that so far back as the days of Moses the emblems of the Unicorn pertained to Judah and Ephraim. The distinction between the two nations of Judah and Israel began before their final separation under Jeroboam, and Rehoboam. You will find in 2 Samuel 2, that David was anointed king over Judah only, while Ishbosheth, Saul's son, was made king over all Israel, this severance continuing for 7 ½ years. Israel was then annexed to Judah under King David (2 Samuel 5: 1), but the two kingdoms of Judah and Israel were finally separated immediately after the death of Solomon, and from that time to the present Judah and Israel have remained absolutely distinct. They were carried into captivity separately, at different times and by different nations, for Israel was taken in captivity by the Assyrians B.C. 721 (2 Kings 17:6), while Judah was carried into captivity by the Babylonians B.C. 588 (2 Kings 25:21). A portion of Judah was permitted to return after seventy years, as had been predicted (Ezra 2:1), but Israel never returned nor was there any prediction that they should return til the final glorious restoration.

In B.C. 721 the ten tribes of Israel drop out of sacred history, and there is no further reference made to them in the historical part of the Bible, but the prophetical portion supplies the sequel, for in these Scriptural prophecies the whole future of the people of Israel is chronicled. Apart from the sacred books we find the last historical record of the ten tribes is given by the great Jewish historian Josephus, writing form Rome, in A.D. 70:

The entire body of the ten tribes is still beyond the River Euphrates, an immense multitude not to be estimated by numbers."

"We see, therefore, that the kingdom of Judah and the kingdom of Israel, ever since the day of Solomon, have been absolutely distinct.

I begin this study of the history of the so-called lost tribes of Israel with this declaration: –The lost tribes, the descendants of the kingdom of Israel, are certainly in existence today. But where? That is the question, and what a wonderful question it is! The discovery of a continent is a great discovery, and Columbus will be celebrated throughout all time as the discoverer of a continent. The discovery of a new star, a new world, is a great discovery. But I venture to think that the discovery of the kingdom of Israel, of the descendants of those ten tribes, would have a

146

greater effect upon the kingdom of God and the hearts and lives of men than even the discovery of a new continent or a new world.

"The descendants of the tribes of Israel certainly exist, the question is, Where? The Jews we know, but where is Israel? Some people assert that God has cut Israel out of His divine programme, and in consequence Israel has become extinct as a nation. In refutation of such a statement let us turn to Jeremiah 31:35-36:

Thus saith the Lord, which giveth the sun for a light by day and the ordinances of the moon and of the stars for a light by night, which divideth (which stilleth) the sea when the waves thereof roar: The Lord of Hosts is His name: If those ordinances (that is the sun and moon and stars) depart from before me, saith the Lord, then the seed of Israel also shall cease from being a nation before me for ever."

This passage distinctly declares that while sun and moon and stars exist the nation of Israel will remain before God.

"Where are the ten tribes? Where is the nation of Israel? Which nation on earth today represents them? How can this be discovered? I have learned that if we really want to know about God's people, the Bible is the book in which to look; let us, therefore, go to the Bible for the history of God's chosen people Israel. Unless God's promises have failed, Israel must be in existence today.

We shall find that the Bible declares that Israel exists as a multitudinous nation, bearing certain marks, inheriting certain blessings, doing certain things for which it was created, and which it was and is its special mission and destiny to perform. The ten tribes are in existence somewhere, and the quest is not so difficult as it at first appears, for although secular history is apparently dumb concerning these tribes– a remarkable fact in itself– Bible prophecy is abundant in descriptive allusions to Israel; and we shall find from the study of Biblical prophecy where the kingdom of Israel is today.

It is perfectly clear that Israel, who had been dispersed for more than 700 years, was much in our Lord's mind during His three years' ministry upon earth, for many were the references to Israel made by Him. As an example, let us turn to the commission He gave to the twelve apostles in Matt. 10:5-6:

These twelve Jesus sent forth, and commanded them, saying, Go not into the way of the Gentiles, and into any city of the Samaritans enter ye not: but go rather to the lost sheep of the house of Israel."

These apostles were not to go to the Gentiles, nor to the Samaritans– who were the descendants of usurpers of Israel–"But to the lost sheep of the house of Israel," and they obeyed this command as far as was then

147

possible. The only tribe that they could reach which had any connection with Israel was Benjamin, and Benjamin as a tribe was won to allegiance to the Lord Jesus Christ. Benjamin had gone into captivity with Judah, and had come back with Judah, but in the prophecies of God Benjamin had always associated with the ten tribes of Israel. It is a remarkable fact that the majority of our Lord's disciples at the time of His earthly ministry were connected with the tribe of Benjamin. It is also of interest that when Jerusalem was afterwards besieged by the Romans under Titus, the members of what had become the Christian tribe of Benjamin escaped.

Christ Himself declared in Matthew 15:24, this was His own mission. *"He answered and said, I am not sent but unto the lost sheep of the house of Israel."*

Again our Lord says in Matthew 21:43: *"Therefore say I unto you* (He was speaking to the Jews), *the kingdom of God shall be taken from you and given to a nation* (the Jews had long since ceased to be a nation) *bringing forth the fruits thereof."*

The Jews themselves evidently so understood His statements, for in John 7:35 we read: *"Then said the Jews among themselves, Whither will He go, that we shall not find Him? Will He go unto the dispersed among the Gentiles, and teach the Gentiles?"*

So the Jews quite understood our Lord to refer to Israel. Israel was evidently in the minds of the apostles themselves. On the day of the ascension they asked Him: *"Lord, wilt thou at this time restore again the Kingdom to Israel?"* Acts 1:6

We may find that the purpose of God has been fulfilled, and the mantle of Israel has fallen upon the British or Anglo-Saxon race.

There are many other remarkable prophecies about Israel which are fulfilled by the British race, but there is yet one more remarkable than any I have given you, and which is also of a specially sacred character.

The observance of a Sabbath has been given by God as a sign which shall mark Israel forever.

The children of Israel shall keep the Sabbath, and observe the Sabbath, throughout their generations for a perpetual covenant: It is a sign between me and the children of Israel for ever." Ex. 31:16-17

Such then are the Scriptures that appear to me to furnish strong evidence in favor of the contention of those who believe that in the Anglo-Saxon race God possesses today the descendants of the house of Israel. If this be true, it adds tremendously to our responsibilities, and opens before us in a way that no human tongue can describe, spiritual

148

possibilities, temporal possibilities, national possibilities, and universal possibilities.

Let none of us, however, be so taken up with the literal fulfillment of prophecy that we forget the spiritual interpretation of it. For this reason it is extremely important that those who study this subject should be filled with the Spirit of wisdom and revelation in the full knowledge of the Lord Jesus Christ, and should themselves be in the full experience of spiritual blessing.

Let us, therefore, claim God's Spirit, and as we learn day by day to see more evidences of the fulfillment of these prophecies, may God possess in us individually, and in the Pentecostal League collectively, and in the thousands of others who are in sympathy with us, body of men and women yielded to Him in heart, and in life, learning His will, proclaiming His truth, and glorifying His name.

149

A LOST PEOPLE
AND
A VANISHED SCEPTRE

GEORGE OWEN BARNES

**As Pastor, Evangelist and Missionary, Rev. Barnes gives a
patriarchal witness to the truth of the Kingdom of God**

INTRODUCTION
By Charles A. Jennings

As further witness to the faithfulness of God in keeping His Word, the
following testimony of Evangelist George O. Barnes is added to a long
list of anointed messengers of God. Throughout his ministerial career,
Rev. Barnes served as pastor, evangelist and missionary, not only in
America but in many countries overseas. During his lifetime he proved
his love and commitment to the Lord Jesus Christ, not only in the life
which he lived, the untiring service which he rendered to others, but also
by his study and written testimony. Even after his formal ministerial
training was completed at Princeton Theological Seminary, he pursued
his intense study of God's Word and desire for further divine revelation
concerning sacred knowledge and truth. The following testimony from
his book, "A Lost People and a Vanished Sceptre," is an example of Rev.
Barnes' interpretational knowledge of the prophecies and fulfillment of
God's holy Word.

In compiling his lectures into printed form in October 1906 in the city
of Washington, D.C., Rev. Barnes clearly stated his purpose in his
preface in the following words.

151

"I print these Lectures, on the "Lost Tribes of Israel," delivered long years ago, for a double purpose. FIRST, to add my feeble protest against what is known, in these day, as the "Higher Criticism"; which, propped by great names, is undermining the Old Testament Scriptures. If unchecked, it promises to leave us without any "Holy Bible," at all.

SECONDLY, I would like to help on, in a small way, the growing good feeling between the two great branches of the Anglo-Saxon family; that now, by constant travel, association, and especially by intermarriages, give promise of ultimate close affiliation, and co-operation in advancing the welfare of "all the families of the Earth."

I think, I prove, in this little booklet, that this is the "manifest destiny," because the scripturally foretold mission, of the English speaking race."

The following brief biographical sketch of the life and ministry of Rev. Barnes is taken from the "LEAVES OF HEALING" magazine of 1902. That same year he stated "at seventy-five I begin what we call, in Kentucky horse parlance, 'the last quarter stretch' of the earthly race." In his untiring zeal, Rev. Barnes expressed his love and devotion to his Lord and Savior Jesus Christ, until the day in which he heard the call for his departure from this mortal life into the presence of his Redeemer.

GEORGE OWEN BARNES

George Owen Barnes was born at Paintlick, Gerrard County, Kentucky, on the 22nd of April, 1827. His father, born in Carshalton, Surrey, England, was a pastor of a large country church. George was the youngest of four children. His mother was a native of Elizabeth City, New Jersey.

In 1836 Mr. Barnes, the elder, removed with his family to Dayton, Ohio, where George received his academic education. This was continued in collegiate work in Centre College, at Danville, Kentucky, from which he graduated in 1845.

Mr. Barnes' early intention was to devote his life to the practice of law, and for two years he studied diligently with this end in view. Then the Mexican war broke out, and young Barnes volunteered, serving for twelve months in the First Regiment, Volunteer Cavalry.

Of his early spiritual life Elder Barnes says: "I was converted in the hard, old-fashioned way in 1843; backslid soon, of course, and was not restored until 1848."

But the good seed had been sown in a good and honest heart, and in 1852, at the age of twenty-five, Mr. Barnes determined to give his life to the ministry of God, and accordingly went to Princeton Theological Seminary to be educated for that work.

His heart turned toward the foreign field, and he longed to carry the Gospel to those in heathen darkness who had never seen the blessed light of Christ.

In July, 1854, he was married and sailed for India, under the Presbyterian Board, in September of the same year.

Hard and faithful toil in a tropical climate broke down the health of the faithful missionary and in 1861 he was obliged to return to America. Knowing nothing of Divine Healing he spent thirteen months at the "Cleveland Water Cure," where he slowly and imperfectly regained his health.

A return to his work in the foreign field being out of the question, he accepted the pastorate of the Presbyterian Church in Stanford, Kentucky. He occupied this pulpit from 1862 to 1872, when he withdrew from the Presbyterian communion. This was a most important step in the life of this man of God.

For five years following his withdrawal from the Presbyterian Church, Elder Barnes alternated between Kentucky and Chicago, spending half his time in each place.

In 1875 John E. Ousley, a millionaire friend, of Kentucky, built a church in Chicago for Mr. Barnes, furnished a house for him, and paid all the expenses of carrying on the work. In the following year occurred another epoch in the life of this wonderful man. He experienced an uplift from the "wave" of spiritual influence which seemed to go around the world at that time.

As a result of this spiritual uplift, Mr. Barnes felt an especial leading of the Spirit to take up the work of an evangelist. He left his Chicago pastorate and returned to Kentucky.

In January of 1877 there was formed a most beautiful, and as the history of the next twenty years showed, a most blessed fellowship in the work of God between Mr. Barnes and his eldest daughter, Marie.

While the father preached the Everlasting Gospel with convincing power, the daughter's clear, sweet voice was raised in divine song, with an inspiration which touched many a heart.

During this twenty-three years, father and daughter circumnavigated the globe, preaching and singing the good news.

As soon as she was through with her school work, Mr. Barnes, youngest daughter, Georgia, made the evangelistic duet a trio and continued with her father and sister, a valued helper until her marriage in 1892.

Mr. Barnes' son also gladdened the heart of his father by entering the ministry. He preached in the mountains of East Tennessee until February 1883, when he joined his father and sisters in the work among the poor in East London, England.

The little family continued for two years in this work, and then sailed for India, where they worked among the British soldiers for a year.

This evangelistic tour was continued for six months, during which the Gospel was preached and sung in Ceylon, in Australia, and in New Zealand. Then the family returned to San Francisco.

During all three and one-half years of work and travel around the world, Elder Barnes and his family depended wholly on the Lord for support, asking no help from any one.

There were five in the family, and the three and one-half years' tour cost sixteen thousand dollars; but Elder Barnes says, "The Lord sent us the money when He wanted us to 'move on.' It almost frightens me to look back at that time. I have never trusted the Lord since as we did then, but at the time it seemed easy to trust Him."

The blessed results of these twenty years of evangelism are well known to many in all parts of the world who have followed the career of this man of God; and especially to those – aged men and women now – who were deeply interested in God's work during those years.

During the first eight years of this twenty-three, Elder Barnes and his helpers kept close count of the confessions until the number exceeded fifty thousand.

In the mountains of Kentucky, where Elder Barnes got the title of "Mountain Evangelist" nearly all the converts were from the class technically known as "sinners."

In 1889 Mr. Barnes, with his family, went to Scotland, where they labored for a year and a half among the Scotch fishermen with continuous success.

In all his work, whether among the rough but sterling mountaineers of Eastern Kentucky or among the working class in the east end of London, or the British soldiers in India, or the Scotch fishermen, God always sent Evangelist Barnes to the poor, "for which" says Elder Barnes, " I praise Him."

Since that time Mr. Barnes' work for God has not ceased, but the advancing years have made it necessary for him to spend them more in quiet, and in study.

Much of his time has been spent in the beautiful island, Sanibel, Florida. Mr. Barnes has also spent some time in New York and Washington, D.C.

During his work in Australia, Elder Barnes heard of the work of John Alexander Dowie, now General Overseer of the Christian Catholic Church in Zion, Illinois.

THE LOST TRIBES OF ISRAEL
By George O. Barnes

Of course, the first appeal, in the discussion will be to Holy Scripture; as the bulk of information springs from that pure source; but all genuine confirmation of its truthfulness, in "profane History," will be gladly used as a secondary matter. Collateral but invaluable proof has been discovered, in records that, while not bearing the stamp of inspiration, contain such self-evidencing testimony of verity, that they produce profound conviction.

And, allow me to impress it upon your minds, at the outset, that it is not the mere establishment of a fascinating theory, that is involved in this investigation; but no less a matter than the grave and vital defense of the character of God. The question indissolubly joined to this discussion is: Does God speak the truth: and does He fulfill His promises after making them? No true lover of God can be indifferent to the answer of such a question: especially when much external evidence to the contrary is adduced by the skeptic. This swings the subject clear of mere human theories and opinions, however elaborate. A demonstration, not a guess, is demanded. That, I propose to give; for, to me, the subject has long gone past the "theory" stage.

When Holy Scripture lands the ten tribes of Israel on the banks of the Caspian Sea, the records of their history cease, and they become, to future ages, the "Lost Tribes." This was about 580 years before our "Christian Era" began. Do not forget the date.

About the first quarter of the 19th Century lived a "gentleman and a scholar" – Sharon Turner by name – who zealously undertook the Herculean, Historical task of tracing his British ancestry; and we have the result in a book (long out of print, but still found in large public libraries) entitled "A History of the Anglo Saxons." This amazingly patient investigator took up, seriatim, the various people who had settled in the British Isles – The Saxons, the Danes, the Normans, the Jutes, the Angles, etc. – and traced them all to one source. He found that, varied as were their names, they were one people, and he traced them to the banks of the Caspian, about the close of the Sixth Century, before Christ. "Here," he declares, "all traces of our ancestors are lost."

155

I need not link Scripture and "Profane" History at this startling point, for my intelligent hearers. It is self-evident that the ten tribes on the banks of the Caspian, as left there by Scripture, are the "Anglo Saxons" of Sharon Turner's book. We may safely shout, "Eureka!" To the vexed question of the ages, viz., "Where are the Lost Tribes of Israel?"

The value of Sharon Turner's testimony lies, chiefly in this: That he died without knowing what he had done. He never dreamed of the amazing identity he had unwittingly discovered. He told to others where he had found his ancestors, while to himself "all traces of them were lost" on the banks of the Caspian. To us, who read the secret as from an open book, it is almost incredible that such an investigator did not see it at once. But he never did.

We now come to the fountain-head of history, and the "reason why" this outcome must needs be, viz., because God is true to His Word. Four thousand years ago, one man earned the proud title of "The Friend of God" and the "Father of the Faithful," because he believed God, under very trying tests: and "it was counted to him for righteousness." And not only so, but God gave to his "Friend" certain promises, some of which have been wonderfully fulfilled, while others remain, yet to be verified.

These promises were unconditional, as St. Paul fully argues out in the 3rd Chapter of Galatians. And they were very specific. They were reiterated, with added fullness of meaning, to Isaac, and Jacob: and in a very special manner to "David the King" –the "Man after God's own heart."

The first promise is in Gen. 12:2-3, where the Lord called "Abram" out of his native land, to go into a strange country. "I will make of thee a great nation, and in thee shall all the families of the earth be blessed."

The second is in Gen 13:15-16, when Abram generously and self-forgetfully, gave his greedy nephew, Lot, the choice of the grazing grounds, willing to take what was left, in order to avoid strife. "All the land – North, South, East and West – to thee and thy seed. I will give it, forever." "And I will make thy seed as the dust of the earth."

At this time, Sarai (not yet Sarah), his wife, was barren, and had never borne him a child; but he believed God, though years passed, until both were "well stricken in years," before Isaac was born. In Rom. 4:17-22, St. Paul makes beautiful mention of this triumph of faith.

In Gen. 15:5, the Lord repeats the promise of multitudinous descendants, comparing them to the "Stars of Heaven for number."

Then in 17:2-8, besides reiterating the promise of "the land of Canaan, for an everlasting possession," the Lord calls him the "Father of Many Nations," and that "Kings should come out of him."

In 22:17, of the same book, the Lord – still comparing Abraham's seed to the "Stars of Heaven" and, the "sand on the seashore" – utters this remarkable promise: vis., "Thy seed shall possess the gates of his enemies." Mark that expression please.

To Jacob, fleeing from his brother Esau, and arriving at the city of Luz, after the gates were closed for the night, the "God of all comfort" gave him, from his stony pillow, a vision of angels, ascending and descending from earth to Heaven, and Heaven to earth; and from the top of this wondrous "ladder" came the voice of the Lord, repeating, in set terms, the identical promises made, before, to Abraham; and adding words of personal good cheer to the forlorn fugitive. That stone – at night a "pillow," and in the morning a "pillar" of witness – we hear of, again, in this romantic story.

In Gen. 48: 4,16, 19, in connection with the blessing of Joseph's two sons – Ephraim and Manasseh, we have the old familiar lesson of the younger being preferred to the elder, another repetition of Abraham's promise, with this variation, that Ephraim should become "A multitude of nations" – a phrase that I call your special attention to.

Gen. 49 is a famous chapter, giving the destinies of the twelve sons of Jacob in the future, of which I only mention for future reference the blessing of Judah, in whom the royal line was to continue unbroken, "until Shiloh comes:" and of Dan, who in some way, not then unfolded, was to "judge" (or rule) "his people." Of these I 'cannot now speak particularly," except to remind you that "Our Lord sprang out of Judah," and thus Spiritual blessing came, pre-eminently, in that line, as all know. If supreme importance as that is, I must call your particular attention to it, for I wish you to notice, especially, Jacob's blessing to Joseph; through whom comes, to the ten tribes, such a superabundance of temporal blessing, that even a careless reader must be impressed by it.

"Joseph is a fruitful bough; even a fruitful bough by a well; whose branches run over the wall. The archers have sorely grieved him; have shot at him, and hated him; but his bow abode in strength, and the arms of his hand were made strong by the hands of the mighty God of Jacob (from thence is the shepherd, the stone of Israel); even by the God of thy Father, who shall help thee, and by the Almighty who shall bless thee, with blessings of heaven above; the blessings of the deep that lieth under; blessings of the breast and of the womb; the blessings of thy father have prevailed above the blessings of my progenitors, unto the utmost bound of the everlasting hills; they shall be on the head of Joseph, and on the crown of the head of him that was separate from his brethren." (Gen. 49:22-26.)

157

This was the birthright blessing –forfeited by Reuben, Jacob's firstborn, because of sin–transferred to Joseph, his favorite and petted son, by Rachel, the beloved. As it is written (I Chron. 5:1-2): "The genealogy is not to be reckoned after the birthright. For Judah prevailed above his brethren, and of him came the chief ruler; but the birthright was Joseph's."

When it is seen, as I shall prove, that this is the germinal promise, from which has sprung England and America, as they exist at this moment, it becomes of thrilling personal interest to us all. It remains then to demonstrate that the promises to Abraham, Isaac, Jacob and Joseph exactly fit the Anglo-Saxon race, and no other people of whom authentic History takes notice.

1. Beginning with the first promise to Abraham (Gen. 12:3), that in him "all the families of the earth should be blessed," one's thoughts at once settle upon the "World's Redeemer" – Jesus Christ, the blessed – a lineal descendant of the "Friend of God": though that proves nothing, directly, in substantiation of the Anglo-Saxon claim.

But taking the distribution of the Holy Scriptures as the only source of information to the "families of the earth," touching their Savior's person and work in their behalf, we point to the fact, that the "British and Foreign Bible Society," and the "American Bible Society" have almost monopolized the stupendous work of translating the Bible into every known tongue, that the world inherited from the "Tower of Babel:" and distributing the same, by immediate agencies, to "all families of the earth." All other benevolent attempts to aid in this work are dwarfed in the presence of these twin parent societies. We are dealing here with facts that cannot be successfully controverted.

2. Take that promise of unique phraseology, in Gen 35:11: "A nation and a company of nations shall thy seed be;" and find me a fulfillment of it, in any Empire that has existed on the planet, save the British Empire, as we see it today. Leaving out Britain's eldest daughter, lost through the stupid folly of an obstinate King, we see, to the north of Manasseh (the United States) a "nation" challenging comparison with any; free, progressive, and prosperous; but proud of her connection with the "Mother Country": held by no other tie than that of kindred love; able if she wished, to sever the connection tomorrow, but holding it as the highest privilege; tell me, is there a parallel in History to it?

Traveling across the Pacific, we land upon the shore of another "nation": also "free, progressive and prosperous": held in the same bond of love: no coercion, no occupying army, but as proud to belong to the imperial race, and as willing to acknowledge suzerainty as her sister across the Atlantic Ocean. New Zealand is as loyal to England as Canada. And Australia with her "United States of the Orient, is just the same.

3. Another quite unique promise to Abraham was that his seed should possess the gates of their enemies. The general meaning of this is clear. In an Eastern city, the one who held the gates, held a victorious position. From the very first moment of imperial expansion, the Anglo-Saxon race have been blindly fulfilling this prophetic word. Their invariable policy has been to "Possess the gates" of other countries.

Thus the globe is girded by the "gates of all countries, not to mention Halifax and Vancouver, Bermuda, Jamaica and the Bahama, which would be valuable bases should Ephraim and Manasseh, ever again, "fall out by the way," from which "the LORD deliver us." But you must acknowledge that there is something worthy of special notice in the fact, that God promised all this to Abraham's seed, 4000 years ago! Why should it fit our race and no other?

4. Again and again, and yet again, the multitudinousness of the race is emphasized almost in the language of hyperbole. As the "stars of the sky": as the "sand of the seashore," are the figures employed to express this increase in population. Not to dwell on the fact that the Anglo-Saxon race controls largely more than one-fourth of the population of the globe.

But, remember, that "blessings of the breast and of the womb" was part of Joseph's birthright," through whom we inherit.

I think I have, fairly made out a case of identity that cannot easily be disproved. We are Israelites, in lineal descent from "Father Abraham," through Isaac and Jacob; and if hereditary descent, if honorable, is a thing to be proud of – which it is, then we ought to be proud to trace our ancestry, in an unbroken line, to the "Friend of God," who in an ancient day, when God's friends were few, was "true" to Him "as steel."

THE VANISHED SCEPTRE
By George O. Barnes

Having traced the blessings of temporal prosperity through Joseph–in the strict Abrahamic descent–to the greatest nations on Earth–British and American–lineal descendants of Ephraim and Manasseh, we come now, to the promise of unbroken royal continuity; first given to Judah by Jacob, speaking as a prophet, and representative of God; and afterwards confirmed to David; who, in Scripture is called by way of emphasis, "the King," because he was the first King, in the legitimate line of descent from Judah; though preceded by Saul of the tribe of Benjamin.

159

After the return from Babylon, for a brief season, the glory of the ancient race shone out in the illustrious Judas Macaboeus, who "ruled in righteousness." But he was a Levite. "Herod the King," who spent large sums of money in restoring the temple, was an Idumaean, and not of Judah. So in Zedekiah, 425 B.C., the promise to Judah of the continuous sceptre (made by God, through the mouth of Jacob) seemed to fail.

But that we may realize the gravity of the question, that involves nothing less than the truthfulness of God, let us read again the specific word of promise to Judah, and afterwards repeated, more fully in connection with the perpetuity of David's throne.

In Gen. 49:10, we read: "The sceptre shall not depart from Judah nor a lawgiver from between his feet, until Shiloh comes; and unto him shall the gathering of the people be." Now, in seeing the royal line, apparently extinct in Zedekiah, 425 B.C., there is no relief in the violent exposition that some have adopted, in a desperate attempt to support the veracity of God, to wit, that the coming of "Shiloh" was fulfilled in the first advent of our Saviour; who, as a true descendant of Judah, then established a spiritual reign, that has continued unbroken ever since. This amiable shift in exposition bears its desperation on its surface and, not to mention the fact that the almost unanimous decision of the soundest interpreters of Scripture assign the coming of "Shiloh" to the second advent of our Lord; what about the hiatus of 425 years, in which there seemed to be "no King in Israel?" Here is a "departing" of the sceptre from Judah, as far as history informs us, and no skeptic will be convinced to the contrary, but will rather be confirmed in his infidelity, by such a makeshift of a theologian. Far better would it be to acknowledge ignorance, and inability to explain the glaring discrepancy, than to expose truth to a subterfuge.

And then, remember, that if God fails in keeping his word of promise in one thing, away goes our faith in his ability to "make good" any pledge that he has given. We see how the present difficulty strikes at the foundation of all trust in God. True, we may not be able to solve all mysteries, and may, legitimately fall back on: "What I know not now, I shall know hereafter." But ought we not to welcome every proof on every doubtful subject?

And let us not forget that we are directly responsible for "giving a reason, to every one for the hope that is in us," as St. Peter says.

"The word of the LORD that came to Jeremiah," in a very dark hour of Israel's history (when the Chaldeans were thundering at the gates of Jerusalem; and when he knew that the city and royal dynasty were doomed), was, first, an assurance that the national existence of

"Abraham's Seed" was impregnably secure. Listen to this word of promise, Jer. 31:35-36: "Thus saith the Lord, which giveth the sun for a light by day, and the ordinances of the moon and of the stars, for a light by night, ... if these ordinances depart from before me, saith the Lord, then the seed of Israel, also, shall cease from being a nation, before me, forever." If there be a God, that settles the national perpetuity of this favored race, and for the method of it, we have seen His "ways" in the previous lecture. This word is as steadfast as the Sun, the Moon, the Stars.

The substitution, or rather the addition of the word "rulers" for the more definite "kings" is significant. Our "presidents," in Manasseh are "rulers" – not "kings." And the Presidents of America and the Kings of England are not rulers over a foreign population, but over the "seed of Abraham, Isaac and Jacob." How good of the LORD, to speak these reassuring words to Jeremiah; with his life threatened by his own people, and everything about him ready to tumble into ruin! But the LORD knows well how to "comfort them that are cast down."

It can readily be seen that in the midst of this scene of destruction, Jeremiah would be exempt, and more than that, high in favor with the Chaldean Monarch. Taking advantage of this, Scripture tells us, he was able to save the "King's daughters:" and from other sources of information, as hereafter related, we learn that he secured the "Ark of the Covenant," the "High Priest's Breastplate" (the "Urim and Thummin," or the "oracle"): the "Stone of Jacob" (the rear guard in the wilderness journey), and the royal banner of the tribe of Judah.

After much vicissitude and adventure, this grand Prophet and Priest, fled the land of his birth, with the "King's daughters," and the priceless mementos of Israel's departed glory; and sailing along the shores of the Mediterranean, in a ship of Dan, after numerous dangers; and, once, a wreck on a stormy coast (probably in the unquiet waters of the "Bay of Biscay"): he, at last, landed–sailing into the Bay of Belfast with his treasures and accompanied by his faithful Levite secretary Baruch–the companion of many days of peril and adventure.

We must leave them, after their trying voyage, for a while, to bring up other parties, intimately linked with this romance of ancient history.

I wish now to speak of Dan, who, according to the "Word of the LORD," by the mouth of Jacob, was in some way to be associated with royalty as a "ruler of his people," though not of the "blood royal." (Gen. 49:16.)

Scripture says a good deal concerning this adventurous tribe. They were the sailors of Israel; their apportioned territory lying along the

161

seashore; and as they constructed a rude navy, they began a work of exploration, and "exploiting," among the aboriginal inhabitants; scraping along the shallows of the Mediterranean Coast, at first; then boldly ascending great rivers; and everywhere, we may be sure, making their voyages profitable.

Recorded in Scripture, and therefore important, is this remarkable peculiarity of this rapacious tribe. They put "the name of their father Dan" upon their various conquests; and this fact enables us to trace these bold "freebooters," in their plundering course. For example, into the Black Sea, in Eastern Russia, we find two large rivers emptying themselves on both of which are the unmistakable brand of the tribe, in the Dan-eiper and Dan-eister: and going westward on the same coast, we find the Dan-ube, showing that Dan had, long ago, explored them all. Whatever "eiper," eister" and "ube" may mean, "Dan" is not to be mistaken. In the first recorded "raid" of this remarkable tribe, in the north of Palestine, Scripture tells us that 600 Danites found an unguarded city, name Laish, that they took a fancy to; slaughtered the male inhabitants, after the ruthless custom of a murderous age; and settled there, changing its old name to Dan; which henceforth became the northern frontier, Beer-sheeba was the southern. From "Dan to Beersheba," meant what "from Maine to Florida" does with us.

Thus was the word of Scripture fulfilled that said: "Dan shall rule his people, as one of the tribes of Israel."

At this time, of which I now speak, a noble young Danite, named Eochaid, had just been chosen the elective "Heremon," and just at this time Jeremiah the Prophet-Priest of Israel (with the two "daughters" of King Zedekiah: the "ark of the Covenant;" the "Stone of Jacob;" the "breastplate of the High Priest;" and the royal standard of Judah) sailed into the Bay of Belfast, in a ship of Dan–with its figurehead a serpent– Dan's Scripture crest, as it is written (Gen. 49:17): "Dan shall be a serpent by the way." One of these fair "daughters of the King" (Jer. 41:10; 43:6) bore the name Tea-Tamar-Tephi; the central title the same as that of Absalom's sister–David's daughter; and Tephi, apparently a pet name, like "beautiful," or "darling," with us. "The inevitable happened," we say (only there is no blind "Fortuna" with God) and Eochaid became enamored with the lovely daughter of Israel, and claimed her for his bride. Jeremiah agreed, with certain sworn provisos, to the union; and the happy young "Heremon" bore his beautiful "Tea-Tephi" to his palace, in Tara.

The provisos, willingly promised by Eochaid–very much in love, and perhaps not as aware of their importance as he might have been–were

1. He was to adopt the religious faith of his new wife. Agreed!

2. There was to be a "School of the Prophets" ("Theological Seminary," as we call it) established at Tara, to instruct the people in the religion of Jehovah.

3. The third proviso was, that the royal descent must be hereditary and always in the female line. Tea-Tephi's blood must be the title to reign.

4. Tea-Tephi was to be crowned queen, as all her royal ancestors were, upon the sacred "Stone of Jacob," to be preserved for the same purpose for all future generations of monarchs.

On that "Stone of Jacob" every King of Israel has been crowned from "David the King" (par excellence) to George V–lineal descendant of David, through Tea-Tephi–daughter of Zedekiah, King of Judah.

In Windsor Castle, today, prepared for Queen Victoria, "of blessed memory," there hangs upon the wall, her royal pedigree, traced, not through Tudor or Plantaganet, but through James I, of England (before that, James VI of Scotland) up through the Kings of Scotland; then through the Kings of Ireland, to Eochaid III–wedded to Tea-Tephi–daughter of Zedekiah, King of Judah.

Thus, "the sceptre" has not "departed from Judah," nor "a lawgiver from between his feet," nor will it, "until Shiloh comes, to whom the gathering of the people shall be."

"The Stone of Jacob!" How wonderful its history! It is the "Stone of Israel" (Gen. 49:24) on which "our Father Jacob" laid his weary head on that memorable night of nights, when God appeared to him, by a vision of angels, and with His own voice from the top of the heavenly "ladder," gave promises to the heavy hearted fugitive, that shaped his future life. That stony "pillow" at night, and "pillar of witness" in the morning, while a worthless thing ("rejected by the builders") became, in after years, the "head of the corner" in Israel's modern history.

With the single exception of the Queen of England, known as "Bloody Mary," all the monarchs of England, of Scotland, of Ireland, have been crowned upon it; as well as all the Kings of Judah in Palestine, up to David, the head of the House Royal.

Well! The beautiful Tea-Tephi died–leaving one child. But the dynasty was under the care of God, and could not fail. "David has never lacked one to sit upon his throne," and never will. God says so. All the powers of earth and hell cannot prevent it. "Scripture cannot be broken." Ezekiel 17:22-23 is also fulfilled. The tender twig, cropped from the highest branch of the high cedar" was "planted in the mountain of Israel" and has become "a goodly cedar," under whose shadow "all fowl of every wing" are sheltered.

163

Tea-Tephi was buried in the Hill of Tara. The Celtic records mention, with great particularity, the size of her sarcophagus, which is called a "Mergech" or Repository. By her side rests the mysterious Box that the Prophet brought with him, and the jewelled breast plate of the High Priest.

Thus far, you will remember, my object has been to defend the character of God for truthfulness, as against the charges of skepticism, by giving historical evidence–sacred and profane: First, that Israel has not ceased from being a nation, of prominence and importance among the nations of the earth; and second, that the royal line of Judah, has been unbroken, through the ages, and that "David has never lacked one to sit upon his throne."

Taking the Jew, as at present known, as the only representative of Israel, the scoffer may make his sneer good, when he points scornfully to a despised people, "scattered and peeled;" without a government, without a Temple, without a King, and asks: "Is this the way your God keeps His word, to His chosen people?"

And let me ask right here, of every "lover of the LORD," is it a light thing with you to be confronted with such a question, and have no answer to give? And yet, "ye are my witnesses, saith the LORD." Think of it. I do not know how your mind is "built." "Many men of many minds," is a true proverb. But to my mind (seeking an answer to the question of an infidel), what I have offered in my two preceding lectures is not a "theory," but a demonstration.

IN THEIR OWN WORDS

Jewish Testimonies Concerning the Ten "Lost" Tribes of Israel

INTRODUCTION
By Charles A. Jennings

Upon examination of Old Testament history, the honest minded Bible student is confronted with the task of explaining some difficult events. There have been volumes written in an attempt to explain such events as the Noahic Flood, the crossing of the Red Sea, Joshua's long day and other miraculous works of God. Yet there remains one natural event, designed by God and executed by human hands, that is still a mystery to the vast majority of Bible students to this day. That event is the alleged 'disappearance' of millions of Old Testament Israelites following the Assyrian captivities of the Northern Kingdom of Israel and the Southern Kingdom of Judah.

The following is the Scriptural account of the Assyrian captivity of the Northern Kingdom of Israel which took place in 721 B.C.

"And it came to pass in the fourth year of King Hezekiah, which was the seventh year of Hoshea, son of Elah king of Israel, that Shalmaneser king of Assyria came up against Samaria, and besieged it. And at the end of three years they took it: even in the sixth year of Hezekiah, that is the ninth year of Hoshea king of Israel, Samaria (the capital city of Northern Israel) was taken. And the king of Assyria did carry away Israel unto Assyria, and put them in Halah and in Habor by the River of Gozan, and in the cities of the Medes: because they obeyed not the voice of the Lord their God, but transgressed his covenant, and all that Moses the servant of the Lord commanded, and would not hear them, nor do them" (II Kings 18:9-12).

165

The Scriptural account is also very clear that ten years after the captivity of Northern Israel, the king of Assyria invaded the Southern Kingdom of Judah. *"Now in the fourteenth year of king Hezekiah did Sennacherib king of Assyria come up against all the fenced cities of Judah, and took them"* (II Kings 18:13). Later on, Sennacherib made a failed attempt to capture the city of Jerusalem, but was defeated by the miraculous intervention of the Lord. It was some 130 years later that the Babylonians conquered and destroyed the city of Jerusalem. One major and very important point that must be kept in mind is that there is no Biblical account which records that these captured people of Israel and Judah ever returned back to the land of Palestine. In fact, the prophecy given many years before was that because of their disobedience the Lord would bring heathen nations against His people and drive them out of the land which had been given unto their fathers. This historical event is known as the ***Diaspora*** or the ***Dispersion*** of Israel. The big question remains; what happened to these people? Were they completely destroyed or did they migrate to other lands, multiply and fulfill their God-ordained destiny elsewhere?

It is very apparent, according to the New Testament account, that the whereabouts of these dispersed Israelites was no mystery. In the ministry of Jesus, when He made reference to His departure back to the Father, the Jews responded by saying; *"Whither will he go, that we shall not find Him? Will he go unto the dispersed among the Gentiles, and teach the Gentiles?"* (John 7:35).

Jesus also made it plainly understood that He also knew that these dispersed Israelites were still in existence and would be reached with the Gospel message. Jesus said; *"I am the Good Shepherd, and know my sheep, and am known of mine. As the Father knoweth me, even so know I the father: and I lay down my life for the sheep. And other sheep I have, which are not of this fold: them also I must bring, and they shall hear my voice; and there shall be one fold, and one shepherd"* (John 10:14-16; fulfilling Ez. 37:15-28).

During the council of the chief priests and Pharisees, the high priest Caiaphas made it known that Jesus not only would die for the Judah nation, but also for the dispersed Israelites scattered abroad (John 11:47-52).

The following are several accounts of various testimonies from Jewish sources, both ancient and modern. They all confirm the fact that the people of dispersed Israel are *not* the same as the modern people now known as Jews.

****

166

Dr. Moses Margouliouth, a Jewish scholar of the 19th Century, in his *History of the Jews* said, "It may not be out of place to state that the 'isles afar off' mentioned in the 31st chapter of Jeremiah were supposed by the ancients to be Britannia, Scotia and Hibernia."

****

An interesting modern reference is to be found in the declaration of principles given in the United Israel Bulletin, a non-Christian, Jewish publication of April 1951 – "We believe that the Ten Tribes of Israel exist within the Anglo-Saxon-Celtic-Scandinavian-American people and that they in fact constitute them and that they are Hebrews in the same sense that Judah, Benjamin and Levi with the Jewish people are Israelites."

FLAVIUS JOSEPHUS

Josephus, the highly respected and reliable Jewish historian recorded in 70 A.D. that: "there are but two tribes in Asia and Europe subject to the Romans, while the ten tribes are beyond the Euphrates till now, and are an immense multitude, and not to be estimated by numbers" (Book 11, Chap. 5, Par. 2).

REV. ELIESER BASSIN

"What I want, dear brethren, in addressing these epistles to you, is to protest against those Christians who, in spiritualising the Holy Scripture, and calling themselves *spiritual* Israel, appropriate all Israel's promises to themselves, and so give infidels good grounds to say that God is not true to His promise and that He is not a covenant-keeping God, for He has broken His *unconditional covenant* which He made with our fathers Abraham, Isaac, and Jacob. In order to stop the mouth of the infidel, and to open the eyes of blind Christians who do not see God's object with Israel in His dealings with His *once-for-ever chosen people*, let us earnestly search for our lost brethren, the Ten Tribes, and, when we have found them, let us not be silent, but proclaim to the whole world God's wonderful dealings with them, and that He is true to His promises, not a changeable God, but still the same Jehovah, the covenant-keeping God of Israel." From "Letter to the Jews Concerning the Ten Tribes," by the Rev. Elieser Bassin, B.S. of Edinburgh.

"Before I became a Christian, I believed as most of my Jewish brethren still believe, that the Ten Tribes of Israel exist, somewhere, as a powerful nation, having a king of their own and that they are hidden from the sight of men until the coming of the expected Messiah. It is my conviction that Britain is the nation with whom God has identified

167

Himself from first to last. I as an Israelite of the House of Judah, claim you as Israelites of the house of Ephraim. As believers in the faithfulness of our covenant-keeping God I call you to awake from your sleep." Elieser Bassin - 1926 (A converted Jew of Russian birth)

THE "JEWISH CHRONICLE" MAY 2, 1890

"The fate of the lost Ten Tribes is a mystery which has a peculiar fascination for some minds. While not a link is missing of the historical chain so far as the remnant of the House of Judah is concerned, the Israelites who were subjugated by the Assyrian power disappear from the page of history as suddenly and completely as though the land of the captivity had swallowed them up. Beyond some vague reference to them in a passage of Josephus, no mention is made by an authentic writer of their surviving the destruction of their nationality. There has always been, however, an unwillingness to admit that a fate that has befallen so many nations has overtaken the Ten Tribes. Why should they have been less tenacious of life than their brethren of Judah? Nay, the Scriptures speak of a future restoration of Israel, which is clearly to include both Judah and Ephraim. The problem, then, is reduced to the simplest form. The Ten Tribes are certainly in existence. All that has to be done is to discover which people represent them."

EX-CHIEF RABBI DR. V. HERMAN ADLER
The Jewish Church of England

"You are quite right in your surmise that the ten tribes did not return to the holy land."

CHIEF RABBI DR. HERTZ

"The people known at present as Jews are the descendants of the tribes of Judah and Benjamin. So far as is known, there is not any further admixture of other tribes. The Jews look forward to the gathering of all the tribes at some future date. And so as we look around the world, we are driven to believe with Bishop Gobat, former Anglican Bishop of Jerusalem, "that a solid ground exists for the Anglo-Israel hypothesis since nowhere else can Ephraim be found fulfilling the required conditions of Scripture."

168

CHRISTIAN LEAGUE OF JEWISH FRIENDSHIP

MARK JOHN LEVY, Minister
President

"In peace the Gentile and the Jew,
Assemble in a happy throng,
Where faces beam with friendship true,
And Goodwill is the only song."

W. H. H. Shelley,
Secretary and Treasurer

Phone Franklin 3601

Office:
1634 K Street N. W.

CHRISTIAN LEAGUE OF JEWISH FRIENDSHIP

WASHINGTON, D. C.

January 1, 1923.

Hon. Warren G. Harding,
The White House

MY DEAR MR. PRESIDENT:

May I not respectfully call your attention, in the present perilous condition of international affairs, to the important truth that the two great Anglo-Saxon nations of the United States and Great Britain are unconsciously fulfilling the prophetic destiny of the Lost Ten Tribes of Israel, and that it is impossible to follow the trend of international events intelligently without we take this truth into prayerful consideration. I have endeavored in the enclosed brief typewritten statement to set forth its Scriptural setting, and am sending same in the hope that you, as the Chief Magistrate of our United States which represents Manasseh prophetically, will be given thereby clearer light in the administration of your presidential duties in international affairs. It is most interesting to note, Mr. President, that the first leader of the tribe of Manasseh bore your own middle name, "Gamaliel the son of Pedahzur, prince of Manasseh" (Numbers 7:54-59; 1:10).

The printed pamphlet enclosed contains my correspondence, as an appointed delegate to the American Jewish Congress and the Paris Peace Conference, with ex-President Wilson, the British Embassy, the Pastors' Federation of Washington, and other representative bodies, regarding the status of Hebrew Christians in Palestine and elsewhere.

With the assurance, Mr. President, that your administration has a part constantly in my prayers for Divine guidance; and as this is New Year's Day, the anniversary of the reception of our Lord Jesus into the Covenant of Abraham, may I not wish your family and official circles, in His Name, a most happy and prosperous New Year.

I am, in His and humanity's service,

Yours sincerely,

(Signed) MARK JOHN LEVY.

"Pray for the peace of Jerusalem: they shall prosper that love Thee."—Ps. 122:6.

DEPARTMENT OF STATE

WASHINGTON

In reply to
WE 700.00119P81/-   January 13, 1923.

Reverend Mark John Levy,
   Christian League of Jewish Friendship,
      1824 H Street, Northwest,
         Washington, D. C.

SIR:

The receipt is acknowledged, by reference from the White House, of your communication with which were enclosed a typewritten statement and a printed pamphlet bearing the caption, "Resolutions and Correspondence on Jewish National Aspirations and the Promotion of Peace in Palestine."

I am, Sir,   Your obedient servant,
                              For the Secretary of State:
                              (Signed) W. R. CASTLE, JR.,
                                 Chief, Division of Western European Affairs.

~~~~~~~~~~~~~~~

HOW A JEW DISCOVERED THAT JESUS WAS THE MESSIAH AND THE ANGLO-SAXONS ARE THE LOST TRIBES OF ISRAEL

This is the story of a valiant Jewish soldier of the Cross. Marcus S. Bergmann was born in Wieruszow, a town bordering Silesia (a small European Country, bounded by Czechoslovakia, Germany and Poland), in 1846. His Jewish father, who was a strong Talmudist and a member of the Chassidim (also called Assideans or Hasidim. A sect which was the most strict adherent of Judaism), did not long survive his infant son's birth, and so the boy was reared by his uncle, Woolf Bermann, who also belonged to the Chassidim. This man saw to it that young Marcus studied the choicest Rabbinical and Talmudic writing, for he too was to become a rabbi to his people.

Marcus was barely twenty years old when a sudden disturbing restlessness came upon him, and he felt a spiritual burden quite strange to him. Disquieted in his thoughts, he was unable to concentrate on his studies, and he longed to leave his comfortable home and his country to wonder he knew not where.

Finally he obeyed the insistent voice, and he made preparation to leave behind him all the people he loved. Marcus Bergmann arrived in England in 1866, where he set up a small synagogue in London. He ministered there for a while without pay, living on monies from the inheritance bequeathed him by his father.

Although Marcus Bergmann had obeyed God by leaving Silesia and going to the land pointed out by His finger, he was not doing the will of God. Because he had not enquired of the Almighty concerning that which he should do, God's hand struck heavily upon him, and he was laid low in grave illness. He was taken to a hospital, where he hovered between life and death for a period of six weeks.

Let Marcus Bergmann's own words tell the story of God's way with him. In later life he wrote an account of his conversion for the "The Hebrew Christian" (New York) which was published in the September 1894 issue of that magazine.

After mentioning his weeks of illness, Mr. Bergmann wrote: 'When feeling a little better I began to look into the Hebrew Bible, which was on the shelf in the ward. As a reader in the synagogue, I knew the letter of the whole of the Pentateuch, and other portions of the Old Testament by heart.

"The portion of scripture that made a great impression on me at the time of my illness was Daniel 9. Several verses of this chapter (the confession of Daniel) are repeated each Monday and Thursday by every Jew; but the latter part of this chapter, which so plainly prophesies of the sufferings of the Messiah is never read. In fact, the Rabbis pronounce a dreadful curse upon everyone who investigates the prophecy of those seventy weeks.

"They say: 'Their bones shall rot who compute the end of the time!'

"On remembering the anathema, it was with fear and trembling that I read the passage about the seventy weeks and coming to verse 26, Messiah shall be cut off, but not for Himself – though we Jews are most careful not to let a Hebrew book drop on the ground – I threw that Hebrew Bible out of my hand, thinking in my ignorance, that this was one of the missionaries' Bibles.

"But, although I threw the Bible away, yet I could not throw away the words I had just read: Messiah shall be cut off, but not for Himself. These words sank deeper and deeper into my soul, and wherever I looked I seemed to see the words in flaming Hebrew characters, and I had no rest for some time!"

"My heart was burdened with a very great load, and yet I dared not open my mind to anyone. In this state I believed, the Spirit of God led me to Palestine-place. (Situated near the junction of Christchurch and Church

171

Roads in Merton an outer suburb of London.) My heart failed me when I reached the door of the late Rev. Dr. Ewald.

After several vain attempts I ventured to knock, and was admitted to see that venerable servant of the Lord. To him I unburdened my soul and told him all that was in my heart. He asked me whether or not I was willing to come into his home for enquirers, in order to be instructed in the truth as it is exemplified in the Lord Jesus.

"I told him that this was just what I needed, and I at once accepted his kindness. This was just one week before the Passover!

While the members of Marcus Bergmann's congregation at the synagogue kept the Feast of the Paschal lamb, he learned of the Lamb of God, who was sacrificed for the salvation of mankind, and the redemption of Israel, and he was comforted.

Not long afterward Marcus accepted our Lord Jesus the Christ as his Saviour, and God's operation upon his soul was finished. The cancerous core of hatred had been cut out, forever, and the Saviour's healing love occupied the place where it had grown.

Eagerly, feverishly, Marcus searched the Scriptures for more evidence of his wonderful revelation. He found it in Matthew 21:42-45, and his heart ached with anguish for his Christ-hating people. He needed no more evidence, for the Judge of judges had said: "The Kingdom of God shall be taken from you (Judah) and given to a nation bringing forth the fruits thereof."

For hundreds of years it has been the custom for the heads of aristocratic British families to dedicate their sons for the service of their country, and to educate them for public office.

A wealthy and titled English gentleman had a beloved and talented son who showed promise of developing into a brilliant and scholarly man of letters. Determined to give his heir every educational advantage available, the indulgent father decided to have him tutored in Hebrew as well as in other languages.

At that time in England there were many Jews who were qualified to teach, and several of them applied for the position. So did Marcus Bergmann. The fairness for which he was noted compelled the nobleman to grant interviews to every man who was interested in teaching his son, but Marcus impressed him most of all, because he was a Christian.

Marcus and his pupil liked each other from the start, and their liking developed in a strong friendship. The chosen course of study involved the reading of the Old Testament, and one day the young nobleman called his tutor's attention to Isaiah 42:6, where it is written: "I the Lord have called thee in righteousness, and will hold thine hand, and will keep thee, and give thee for a covenant of the people, for a light of the Gentiles; to open the blind eyes, to bring out the prisoners from the prison, and them that sit in darkness out of the prison house."

Then, turning to Isaiah 49:8 the youth read the prophet's inspired words: "Thus saith the Lord, In an acceptable time have I heard thee, and in a day of salvation have I helped thee; and I will preserve thee, and give thee for a covenant of the people, to establish the earth, to cause to inherit the desolate places."

As the dear young voice uttered these glorious words, Marcus Bergmann's heart leaped within him, and his blood churned so loudly in his ears he could hardly hear the lad say, *"then Christ is given to Britain."*

Bergmann stared in surprise at his pupil, who confessed, "I am a British Israelite, sire." Marcus was stunned. What had the boy said? Was it possible that the Almighty had forsaken Judah? Had the Messiah given Himself to Gentile Britain?

He fell upon his knees, beseeching Jehovah to take the veil from his eyes and show him the truth of the matter. And God sent His servant to consult His Book.

And Britain had brought forth the fruit, which was the spreading of the Gospel of Salvation! Was not the British and Foreign Bible Society busy bringing out translations of the Bible in many languages – his own Yiddish translation among them? What of the hundreds of British missionaries who had gone to far lands to carry the Word and to suffer for the Lord?

Christ was the first fruit of the Kingdom and the British were proclaiming Him everywhere as the King of Kings "They were God's Israel!" Humbly Marcus Bergmann prayed God for the honour of teaching this glorious, shining Truth. And God heard, and granted to him the coveted privilege.

It was not long before Marcus was standing before large groups of people, telling them the reason they had been so richly blessed was because they had accepted the Messiah. The Jews, he said, were a persecuted, miserable people, whose sufferings would continue until they too accepted Him.

He contended that Britain's mighty power was derived from her belief in the saving grace of Jesus, and that she would inherit the Kingdom because of it. Marcus Bergmann made no secret of his Jewish background, and he exulted in his confession of Christ as Saviour. As a member of the British Israel Association he witnessed steadfastly and strongly for the rest of his days, happy and proud to be serving the Lord.

He died in 1923, at the age of 76, glorying in the Crucified One to the last, praying that the time soon would come when Judah would love Him, and breathe His Holy Name in reverence.

The above testimony is composed of excerpts from an article by Mary Hughes and is reprinted from *THE ENSIGN MESSAGE*.

"James...to the twelve tribes which are scattered abroad..."   James 1:1

Elieser Bassin, C.M., Ph. B.

With an additional testimonial by Cyril Leach

Elieser Bassin was born in Russia in the nineteenth century of pious and wealthy Jewish parents. While still a young man, he moved to Great Britain in 1876. Bassin accepted Jesus Christ as the true Messiah of Israel and became a most scholarly and devoted Christian.

In his sincere search for truth, he was confronted with the mystery of the "lost" ten tribes of Israel. After extensive research, he became thoroughly convinced that the Anglo-Saxon and related peoples are the literal descendants of those ancient Israelites who were taken into Assyrian captivity so long ago. In his book, "British and Jewish Fraternity" he writes, "The Hebrew Scriptures point to the British Isles as the home of God's firstborn".

Bassin gave a series of lectures entitled, "God's Dealings With His Chosen People Israel", in which he presented his proofs that the Anglo-Saxon and related peoples comprise the true house of Israel. The following is the text of a lecture given by Elieser Bassin in Portobello, Scotland in 1884.

The Lecture

by Elieser Bassin

DEAR friends, – In compliance with the request of many Christian friends that I should communicate my views on the subject of the Identity of the British people with the Lost Tribes of Israel, and how I came to believe it, I have agreed to deliver the following lecture, hoping by it, through the blessing of God, to awaken among the true disciples of Jesus a deeper interest in searching the Scriptures as to God's dealing with Israel.

Before I became a Christian, I believed, as the most of my Jewish brethren still believe, that the Ten Tribes of Israel exist, somewhere, as a powerful nation, having a king of their own, and that they are hidden from the sight of men until the coming of the expected Messiah.

This tradition is probably founded upon the Second Book of Esdras 13:10, where we are informed that "the Ten Tribes were carried away prisoners out of their own land, in the time of Osea the king, whom Shalmaneser, the king of Assyria, led away captive, and he carried them over the waters, and so they came into another land. But they took counsel among themselves that they would leave the multitude of the heathen, and go forth into a further country, where never mankind dwelt, that they might keep their statutes, which they never kept in their own land. And they entered into Euphrates by the narrow passage of the river. For the Most High then showed signs for them, and held still the flood till they were passed over. For through that country there was a great way to go – namely, of a year and a half, and the same region is called Arsareth. They dwelt there until the latter time, and now, when they shall begin to come, the Highest shall stay the springs of the streams again. That they may go through." I believe also another Jewish tradition, that the Ten Tribes went away West beyond the river Sabbatyon – *i.e.,* rest.

On my arrival in England, for the first time, in 1876, I heard of the theory that the British people are the descendants of the Ten Tribes of Israel. Many a time Christian friends asked me what I thought of that theory and my answer generally was, I would gladly accept the British as my brethren, the children of Abraham, but I do not know how such a theory can be established. How is it possible that such a mixed race, like the British, made up of the Welsh Kymry, the Keltic ancient Britons, the Picts and Scots, and Scythian Angles, the Teutonic or Gothic Saxons, the Danes and Normans, could ever have been brethren, the children of one father, Israel? Until the beginning of 1884, I looked upon the theory as curious, and only a crotchet, although I had never meditated on the subject for ten minutes, because I thought that it was not worth while to

175

give the slightest attention to such an apparently ridiculous theory. But now that I have given great attention, both in reading and reflection, to the subject of the Identity of the British nation with the Ten Tribes of Israel, I have come to the conclusion that the subject is highly interesting, and of great importance to Christians and to Jews.

I cannot enter fully into the particulars of my views in the limits of one lecture; but I hope, by the help of God, to bring them out clearly in my lectures on "God's Dealings with His Chosen People Israel," which I intend to deliver by-and-by. Meanwhile, I will endeavour to give you an outline of the reasons why I believe that the British nation is identical with the ancient kingdom of Israel. And I entreat you, dear friends, in the words of the Right Rev. Dr. Ryle, Bishop of Liverpool, in his tract, "Scattered and Gathered," "not to dismiss the subject as speculative, fanciful, and unprofitable." The world is growing old; the last days are come upon us; the foundations of the earth are out of course; the ancient institutions of society are wearing out and going to pieces. The end of all is things at hand. Surely it becomes a wise man at a time like this, to turn to the pages of prophecy, and inquire what is yet to come? At a time like this the declaration of God concerning His people Israel ought to be carefully weighed and examined. At the time of the end, says Daniel, "the wise shall understand" (Daniel 12:10).

The words just quoted from the Bishop of Liverpool are of great value to us, although the venerable Bishop applies it to the Jews, who are only a small part of Israel. The tract is very interesting, but I am sorry that the author makes no difference in it between the two Houses of Israel and Judah. We know, from 1 Kings 12, of the separation between Judah and Israel: but we know of no union that took place between them.

The Lord, for His wise ends, separated and kept them apart for nearly three thousand years: and during most of the time Israel was unknown, according to Hosea 1:9, while the Jews were known as a by-word and reproach, according to Jeremiah 24:9. One part of the prophecies has been fulfilled in the case of one section of Israel; and a second part has to be fulfilled in the case of the other section of Jacob's descendants.

The time of their union has not yet come; but there is a glorious and blessed union still in store for Judah and Israel. According to Zechariah 10:6-12. The House of Israel, which is now lost and hidden from the sight of men, must be found before the glorious union of Judah and Israel takes place. Israel will be found by the world; and it has been found in these latter days by many, and also by me.

And now, after these few introductory remarks, I will tell you how and where I found the Lost Tribes of the House of Israel. Some of you

176

will remember the lecture I had the privilege of delivering last February in the parish church of this town on behalf of my persecuted brethren. After that lecture a lady whom I now see in the hall handed me the Rev. Dr. Poole's "Fifty Reasons Why the Anglo-Saxons are Israelites." The Rev. Mr. Jameson, your parish minister, who presided on that occasion, and my friend, General Hogan, who is now in the chair, will perhaps recollect my jesting on the subject of Identity, which I then considered to be an absurdly extravagant theory.

Next morning I left for Aberdeen, and being about six hours in the train, I had time to read carefully Dr. Poole's pamphlet. I took my Hebrew Bible and began to examine the passages referred to, and was so intent on studying the subject, that for some minutes after the train had stopped I did not notice its arrival in Aberdeen. With all the arguments in that pamphlet I could not agree, but from that time I began to think over the subject with an unprejudiced desire to discover the truth in regard to the matter for its own sake. I was very much encouraged to search for the Lost Tribes in Britain by the quotation of Rev. Dr. Poole from Dr. Abbadie, of Amsterdam, who said in 1723, "Unless the Ten Tribes have flown into the air, or have been plunged to the centres of the earth, they must be sought for in the North and West and in the British Isles." For some months I studied the subject carefully from a Scriptural standpoint, and I found that the predictions of the Bible are much more easily interpreted on the supposition that the Identity theory is true than on any other supposition. The great difficulty to me was, how the theory could be established from philology, ethnology, and history; and this difficulty still prevented me becoming a convert to the Anglo-Israel belief.

A few months later I had the honour of making t he acquaintance of Mrs. Geils, of Ardmore, who is a firm believer in the Identity and full of zeal in promoting her views. She supplied me with a large number of books on the subject. I read also pamphlets written in refutation of the theory, and I found that both parties run into extremes and equally fall into grievous mistakes! However, one who wishes to find truth for its own sake will notice in reading the books written in defense of Anglo-Israelism that each book throws more or less light on the subject.

I shall now relate how my difficulties about the various British peoples were removed: I resolved to trace carefully the various races of Britain from their original habitations.

We have (1) the Keltic Britons; (2) the Romans; (3) the Picts and Scots; (4) the Angles; (5) the Saxons; (6) the Frisians; (7) the Danes; (8) the Normans. Now I put aside the Romans, who never mingled with the Britons. They encamped in the island, and were the rulers over the country, but left it, after 400 years of occupation, in A.D. 418 in the same manner as they had entered it, leaving behind them only traces of military camps and forts, but no colonies.

I then began to trace the Keltic Britons, and found them to be the first Israelitish emigrants, who emigrated from Palestine to Spain (then called Tarshish) perhaps as early as 1285 BC; for we know from Judges 5: 17, that Dan had ships at that time, and it is most probable some of the Danites emigrated to another land, when Israel was under the yoke of Jabin, king of Canaan, of the king of Moab, the king of Mesopotamia, and of the Philistines. There can be no doubt that there were Hebrew colonists in Spain during Solomon's reign; for we read in 1 Kings 10:22, that Solomon had at sea a navy of Tarshish, bringing gold and silver, ivory and apes, and peacocks. I think it is quite reasonable to suppose that Solomon must have had in that country a colony of Hebrew merchants and labourers. In confirmation of the fact, that there were Hebrew colonists in Spain in the reign of Solomon, Bishop Titcombe tells of an extract he took from a learned Latin commentary on Ezekiel, by Father Vilalpandus, where, after quoting from Philo, Josephus, Seneca, and Cicero on the subject of Hebrew colonization in Spain, he mentions the remarkable fact that a stone had been found at Saguntum, having an inscription in Hebrew characters sculptured upon it, running thus: "This is the tomb of Adoniram, the servant of King Solomon, who came to collect tribute and died here." (See 1 Kings 4: 6.) From the voyage of Jonah, as we read in Jonah 1:3, we learn that the ships of commerce traded regularly between Tarshish and the coast of Palestine, for he found at Joppa a vessel ready for the voyage at the very moment he wished to set sail. And why should Jonah flee to Tarshish if no Hebrew colonists were there? It cannot but be supposed, therefore, that at the impending invasion from Assyria tribes like those of Dan and Asher, which were used to navigation, availed themselves of the same means of escape as Jonah.

Tacitus says that the Silures, or inhabitants of Wales in his time, resembled the people of Spain, from which he concluded that they were of Spanish origin (Vit. Agr. § 11). I was still more confirmed by the assertion of Strabo, who says of the Aquitani, on the shores opposite to Britain, that they resembled the *Iberi* of Spain, more than they did the other Gauls, in language and appearance (lib. 4 § § 1, 2). There is a great similarity between the words Iberi and Hebrew, and a still greater between Iberi and the original [Hebrew] form [of] Ibri, which is without the aspirate. There is a frequent interchange of *e* and *i* in the spelling of ancient names, and the prefixing of the aspirate *h* is quite common:

hence we have Heber for Eber, Hibernian for Ibernian. After collecting all the information I could get on the subject, I came to the conclusion that some of the Israelites escaped about BC 720 from the coasts of Palestine to Spain, where a Hebrew colony already existed, and that the Spanish Kelts who were Israelites, migrated to Cornwall and Ireland even before the kingdom of Israel was carried away captive by Shalmaneser.

Having found who the Keltic Britons were, I proceeded with my enquiry as to who the Welsh Kymry were, and read what Thomas Stephans, in his work on "The Literature of the Kymry," says: They are the last remnant (he says) of the Kimmerioi, of Homer, and the Kymry (Cimbri) of Germany. From the Chersonesus (Jutland) a portion of them landed on the shores of Northumberland, gave their name to the county of Cumberland, and in process of time followed the shore to their present resting-place, where they still call themselves Kymry and give their country a similar name. Their history, clear, concise, and authentic, ascends to a high antiquity. Their language was embodied in verse long before the languages now spoken rose into notice: and their literature, cultivated and abundant, lays claim to being the most ancient in modern Europe. Professor Rawlinson, following Sharon Turner, admits that "the identity of the Cymri of Wales with the Cimbri of the Romans seems worthy of being accepted as a historical fact, upon the grounds stated by Niebuhr and Arnold."

Next I sought to discover the origin of the Kymry of Wales, and from which family of the human race they sprang. But having no longer the classic historians of Greece and Rome to guide me, I was obliged to consult the books which existed before the use of the papyrus was general, and when the sun-dried brick was the common table and the Imperial Blue-Book. Such books have been recovered in the mounds of Assyrian ruins, and among other inscriptions is the "Nimroud Obelisk," now in the British Museum. It records the annals of Shalmaneser, king of Assyria, whose rule was between 858 and 823 BC, and one of the items runs thus: –

"The tribute of Jehu, the son of Omri *(Jahua Abil-Khumree)*, silver, gold, bowls, vessels of gold, &c., with sceptres for the king's hand, all these have I received."

Another set of inscriptions, which tells the story of Tiglath-Pileser's reign, gives us the following, unfortunately broken, record: – "The land of Samaria *(Beth Khumree)* . . . the population . . . the goods of its people . . . I sent to Assyria. As they had slain Pekah, their king, I appointed Hosea over the kingdom."

179

The palace walls of Sargon, a successor of Tiglath-Pileser, display these words: – "By the aid of the sun I captured the city of Samaria (Khumree), and carried into captivity 27,280 of its inhabitants."

I believe that you will agree with me that, from what has already been said, it can be satisfactorily concluded that the kingdom of Israel, of Scripture, and the *Beth Khumree* of the Assyrian inscriptions, are identical. History presents these people as having been carried captive by the Assyrians at various periods between the year 740 and 721 BC; and they were settled in the "cities of the Medes," near the shores of the Caspian Sea, east of the river Araxes, where, in a Russian fortress termed "Gumri," their name is to be found on the banks of the Araxes till the present day.

The meaning of the name Gimiri or Khumree is, according to Sir Henry Rawlinson, "The Tribes," which was the most common appellation of the people of Israel.

Being convinced that Welsh Kymry, as well as the Keltic Britons, belonged to the Hebrew race, I began to consider the case of the next nation that came to Britain, and found that the Jutes from Jutland arrived about AD 449, and 98 years afterwards, in AD 547 came the Angles. This brought me to the great Anglo-Saxon race. I then turned to Sharon Turner's celebrated work, on the "History of the Anglo-Saxons," and I found him saying in book 2, chapter 1: "The Saxons were a Gothic or Scythian tribe; and of the various Scythian nations which have been recorded, the Sakai, or Sacae, are the people from whom the descent of the Saxons may be inferred with the least violation of probability. Sakaisuna, or the sons of the Sakai, abbreviated into Saksun, which is the same sound as Saxon, seems a reasonable etymology of the word Saxon. The Sakai, who in Latin are called Sacae, were an important branch of the Scythian race. They were so celebrated, that the Persians called all the Scythians by the name of Sace; and Pliny, who mentions this, ranks them as among the most distinguished people of Scythia. Strabo places them eastward of the Caspian, and states them to have made many incursions on the Kimmerians and Treres, both far and near. They seized Bactriana, and the most fertile part of Armenia, which from them derived the name Sakasina; they defeated Cyrus; and they reached the Cappadoces on the Euxine. This important fact of a part of Armenia having been named Sakasina is mentioned by Strabo in another place; and seems to give a geographical locality to our primeval ancestors, and to account for the Persian words that occur in the Saxon language, as they must have come into Armenia from the Northern regions of Persia.

"That some of the divisions of this people were really called Sakasuna, is obvious from Pliny; for he says, that the Sakai, who settled in Armenia, were named Sacassani, which is but Saka-suna, spelt by a person unacquainted with the meaning of the combined words. And the name Sacasena, which they gave to the part of Armenia they occupied, is nearly the same sound as Saxonia. It is also important to remark, that Ptolemy mentions a Sythian people, sprung from the Sakai, who reached Armenia, who were called Sacassani; they may have traversed Europe with the same appellation; which being pronounced by the Romans from them, and then reduced to writing from their pronunciation, may have been spelt with the x instead of the ks, and thus Saxones would not be a greater variation from Sacassani, or Saksuna, than we find between French, Francois, Franci, and their Greek name, or between Spain, Espagne, and Hispania."

In tracing the earliest mention we have of the word "Saxon," I found it in its first shape, Sakae, in the inscriptions on the Behistun Rock, which Sir H. Rawlinson concludes must belong to the date 516 BC. This writing is 300 feet above the level of the plain, in the face of a precipitous rock, which rises perpendicular to a height of 1700 feet. Rawlinson first deciphered the letters by the aid of a telescope. The portion specially referred to here is a sculpture representing Darius Hystaspes trampling on the body of one captive, while eight others are standing before him, tied together by their necks; each one having his name and his crime recorded on a tablet over his head. The last figure of the eight is "represented with a high-peaked cap, exactly like that worn by the ancient Israelites and a cast of countenance totally unlike the rest," and is described as follows: "This is Esku-ka, the chief of the Sakae."

It was not the first time that the Hebrews were called by another name. They were called "Children of Abraham," then "sons of Jacob" and "children of Israel," then "Beth Omri," or Khumree, and in Amos 7:16, and Psalm 105:9, they are called [in Hebrew] "the house of Isaac".

The [Hebrew] name has been undergoing a change in writing and pronunciation. Even in the Bible, for in Amos 7:16, and Psalms 105:9, we see that instead of (*yits-chak*) we read (*yis-chak*), the [Hebrew] letter (*Tsude*) being changed into a (*sin*). It is very common in the east to drop the letter *I* and so we have Schaek for Ischaek, and in dropping the guttural (*ch*), we have Sak or Saac; the letter *k* or *c* is often changed to *x*, and thus we have Saax, and with the termination *ons*, which means son, we have Saaexons. Seeing so good historical, philological, etymological, and ethnological authority for connecting Israel, after the great captivity and complete deportation, with a people whom we can trace throughout

181

the later historical records, I do not hesitate to confess that I firmly believe that the Anglo-Saxons are of the Lost Tribes of the House of Israel – the House of Isaac, the children of Abraham, the friend of God, to whom God has given an unconditional promise that his seed shall be as the dust of the earth, the stars of heaven, the sands on the sea shore, and that a nation and a company of nations shall descend from him.

After the Saxons came the Danes to Britain in AD 787, and the Normans in AD 1066. In enquiring as to the origin of those people, who helped to make up the present British nation, I found that Sharon Turner, who supports his opinions by quotations from Herodotus, Strabo, Pliny, and Josephus, says: "The Anglo-Saxons, Lowland Scotch, Danes and Normans, all sprang from the same stock."

Thierry, in his History of the Norman Conquest, Book 2, says: – "Such was the first appearance in England of the Northern pirates, called Danes or Normans, according as they came from the island in the Baltic Sea, or from the coast of Norway. They descended from the same primitive race as the Anglo-Saxons."

On these and many other grounds, which I do not now quote, because it is impossible to do so in the limits of a lecture, I came to the conclusion that the Keltic ancient Britons, the Picts and Scots, the Scythian Angles, the Gothic Saxons, the Frisians, the Danes and the Normans have in truth been brethren, the Lost Ten Tribes of Israel. But in spite of all that I had discovered, there remained a dark and insoluble riddle, how they should so nicely and trimly have been united into one people in Britain in order to represent the Lost Ten Tribes of Israel. This riddle cannot be solved by the aid of ordinary analogies or of common ethnic migration. But when I recollected that I was considering the history of God's chosen people, who were subjects of divine prophecy, I felt sure that He who guides the course of Providence would be fully able to work out His own designs, and bring these masses of Israelites, who were scattered, into such lines of forward movement as would place them just where He meant them to be collected together. Therefore I resolved to study again the Bible carefully to see what the Scripture indicates concerning the Ten-Tribed kingdom of Israel.

I began the investigation of the prophecies with Hosea, who had a special mission to the Ten Tribes of Israel. In the first chapter the prophet represents the Ten Tribes under the figure of the children Jezreel, Lo-Ruhama, and Lo-Ammi, being symbolical of their approaching condition of exile, when they were to be judged, cast off, and made uncovenanted as Gentiles. Hosea says, further, in chapter 2:8, that God will hedge up the way of the Ten Tribes with thorns, and make a wall, so that they shall not find their path. Again, in chapter 8:8-9, he says: *"Israel is swallowed up; now shall they be among the Gentiles as a vessel wherein is no pleasure"*– that is, they shall be hidden from view, or put out of sight. "For they are gone up to Assyria, a wild ass alone by himself." In the book of Hosea, from beginning to end, we see that Ephraim-Israel were to be lost to themselves and to other nations.

From Ezekiel 20:32-39 it would seem that the Israelitish captives in Assyria were anxious to obliterate all mark of their origin, but God vows to prevent their utter corruption, and assimilation with the heathen by whom they are surrounded, and addresses them in the following words: "And that which cometh into your mind shall not be at all: that ye say, We will be as the heathen, as the families of the countries, to serve wood and stone. As I live, saith the Lord God, surely with a mighty hand and a stretched-out arm, and with fury poured out, will I rule over you; and I will bring you out from the people, and gather you out of the countries wherein ye are scattered, with a mighty hand and with a stretched-out arm, and with fury poured out; and I will bring you into the wilderness of the people, and there I will plead with you face to face; like as I pleaded with your fathers in the wilderness of the land of Egypt, so will I plead with you, saith the Lord God, and I will cause you to pass under the rod. And I will bring you into the bond of the covenant."

God has cast Ephraim-Israel away, but their case was still entirely in His hand. Although divorced, and sent away from the land which He calls His own, they were not cast out of His care or beyond His control, and in spite of the enormity of their wickedness, which caused Him to cast them out of His land, He had determined to keep a watchful care over them; for "God is not a man that He should lie," or not fulfill the unconditional special blessings He promised to Abraham, that his descendants should become great, mighty and prosperous.

After God had scattered Israel in many countries of Asia and Europe, the time came that the promise of God in Hosea 2:14 was to be fulfilled: *"Therefore I will allure her and bring her into the wilderness* (i.e., the then thinly inhabited Britain, which was like a wilderness), *and* (I will) *speak comfortably to her."* And again: *"Hear the word of the Lord, 0 ye nations, declare it in the isles (of Britain) afar off (from Palestine), and say, He that scattered Israel will gather him and keep him"* (Jeremiah 31:10).

When the main body of Israel was by the providence of God gathered to the British Isles, and after a time of fighting among themselves, they returned unto the Lord, for the time had then come that the prophecy of Hosea 1:10 should be fulfilled, which says: *"And it shall come to pass, that in the place where it was said unto them, Ye are not My people, there it shall be said unto them, Ye are the sons of the living God."* Through Christ the British-Israel are the children of the living God, children of Abraham according to the spirit as well as according to the flesh, and therefore from that time they began to enjoy all the earthly blessings promised to Abraham and to his seed for ever, which are only a shadow of the heavenly blessings.

Since that time the birthright promises began to be realized, that the seed of Abraham, Isaac, and Israel were to be more than ever as *"the dust of the earth"* (Gen. 13:16), and as *"the stars of heaven"* (Gen. 15:5) and to become *"a company of nations"* (Gen. 35:11).

Israel has been blessed in Britain, so that the Isles have become too strait for his children, and he required new territory. This was foretold in Isaiah 49:19, 21, and another Scripture had to be fulfilled that declares of Israel, *"Thou shalt break forth on the right hand and on the left, and thy seed shall inherit the Gentiles, and make the desolate cities to be inhabited "* (Isaiah 54:3).

Among the many marks which the British people have to show as proof that they are the lost Israelites, is the possession of the "Gates" or strongholds of their "enemies," according to the promise of God (see Gen. 22:17). When we take the atlas, we see that Britain possesses, as Philo-Israel describes it, the grand points all over the world, which give her power and influence in all the countries. These are:

1. Gibraltar, in Spain, a true Gate of the Mediterranean.

2. Malta, which was formerly the property of the French, and is a sort of door or Gate to the Mediterranean Sea Eastwards.

3. A large share of the Suez Canal, a Gate of the Red Sea and of Egypt.

4. The Island of Perim, a place which is at the South of the Red Sea, and whoever has that can shut up the road into that sea, or open up the passage towards Egypt from India as he likes.

5. Aden, a port in Arabia, which is a Gate of entry into that country.

6. The island of Socotra, close to Aden, which is another Gate to guard the entry into the Red Sea, the road to the land of Israel from the East and from India.

7. The seaport town of Bombay, and that Gate gave Britain all Western India.

8. Madras, and the possession of it has enabled Britain to take all South India, and hold Ceylon besides.

9. The great Gate Calcutta, in North India, which is the chief city of all those parts.

10. There is Burma, too, a country of which we have taken a great portion, because we seized the town of Rangoon some years ago; and Rangoon is a Gate of the Burmese Empire.

11. On the other side of India, up to the far North-east you will see on the maps a town called Peshawur, which is the door of the road into Afghanistan from India, and this is a Gate also which God gave to our nation in 1849.

12. Then ,in the Straits of Malacca there are three places you will find—Penang (an island), Malacca and Singapore—all three Gates or strongholds, giving the owners "command" of that passage; and we British have been made by God to possess them all three.

13. Beyond these spots there is the Island of Labuan and the town of Sarawak, in and off the large continent Island of Borneo; and these two Gates we hold.

14. Off the coast of China there is the strong Island of Hong Kong, which God gave us to possess, and there are many seaport towns on the East Coasts of China where He has made us very powerful, because of our Navy, and these places are, I think, going to be "Gates" for the destruction of the Chinese Empire, and the transfer of it, perhaps, to the British nation.

15. Sydney, Melbourne, Adelaide. and Perth are Gates in Australia, which God gave to Britain.

16. The islands of New Zealand are great Gates.

17. Then there is Tasmania, which is British; and we got that by having the Gates of Australia.

18. Going round to Africa we have a large slice of that country to the South; and we got "possession" because of our hold on "the Gates," Cape Town and Natal.

19. Further North-west, there is Cape Coast Castle—a Gate which enabled us lately to conquer the Ashantee kingdom and destroy Coomassie.

185

20. St. Helena is a true British Gate, because it gives us influence at sea on the ocean road to India.

21. And finally, we have Gates in the Falkland Islands, at the very South of South America, besides Ushuwia, in Tierra del Fuego. We have also Gates in the West India Islands and in Georgetown, British Guiana.

It seems to me that in accordance with common sense and Scripture truth, the British are the main body of Israel indeed, for if not, why are the blessings promised by God to Abraham and his seed for ever now inherited by Britain? It is my conviction that Britain is the nation with whom God has from first to last identified Himself, in which He has been pleased to show forth the glory of His divine attributes, and that He is doing so at the present moment, and will do so until the end of time. *"God has not cast away His people whom He foreknew"* (Romans11:1). God has foreknown Israel and has chosen them as a nation to enjoy supremacy and preference before all nations in the world, to be a holy nation unto God, as it is written: *"For thou art an holy people unto the Lord thy God. The Lord thy God hath chosen thee to be a special people unto Himself, above all people that are upon the face of the earth"* (Deuteronomy 7:6). No one can deny that Britain, as a nation, is holier than any nation in the world. I do not say a perfectly holy nation, but holier in every respect than other nations, a more special people unto God than any other people on earth, with the exception of the Jews, who are the brethren of the British people, with whom God's dealings are as marvelous as His dealings with the British. The reason of it we have clearly given to us in God's Holy Word, in Deuteronomy 7:8, in order to keep His vow to the fathers Abraham, Isaac, and Israel.

Judah-Israel, or as they are better known now, *the Jews,* are a special people unto the Lord, who have their part in being God's witness on earth, in the same manner as Ephraim-Israel or Britain; but they cannot inherit the *"unconditional"* *temporal blessings* unless united with Ephraim, as they cannot be partakers of the *spiritual blessings* unless they accept Jesus as their Messiah.

The birthright of the blessings was bequeathed by Abraham to his son Isaac, and the bequest was confirmed by God, as we see from Genesis 26:2-5, 24. Isaac bequeathed the inherited blessings to one of his sons, to Jacob (Genesis 28:3-4), which were confirmed by God, and even increased (Genesis 28:13-14). Jacob, who had twelve sons, bequeathed the spiritual blessing, which is the Messiah, to Judah, and with the blessing the sceptre was given to Judah, with the promise that it shall not depart from the seed of Judah for ever (Gen. 49:10).

So, accordingly, "Judah prevailed above his brethren, and of him came the chief *Ruler,* but the birthright belonged to Joseph" (1 Chronicles 5:2). Reuben was the first-born, but his birthright was taken away from him and given unto the sons of Joseph.

Now, what was the birthright that Jacob bequeathed to the sons of Joseph? We read of it in Genesis 48:3-5, 15, 16, & 20, where Jacob hands down the temporal blessings, and the name *Israel,* which God had given him, to Ephraim and Manasseh, and ". . . set Ephraim before Manasseh." That God has confirmed the bequest Jacob made to Ephraim we see from Jeremiah 31:8, *"Ephraim is My first-born,"* and as such he was the national representative, both in history and prophecy, from the time Israel became a nation, and especially since the disruption of Judah and Israel.

No tribe can inherit the *"unconditional temporal* blessings," unless united with Ephraim. Is it, then, not reasonable to assert that, as the British Empire is in possession of all the grand promises given to "Abraham and to his seed for ever," it is Ephraim-Israel, the promised *"nation"* in Britain, and the *"company of nations"* in the colonies?

And now, in conclusion, dear friends, I, an Israelite of the House of Judah, claim you as my brethren, as Israelites of the House of Ephraim, and ask you to remember your brethren, the Jews, more earnestly in your prayers before the Lord, that the time may soon come when *"The House of Judah shall walk to the House of Israel and they shall come together out of the land of the North to the land that 1 have given for an inheritance unto your fathers"* (Jeremiah 3:18). Yes, dear brethren, I firmly believe that the Jews, who are called by Jeremiah the House of Judah, will in due time recognize the British people as their own kindred of the House of Israel; and in joy at seeing their lost brother Ephraim raised in the marvelous providence of God to a position of such preeminence in the world, will come and ask Britain to restore them to the land of promise. At that time the Lord will order events, so that Palestine, with the Euphrates as a boundary, will come into British possession, and the land will become inhabited by Britons who are of Ephraim-Israel, and by Jews who are Judah-Israel.

The Jews, in uniting themselves with their brother Ephraim, will get a share in the temporal blessings, and through Christ they will become partakers of the spiritual blessings. Through the instrumentality of the British people the Jews will recognize in Jesus the Messiah of Israel, the Son of David, the Son of God, Jehovah their Righteousness. The Jews, in recognizing the Britons as their brethren, will gain confidence in them, and listen to their teaching. But while Judah and Israel are in the land of promise, the great trouble of Jacob will come, of which we read in Zechariah 13:9, "And I will bring the third part through the fire, and will refine them as silver is refined, and will try them as gold is tried: they shall call on My name, and I will hear them; I will say, It is My people; and they shall say, The Lord is my God." When the refining is over, *"then shall the Lord go forth and fight against those nations, as when He fought in the day of battle. And His feet shall stand on that day on the Mount of Olives, which is before Jerusalem on the East"* (Zechariah 14: 3, 4*)*. *"And it shall come to pass in that day, that I will seek to destroy all the nations that come against Jerusalem. And I will pour upon the House of David, and upon the inhabitants of Jerusalem, the spirit of grace and supplications, and they shall look upon Me whom they have pierced, and they shall mourn for Him as one mourneth for his only son"* (Zechariah 12:9, 10). Then will Judah and Israel join in one harmonious "Hosannah! Blessed be He that cometh in the Name of the Lord." Christ will then re-establish the theocracy which was once the glory of Israel, and that in a much more glorious form than Israel ever saw under any of its kings, and the people will enjoy fully all the blessings promised to the fathers and revealed by the prophets.

That glorious time, dear brethren, I believe near at hand, and therefore the Lord has ordained in these latter days the movement which teaches the Identity of the British people with the Tribes of Israel, and we are called upon to help onward this movement to its consummation in these days. Depend upon it, God's purposes will be accomplished in spite of all opposition. Let us also remember that God is independent of human agency; but He has bestowed grand privileges on men in permitting them to work with Him in bringing about the results that He has decreed. Let us thank God that to our lot has fallen the high honour of aiding in the fulfilling of God's great and glorious purpose in bringing to light the Ten Tribed Kingdom of Israel, which has been hidden so long from the sight of men, in order to enable "the House of Judah to walk to the House of Israel," and help them to *"return and seek the Lord their God and David their King"* (Hosea 3:5).

As believers in the faithfulness of our covenant-keeping God, I call to you to awake from your sleep. The coming of our Lord bids you rise up from your slumber, listen for the sound of His feet, watch for Him, have all things ready, and to "watch and pray." Let us make our whole life an advent, a season of preparation for the Lord's coming; and may God help us, through His Holy Spirit, in this wise and blessed work of godly preparation to meet the King of glory, when He comes to "restore again the kingdom to Israel."

"And He shall judge among the nations, and shall rebuke many people: and they shall beat their swords into plowshares, and their spears into pruning-hooks; nation shall not lift up sword against nation, neither shall they learn war any more. O House of Jacob, come ye, and let us walk in the light of Jehovah" (Isaiah 2: 4, 5). And let us say; *"For Zion's sake I will not hold my peace, and for Jerusalem's sake I will not rest, until the righteousness thereof go forth as brightness, and the salvation thereof as a lamp that burneth"* (Isaiah 62:1).

With such a resolution I close my first lecture on the Identity of the British people with the Ten Tribes of Israel, and may the God of our fathers, Abraham, Isaac, and Israel, be our help to carry out our resolution to His glory. Amen.

"THE ACID TEST"
by Cyril Leach

"I, Cyril Leach, a Jew of pure extraction, write testifying to the great light given me by British-Israel Truth, and how through this wonderful key to the Bible, I came to the belief that Jesus Christ is of a truth the Son of God and the Redeemer of Israel . . . I come from a line of Rabbis on both my father's and my mother's side known far and wide in Palestine for their piety, charity and wide learning. Indeed to this day one of my great grandfathers has a synagogue dedicated to his name in the Holy City . . . it was not until I reached the age of sixteen that I began to reflect at all seriously or deeply about religion. One of the first things that sorely perplexed me was the position of my own people in the world . . . I began to wonder if the words 'God's chosen people' were not mere platitudes . . . why had our people no King when God had sworn to David "Thy throne shall be established for ever"? God said to Abraham "Behold my Covenant is with thee and thou shall be the father of many nations." These and other points let me to doubt whether the Bible was after all God's Word . . . I was assured that the Saxon people were a Gentile people, inferior as regards race to the Jews, and I remember asking my father "If the Jews are God's chosen people, why is such a wonderful Empire (Britain) . . . doing the very work the Jews should be doing" . . . One day a book was lent me, setting out what appeared to me at the time a preposterous idea, that the Saxon race is the continuation of the Northern Kingdom of Israel carried into captivity in 721 B.C. a long time before the Southern Kingdom of Judea was shattered by Babylon. I laughed at the notion that an uncircumcised people who believed in an imposter called Christ who set Himself up as the Son of God, could be the Seed of Abraham. For the first time in my life I began a most careful search of the Word of God - the acid test of all religious movements to see if there was any truth in this astounding assertion. To my intense surprise I found that prophecy after prophecy had materialized and was in the process of materializing in the Saxon people. I now saw quite clearly that it is discrediting God's Holy Name, and His reputation as a God who fulfils His promises, to assert that the Jews form the whole Seed of Israel."

~~~~~~~~~~~~~~~~~~~~~~~~~~~~~~~~~~~~~

ISRAEL'S PRAYER

Now may God of power and grace
Attend His people's humble cry;
Jehovah hears when Israel prays
And brings deliverance from on high.
The Name of Jacob's God defends,
Better than shields and brazen walls;
He, from His sanctuary sends
Succour and strength when Zion calls.
Well, He remembers all our sighs;
His love exceeds our best deserts;
His love accepts the sacrifice
Of humble groans and broken hearts.

In His salvation is our hope.
And in the Name of Israel's God;
Our troops shall lift their banners up,
Our Navies spread their flags abroad.
Some trust in horses trained for war,
And some of chariots make their boast;
Our surest expectations are
From thee, the Lord of Heavenly hosts.
Now save us, Lord, from slavish fear;
Now let our hopes be firm and strong;
Til thy salvation shall appear,
And joy and triumph raise the song.

By Isaac Watts (1674-1748)
(Watt's prayer, beseeching God's help for England, his native land.)

190

CONTROVERSY IN ZION

FOR THE BENEFIT OF OUR PENTECOSTAL BRETHREN

By George W. Southwick

God is moving by His Spirit,
Moving in all the earth;
Signs and wonders when God moveth,
Move, O Lord in me!

In his dynamic classic book entitled "TONGUES OF FIRE", William Arthur wrote the following words; "A religion without the Holy Ghost, though it had all the ordinances and all the doctrines of the New Testament, would certainly not be Apostolic Christianity..."

Among recent religious trends in America which has seriously altered the spiritual climate of this nation is "The GREAT CHARISMATIC RENEWAL". People within the mainline historic denominational churches almost everywhere claim Divine anointings in supernatural power.

In ever increasing numbers the very same things that brought persecution and ostracism against the 'little flocks' of 'Pentecostals' in the first part of the 1900's are now happening today. Those unusual events include 'Divine Healing meetings', 'speaking in tongues' (called Glossolalia), 'miracle meetings', where fervent testimonials are related concerning miraculous happenings and other supernatural demonstrations of 'Gift Ministries'. All these and more are now common place in many of the established denominational churches.

For all these 'happenings', long time Pentecostals and groups are rejoicing at this amazing turn of events. Pentecostal-Full Gospel people in America are no longer suffering bitter persecution and rejection against their 'experimental' position of receiving the Baptism of the Holy Ghost as they once did starting almost 100 years ago. The old stigma of 'Holy Roller' seems to be gone for good; for which we praise the Lord!

This remarkable world-wide 'move of God' is now vindicating the **BIBLICAL AND APOSTOLIC PENTECOSTAL EXPERIENCE** and proves that investigation of Holy Scripture will bring to light hidden truth no matter how deeply buried away from sight.

Church history constantly has revealed that the 'Spirit of Truth' will remove the darkness and power of spiritual ignorance and break the

191

bondage of the human will into a state of glorious liberty. That 'Spirit of Truth' always destroys the captivating wand of the Babylonian Enchantress and thus freeing the Lord's people; enabling them to 'follow on to know the Lord'.

How wonderful in these 'Last Days' to know, believe, see and experience things long 'lost' to God's people who are the 'Sheep of His Pasture', to whom these promises are now being restored. Every Christian should know the Lord cannot be arrested in His work regardless of individual opposition and rejection. Yet the sad fact remains, many fine Christian people have gone into their graves since the end of the 19th Century, having 'lost out' in refusing to believe and receive the blessings of this 'latter rain' outpouring upon Western Christianity and our American Nation!

THE WOLF AND THE SHEEP

Since this message is addressed directly to PENTECOSTAL PEOPLE, we point out a most vital and dynamic revelation from the mind of God that has been 'lost' to our now highly organized PENTECOSTAL DENOMINATIONS.

The late Pastor Charles G. Weston once said to me, "THE SCOFIELD REFERENCE BIBLE IS NOT THE BIBLE THE HOLY SPIRIT GAVE TO US..."

The Scofield Bible contains the ideas and the interpretations of men in marginal comments on the same page as Holy Writ. It is the Holy Spirit who is the interpreter of the WORD. Not mortal man.

The marginal comments are only the interpretations, ideas, beliefs and teachings of Dr. C.I. Scofield. THEY ARE NOT THAT WHICH IS GOD-BREATHED FROM THE SPIRIT OF GOD.

Now, at present a great and frightful wonder has 'happened'. A large number of Pentecostal evangelist and television preachers have published Bibles with their own names and notes on them.

It is very obvious that Pentecostals have forsaken the wisdom of the past and have been misled far afield. The DISPENSATIONAL interpretation of Holy Scripture has taken hold in the evangelical world. The Plymouth Brethren teaching of DISPENSATIONALISM is the 'Wolf' and Pentecostalism is the 'Sheep'!

We cannot be silent in the face of this great evil which has been committed against our brethren! A friend called telling me of a television preacher asking 13 well-known ministers the following question: *What is the greatest thing in Prophecy today?*

192

Twelve ministers responded by saying: 'The manifestation of the Israeli state in 1948'. Only one minister responded by saying: 'The greatest thing in Prophecy is the 'Deception' in every facet of our lives! Revelation chapter 12 states that fact!' To be explicitly honest we must ask ourselves two questions. *1) Have we correctly interpreted Prophecy? 2) Could it be possible that a movement of makers and shakers have embraced error?*

As a whole the Pentecostal movement has become a Prophetic 'cult' and the rapture teaching is the lollipop! This is why the Lord is now raising up anointed men to speak the truth in love as to our early beginnings. Multitudes of good and sincere Pentecostal believers are in total darkness concerning these things. Our desire is to reach believers who love Holy Spirit inspired revelation and hate the darkness of ignorance. The great need of the modern day church is for saints who will turn to light when it is shined upon their pathway.

We are firmly convinced that Holy Spirit filled, led and taught Pentecostal people are capable of believing the greatest truths from out of the Word of God because of 'the Anointing' I John 2:26-27.

Someone has said concerning error . . .
"An error no wider than a hair will lead a hundred miles from the goal". And again, *"Heresy is the leprosy of the head."*

It was Martin Luther who said: *"Proper understanding of the Scriptures comes only through the Holy Spirit".* Andrew Murray said, *"As all the Word of God is given by the Spirit of God, so each word must be interpreted to us by the same Spirit."*

I have learned in more than sixty years of Christian ministry that it is not controversy we have to dread as much as the *spirit of controversy.* I have learned that the worse thing we can bring to a religious controversy is **anger** because it is only one letter from **danger.** We beseech you brethren...LISTEN!

Time has proven that Pentecostalism as a movement generally has stumbled at cardinal questions and fumbled at points which are extremely critical. It has not come to grips with all the issues involved. As a result, ominous rumblings of underground tremors are now distinctly heard by 'Him who hath an ear to hear what the Spirit saith to the churches'. Let it be known far and wide that religious 'booms' always turn out in the end to be spiritual 'busts' causing embarrassment and egg on the face.

What great truth has been lost to the vast majority of present day Pentecostal saints! We speak of the Anglo-Israel message which is now spreading among American Christian people. This 'revelation knowledge' is just as much a work of the Holy Spirit as any other 'move of God'. Most of our modern second and third generational Pentecostal people do not know that the Anglo-Israel message is a heritage of theirs from out of the past.

It is true that a number of early pioneer Pentecostal preachers, who had great influence upon the movement in its early beginnings, who are now looked upon with great respect, were committed believers in the Anglo-Israel message of the Holy Scriptures.

This historical insight comes as a terrible shock to many Pentecostals, especially the modern stereotyped preachers, regardless of their respective Bible College training, who are all made from the same mold. These are the ones who seemingly 'with one accord' bitterly denounce the Anglo-Israel truth as a most pernicious and devilish doctrine. These same stereotyped 'scholars' denounce in the most bitter terms those who advocate this prophetic interpretation as members of the Protestant underworld! All the while these rapture chasers are in complete ignorance to the fact the Anglo-Israel message was preached, believed and advocated in the Pentecostal past!

How have the mighty fallen! *What wisdom and blessing have been lost!* One of the greatest sermons of the late Aimee Semple McPherson was, "Lost and Restored". She pointed out that great things from Apostolic days were lost during the last 2,000 years, but are now being restored to the people of God in these latter days.

CHARLES F. PARHAM

In any historical study of the whole Pentecostal movement, the very first name that comes into view is that of Rev. Charles F. Parham. Regardless of the credit he receives or does not receive for the genesis of the movement; *did you know that he was an earnest believer and a strong advocate of the Anglo-Israel message of the Bible?* Here was a man with a challenging message coupled with a passion for spiritual truth.

The following are the opening and closing paragraphs of an article authored by Rev. Parham which appeared in the APOSTOLIC FAITH MAGAZINE for July 1927. The article is entitled, "THE TEN LOST TRIBES." Brother Parham writes:

"I want to write a short sketch to introduce to our readers one of the most important topics of the day, commonly known as Anglo-Israel, or The Ten Lost Tribes. I do not think that any Full Gospel preacher ought to longer delay in acquainting himself with this subject as I believe it

194

belongs with the Full Gospel Message and that the message of the last days must include this subject or we are not preaching the Full Gospel.

"Now, if the reader will carefully read Jacob's blessings upon his children for the last days, and all the prophecies concerning Israel in the Old Testament, knowing they refer to the above named nations (ie: Anglo-Saxondom) and belong to us as a people, (ie: Protestants) the Old Testament will become a new book to you full of vital importance and interest."

READER HARRIS AND D.H. MACMILLAN

Two outstanding men in Great Britain were Reader Harris, K.C. and the late Commander D. H. MacMillan. Both men were Pentecostal in belief, experience and practice, yet very active in the Anglo-Israel Movement. Both held official positions and their writings are still available. Greatly respected and beloved by British Pentecostals, neither of these men could be accused of being unbalanced or fanatical. Brother Harris was a well known King's Counselor and Brother MacMillan and his wife were ordained ministers in one of Great Britain's active Pentecostal Churches. Keep in mind these good men, my fellow Pentecostal Kingdom believer, the next time you are given "cold shoulder and bitter tongue" from your fellows, because of your belief in this Israel message.

GEORGE AND STEPHEN JEFFREYS

Another name which will always be high on the honor roll of Pentecostal Evangelists and churchmen of Great Britain is that of the late beloved Principal George Jeffreys. He was the founder of the Elim Foursquare Alliance, one of the largest Pentecostal groups in Great Britain. (Somewhat comparable to the Foursquare Gospel Church in America.) Subsequently, Principal Jeffreys was instrumental in founding the Bible Pattern Church Fellowship.

This group came forth because of a desire of many to return to *Local Church Order* as they saw it in the New Testament. No man in modern times, up to Billy Graham, ever spoke to larger crowds than did this great evangelist, Principal George Jeffreys. He filled the greatest halls and auditoriums in Great Britain. Upon his death, tributes came from all over the world, especially from Pentecostal leaders. They all gave high honor to this man as an outstanding leader and preacher among Pentecostals.

What is significant to Pentecostal believers is that Pastor George Jeffreys was a strong committed believer in the Anglo-Israel message. He gave outstanding witness to this truth all through his ministry of many years. Students who attended the Bible College which his church started were told the truth on this vital matter. What can we say to these things?

One article by Brother Jeffreys, which was given wide circulation is called, "THREE SCHOOLS OF THOUGHT." In this message he tells us that there are only three schools of Bible interpretation concerning Israel.

1.   That the Jews are all Israel (which is commonly known as Dispensationalism. It is advocated by the Scofield Bible. American Pentecostalism is saturated and smothered by this viewpoint.)

2. That the Church is the inheritor of the promises made to Israel and therefore Israel and the Church are interlocked. This is known as "spiritualizing" and it is the historic view of the Reformers. Most of the old line denominations hold to this view.

3. That the Anglo-Saxon and kindred people of Western Europe are literally the Israel people of the Bible. (The Ten Lost Tribes who are restored in the "latter days" and "redeemed" as a result of the Incarnation, Crucifixion, Resurrection and Ascension of our Lord Jesus Christ, and that all the history and prophecy of the Bible bears this out.) Principal George Jeffreys leaves no doubt in the readers mind as to his confirmed belief in this third position of Bible interpretation.

Principal George Jeffreys' brother, Stephen Jeffreys, was also a committed believer in the Anglo-Israel message. He too was a Pentecostal pioneer who was active in the proclamation of divine healing until his death in 1941.

Isn't it strange that our Pentecostal brethren from all groups are supremely proud of this great man of God but bitterly denounce what he lovingly believed? Somehow Pentecostal preachers, especially in America have failed to "catch the flame" in getting in their hearts and heads the message of the identification of God's true Israel people, which he gave under the inspiration of the Holy Spirit. We can only say, surely "an enemy hath done this."

F.F. BOSWORTH AND JOHN A. DOWIE

Let us return to America, where we pick up the name of Evangelist F.F. Bosworth. This man died a most triumphant death in January 1958 at age eighty-one. He also was dearly beloved by all Pentecostals. Brother Bosworth was active in the Assemblies of God in its early days. Later he joined with the Christian and Missionary Alliance where his name remained until his death. In experience he was fully Pentecostal. Let us now look at a few outstanding things about this great man of God.

196

First, let us remember him as an evangelist, for that is the title he used, Evangelist F.F. Bosworth. He will ever be remembered as one of America's greatest. When we think of Finney, Moody, Torrey, Sunday, Beiderwolf, don't omit the name of Bosworth. Multiplied thousands heard him preach. His sermons were superb. We can only hope that some day someone will have the vision to republish his sermons in a book. They would be comparable to his supreme effort – *"Christ the Healer."* This is acclaimed by many as the greatest book on Divine healing ever written. It has been republished by Oral Roberts' Abundant Life Ministry, for this many are grateful. Sermons like these should never die or fade away. Evangelist Bosworth's book, *"Christ the Healer"* is considered a classic on divine healing.

Second, let us remember Brother Bosworth as a pioneer in the Divine Healing Ministry we hear so much about today. Long before such names as Oral Roberts, T.L. Osborn, Gordon Lindsay, Kathryn Kuhlman and many more were ever heard of, Evangelist Bosworth was receiving great persecution for his firm stand on this subject. His early years were with John Alexander Dowie of Zion, Illinois (who also was a believer in the Anglo-Israel truth). Evangelist Bosworth greatly helped make it possible for men and women today to get the large receptive audiences that come to hear the message of salvation and divine healing.

Third, Let us remember Brother Bosworth as a missionary statesman. The latter years of his life were spent in world travel. One prominent evangelist he traveled with was the late William Branham of Jeffersonville, Indiana. Brother Branham was a gifted man and well known in all Pentecostal circles. Together they visited many nations with a message of salvation and healing with Apostolic 'signs' following.

Fourth, and most important was Brother Bosworth's knowledge of the fact that the Anglo-Saxon and related people are the direct literal descendants of ancient Israel and his lifelong contributions to spreading this great truth. His radio ministry in Chicago will long be remembered by thousands in the middle west who first learned about this Bible truth through him. His presentation of this great truth was so profound and Biblical that it stands as a witness to this very day.

To give some idea and insight into his study habits, it was only after a thorough investigation, taking him through 100 books, would he openly commit himself on the Anglo-Israel subject. He never "jumped off the deep end" on this matter. As a lasting contribution to the Anglo-Israel belief, Brother Bosworth has left on hand a booklet called, *"The Bible Distinction Between the House of Israel and the House of Judah"*. At least eight printers have published it, totaling over 100,000 copies. This is a conservative estimate and is no little accomplishment for such a booklet.

He also published another booklet, which is now unfortunately out of print, which shows his grasp of the Prophetic Word. This was called, *"The Prophecy of Daniel's Seventy Weeks."* In this brief, Brother Bosworth showed, not only his ability to properly interpret prophecy, but also his knowledge of the history of prophetic interpretation. Needless to say, he showed that the prophecy of "the seventy weeks nation" has long been fulfilled and that the *"gap"* or *"Parenthesis"* theory is totally without foundation in the Holy Scriptures. He also tells us this theory is without support in the teachings of the Church until comparatively recent times.

F.F. Bosworth maintained this same position on Prophecy to his triumphant home going. Evangelist Bosworth was a personal friend with Rev. Charles O. Benham, who also strongly believed the Christian Anglo-Israel message of the Bible. Rev. Benham was a very prominent Pentecostal pioneer who blazed the Gospel message of the Baptism of the Holy Ghost and divine healing.

Now, dear Pentecostal friends, after this enlightening and breathtaking trip – please don't be so conceited as to think you have all the truth. Why are you so frightened when someone identifies the Anglo-Israel nations of Western Europe and North America as the TEN LOST TRIBES? You ought to rejoice! How true it is, the human heart "draws back" in fear of the unknown (especially along spiritual lines). Is it not true that a screech owl hooting in the dead of night has often alarmed someone into a state of complete consternation? A pip-squeaking church-mouse will often strike as much terror in some human heart as the roar of a mighty lion!

My dear Pentecostal preacher friend, are you fearful this message will tip over your offering basket? Perish the thought. The Lord commands, "preach the preaching I bid thee!" We are called to obey, not to organize. Why do you so persistently reject a truth which the Holy Spirit so faithfully revealed to these men of God? It was the fact that God was true to His Covenant promises to Abraham that made these men such examples of faith and fortitude by which they accomplished so much for the Kingdom.

Isn't it somewhat presumptuous for you to turn up your heels and kick out at some teaching you have never really examined? I pray you will listen with both ears before you judge! Why not pray about this matter in all seriousness that the Holy Spirit would enlighten your understanding? It is much too late in the day to reject this truth, which will not only make a new Bible unto you, but make a new preacher of you as well. Understanding the Anglo- Israel message will show the way out of a terrible confusion existing in our nation and in the whole world.

My Pentecostal friend, has it ever occurred to you that you have accepted a false premise advocated by Pentecostalism's worst enemies, the advocates of DISPENSATIONALISM? *Futurism* is a false interpretation of prophecy and you are caught in its net. Open the Word of God, my friend, and let the Spirit of God deliver you. You are believing a false expectancy which will never be realized. Then where will your faith be? I challenge you to seriously make this a matter of prayer and study. Tell the Lord you are willing to have your eyes opened and that you will be willing to take your 'place' with the truth and not "hold the truth in unrighteousness" Romans 1:18.

We could name several outstanding evangelists and preachers who were and are silent believers in this Anglo-Israel truth. Many pastors could also be named, but for fear of opposition they have chosen to remain silent. What will be their end?

GEORGE R. HAWTIN
February 27, 1909 - June 21, 1994

The name of George R. Hawtin was once widely known throughout North America's mid-twentieth century Pentecostal and Latter Rain movements. He was a prominent leader in the 1948 Latter Rain outpouring which first took place at Sharon Orphanage and Bible School in North Battleford, Saskatchewan, Canada. He was previously a pastor in the Pentecostal Assemblies of Canada, where he pioneered Bethel Bible Institute at Star City in 1935. He resigned from that denomination in 1947 and joined Herrick Holt of the North Battleford Church of the Foursquare Gospel in an independent work that Holt had established. Hawtin became president of Sharon's Global Missions.

On February 12, 1948 spiritual revival broke out at the Bible School at Sharon, which put both George and his bother Ern into prominence during the resulting Latter Rain movement. This revival was characterized by many reports of divine healings and other miraculous events. Ern Hawtin reported that the Lord demonstrated his majestic power at the Sharon school in a "strange new manner. Some students were under the power of God on the floor, others were kneeling in adoration and worship before the Lord. The anointing deepened until the awe of God was upon everyone." George Hawtin later reported, "That all heaven broke loose upon our souls and heaven above came down to greet us." These types of spiritual phenomena would be experienced by thousands of people all across the United States and Canada. This spiritual outpouring would be a major factor which helped to precipitate the prominence of many evangelists in the divine healing movement.

George Hawtin went on to write and publish a series of 32 books on various vital subjects dealing with deep Biblical truths. Many of these books first appeared as articles in his monthly publication called, *"The Page."* One of the subjects which the Lord revealed to him was concerning the true identification of God's people Israel, the family of Abraham. In his book *"The Abrahamic Covenant"*, he confessed that he once avoided the questions that challenged his traditional beliefs. Then by the profound truth of God's Word he had to accept the plain truth concerning God's true people Israel. He writes: "For many years I have felt that the day would come when it would be my God given task to unfold, at least in part, some of the hidden mysteries concerning God's chosen people, who are the seed of Abraham. Not many people now reading this message are fully aware that the entire Old Testament from Genesis to Malachi, together with much of the New Testament concerns itself with that chosen people – all twelve tribes of them, who are the seed of Abraham, Isaac and Jacob. This fact in itself should be enough to demonstrate the vast importance connected with the subject. In God's holy word this chosen race is described in such endearing terms as these:

My People Israel	Ezekiel 39:7
Mine inheritance	Isaiah 19:25
My heritage	Joel 2:3
My glory	Isaiah 46:13
My servant	Isaiah 41:8
My witnesses	Isaiah 43:10
My called	Isaiah 48:12
My nation	Isaiah 51:4
Mine elect	Isaiah 45:4
My redeemed	Isaiah 43:4
My firstborn	Jeremiah 31:9

George Hawtin became a strong proponent of the teaching that identified the Anglo-Saxon and related people as the true literal descendants of Abraham.

LEAVES OF HEALING

JOHN ALEXANDER DOWIE
1847-1907
Though "he being dead yet speaketh" Heb 11:4

Compiled by Charles A. Jennings

As a forerunner of what God has prepared for His people in the next generation, He always sends a messenger *"to make ready a people prepared for the Lord"* (Luke 1:17). Usually, that messenger is thought of as being strange by the religious standard of the day and often strongly rejected by the ruling church authorities. One such God-ordained messenger who was the forerunner in preparation for the Twentieth Century ministry of divine healing was John Alexander Dowie. One writer recalls:

"John Alexander Dowie holds a unique and definite place in the development of apostolic ideals for the Church of the Twentieth Century. His life mission and work present a fascinating, romantic object lesson for those interested in progressive Christianity. Single-handed, as Elijah of old, he denounced the decadent order of the day, and protested mightily against apostasy, both of the Protestant and Catholic divisions of the Church and heralded a New Day of a Thousand Years when Jehovah would hold sway over a redeemed people on the renewed earth."

On May 24, 1847 Dowie was born into the home of highly educated and devout Christian parents in the city of Edinburgh, Scotland. It was there he attended church and was converted to Christ at the early age of seven years old. Later he recalls the story of his early conversion in the following testimony.

"I feel to witness first of all today to the fact which myself and my God know is true. I am in my 49th year; and I was in my seventh when in the city of Edinburgh, Scotland, where I was born, I was converted. A good and holy man, now passed into the heavens, who was the means of the conversion of my father, and who made him one of his earnest co-workers. That good man was standing in a quaintly constructed street pulpit. He was a man of great capacity, great wit, and much sympathy, but above all, a man of astonishing piety. An advocate by profession.

That is a barrister pleading before the courts. But being wealthy he did not pursue his profession. In a remarkable way God saved him; and he became a preacher. On the night I was converted, my father took me for the first time to hear him preach; and he lifted me in his pulpit and caused me to sing. He knew me well. He got me to sing; and that night I gave my heart to Christ, whilst the multitude in the streets were listening to the hymn that the bairn was singing.

"Come let us to the Lord our God, with contrite hearts return, Our God is gracious; nor will leave, the desolate to mourn."

I also sang, *"Long hath the night of sorrow reigned."* I had never seen the stars to my remembrance before; or at such a time. It was a summer night. The daylight had long faded. The twilight was with us; and the stars were peeping out, as I sang, *"Long hath the night of sorrow reigned."* My voice echoed and reechoed. I was standing near where John Knox used to stand and preach, on the steps of his own house. Not far from St. Charles Cathedral, perhaps the oldest church in Scotland. Not far from where the martyrs had died for the cross; and not far away was the great Friar Church where most of my name and family had given their lives for Christ. And that night I gave my life to Christ. In a few days after that, I asked my father what my name meant. I asked him what John Alexander meant. And he said he did not know. And he said, 'you ask so many questions, I am getting tired. Look it up in the family Bible.' I hunted through the family Bible; and I found that John meant, 'by the grace of God' and the Alexander meant, 'a helper of men.' And I said, I will be that by the grace of God."

When at the age of thirteen years old, his family moved to Australia where he began working and earning his own money as a salesman in his uncle's shoe shop. At the age of sixteen, he was divinely healed of chronic dyspepsia. At the age of twenty, he surrendered to a divine call for Christian ministry and returned to his native Scotland to attend Edinburgh University. While there he studied at the Free Church School for three years and then returned to Australia. In the spring of 1872 he accepted the pastorate of the Congregational Church in Alma. The following year he accepted a pastoral call to a church in the city of Manly Beach. In 1875, Dowie moved again and accepted the pulpit at a church in the Sydney suburb of Newtown. On May 26, 1876, he married his wife Jeanie, in the city of Adelaide, South Australia.

In the August 31, 1894 edition of his paper, *Leaves of Healing*, Dowie gives a resume of his life in the following words:

"The editor was born in the city of Edinburgh, Scotland on the 24th of May, 1847. He received his early education in the academies of that city and went with his parents in 1860 to Adelaide, South Australia. After spending seven years in business pursuits he entered upon a course of study beginning in 1868, and left Australia for his native city shortly afterwards. He studied for a time in the University and the Theological Halls of Edinburgh. He returned to South Australia and was ordained into the ministry in 1872, becoming pastor of the Congregational Church of Alma. He removed to Sydney, New South Wales, in 1873 and became pastor, first, of the Manly Congregational Church, and then of the Newtown Congregational Church. The latter position was one of great influence, being at that time the collegiate church of the Congregational Denomination, and so he had the duty of ministering to the resident professors' public offices in connection both with his own denomination and general religious, temperance and educational work, and took part in the origination of many religious and social organizations. In 1878, after long and prayerful consideration, he resigned his pastoral charge and his ministerial membership in the Congregational Union of New South Wales, not without a unanimous protest on the part of the Ministerial Association of Sydney, but he felt called of God to devote himself wholly to evangelistic work amongst the masses of the people, and had become convinced, among many other things, that it was wrong for a minister to sale and for a church to buy any man's spiritual power or services. Accordingly, until this day he has ministered at all times and at all places without money and without price, depending entirely upon the free will offerings of God's people for the maintenance not only of himself and family, but for the large sums of money which have been necessary to carry on the work in which he has been engaged. It is impossible in this column to give an outline even of that work, but suffice it to say, that he removed to Melbourne, the capital of Victoria, Australia, in 1882, and continued his ministry there until 1888, having established a large church, and built a tabernacle, and founded the International Divine Healing Association. He conducted missions in many parts of Australia and for about six months throughout the beautiful islands of New Zealand. He left Australia finally in March 1888, and after spending several months in the islands of New Zealand, he arrived at the Golden Gate, San Francisco, on June 7, 1888. Since that time he has conducted a long series of missions and established branches of the Association throughout all the Pacific Coast states and in many other parts of the United States and Canada."

While pastoring the Congregational Church in Newtown, Dowie experienced his first miracle of divine healing that would revolutionize his life and ministry. In his own words, he relates the following account.

"At noontide, sixteen years ago, I sat in my study in the parsonage of the Congregational Church, at Newtown, a suburb of the beautiful city of Sydney, Australia. My heart was very heavy, for I had been visiting the sick and dying beds of more than thirty of my flock, and I had cast the dust to its kindred dust into more than forty graves in a few weeks. Where, oh where was He who used to heal his suffering children? No prayer for healing seemed to reach his ear, and yet I knew His hand had not been shortened. Still it did not save from death even those for whom there was so much in life to live for God and others. Strong men, fathers, good citizens, and more than all true faithful Christians sickened with a putrid fever, suffered nameless agonies, passed into a delirium, sometimes with convulsions and then died. And oh, what aching voids were left in many a widowed, orphaned heart. Then there were many homes where, one by one, the little children, the youths and the maidens were stricken, and after hard struggling with the foul disease, they too lay cold and dead. It seemed sometimes as if I could almost hear the triumphant mockery of fiends ringing in my ear, whilst I spoke to the bereaved ones the words of Christian hope and consolation. Disease, the foul offspring of its father, Satan and its mother, Sin, was defiling and destroying the earthly temples of God's children, and there was no deliverer.

And there I sat with sorrow bowed head for my afflicted people, until the bitter tears came to relieve my burning heart. Then I prayed for some message, and oh, how I longed to hear some words from Him who wept and sorrowed for the suffering long ago, the Man of Sorrows and Sympathies. And then the words of the Holy Ghost inspired in Acts 10:38 stood before me all radiant with light, revealing Satan as the defiler and Christ as the Healer. My tears were wiped away, my heart was strong, I saw the way of healing, and the door thereto was opened wide, and so I said, 'God help me now to preach that word to all the dying round, and tell them how 'tis Satan still defiles, and Jesus still delivers, for He is just the same today.'

A loud ring and several loud raps at the outer door, a rush of feet, and then at my door two panting messengers who said, 'Oh, come at once, Mary is dying; come and pray.' With such a feeling as a shepherd has who hears that his sheep are being torn from the fold by a cruel wolf, I rushed from my house, ran hatless down the street, and entered the room of the dying maiden. There she lay groaning, grinding her clinched teeth in the agony of the conflict with the destroyer, the white froth, mingled with her blood, oozing from her pained distorted mouth. I looked at her and then my anger burned, "Oh," I thought, "For some sharp sword of heavenly temper keen to slay this cruel foe, who is strangling that lovely maiden like an invisible serpent, tightening his deadly coils for a final victory."

In a strange way it came to pass; I found the sword I needed was in my hands, and in my hand, I hold it still, and never will I lay it down. The doctor, a good Christian man, was quietly walking up and down the room, sharing the mother's pain and grief. Presently he stood at my side and said, "Sir, are not God's ways mysterious?" Instantly the sword was flashing in my hand, the Spirit's Sword, the Word of God. "God's way!" I said, pointing to the scene of conflict, "How dare you, Dr. K——, call that God's way of bringing His children home from earth to heaven? No, sir, that is the devil's work, and it is time we called on Him who came to "destroy the work of the Devil," to slay that deadly foul destroyer, and to save the child. Can you pray, Doctor, can you pray the prayer of faith that saves the sick?" At once, offended at my words, my friend was changed, and saying, "you are too much excited, sir, 'tis is best to say, God's will be done," he left the room. Excited! The word was quite inadequate for I was almost frenzied with divinely imparted anger and hatred of that foul destroyer, disease which was doing Satan's will. "It is not so, I exclaimed, "No will of God sends such cruelty, and I shall never say God's will be done to Satan's works, which God's own Son came to destroy, and this is one of them." Oh, how the Word of God was burning in my heart: "Jesus of Nazareth went about doing good, and healing all that were oppressed of the devil: For God was with Him." And was not God with me? And was not Jesus there and all His promise true? I felt that it was even so, and turning to the mother, I inquired, "Why did you send for me?" To which she answered, "Do pray, oh, pray for her that God may raise her up." And so we prayed. What did I say? It may be that I cannot now recall the words without mistake, but words are in themselves of small importance. The prayer of faith may be a voiceless prayer, a simple heartfelt look of confidence into the face of Christ. At such a moment words were few, but they mean much, for God is looking at the heart. Still, I can remember much of that prayer until this day, and asking God to aid I will endeavor to recall it. I cried:

"Our Father, help! And Holy Spirit teach me how to pray. Plead thou for us, oh, Jesus, Saviour, Healer, Friend, our Advocate with the Father. Hear and heal Eternal One! From all disease and death deliver this sweet child of thine. I rest upon the Word. We claim the promise now, The Word is true, "I am the Lord that healeth thee." Then heal her now. The Word is true, "I am the Lord, I change not." Unchanging God, then prove Thyself the Healer now. The Word is true, "These signs shall follow them that believe, in my Name they shall lay hands on the sick and they shall recover." And I believe and I lay hands in Jesus Name on her, and claim this promise now. The Word is true, 'The prayer of faith shall save the sick.' Trusting in Thee alone, I cry, oh save her now, for Jesus sake, Amen!"

And lo, the maid lay still in sleep, so deep and sweet that the mother said in a low whisper, "Is she dead?" "No, " I answered in a whisper lower still, "Mary will live, the fever is gone. She is perfectly well and sleeping as an infant sleeps." Smoothing the long dark hair from her now peaceful brow, and feeling the steady pulsation of her heart and cool, moist hands, I saw that Christ had heard and that once more, as long ago in Peter's house, "He touched her and the fever left her." Turning to the nurse I said, "Get me at once, please, a cup of cocoa and several slices of bread and butter." Beside the sleeping maid, we sat quietly and almost silently until the nurse returned, and then I bent over her and snapping my fingers said, "Mary!" Instantly she woke, smiled and said, "Oh sir, when did you come? I have slept so long, then stretching out her arms to meet her mother's embrace; she said "Mother, I feel so well." "And hungry too?" I said, pouring some of the cocoa in a saucer and offering it to her when cooled by my breath. "Yes hungry too," she answered with a little laugh, and drank and ate again and yet again, until all was gone. In a few minutes she fell asleep, breathing easily and softly. Quietly thanking God we left her bed and went to the next room where the brother and sister also lay sick of the same fever. With those two we also prayed, and they were healed. The following day all three were well and in a week or so they brought to me a little letter and a little gift of gold, two sleeve links with my monogram, which I wore for many years. As I went away from the home where Christ as the Healer had been victorious, I could not but have somewhat in my heart of the triumphant song that rang through heaven, and yet I was not a little amazed at my own strange doings and still more at my discovery that *He is just the same today*. And this is the story of how I came to preach the Gospel of healing through Faith in Jesus." (Leaves of Healing, February 15, 1895)

"In 1882, I was called to an almost precisely similar case in Melbourne. The child was instantly healed, a girl. From that moment the ministry came in Power. And since then I have been praying with the sick, I may say, everyday of my life, so that now in some years I have prayed as many as fifty thousand times, and in others as many as seventy eight thousand times in one year." (Leaves of Healing, March 20, 1896)

In 1878, Dowie left the Congregational Church and launched his own independent ministry in the cities of Sydney and Melbourne. He ran unsuccessfully for a seat in the Australian Parliament, but gained widespread notoriety for his strong opposition to the liquor traffic. In 1888, Dowie and his wife with their two children, William Gladstone and Esther, moved to the United States. He held evangelistic meetings on the Pacific Coast and other parts of the United States for two years before establishing his base of operations in Evanston, Illinois. During that time the membership of his *International Divine Healing Association*, of which he was president and founder, had increased to over five thousand members. The *Voice of Healing* of May 1949 gives the following account of Dowie's early years in America.

"Leaving Australia in March, 1888, he went through New Zealand, crossed the Pacific, and passed through the Golden Gate at San Francisco on June 7, 1888. Dowie did not have long to wait after landing at San Francisco to have an opportunity to minister to suffering humanity. Among those who came to interview him during his stay at the Palace Hotel, an aged woman appeared who had come with her crutch all the way from Sacramento to interview Dr. Dowie. Her husband having read of Dowie in the newspapers, urged her to go, saying, "This is the old time religion, or else it is all a lie. Go down and see if the Doctor is what they say he is, and if he is, you will come back cured."

She looked at Dr. Dowie with tears in her eyes, ready to yield her heart to the Savior after he had made plain the way of salvation to her. "Now, will you trust Jesus as your Healer?" Dr. Dowie asked. The woman responded in the affirmative after he had explained to her the fact that Jesus was invisibly present that very moment in spirit and power.

Without another word, Dr. Dowie knelt at her feet and put the diseased foot in his hand and prayed for her healing, saying to her: "In Jesus' Name, rise and walk." She arose and walked several times across the room. Her daughter, who was a backslider, was restored to God.

As they were leaving, Dr. Dowie said, "You have left something behind, your crutch." "I don't need it anymore. I am healed," she said. Then she walked away without it, more than eight blocks to her daughter's house.

Chicago newspapers attacked him as an imposter, and informed him that he was not needed nor wanted in the city of Chicago. At this particular time, as he was about to close a convention on Divine Healing and was delivering the final address on August 7, 1890, a lady brought a prayer request to him, asking prayer for Mrs. Jennie Paddock, who was lying at home suffering from fibroid tumor - the doctors having abandoned the case because mortification had set in.

Dr. Dowie took this as a test of whether he should open a mission in the city of Chicago. Then and there he knelt down and prayed for the dying woman. She was instantly healed and lived for many years. This wonderful miracle startled many people in Chicago; and even the *Chicago Inter-Ocean* published the details of the case in the issue of August 28, 1891.

Dr. Dowie conducted evangelistic divine healing services during the 1893 Chicago World's Fair across the street from some of the most popular attractions such as the Buffalo Bill Wild West Show. Many people who attended his meetings testified of being divinely healed and his ministry began to grow as he gained popularity among the common people. Shortly thereafter he opened *Healing Homes* throughout the city to accommodate the hundreds of people who would come to receive physical healing, spiritual counsel and training in the Christian Faith. He then started his publication, *Leaves of Healing* in 1894 which was printed by his own Zion Publishing House. He began conducting services in his spacious Zion Tabernacle in Chicago and in 1895 organized the *Christian Catholic Church.*

Major controversies, lawsuits and even arrests were sparked by Dr. Dowie's stand against unscrupulous medical doctors, the use of all pharmaceutical drugs, the consumption of all pork products and membership in all secret societies such as Freemasonry. Thousands of people flocked to his meetings and acclaimed him as their spokesman while he openly criticized both British and American crooked politicians, corrupt corporations and liberal clergymen. By 1901, he had become such a dynamic influence upon the Christian people of America that he had baptized over 10,000 converts in four years and had over 40,000 subscribers to his *Leaves of Healing* magazine which was published in English, Dutch and German. In 1901, he secured a two year lease on the

Chicago Coliseum and was speaking to capacity crowds of 12,500 people each week.

The divine healing miracles that the Lord performed under the ministry of Dr. Dowie ranged from instantaneous cures of every disease and malady from simple broken bones to cancer and gun shot wounds to insanity. One of the most prominent and publicized miracles was the healing of Miss Amanda Hicks of Clinton, Kentucky. She was instantly healed of terminal cancer in the final stage. Miss Hicks was the president of a denominational church college and the cousin of President Abraham Lincoln. Her church authorities summarily dismissed her from her position in their denial and protest against modern day divine healing miracles.

The following is the account of two prominent healing miracles and subsequent legal difficulties early in the Dr. Dowie's ministry in Chicago.

Miss Amanda Hicks "was suffering from a cancerous tumor which had burst and discharged into the alimentary region with adhesions in many places, and had been given up by the doctors to die. Brought to Chicago on a stretcher, a terrible victim of morphine, Miss Hicks made the promise never again to touch the diabolical drug, and prayer was offered by John Alexander Dowie on her behalf. In a moment, the terrible agony of months departed, and later in the evening she arose and walked about, and during the next few days, large quantities of cancerous material passed from her body. She returned home entirely healed, and the *Clinton Democrat* of March 8, 1894, published her testimony.

As Providence would have it, John Alexander Dowie, having been tormented by the diabolical din of Cody's "Wild West Show," near his tabernacle in 1893, was given the joy of capturing a Cody from the murderous demon of disease. On November 1, 1893, Sadie Cody, niece of Colonel W. F. Cody, known as 'Buffalo Bill,' was brought in a dying condition to the servant of God. A police ambulance received her and carried her to the Divine Healing Home. Many of her friends expected her to be brought home a corpse as she was dying of a spine tumor. After Dr. Dowie prayed for her, she was able to stand on her feet–something she had not done for eight months. Within a short time she was completely restored, and after five weeks was able to return home and resume her usual duties there.

The year 1895 stands out as a banner year in John Alexander Dowie's ministry in the city of Chicago. He opened several Divine Healing Homes and thus drew the fire of the Chicago Council and Aldermen upon himself. They demanded he take out a license for conducting a hospital or sanitarium, which he refused to do. As a result, he was arrested over a hundred times in that year. Frequently being taken from the platform while delivering addresses, put in the worst jails in Chicago, and many so hated him that they were even plotting to murder him.

John Alexander Dowie fought the battle single handedly for the right, under the constitution of the State of Illinois to pray for the sick without medical interference; and this laid the foundation for the founding of the Christian Catholic Church (the term Catholic means universal and has no connection with the Roman Catholic Church) , which with five hundred charter members took place February 22, 1896." (Voice of Healing - May 1949)

Multiplied thousands of testimonies were recorded and noised abroad throughout North America and around the world. His ministry attracted many ministers and evangelists who were personally or whose family members were healed or blessed and later became very prominent in the Divine Healing ministries throughout the first half of the twentieth century.

Evangelist John G. Lake, whose ministry later on greatly impacted South Africa for Christ, was a deacon in the *Christian Catholic Church* in Zion City, Illinois. He related the following testimony:

"Were it not for Zion I should be the most unhappy of men. I had a brother healed in Zion about four years ago, who had been an invalid for several years.

I had a sister, Mrs. William Otto, of Wyandotte, Michigan healed in Zion. She had five cancers. She had been in the Hospital and had many operations. The Lord healed her. I have a sister present here tonight, Mrs. Moffat, who was healed when she was very low.

My wife was healed in February, 1898 of heart disease. The disease developed gradually for five years. She was treated by a specialist, who said it was impossible for her to recover. The Lord healed her, and healed her instantly.

About two months after that, my little boy was dying. We did not know how to pray the prayer of faith then as well as we do now. We had not made everything right, and the Lord did not answer our prayer. We went to Zion and the boy was healed. He is now a healthy, happy boy. In our neighborhood there have been at least 56 cases of healing.

Mrs. Janet Currie, living near Sault Ste. Marie, broke her limb at the ankle. The bone decayed and mortification set in. The limb was discolored, and her brother said it was swollen twice the size of a stove pipe. It took two men to hold her in bed, she suffered so. The skin on the limb split open. The physicians were going to operate on her, but she decided that an operation would be useless. She heard of my sister and wrote to her. A time for prayer was appointed in Zion, and at the time of prayer she was healed instantly. She took a basin of water and washed the limb, and the old skin all peeled off. The new skin under it was perfectly formed, and the two limbs are exactly alike. The limb was absolutely made new.

Another healing was the case of a little boy who had convulsions for 48 hours. He was kept in a nursery close to my home. He had been unconscious for four days. I made an appointment for prayer in Zion that night by telegraph. I also notified the members and friends in the neighborhood to pray. The child was instantly healed at the time of prayer, and is well today." (Leaves of Healing - July 28, 1900)

Among the many others who were greatly blessed and influenced by the ministry of Dr. Dowie were: F.F. Bosworth (1877-1958), Eli N. Richey and family including his famous evangelist son, Raymond T. Richey (1893-1968), Gordon Lindsay (1906-1973), William H. Piper, Zion's Overseer At Large (1868-1911), who later became founder and pastor of the old *Stone Church* in Chicago and the popular song writer/evangelist F. A. Graves whose daughter married a prominent Assemblies of God college professor.

The list also includes such men of God as Fred Vogler and J. Roswell Flower (1888-1970) who was instrumental in the founding of the Assemblies of God in 1914.

For many years following his death in 1907, Dr. Dowie was honored by many prominent 'healing' evangelists including William M. Branham and F. F. Bosworth, as pictured above. As reported in the *Voice of Healing* magazine of May 1949, Branham and Bosworth held a joint healing campaign in Zion City for eleven nights in April 1949.

Thousands of earnest minded Christian people rejoiced in the ministry, wholesome fellowship and the 'Bible Days are here again' type of atmosphere generated at Dowie's Zion Tabernacle in Chicago. Thousands of men quit there jobs elsewhere and moved their families to the Chicago area in order to be a part of the assembly of believers where Jesus Christ was proclaimed as Savior, Healer and Sanctifier.

In the May 4, 1901 issue of *Leaves of Healing* is a description of a typical scene as thousands gather for a Lord's Day afternoon service.

"The assembling of a Zion audience on a Lord's Day is a most interesting sight. It is a faithful commentary of the character of Zion herself. Especially is this true at *Central Zion Tabernacle*, at the

211

headquarters of the work, where the attendance can be numbered in thousands.

The principal service of the day is at three o'clock in the afternoon. At this service the General Overseer presides and speaks, and Zion's White robed Choir and Robed Officers are in attendance.

Although this service is held in the afternoon, a large part of the audience assembles at the morning service. They come from all parts of the city, from all the suburbs, and some come from cities so far out from Chicago that they can scarcely be called suburbs.

At the close of the morning service, some go to Zion boarding houses in the vicinity while others gather in the refectory in the basement of the Tabernacle. All eat their food with gladness and singleness of heart, praising God and talking over the services of the morning. Hardly has lunch been finished when the great auditorium of the Tabernacle begins to be filled.

Zion's people have learned that the crowds are coming and that if they wish to obtain seats, they must take them early. At two o'clock there are thousands in and around the Tabernacle. The broad pavement in front, extending from the Tabernacle doors down to the sidewalk on Michigan Avenue, is a great forum at this time, especially in warm weather. Here are hearty handshakings, renewals of old acquaintanceships and forming of new ones." (Leaves of Healing - May 4, 1901)

In 1900 Dowie unveiled plans for the acquisition of property and the building of the city of Zion about forty miles north of Chicago. The size of the city was ten miles square and was built as a totally Christian society. It provided services of all kinds (except medical, drugs, tobacco, liquor and swine) including factories and stores as employment for the members of Zion Tabernacle. By the end of 1901, construction was well underway and plans were materializing toward the development of Zion City. Dr. Dowie announced that his ministry in Zion was basically three fold with the Christian Catholic Church as being the *ecclesiastical branch*, Zion College, as the *educational branch* and the factories and stores as being the *commercial branch*.

His ministry also provided spiritual and physical help for homeless and wayward women, plus an educational program for children. Dr. Dowie felt that the public school system had become anti-Christian and morally corrupt.

Dr. Dowie with an entourage of family and friends took a five month tour of Great Britain and Europe starting in the fall of 1900. While there, he visited and/or established Zion Churches and a Zion Publishing House

212

in London. He was well accepted by the common people as his public meetings were well attended. From October 10 -31, 1900 he held capacity crowd meetings at St. Martins Town Hall, Charing Cross, London, each weekday afternoon and evening. While there, a gang of ruffians opposed to his message, attacked him and his party and attempted to kill him.

Upon his return to his home base in Illinois, Dr. Dowie continued to pursue the construction of Zion City and promote his ministry throughout the United States and overseas. He suffered a stroke in September 1905 following several major confrontations with his critics in New York and Australia where his attacks on the vices of the reigning British Monarch gained international press attention. He continued his travels on behalf of Zion City in 1906, but suffered a fatal stroke and went to his eternal reward on March 9, 1907. He was buried in Zion City, Illinois.

Forty-two years after Dr. Dowie's death, *Voice of Healing* editor, Gordon Lindsay in the May 1949 issue, reflects upon the life and ministry of Dr. Dowie, that stalwart preacher who proclaimed Jesus Christ both Savior and Healer. Lindsay states that:

"In a single-handed crusade in Chicago, and against great odds, Dr. Dowie established the right to pray for the sick without interference from civil authorities. Tens of thousands testified of healing under this man's ministry and Dr. Dowie conceived the idea of building the city of Zion, on the shores of Lake Michigan, in which conditions would approximate as nearly as possible those of the Millennium. But he failed to take into consideration that the multitude of details involved in the consummation of this plan, would tax his strength to the point of breaking down his health. It is interesting to note, that of the many who lost in the decline of real estate values after the death of Dowie (the editors parents were among these) we have yet to find one who did not believe that the rich legacy of faith they inherited from Dowie's ministry more than compensated their temporal loses.

Like a clap of thunder out of a clear sky, John Alexander Dowie started on his world wide mission of setting forth from the Word of God, and putting into practice, the ideas, ideals and principles of the coming Messianic Kingdom; and thereby succeeded in making "Zion" a household word throughout the whole world.

It has been said that in him were treasured up the rarest gifts and talents ever given to man. As an iconoclast, he denounced evil in high and low places, tore off the mask of hypocrisy from unfaithful shepherds behind the pulpit, protested against the shams and fads of a giddy world, and heralded the death-knell of the dying age.

Sudden and unexpected as was his entry upon the public arena, so sudden and unexpected, also, was his exit and demise, compelling thousands of devoted followers to whom God's inspired Word was a sealed book, to acknowledge that his faithful ministry had resulted in making the Bible a new Book to them."

While in his pulpit, Dr. Dowie commented on many subjects, even though they were of an extreme controversial nature. Even before the major Pentecostal outpouring in 1901, he made the following comment concerning "speaking in tongues".

"Well, I do not know. I think some of you are getting a new tongue. You are getting a tongue that gives praise to the Lord, for a new blessing that has come into your homes, and He is giving us new tongues. We have not everything yet, that is true, but He gives the Word of Wisdom, and the Word of Knowledge, and Faith, and Gifts of Healing, and Workings of Miracles, and Prophecy and Discernings of Spirits, and He will give us in due time Tongues and Interpretation of Tongues. He will. That is coming in its right time." (Leaves of Healing - April 10, 1897)

The proclamation of *theocracy* was a major topic in Dr. Dowie's sermons. He boldly proclaimed that he was not a Democrat or a Republican, but a *Theocrat* who had a strong belief in a *government by God*. He stated that:

"God's rule is the only government that brings peace. There is no doubt whatever that the Kingdoms of this world must become the Kingdoms of our God and His Christ, and in that day it will not be Democracy, nor Aristocracy, nor Oligarchy, nor Autocracy, but the form of government will be Theocracy.

God will rule, and that is the only form of government that will bring peace to this world. Unless you are governed by God in your heart, in your home, in your workshop, you will not have peace. And, unless God governs in this city, and in this land, there is no possibility of peace." (Leaves of Healing - August 13, 1898)

Dr. Dowie was also a strong believer in and took a firm public stand in favor of the *Christian Anglo-Israel* message of the Bible. He was a personal friend of Dr. Joseph Wild, pastor of the Bond Street Congregational Church of Toronto, Ontario. By invitation of Dr. Wild, an evangelistic healing service was conducted by Dr. Dowie in the Toronto Church. Dr. Wild was a strong believer in both divine healing and the Anglo-Israel message. He was well known throughout the city and would preach to capacity crowds his convictions on these subjects based upon the Scriptures. His sermons were often printed in the *Toronto Evening News*. He authored two books on the Anglo-Israel topic entitled;

The Future of Israel and Judah - Being the Discourses on the Lost Tribes and *The Lost Ten Tribes.* At this time during the closing years of the Nineteenth Century and the beginning of the Twentieth, many prominent pastors and evangelists were proclaiming this end time message concerning the Scriptural destiny of the Anglo-Israel people. Among them was the eminent evangelist, George O. Barnes of Sanibel, Florida who was ordained as an Elder in the Christian Catholic Church of Zion City. He too, authored a book on this topic entitled, *A Lost People and a Vanished Scepter.* Evangelist Barnes was one of the many ministerial supporters of Dr. Dowie.

The following are public statements that were made by Dr. Dowie before thousands of church attendees and published in his *Leaves of Healing* magazine. It is very obvious, in spite of the fact he believed that the modern day Jews comprised the House of Judah, that he definitely believed that the Anglo-Saxon, Germanic and related people are the literal descendants of the ancient Israelites. One Scriptural fact that Dr. Dowie failed to point out is that the Israelites that were carried away into the Assyrian captivities of 745 BC to 721 BC also included thousands of people from the Southern Kingdom of Judah. This included people of the tribes of Judah, Benjamin and Levi. The Assyrian kings took captive people of the southern tribes but left the city of Jerusalem untouched. The inhabitants of Jerusalem were later taken captive by Babylon and they are the people that became known as Jews. The lost 'ten' tribes actually include members of all twelve tribes of Israel, including Judahites, Benjamites, and Levites. As one reads the following statements of Dr. Dowie, considering his wide spread influence throughout the Western world, it compels the reader to honestly admit that the Anglo-Israel truth was well known and believed by multiplied thousands of Christians. There is further evidence that the Anglo-Israel truth was a Scriptural viewpoint held by many of our Pentecostal Pioneers, both ministers and laymen.

" I AM A FIRM BELIEVER"
By Dr. John Alexander Dowie

(The date following each of Dr. Dowie's direct statements below indicates the issue in which they were published in the *Leaves of Healing* magazine.)

The war in the East was checked by the great powers of Europe; who would not allow it to go further because Europe must have been drawn into the war, and it had to be stopped. That could only last a short time. But meanwhile, such an opportunity is given to the Church of God to proclaim the Gospel of Jesus Christ in the times of this profound peace; when the nations can listen to the voice of God; I tell you such an opportunity is given as this earth, until its last battle has been fought will never again see. It seems to me we have everything in our favor in preaching the Gospel of the King. Let me show you what we have in our favor. We have the British Empire, with the flag of the 'Cross' floating over nearly 400,000,000 of this earth's inhabitants. We have the 'Stars and Stripes' of the same people, of the Anglo-Saxon race, floating over 70,000,000. We have defended and protected people to the number of 30 or 50 millions, protected by the great nations, Britain and America; and the Anglo-Saxon people have therefore directly and indirectly over 500 million of earth's people beneath their flags. More than one third of the whole population of the world, and by far more than one third of its intelligence and power. For practically the money and the manliness and the strength and the religion and the power with God that is given on this earth is within, with a few exceptions, the Anglo-Saxon nations. I want to say this; that I am an Anglo-Israelite. The blood of the Hebrews is in my veins. My fathers in the Roman age were Hebrews. They came from the ancient Israelites; and before the Romans settled in Scotland, our family gathered under the mountain of Ben Macdhui; which is my name in Scotch. Not Dowie, but Dhui. And to this day our language under that mountain is Hebraistic. Our customs are Hebraistic. Our spirit is the spirit of Israel. And ye my brethren who belong to the Anglo-Saxon nation, or who are engrafted into them through other nations, let me tell you that you are the Israel of God; and the Kingdom of God must first be established through Isaac's sons. And that is the Anglo-Saxon race of this day. The seed is becoming manifest in Isaac's son. 'In Isaac shall thy seed be called.' And in Isaac God is calling His people. (September 27, 1895)

****

Now 3,380 years ago, nearly 3400 years ago, God wrought the mighty deeds which today we have read about. And today God has got to work them again. Not exactly the same way; but with the same essential circumstances. In manner different; but in power the same. It seems to me today that the children of Israel are in bondage; and very largely, of a diabolic power. There has been in my mind for a long time this conviction, that is the children of Israel - now you know my views concerning that.

216

I believe the Anglo-Saxon race to be Isaac's sons. I believe that the British and American people form one great Israel; not Judah. That they are the descendants of the ten tribes of Israel. That you can trace the migration of Dan that took to the sea in ships, from the Danube to Dan's mark,

(Denmark) and therefore the whole great British nation; that, if we were not the natural descendants of Abraham according to the flesh, we have all the rights, all the claims, all the privileges, because 'if we are Christ's,' then we are Abraham's seed and heirs, according to the promise. Hence I speak to Israel; and I say, 'Hear, O Israel. Jehovah thy God, the one God that in the days of Moses led thee out of Egypt, and through the howling wilderness into the land of plenty, gave thee liberty, and has taken thee out of slavery; given thee healing when thou wert sick, established the covenant of God, and given thee the great rich land. Hear, O Israel, the Lord thy God is still thy deliverer.'

Where the Church and the people of God are today, I believe that we can see that the Church of God, the Israel spiritually, is within Israel nationally, for they are not all Israel that are of Israel. There is the Israelite in whom there is no guile. Whose heart is cleansed by faith in Christ. They are the Nathaniels. There are the Israelites according to the flesh. I want you to distinguish between the two. I speak now concerning the spiritual Israel. I want to say to you today, as good Israelites, that I am glad with all my heart to see the Israel of God everything longing to escape, and are fast escaping from the Egyptian bondage of a false ecclesiasticism. (October 11, 1895)

****

I love the Jews. I have some reason to believe that I am myself of Israelitish descent. A series of articles upon ancient Israelitish families in Great Britain was written some time ago in the London *Leisure Hour*, a paper that has a circulation of several hundred thousand every week and published by the *Religious Tract Society*, by a gentleman bearing my name, Dowie, and it agreed with my own researches and convictions that our family was Israelitish. He went so far, indeed, as to say that the family were descendants of Jehoram, King of Israel, but that is farther than I would be inclined to go; and besides, Jehoram was a rascal, and I hope we are of more honest stock in Israel. But all lines lead back to Abraham, the Father of the Faithful, however, degenerate or good his descendants might be, and to whom God said, "In thee and in thy seed shall all nations of the earth be blessed." I rejoice in the thought that I belong to the Race in whom God blesses the world. Therefore, I greatly love Israel. Consequently I love the Jew, who is an Israelite. The Jews

217

are composed principally of the two tribes, Levi and Judah, and probably part of Benjamin, but Israel was the name given to the ten tribes who broke away from Judah; but the word Israel also covers the whole twelve tribes. The ten tribes no doubt are scattered among the Anglo-Saxon nations, and the Saxon is Isaac's Son. I believe with all my heart in the identity of the Anglo-Saxon with Israel fulfilling the prophecy, "In Isaac shall thy seed be called." (March 6, 1896)

****

"Israel is a scattered sheep; lions have driven him away; first the king of Assyria hath devoured him, and last this Nebuchadrezzar king of Babylon hath broken his bones."

You see you have got to hunt for this Israel that has been dispersed. You have got to look for the tribe of Dan. You have got to look after the ships of Dan of which the Scripture speaks, and go down the Mediterranean with these ships, and go down to Danube, which is Dan's River, and go right through the whole of Europe and you will find Dan's name on every place they went. They called every place, as the Scripture says, by the name of their father Dan until they came to Dan's-Mark; then they did not go any further, that is Denmark, and they crossed over to England and fought, and got a great big footing there, and the Danites were everywhere, the Dons, and the Danes, and the Dans all over Great Britain and Ireland, and driven back at last into the mountains, there they have held their language unto this day; for you have got the descendants of Israel in a very pure condition, in the Highlands of Scotland and in some parts of Wales and Ireland.

The Celtic languages are full of Hebrew, and with customs that are Hebraistic. You have got to search for this Israel, and you see it was to be driven away.

"Therefore thus saith Jehovah of Hosts, the God Israel; behold I will punish the king of Babylon and his land, as I have punished the king of Assyria. And I will bring Israel again to his habitation, and he shall feed on Carmel."

Now that has not been done. They were not brought back again in the time of Christ. They have never been brought back again since, but they are getting near there now. Israel is in Egypt, and holding it with a firm grasp. The Lion of Judah is sitting on the throne of Britain, and it is only a step to Palestine, and only a few days when the Crescent will fall before the cross, and instead of the Mohammedan flag from the hill of Zion, the cross of Jesus will float. (August 7, 1896)

Therefore thy gates shall be open continually; they shall not be shut day or night."

The gates of British and American nations are open all the time in different lands. In heathen lands and Mohammedan countries they shut their gates at night, and they are afraid. They guard them closely, but in Anglo-Saxon lands the walls of our cities are brave men's hearts. There are no other walls; we do not build up walls, and the gates of our ports are open day and night continually, but you go to godless lands and you will find all kinds of restrictions. You cannot enter a port in darkness; you cannot go into it without going through all kinds of difficulties, but everything is done under this and under our own flag to facilitate the going in and out day and night continually. The gates at New York and San Francisco; the Golden Gate at San Francisco and the Great Eastern Gate at New York, are open wide. It is so with the gates of all our cities and all our ports throughout the world, they are open day and night continually, but the difference is very marked when you go into the lands that are not belonging to God's Israel, as I consider the English and American people to be.

"That men may bring unto thee the forces . . ."

The Word **'Forces'** in the margin you will find is translated "wealth;" the wealth of the Gentiles; that is, of the Nations.

"And that their kings may be brought. For the nation and kingdom that will not serve thee will perish; yea, those nations shall be utterly wasted."

Now, that is just the position. The nation and the kingdom that will not serve God and God's people shall perish. The nation that will not fall into line with God's Israel is going to perish. The day is coming; it will not be long until it is seen that every nation has got to fall in line with God's Israel in these latter days. Israel is a Nation as well as a Church. It is God's great people as a National Israel.

"In Isaac shall thy seed be called"

Isaac's sons, Saxons, are God's national children. (August 21, 1896)

I thought there was nothing on earth more inspiring when I returned to Scotland, after a long absence, and I heard in one of the great churches in my native city, Edinburgh, the people sing that **Old Hundred**, as we call it, to the grand old swinging march that they have for it in Scotland - there is not a child that does not know it; there is not a man or woman that does not know it. That great hymn of praise: **"All People That On Earth Do Dwell."**

That metrical version in the old Scotch translation is very much better than the prose version that we read, and it has this advantage too; It was very directly taken from the Hebrew. As some of you know, there is a great deal of Hebrew in the Gaelic tongue, and the Scotch people have a

219

great deal of Hebrew in their makeup, and in their tongue too, the Highlanders especially, and it entered into the translation in a poetic form, which is much better. (October 2, 1896)

****

Rich as the Jewish people were, the Anglo-Saxon race today controls the gold of the world. Ninety-three percent, of the commerce of the world passing through the Suez Canal is under the British flag. Under that flag today there are four hundred and fifty, perhaps five hundred, millions of people, and under the flag of the United States, the sister nation, there are say seventy millions; there are therefore five hundred and twenty millions and with protected people, nearly six hundred millions of people today are denominated by the Anglo-Saxon race.

Therefore God's Israel, which I hold the Anglo-Saxon race to be, is today the richest and most powerful, and most educated and most blessed of all the families of the earth. (October 9, 1896)

****

Now, she is a Canaanite; she belongs to the accursed race, and almost in despair, she looks at His retreating figure. Oh, how hard it is! How hard the answer is! **"I am not sent but to the lost sheep of the House of Israel."** She does not belong to Israel at all. She has not learned the truth that the world has not learned yet; that God must first bless His Israel, and that through Israel every nation is to be blessed; and that every man in his nation, no matter of what tongue or color, or clime, in coming to Christ, must come through Jesus, the Messiah of Israel, the son of Abraham.

He must be spiritually regenerated, and divinely ingrafted into the stock of God's Israel. You cannot be saved outside of Israel, and I hold today that the descendent of God's Israel is not the Jew alone, they are only two tribes, but the Anglo-Saxon race, Isaac's sons, the ten tribes of the Israel of God who rule in the islands and on this great continent, and whose two flags cover 550,000,000 out of the 1,400,000,000 on the earth; they are God's national Israel, and God's spiritual Israel is His Church. (November 27, 1896)

****

I want you to notice that this expression that I used today for my text, "He that toucheth you toucheth the apple of His eye" is spoken concerning God's Zion. Which is now spread abroad throughout the earth by the distribution of Israel from the North, by the distribution of the Anglo-Saxon race, Isaac's sons, throughout the earth in accordance with his prophecy, "Ho, ho, come forth, and flee from the land of the north, saith the Lord; for I have spread you abroad as the four winds of the heaven, saith the Lord." (January 22, 1897)

****

Friends, I am thankful that if the contest is to come, it shall come quickly. I am thankful that if it has to come it finds Great Britain today, at the head of God's Israel, in the possession of the Imperial Power that God has given to the race of which the United States of America are a part - Anglo-Saxon. (April 17, 1897)

****

The devil is always trying to destroy the Israelitish race, and I belong to Israel. I do not mind telling you that I believe the blood in my veins is directly Israelitish. I believe that most of you here are Israelitish; that the Saxons are Isaac's sons. That the Danes are Danites of the tribe of Dan, and that we, although not Jews, are Israelitish by race as well as Israelitish by religion; for, *"If ye be Christ's, then are ye Abraham's seed, and heirs according to the promise."* (May 29, 1897)

****

Concerning Queen Victoria, Dr. Dowie said the following: (editor)

On June 28, 1837, a girl who had been born on May 24, 1819, and who had therefore, just passed out of her eighteenth year, was suddenly called upon to succeed a line of kings that stretches away back into the historic past, some of us think to the throne of ancient Israel, and under a royal banner which has waved for a thousand years and more, and which today after sixty years of reign is the most unsullied banner that waves over man on any part of this earth. (July 10, 1897)

****

I personally am not a monarchist, and when Her Majesty had reigned fifty years, I was the only minister in Melbourne who preached against monarchy, while I preached thanking God for the Queen. I preached from the text on that occasion, God said, *"I gave thee a king in my anger, and took him away in my wrath."* I believe it. I believe what God said to Samuel is true. **"They have not rejected thee, but they have rejected me that I should not rule over them."** And I believe at the same time that God hath made a covenant with the British people and with the British race. Are we not Israel? Do not Paul's words apply? **"Who are Israelites; to whom pertaineth the adoption, and the glory, and the covenants, and the giving of the law, and the service of God, and the promises; whose are the fathers, and of whom as concerning the flesh, Christ came, who is over all, God blessed forever. Amen."**

Who are we, if we are not Israel? Whence came we, this imperial Anglo-Saxon race? The Saxons are Isaac's sons. I-sax-sons. The Danes

221

are of the tribe of Dan which landed at the Danube, and went through Europe and through Denmark, and passed no further they stopped and called their land Dan-mark. Our native islands are where Donald Morrison comes from, and he who is talking to you today comes from, because if I were in the Highland they would call me Ian Dhui.

I am of the clan from which Ben MacDhui takes its name, the second highest mountain in Scotland, not Dowie, Dhui, as every Gaelic scholarly Scotchman knows. It was at that Ben where the last of the Israelitish kings found a refuge, as tradition says.

Perhaps it is so. Perhaps it is not, but whether it was Jehoram, the last king of Israel, that gathered his family under Ben MacDhui or not, this I do know, that my fathers speak Hebrew in our Gaelic today and the customs and practices and forms of our Highland men are Israelitish, and that today it is an Israelitish descendent who sits upon the throne of her father David, King of Israel. I believe it.

Many of you, perhaps, have not sufficiently studied the Anglo-Israelitish theory, as it is called, to be able to follow me very closely, but let me tell you this: those who have studied have no doubt at all about the matter that we today are God's Israel, and that the latter day promises are fulfilled, that in the Isles He would reign, and that from the Isles His law would proceed. **"Harken unto me, my people, and give ear unto me, oh my nation; for a law shall proceed from me, and will make my judgment to rest for a light of the people. My righteousness is near; my salvation is gone forth, and mine arms shall judge the people: The Isles shall wait upon Me, and on mine arm shall they trust."**

And from that little group of islands on the shores of Europe, today there proceeds the law and the Gospel of the Everlasting God, and for good or ill the mightiest empire the world has seen is beneath the British flag today. (July 10, 1897)

****

I tell you these nations are going down into the pit of hell that they have dug for themselves; and if they fight Great Britain and America, their doom will be swift. I tell you why; because Great Britain and America today are the Anglo-Saxons. They are Isaac's sons, and God has said; **"In Isaac shall thy seed be called."**

And today we stand here with the consciousness that the blood of the Israelite flows in our veins. (July 30, 1898)

Only the Scandinavian and the Saxon and the Anglo-Saxon people are advancing. The Danes are of the tribe of Dan, and Denmark was the limit to which the tribe of Dan went. Dan took to the sea in ships, landed at the

222

Danube River, and everywhere they went, they called the place by the name of their father Dan.

They crossed to England, Scotland, and Ireland, and there the Danites are to be found everywhere. Israel in many of its scattered tribes found a home in the British Islands, and in the Anglo-Saxon countries which now exist.

The British and the American are one, God-appointed people. May God hasten the day when the two nations shall realize that they are one, God-appointed people. (August 13, 1898)

My contention is that the time will come when in the Church of God the foolish and the wise shall be separated; when the wedding feast shall be spread and the supper of the Lamb, and of the Lamb's wife, the Church of God, shall be held upon Mt. Zion; when the foolish shall be shut out, and the wise shall be brought in. The parable represents Israel apart from Judah. It is the ten virgins, not the twelve. It is something that occurs before the final ingathering of the Jews. All Jews are Israelites; but all Israelites are not Jews. All Israel includes Judah, but Israel is known as the ten as well as the twelve tribes. We are of the ten. The dominant blood in the Anglo-Saxon race today is the Israelitish blood.

I believe with all my heart in the Israelitish origin of the Anglo-Saxon race, because of the promise of God. Hence it is that I hail with intense delight the understanding that is swiftly being arrived at between the Australian, the American, the African and the Asiatic Anglo-Saxon. The great headquarters of the race are in Great Britain, and its magnificent outgrowth in America.

Admiral Dewey sounds the true note when he says that the understanding of the Anglo-Saxon race is essentially for the dominance of law and order, and I dare say he means, for the extension of the Gospel of the Kingdom of God on earth; for no law and no order can exist where the Gospel is not supreme. (September 16, 1899)

****

That meant that every tribe of the ten, for Judah was not in this thing at all. It was the ten tribes - our fathers as I believe, according to the flesh: for we are Israelites.

Israel today is to be found in the Anglo-Saxon and Scandinavian races. It is that Israel which God has promised to bless, to call by a new name. (May 19, 1900)

I believe that the Anglo-Saxon people are the Israel of God; that nationally we are Israelites. We are not Jews, for Judah consisted simply of two tribes but there were other ten tribes which composed the Kingdom of Israel when the Kingdom was divided into Israel and Judah.

All Israelites are not Jews; but all Jews in the broad racial sense are Hebrews and Israelites. It was only after the death of Solomon, through the folly of his son Rehoboam, that the ten tribes separated from Judah, and became known as the kingdom of Israel. (July 7, 1900)

****

The Stars and Stripes, the Union Jack and Zion's Flag, borne before Zion's Guard, were symbolic of the Israelitish origin of the Anglo-Saxon race and their going forth, with Zion, to the preparation for the coming of God's Kingdom. (July 21, 1900)

.

There is a Fountain of Eternal Life which springs up in this land. The same is true in the British Empire and true of the Anglo-Saxon people. It seems sometimes that it is in the Anglo-Saxon people only that this salt of high spiritual and moral principle is to be found. God has sent faith to his people that they may be like salt; that they may preserve all that is best, all that is Divine in connection with family and city and national and world life. (October 20,1900)

****

God still blesses the world only through Israel. God confines His workings among the nations to His Israel still. You will notice that the nations which are not Israelitish are in darkness.

We are Israelites. I know it. If I could not prove it any other way, I have the feeling in my very flesh and blood and bones that I belong to the Israelitish race. My own sympathy is with all the Covenants and promises of God which are made in Christ Jesus to the glory of God the father. (December 15, 1900)

****

Ephraim stands, in my opinion, for that portion of Israel which is found in these United States, and upon this American continent. I will not enter upon that at great length. *I am a firm believer*, and have been for thirty years, in the Israelitish origin of the Anglo-Saxon race. There was no part of my recent journey which I viewed with more interest than my visit to Iona and Staffa. I am studying concerning what I then saw. I am intensely interested in the whole story of St. Columba. Columba means a dove. Columba was the first preacher of the Gospel in the Eighth Century to Scotland. He came from Ireland.

I was led to make a number of examinations and to follow up some clues by reading of ancient history, and I am not through yet. Everything I read and see and experience confirms me in the conviction that the Anglo-Saxon race is the lineal descendant of the Ten Tribes of Israel

224

who were scattered abroad. That in this land it is the dominant race, is of course without question. (February 9, 1901)

****

I gladly record my profound conviction that every prophecy which God said would be fulfilled in National Israel is being fulfilled in the Anglo-Saxon race today. (September 28, 1901)

****

Now these Israelites are essentially Danites everywhere they go, it is just as Sir Walter Scott put it; his motto was the prevailing practice of the Highland Clan, and by the way the Highlanders of Scotland are clearly Hebrews. The Gaelic language is full of Hebrew. John Stuart Blackie, who founded the Gaelic chair in my own native city University, where I also studied declared that his conviction was that Gaelic was essentially Hebrew. All good Hebraists, I think without exception, find the same conditions to exist. (December 14, 1901)

****

I love you, my brothers and my sisters. I believe I have the same blood in my veins that you have. I am not a Jew, but I am an Israelite, and I say to you this, brothers; the God of Abraham, the God of Isaac, the God of Jacob, the God who led our fathers through the weary wilderness, is a God of Purity and Love. (January 11, 1902)

****

Our Lord Jesus Christ came to establish a kingdom. The Gospel of the Kingdom of God is the Gospel that He preached. In every parable, in every simile in which He put his Gospel before His disciples in the world, He used that expression, the "Kingdom of the Heavens," or "The Kingdom of God" is like unto this or that. The Kingdom of God is the whole aim and purpose of God's Great Gift to humanity. (April 19, 1902)

****

I hold to the Israelitish origin of the Anglo-Saxon race. (June 28, 1902)

As we look into the faces and hear the testimonies of those who have been blessed and healed spiritually, psychically, and physically, we see that their hearts have been touched, that their habits and manner of living have been changed. They now hate the destructive things they once loved.

Without a doubt they have come into their inheritance under this New Covenant. We ask how they came into possession. The reply is invariably LEAVES OF HEALING.

225

"We could not find the straight gate and narrow way. We were shown it by God's Message through these printed pages."
THIS NEW COVENANT IS THE MESSAGE BORNE BY "LEAVES OF HEALING."

One of the difficulties through all the ages since it went into effect is to make it known to the inhabitants of the earth and overcome the false teachings by which so many millions are deceived.

If each Christian in Zion today can present these truths to just one person each year and convince and convert him, and, when that one is converted, if he will turn and help in the same way, the 1,500,000,000 people on the earth can be taught the Gospel in twenty years.

Distinction Between "The House of Israel" and "The House of Judah"

Radio Address by F. F. Bosworth

INTRODUCTION
By George W. Southwick, D.D.
Pastor, Bible Teacher
Conference Speaker

I can say with deep and humble gratitude that I heard him speak! It was at a William Branham healing campaign in Eugene, Oregon. Evangelist Bosworth believed that Branham was "a man sent from God." In fact, he became a member of the Branham team.

His was a commanding presence. He was brilliant in the pulpit. His messages were clear and full of revelation knowledge. He was a Teacher-Preacher, a true scholar and his message was understandable. He became a great Christian Statesman.

Evangelist F. F. Bosworth learned to preach under the late Alexander Dowie of Zion, Illinois. There is where his famous book, "CHRIST THE HEALER" was hammered out on the anvil of experience and Bible instruction. It is said that each chapter of the book was a sermon of his.

An elderly couple which attended my services for several years, knew him as a youth. They said he was the Band Leader of Zion Tabernacle and worked in an ice cream store!

227

In the 1920's and 30's great crowds attended his Healing Crusades. He was also a pioneer preacher in radio ministry. Evangelist Bosworth had one of the most powerful ministries the 20th century has ever known.

Evangelist Bosworth's sermon contained in this booklet is a Bible teaching message that is a real gem. It is a corrective teaching message that cannot be refuted. The work of a 'rightly dividing' of Scripture. How easily the Holy Spirit uses this dedicated vessel to unravel a most difficult topic in the Bible and make it easily understandable.

Read this carefully, assimilate its contents and your life will never be the same!

RADIO ADDRESS

By Evangelist F. F. Bosworth

Today there is much teaching on the subject of prophecy, and it is important that there should be. It is very important for every student of prophecy, in fact, it is absolutely necessary for their understanding, to see the distinction the Bible makes between the Jews and the other Tribes of Israel. Until this distinction between the two Houses, Israel and Judah, as that distinction is taught in the Scriptures, is clearly understood, a great portion of the Bible will remain a closed book. This clear distinction between the two Houses is never lost sight of in the Bible, and until it is understood, it is impossible to follow the truth of Scripture on this subject, or to understand the Bible story of Israel. If we had time we could show you that ignorance of this distinction is responsible for much of the infidelity today. Because the pre-millennial promises God made to the "House of Israel" have not been fulfilled to the "House of Judah," they have accused God of unfaithfulness.

Many people today suppose that where Israel is mentioned in the Bible, it means the Jews. We read articles and hear sermons today in which the writers and speakers refer to "Abraham, the Jew." Isaac and Jacob are often called Jews, the most absurd and impossible thing as we shall see from the Scriptures. It is a common thing today to hear ministers and writers use such phrases as the following:

"The Jews in Egypt"
"The Exodus of the Jews"
"The Jews at Mt. Sinai"
"When the Jews entered Canaan"

"12 Tribes of the Jews"
"Abraham, the Jew"

Thousands of Christians use the terms "Israel," and "Jew," "The House of Israel," "The House of Judah," employing these and similar words and phrases as if they always referred to the same people. They do not know that according to Biblical history, there were no "Jews" known as such until about 15 centuries after Abraham was born, and until 600 years after the death of Moses.

Most Hebrews Not Jews

Beginning with Adam, we have the start, not only of chronology, but of the genealogical tables of the Bible. There are ten generations from Adam to Noah, and ten generations from Shem (Noah's son) to Abraham. Eber or Heber was the fourth in generation from Shem. All of the descendants of Heber were Hebrews. Abraham was six generations later. He, therefore, was a Hebrew. The Hebrews were not Jews, because Judah, from whom the Jews descended, was not yet born. When the time came that there were Jews on the earth, of course, they also were Hebrews - a very small portion of them - but the great mass of Hebrews were not Jews, and are not today. Let us closely follow the facts.

"Abraham had eight sons. One son was Ishmael whose mother was Hagar. One son was Isaac, whose mother was Sarah. After Sarah's death, Abraham married Keturah, and she bore unto him six sons. Abraham, being a Hebrew, or descendant of Heber, his descendants would of course be Hebrews, and their descendants would also be Hebrews, but their descendants are not Jews. If they are, then Ishmael, that would make the Arabs Jews. The descendants of Keturah's six sons became the Brahmins of India. It would be foolish to declare that they are Jews, although as the descendants of Abraham, they are of the stock of Heber, and therefore Hebrews. The same reasoning applies to Isaac, Isaac was a Hebrew, the son of Abraham. Now Isaac had two sons, Esau and Jacob. If Isaac was a Jew, then both Esau and Jacob would be Jews. This would make the descendants of Esau also Jews, but the descendants of Esau became the Edomites, later the Turks; also the Pharaohs of the oppression were of the Esau line, but none of these people are Jews."

To call Abraham a Jew would make him a descendant of Isaac's yet unborn grandson Judah. The Tribe of Judah had no existence on earth during the time of Abraham and Isaac. If Isaac was a Jew, then surely his twin sons, Jacob and Esau would be Jews. We all know that Esau,

Jacob's twin brother, became the progenitor of the Turks, as they are known today. If Jacob was a Jew, how could it be that his twin brother would not be, since they were both born of the same father and mother?

Descendants Do Not Name Their Ancestors

Jacob, one of these twin brothers had 12 sons, which came from four different mothers. None of these 12 sons were Jews. One of his 12 sons was Judah, but in the sense in which we use the word "Jew" today, the term cannot be applied to Judah, for "he was not a Jew," because of the fact that they whom we call Jews today have certain characteristics and are racially a type that came into existence hundreds of years after Israel left Egypt. This racial type or remnant we know as the Jews is only a small portion of the descendants of Judah, who was only one of the 12 sons of Jacob. There are no Jews among any of the descendants of Jacob's other 11 sons. Now Judah had three sons. "The descendants of one son, Zarah, peopled the shores of the Mediterranean, leaving Egypt before the exodus of the children of Israel." Pharez, the twin brother of Zarah, became the progenitor of the tribe of Judah. The tribe of Judah descending from Pharez was divided by the Lord into two Houses - the "House of David" and the "House of Judah."

Abraham was the father of Isaac; Isaac was the father of Jacob; Jacob, who was later named "Israel," became the father of Reuben, Simeon, Levi, Judah, Dan, Naphtali, Gad, Asher, Issachar, Zebulun, Joseph and Benjamin. The 12 sons each became the head of a Tribe called after his own personal name. From Judah, the fourth son of Jacob, are descended the Jews; the word "Jew" being simply an abbreviation of the name "Judah." A glance at the genealogy will show that it is impossible for Abraham, or Isaac, or Jacob, to have been Jews. Only the descendants of Judah - those coming after him, could be called by his name - not his ancestors. No one had ever been named "Judah" until more than 200 years after Abraham was named. Suppose your parents gave you the name of Charles. That does not name your ancestors, who lived two hundred years before you, Charles. And naming Jacob's fourth son Judah would not make Abraham, his great grandfather, a Jew.

Israel and Judah Separate Nations

The 12 Tribes of Israel became two nations, with widely different destinies, until the time when they will be united in the coming age. (Ezek. 37:22) The distinction or separation between Judah and Israel was

230

foreshadowed at an early date. We read in Psalm 114:1, 2 "When Israel went out of Egypt...Judah was His sanctuary and Israel His dominion." In Samuel's day, the two Houses, Judah and Israel, were numbered separately. In I Samuel 11:8 we read "And when he numbered them in Bezek, the children of Israel were three hundred thousands and the men of Judah thirty thousand." Notice that even at this early date, Israel numbered ten times more than Judah. The Numerical contrast today is very much greater. The Bible tells us that the Jews would be "few in number," but it tells us that Israel would be as the sands of the sea for multitudes (Hosea 1:10). The Scriptures tell us that David reigned seven years over Judah before he was made King over Israel. If Judah and Israel are the same, how could David be king for seven years over Judah before he was made King over Israel? Until the year 975 B.C. the descendants of Jacob formed one nation. But they are spoken of as "the two families which the Lord hath chosen" (Jer. 33:24).

In the year 975 B.C. at the death of King Solomon, the nation was divided into two nations. In I Samuel 18:16 the expression "All Israel" is used, when Judah is excluded. I will quote you this passage: "But all Israel and Judah loved David, because he went out and came in before them." In II Chronicles 10:12-14 we are told that when Solomon died, and his son Rehoboam came to the throne, the ten tribes rebelled, and under Jereboam, formed the NORTHERN NATION; while Judah, along with Benjamin and certain Levites, formed the SOUTHERN NATION.

The NORTHERN NATION, which consisted of the Ten Tribes, was known under the following national titles: Israel, Ephraim, Isaac, Samaria, The House of Israel, The House of Judah and The Ten Tribes.

THE DIVISION WAS OF GOD

The SOUTHERN NATION, which consisted of the two tribes of Judah and Benjamin, was known as "Judah," "The House of Judah" or "The Jews." The capital of the SOUTHERN NATION was Jerusalem. If I had more time, I would quote you the Scriptures which show that this division of the Tribes of Israel into two nations was Divinely Predetermined, Divinely Predicted, Divinely Emphasized, Divinely Maintained, Divinely Accomplished, Divinely Explained, Divinely Approved. The Scriptures show that this division into Two Kingdoms had behind it and controlling it, the fore-ordaining eternal councils of God; and it took place for great, beneficent, well-defined and Divine reasons.

231

In Jeremiah the 3rd chapter, Israel is five times called "Backsliding Israel," a term never once applied to Judah, and Judah is four times called "Treacherous Judah," a term not once applied to Israel. I will read you this passage: "And I saw, when for all the causes whereby BACKSLIDING Israel committed adultery I had put her away, and given her a bill of divorce; yet her treacherous sister Judah feared not, but went and played the harlot also." (Jer. 3:8) Ask those who declare that Israel and Judah are the same people to read that passage, analyzing it in the light of their belief. And there are many such passages showing the clear distinction between Israel and Judah. There are more than 2000 references to Israel in the Bible that have no reference whatever to the Jews. On the other hand, there are more than five hundred references to Judah that have no reference to Israel, and yet there are those continually trying to tell us there is no distinction between Israel and Judah, and continually refer to Israel as Jews, and even change the name of Judah to Israel. It is absurd as to use the words America and England interchangeably.

Here is another quotation for them to explain: "Backsliding Israel hath justified herself more than treacherous Judah." Make Israel and Judah one and the same people referred to, and the statement becomes ridiculous. Many today are evidently unacquainted with the fact that, according to Biblical history, there was not a single "Jew" known as such upon the face of the earth earlier than 600 years after the death of Moses, or about 1500 years after Abraham was born. There were, of course, Hebrews and Israelites long before that time; Abraham and Isaac were Hebrews; but they were neither Israelites nor Jews. The 12 sons of Jacob were Hebrews and Israelites, but they were not Jews. The same may be said of Moses and Aaron, of the people of the Northern Kingdom, of Elijah and Elisha. To avoid confusion over the expression "Israel" it is necessary to determine in which sense it is used in any particular passage, whether it means: (1) "The whole of the Twelve Tribes; (2) Or the House of Judah alone as being a part of the Twelve Tribes; (3) Or the Ten-Tribed Kingdom."

Ten Tribed Israel Never Called Jews

Nothing can be more unscriptural than to call all Israelites "Jews;" it is as absurd as calling all Americans Californians. Most of Israelites are not Jews because they are the descendants of the other tribes of Israel. There is just as much reason for calling all Israelites "Danites" or "Gadites" or "Ephramites" as there is for calling them Judahites or "Jews." It is just as reasonable to call all "Jews" "Danites" as it is to call all "Danites" "Jews." The term Jew is never used until more than a thousand years after Abraham. It appears for the first time in II Kings 16:6, where we are told that the King of Israel, together with the King of Assyria, made war against the King of Judah. Now since in this passage Israel, one Kingdom, made ware against the Jews, another Kingdom, how can they both be the Jews? The Scriptures never once refer to the Ten-Tribed House of Israel as "The Jews;" neither past, present, nor future. The term "The Jews" is never, in God's Word, applied to the 12 Tribes, collectively, or to the Ten-Tribed House of Israel.

Bishop J. A. Allen of California, speaking of this modern confusion which we are discussing writes: "For ecclesiastical writers to ignore the national and racial representative Israelitish names of Joseph, Ephraim, and Samaria (The name of Israel's former capital city, as used in history and prophecy,) and to substitute "The Jews" either as a name or as a people, calling them the sole representatives of Israel's race, is not only the height of ignorance, but THE GREAT ECCLESIASTICAL CRIME OF THE AGES. Truly an enemy hath done this."

In Jeremiah 13:11, nearly 400 years after the tribes were divided by God into the two kingdoms, "The Whole House of Israel" and "The Whole House of Judah" are both spoken of in the same verse, proving that neither House without the other constitutes all of the Lord's chosen people. "The Whole House of Judah" are not all of the Lord's people, and "The Whole House of Israel" are not all of the Lord's people. It takes "The Whole House of Israel" together with "The Whole House of Judah" to make all of God's chosen people; and comparatively few of these are Jews. This text proves conclusively that there is a people called the "Whole House of Israel" of which the "Whole House of Judah" is regarded as neither part nor parcel. The Holy Spirit has never either in Biblical history or prophecy, called the 10 Tribed House of Israel "Jews". They have never been called "Jews" except by uninformed and unscriptural teachers.

Birthright People Are Not Jews

The fact that Jacob's two wives, Leah and Rachel, are spoken of as "building the House of Israel," of necessity divides the immediate household of Jacob into "two families." In Jeremiah 33:24 they are spoken of as "the two families which the Lord hath chosen." The Covenant promise of the BIRTHRIGHT was given to one of these families, and that of the SCEPTRE to the other family. Rachel was to be

233

the mother of "thousands of millions" while Leah was to be the mother of royalty. Genesis 49:10 shows us that Judah represents the SCEPTRE family; and I Chronicles 5:2 tells us "THE BIRTHRIGHT is Joseph's." Never try to apply a BIRTHRIGHT blessing to the Jews. Judah and the Jews were excluded from the BIRTHRIGHT promises, Joseph from the SCEPTRE. The BIRTHRIGHT people are not, and are never in the Scriptures called Jews.

In Ezekiel the 37th chapter we are told that "the two sticks" which are still separate, but which are yet to be reunited, represent Judah on the one hand, and Joseph and the "House of Israel" on the other. One of these sticks represents the SCEPTRE people and the other the BIRTHRIGHT people. Judah, the inheritor of the SCEPTRE, is only a half bother to Joseph, the inheritor of the BIRTHRIGHT. The SCEPTRE and the BIRTHRIGHT inheritors are "two-families" with different mothers. How could the distinction between the SCEPTRE and the BIRTHRIGHT families Judah and Israel be more emphatic?

Israel Distinct From Judah

Unless we see the distinction between the "House of Israel" and the "House of Judah" from the time of the division till the final and glorious reunion of the Two Houses, which will take place at the end of the "latter days," the prophecies concerning Israel cannot be understood. From the time of the division into two kingdoms until now, Judah and Israel have remained absolutely distinct. They were carried into captivity separately, at different times and by different nations, because Israel was taken into captivity by the Assyrians, 721 B.C. (II Kings 17:6); while Judah was carried into captivity 133 years later by the Babylonians 588 B.C. (II Kings 25:21). A portion of Judah returned after 70 years, as had been predicted (Ezra 2:1), but Israel never returned, nor was there any prediction that she would return until the final, glorious, restoration in the near future. All the prophecies were written after the division of the tribes into two nations; and these prophecies give the whole future of Israel as entirely distinct from Judah.

The great Jewish historian Josephus, writing from Rome in the year 70 A.D. which was nearly 800 years after Israel was taken into captivity by the Assyrians says: "The entire body of the 10 Tribes are still beyond the Euphrates, an immense multitude not to be estimated by number." It is estimated that there were 50 million in Israel at the time of the division, and this was 800 years later.

Rev. Canon Faucett M.A. says in his "Critical and Expository Bible Encyclopedia" The idea that the House of Israel has been amalgamated and incorporated with the "Jews," is one of the most amazing errors in Biblical History.

The prophets write of Israel and Judah still being separate people in "the latter days," or the days of the Gospel dispensation. In the 37th chapter of Ezekiel is a prophecy yet to be fulfilled. God promising to unite the stick of Joseph, representing the House of Israel with the stick of Judah, and make them one stick in His hand. This and many other Scriptures require that Israel and Judah be kept separate until this union which has not yet taken place.

According to the prophet Hosea, the House of Israel in the last days was to become as the sands of the sea for number, before their reunion with the House of Judah, and their return, representatively, to Palestine (Hosea 1:10, 11). Also Jeremiah writes: "When ye be multiplied and increased in the land in those days...the House of Judah shall walk with the House of Israel and they shall come together out of the land of the north, to the land that I gave for an inheritance unto your Fathers" (Jer. 3:16-18).

In Jeremiah 30:3, 4 we have a prophecy yet to be fulfilled concerning the uniting of the two Houses. Here we read: "For the days come, saith the Lord, that I will bring again the captivity of MY PEOPLE Israel and Judah; and I will cause them to return to the land that I gave to their fathers and they shall possess it. And these are the words that the Lord spake concerning Israel and concerning Judah." Here God calls Israel and Judah "My People Israel and Judah." So if Judah, the Jews, are the people of the Lord, then the Lord has a people besides the Jews whom He calls Israel and who are not counted among the Jews.

Long before the division took place, Moses, while prophesying unto the seed of Jacob, cried out: "Hear, Lord, the voice of Judah and bring him unto his people: (Deut. 33:7). This plainly shows that Judah was to be separated from his people and finally brought back to them. And the Scriptures tell us that shall not be until at the end of "the last days."

No Evidence For Amalgamation Theory

Orthodox Jews, even to this day, know that they do not represent the Ten-Tribed House of Israel. On the day of the Feast of Trumpets and on the Day of Atonement, they include in their prayer Jeremiah 31:20, and pray that Ephraim Israel (the Ten-Tribes) may be united with them. If we had time, we could quote from the testimony of Jewish scholars, and from their literature, showing that they know they are not representatives of the Ten-Tribed House of Israel. We have quotations from the "Jewish Encyclopedia," "The Jewish Religion," "The Jewish Chronicle," Rabbi Gershom, Prof. Neubauer, "The History and Literature of the Israelites," "The Jewish Quarterly Review," etc. The Rabbi Dr. Hertz, of London, says: "People known at present as Jews are descendants of the Tribes of Judah and Benjamin...we look forward to the gathering of all the Tribes at some future date." The learned Isaac Leiser says that "The Israelitish nation was left in banishment after the return of the Jews from Babylon." Professor Neubauer wrote: "The hope of the return of the ten tribes has never ceased among the jews in exile." Josephus, a Jew, and loyal to Jewish history and tradition, wrote about 70 A.D. or about 800 years after the captivity of Ten-Tribed Israel as follows: "The 10 Tribes did not return to Palestine; only two Tribes served the Romans after Palestine became a Roman province."

Jeremiah prophesied that only they who were taken by Nebuchadnezzar to Babylon were to return. Then the historical fulfillment of that prophecy must see only a return of those taken to Babylon. Both Ezra and Nehemiah testify to the fact that historically only those taken by Nebuchadnezzar to Babylon did return (Ezra Chapter 2: Nehemiah Chapter 7).

The return to Palestine of the 10 Tribes at any time in the past is contrary to Kings and Chronicles, contrary to Ezra, Nehemiah, Zechariah, Jerome and Josephus, and to history. In the prophecy that the "Two Sticks," Judah, and the House of Israel will become "one nation in the land upon the mountains of Israel; and one King (the Lord Jesus Christ) shall be King to them all" we have Divine proof that the two Houses are still separate, because Christ is not reigning over them as King at the present time.

In connection with the return of the Jews from Babylon, Nehemiah says: "I saw Jews that had married wives of Ashdod, and of Ammon, and of Moab," (Nehemiah 13:23). Ezra declares the same fact, naming the Hittites as among those with whom marriages were consummated. In Ezra 9:1 - Ezra says "They have taken of their daughters for themselves, and for their sons: so that the holy seed has mingled themselves with the people of those lands: yea, the hands of the princes and rulers hath been chief in this trespass." You can see how the facial expressions of all the descendants of these intermarriages would differ from that of the pure descendants of Judah, and still more from the BIRTHRIGHT TRIBES who were only half brothers of Judah to begin with.

236

When Jesus told the Jews in his day that he would go where they could not find Him, though they should seek for Him, the Jews, knowing of Israel still in dispersion, inquired: "Will He go to the dispersed among the Gentiles? (John 7:35). This passage shows that the Jews knew that the Ten Tribes were still in dispersion among the Gentiles.

God divided the Abrahamic promises among Jacob's twelve sons, and when He said through Jacob that Ephraim's "Seed shall become a multitude of nations." He was not referring to the Jews who never have or ever will be "a multitude of nations," God was speaking to the BIRTHRIGHT heirs. The "Nation and a Company of Nations" promised in Gen. 35:11 was a BIRTHRIGHT BLESSING TO BE FULFILLED" in the last days before Christ's Return (Gen. 49:1) to Joseph and his descendants (I Chron. 5:1), none of which are Jews. In Jer. 31:9, God said, "Ephraim is My firstborn," and in Gen. 48:19, Jacob said of Ephraim, "His seed shall become a multitude of nations" - just the opposite of what was said of Judah - "He shall become a remnant." That this promise to Israel was not to Judah is proven by the fact that Judah has never been a multitude of nations, and never will be. And so, more than 2,000 times God refers to Israel when what He says has no more to do with the Jews than with the Germans, or the Italians or the Chinese, or the Russians. On the other hand, the word "Jew" is mentioned 265 times, and in no instance does it refer to the Northern Kingdom of Israel or to any of their descendants.

The Amalgamation Theory Receives No
Support From Holy Scripture

The book of Micah plainly teaches that the Jews who "halted" were to become "A remnant," while Israel "that was cast far off," was to become "a strong nation" (Micah 4:7). The bringing together of these "two families" is to be associated with the Kingdom-Age. Till then, they would be separate. Some errors are slow in dying but this amalgamation-assumption which falsifies hundreds of Scriptures is now only lingering upon its death bed.

It is important to notice that neither the Major nor the Minor Prophets appear in the Old Testament until about 200 years after the division of the Twelve Tribes into two nations. What then did they find was the condition of God's chosen race? Was there any sign of amalgamation among them? Not a scintilla. The prophets found them still divided into two nations; as separate as France and Italy, or Britain and America. They had separate Kings, separate administrations, separate national alliances, and of course, separate national titles. The National title of the Ten Tribes was "Israel," or "Ephraim," because the Tribe of Ephraim had become the Tribe of the Birthright owing to the sin of Reuben. We have seen that the national title of the other two tribes was "Judah," a remnant of which were later called "The Jews."

It was during this state of affairs that the prophets commenced their ministry - some residing in the territory of Israel, and others in that of Judah. The Prophets addressed these two nations by the names that God gave them - "Israel" being the title which the Northern Nation had decided to retain; and "Judah" being the title which the Southern Nation had decided to assume. Hence we find that all through their writings, whether of warning, of rebuking, or directing, or consoling; and whether their words were historical or prophetical, the prophets recognized the separate condition of the Two Nations, and accordingly addressed them by their chosen and well-known national titles.

Ten Tribed Israel a Non-Jewish People

The separation into the Two Nations took place many years before any of the major or minor prophets wrote; therefore, the "Israel" known to Isaiah, Jeremiah, Ezekiel, the minor prophets, our Lord, the evangelists, and the apostles, had no Tribe of Judah in it. Israel, as known to all of these writers, was a non-Jewish people. Israel has remained a non-Jewish people to this day. The amalgamation theory is hopelessly discredited in the presence of the Bible. The closing books of Bible history leave Israel and Judah in separation from each other, while Bible prophecy keeps them separated until reconciled and united in the Kingdom-Age, and are dwelling representatively in the Holy Land under the personal reign of the Lord Jesus Christ, their welcomed and Crowned Messiah.

Hosea's statement that Israel shall be "as the sand of the sea which cannot be measured nor numbered" is not made concerning Judah (Hosea 1:10). In the first chapter we read "Then shall the children of Judah and the children of Israel be gathered together, and appoint themselves one head, and they shall come up out of the land: for great shall be the day of Jezreel." Did the two nations of captives "gather together" and amalgamate while in the land of their captivities? Did they "together appoint themselves one head" when the small remnant of Judah returned from Babylon? Both Ezra and Nehemiah, who were the historians of the Babylonian return, inform us that this was not the case.

That this uniting of Judah and Israel did not take place when the remnant of Judah returned after the Babylonian captivity, is clearly proved by Jeremiah's prophecy in the third chapter where we are told that "The House of Judah shall walk with the House of Israel and they shall "come together out of the land of the North to the land that I have given for an inheritance unto your fathers" (Jer. 3:18). Nothing like this has yet taken place. The 17th verse of this chapter shows us that when Israel and Judah unite, Jerusalem will be so fully under Divine truth and influence that she will be called "The Throne of Jehovah." This shows us that this uniting of the Two Houses has not yet taken place, and when it does it will not be a Jewish Nation. It will be the Israel Nation.

Of this reunion of Israel and Judah, Jeremiah in the 50th chapter and 4th verse says, "In those days, and in that time, saith the Lord, the children of Israel shall come, they and the children of Judah together: They shall go on their way weeping, and shall seek the Lord their God." It was not in "the former days" but at the end of "the latter days" [after the "seven times" or 2520 years punishment of both Houses has run out] that this is prophesied to take place; and if Israel is already amalgamated with Judah - this and other prophecies can never be fulfilled. Jeremiah goes on to say in the 20th verse, "In those days, and in that time, saith the Lord, the iniquity of Israel shall be sought for, and there shall be none; and the sins of Judah, and they shall not be found; for I will pardon them whom I leave as a remnant." We all know that such a return and union of Israel and Judah has never yet taken place.

Return "Together Out of the Land of the North"

According to the amalgamation theory, which has no support of the Scripture, Israel would have gone south to join Judah instead of Judah going north to join Israel for Jeremiah says "In those days, "The House of Judah shall walk with the House of Israel, and they shall come together out of the land of the north to the land that I have given for an inheritance unto your fathers." We know that this has never yet happened. This is not true even of Judah's return from Babylon. They returned from the south. When Israel and Judah become "one nation in the land upon the mountains of Israel, they are to have one King and be no more two nations" says Ezekiel (37:22). That this uniting of Israel and Judah was not in the past is again proven by the fact that the Jews have never had a King since they went into Babylonian captivity. As a matter of undeniable fact, there never has been, to this very day, a Davidic King reigning in the Holy Land from the year B.C. 586, when the temple was destroyed, and the House of Judah was carried away captive to Babylon. Anyhow it was not of any human monarch that Ezekiel wrote when his prophetic vision spanned the gulf of ages, and he beheld the glories of the Crowned Redeemer and of His ransomed, restored, and united Israel. Ezekiel had reference to Him of whose Second Coming we read; "And He hath on His vesture and on His thigh a name written: KING OF KINGS AND LORD OF LORDS" (Rev. 19:16).

And then, I ask, did the returned captives abide in the land "forever"? The prophet tells us that when Israel and Judah are reunited, their descendants were to be in perpetual occupation of the land. We know that this has never taken place because the Jews were suddenly driven out in A.D. 70, and have been wanderers for 18 centuries. This shows again that the Ten Tribes did not go back with the Jews when they returned from Babylon.

Jerome was one of the most eminent of the early fathers of the Church. He wrote, in the 4th century, which was more than a thousand years after Ten Tribed Israel went into captivity as follows: "Unto this day, the ten Tribes are subject to the Kings of Persia" -- "The Ten Tribes inhabit at this day the cities and mountains of the Medes." He knew that Israel had not returned to Judah, that the ten tribes were still separated from the Jews.

Ezra, in the 2nd chapter and the 1st verse, shows us that those who returned to Jerusalem were all from one "province." This word is in the singular. This is proof that the House of Israel who were captive not in this "province," but in another country, did not return.

In the book of Ezra, which mentions the two tribes that returned, none of the Ten Tribes were listed. And in the book of Nehemiah, which says that only Judah and Benjamin returned, none of the ten tribes are mentioned.

In Zechariah the 10th chapter, which was written 18 years after the Jews had returned from Babylon, the prophet shows that when he wrote, the Two Houses of Israel and Judah were still separate. And then all His prophecies concerning Israel require that they shall be kept separate from Judah as a people until their future uniting. On page 500 of the Scofield Bible, Dr. Scofield says, "The two Kingdoms are to be reunited in the future Kingdom" and then cites a number of Scriptures to prove the assertion.

The amalgamation-theory is hopeless. It is a mere assumption. All who hold that theory will have to abandon it if they follow the testimony of Holy Scripture. If they adhere to their theory they will be in conflict with the Word of God, and with all the historical facts. Their theory breaks down at every point. None of those who hold that Israel was amalgamated with the Jews can tell you when the amalgamation took place. Just so the Scriptures, which require that Israel shall be a great military power in the last days, cannot be applied to the Jews; and they are not applicable to Israel during the Millennium when there will be no wars. These promises are pre-millennial, and not consistent with millennial times.

The many Scriptures also which require that Israel in these last days shall be a maritime people "whose seed shall be in many waters" cannot be applied to the Jews; but they apply perfectly to the BIRTHRIGHT section of Isaac's descendants to whom the promises were made.

We have seen in other broadcasts that Jerusalem was trodden down of the Gentiles exactly "seven times" or 2520 years to the very day. Obadiah in the 17th verse speaks of the soldiers under General Allenby, who delivered Jerusalem from the Turks on the exact day and in the exact manner in which God says Jerusalem would be delivered, as belonging to the House of Jacob (verse 17). The next verse shows us what part of "The House of Jacob" they were - "The House of Joseph." And the next verse shows what part of the House of Joseph they were - "Ephraim;" and in the same verse He speaks of them as "the children of Israel." Also in Ezekiel 25:14 God shows us that it would be Israel who would drive out the Turks and end the "treading down of the Gentiles" in Palestine. To insist that these Scriptures addressed to Israel are to be applied to the Jews is to call the soldiers of General Allenby Jews.

Thus, you see that if we were to discuss each of the hundreds of Bible references to Israel as distinct from the Jews, it would furnish matter for a large volume.

In the authorized daily prayer book of the United Hebrew Congregation of the British Empire, there are three prayers which they pray for Israel as distinct from themselves. They pray both for "Judah" and "Israel." In one of these prayers they speak of Ephraim-Israel as "our brethren." Dr. V. Herman Adler, who in the past was chief rabbi of the Jewish Church in England, wrote: "The Ten Tribes did not return to the Holy Land."

In this discussion over the air, we have given you but a small part of the Biblical and historical proof of the distinction between Israel and Judah. We have scarcely touched upon the many wonderful prophecies concerning "Israel" which have no reference to the Jews, nor upon those relating to "Judah" which have no reference to Israel. To discuss these even briefly would furnish material for a good sized book.

For instance, to apply to the Jews the many Scriptures which require that the descendants of Ephraim shall be "a multitude (or Commonwealth) of Nations" (Gen. 48:19) in these "last days," before the

241

union of the Two Houses, Judah and Israel, would be equivalent to saying that the only "Commonwealth of Nations" on earth today are Jews. The Anglo-Saxon Nations are Isaac's sons or Saxons, but they are not Jews. Only one of the twelve Tribes are descendants of Judah. The Promise of "A Multitude of Nations" was made to Ephraim, not to Judah. Again, Gen. 48:19 shows us that two great rival nations were to spring from Joseph "in the last days." To insist on applying this Scripture to the Jews, is equivalent to calling these great rival nations Jews.

****

Publisher's note: Among many modern day Bible teachers there is a lack of proper understanding concerning the distinction between the House of Israel and the House of Judah. As a result of this wrong historical understanding, the popular theories of 'Dispensationalism' and 'prophetic' Futurism have created a false hope and a misguided allegiance among millions of God's people.

****

Fred Francis (F. F.) Bosworth was a pioneer evangelist in the ministry of divine healing during most of the first half of the 20th century. He also had a profound understanding of the Holy Scriptures and was a believer in the Anglo-Israel message as stated in his sermon contained in this booklet. The following is a comment by Evangelist Bosworth written in 1952 concerning his ministry of proclaiming Jesus Christ as both Savior and Healer.

"For more than thirty years during great evangelistic campaigns, I have overworked, praying for the sick and afflicted. During fourteen years of this time, we conducted the National Radio Revival during which time we received about a quarter of a million letters, most of them containing prayer requests from sick and suffering people who could not have recovered without the direct action of the Holy Spirit in response to the "prayer of faith". We have received multiple thousands of unsolicited testimonies from those who have been miraculously healed of every bodily affliction I know anything about, including leprosy. To God be all the glory because these results are impossible to anyone but Him. As a result of these miracles, many thousands have been joyfully converted, whom we would have missed had we not preached the healing part of the gospel once a week in all our evangelistic campaigns."

The following are typical testimonials that were written by pastors concerning the ministry of Evangelist Bosworth.

"Neither shall we forget the precious teaching of that Apostle of Faith, Rev. Bosworth, which played an important part in each campaign, in creating and stimulating trust in the Great Physician. Again and again, under his ministry, we saw deaf spirits cast out and eardrums recreated. No case of sickness daunted the enthusiastic faith of this veteran warrior. He labored unceasingly and we certainly learned to love him."
Pastor A. H. Cooper

"The constructive teaching on Divine healing given by Brother F. F. Bosworth whom we regard as a 20th century pioneer of the ministry of the miraculous, inspired and established the faith of many. His undaunted faith in prayer for deaf mutes and the results which followed became an incentive to thousands to trust God for their healing."
Pastor John F. Wooderson

Queen Victoria
Heir To King David's Royal Throne

Rev. Charles Fox Parham
1873-1929

American Pentecostal Pioneer, Pastor and Prolific Author Confirms the Truth of God's Word in Tracing the Biblical, Genetic Connection of the Royalty of Great Britain to the Throne of King David

INTRODUCTION
By Charles A. Jennings

Of all the spiritual revivals that have taken place on the American Continent, none has been so influential, far- reaching and enduring as the Pentecostal Spirit-outpouring of the early 20th century. There were earlier revivals such as the mid-eighteenth century First Great Awakening of New England and the Second Great Awakening of the Midwest at the turn of the nineteenth century. They helped to preserve the moral and spiritual standards of Biblical Christianity in the American people in preparation of greater things to come. One of the most phenomenal and sovereign spiritual awakenings ever to occur in American history is the spiritual revival which took place among the Southern Army during the war years of 1861-1865. The fruits of this revival eventually spawned the establishment, growth and expansion of more churches, Bible schools, camp meetings and evangelistic efforts than any previous revival. As a natural result, this created the perfect climate for the Holiness revival which was soon to follow in the 1880's and 1890's. These revivals of the past were not the only thing that God had in store for the Body of Christ that would revolutionize the lives of millions, both at home and abroad.

Soon after the turn of the twentieth century, an event would take place in the very heartland of America that would be both miraculous and most influential upon the institution of the modern church. That event would be the outpouring of the Holy Spirit in fulfillment of the words of the prophet Joel (2:28-29) and the affirmation of the Apostle Peter as recorded in Acts 2:14-18.

Whenever the history of the latter-day spiritual outpouring is studied, the Rev. Charles F. Parham is most likely always considered as being the father of the modern Pentecostal movement. At the age of nine years old, Parham felt a divine call to the ministry and soon had a strong attraction to Christian evangelism. He was converted to Christ in a Congregational Church and in 1890 entered Southwest Kansas College for three years. He pastored a Methodist church for two years from 1893-1895 before joining the Holiness movement and opening the Bethel Healing Home in Topeka, Kansas in 1898. Here he began publishing his bi-monthly Holiness journal, entitled "THE APOSTOLIC FAITH."

After some time of further research into the Holiness movement and earnestly seeking for a greater personal manifestation of spiritual power, Parham returned to Topeka in September 1900. Here he opened a Bible school in an old mansion, where he encouraged the students to seek for a greater spiritual experience as recorded in the Book of Acts. One of the students, Agnes Ozman, received the expected blessing and spoke in 'tongues' as a sign of its reception. This greatly encouraged Parham and the rest of the student body and within a few days he and about half of the students testified as to receiving the "Baptism of the Holy Spirit."

A similar revival experience occurred in Galena, Kansas in 1903. From there, Parham went to Houston, Texas and held a ten-week training session which fanned the flames of the Pentecostal message throughout Texas. Soon afterward, the outpouring in Los Angeles, California occurred and quickly spread throughout the country. Among all the early leaders of the modern Pentecostal movement, Charles F. Parham is credited with formulating classical Pentecostal theology and is recognized as being its principle pioneer and founder.

As early as 1899 or before, Parham had recognized and was teaching the truth of the Christian Anglo-Israel message of the Bible.

He earnestly contended for this truth until his death in 1929. As late as two years before his death, he published an article in *"THE*

246

APOSTOLIC FAITH" magazine of July 1927 affirming his belief in this truth and encouraging his readers to accept it as being a part of the Full-Gospel message. The following are the opening and closing paragraphs of that article entitled, *"The Ten Lost Tribes."*

"I want to write a short sketch to introduce to our readers one of the most important topics of the day, commonly known as Anglo-Israel, or The Ten Lost Tribes. I do not think that any Full Gospel preacher ought to longer delay in acquainting himself with this subject as I believe it belongs with the Full Gospel Message and that the message of the last days must include this subject or we are not preaching the Full Gospel.

"Now, if the reader will carefully read Jacob's blessings upon his children for the last days, and all the prophecies concerning Israel in the Old Testament, knowing they refer to the above named nations (ie: Anglo-Saxondom) and belong to us as a people, (ie: Protestants) the Old Testament will become a new book to you full of vital importance and interest."

The following article entitled, *"Queen Victoria's Descent From Adam,"* was published in *"THE APOSTOLIC FAITH"* magazine of March 22, 1899.

On the following pages are facsimiles of this article and of the masthead of Parham's magazine.

QUEEN VICTORIA'S DESCENT FROM ADAM

The following genealogy was first studied by Rev. F. R. A. Glover, M.A., of London, in 1861, but no depths of facts were reached, when others took it up, until Mr. J. C. Stevens, of Liverpool, compiled this evidence which resulted in bringing to light the wonderful fact that God has proved His oath to David that he would never want for an heir to sit on the throne, and infidelity is nonplused.

This, then, was discovered to be no new fact; that the Saxon kings had done the same was found in MS, in Herald College, London, and in Sharon Miner's History of Anglo-Saxons, vol. I.

At the capture of Jerusalem Zedekiah was taken to Babylon and died there, but Jeremiah, his father-in-law, fled with the heir to the throne, Tea Tephi, to Egypt, and when Egypt fell fled on board a ship carrying tin from Britain, and thus reached Ireland, and there died.

"In the following genealogy those who reigned have K fixed to their names. The dates after private names refer to their *birth* and *death*; those after sovereign's names to their *accession* and *death*. Wherever known, the wives have been mentioned. Besides those mentioned in Genesis, some have been obtained from Polano ("The Talmud." London, 1877.) b, and d. stand for *born* and *died*."

ADAM TO VICTORIA

Generations

1. Adam, b c 4000, 3070, Eve.
2. Seth, b c 3870, 2978
3. Enos, b c 3765, 2860
4. Cainan, b c 3675, 2765
5. Mahalaleel, b c 3605, 2710
7. Enoch, b c 3378, 3013
8. Methusaleh, b c 3313, 2344
9. Lamech, b c 3126, 2344
10. Noah, b c 2944, 2006, Naamah
11. Shem, b c 2442, 2158
12. Arphaxad, b c 2342, 1904
13. Salah, b c 2307, 2126
14. Heber, b c 2277, 2187
15. Peleg, b c 2243, 2004
16. Reu, b c 2213, 2026
17. Serug, b c 2181, 2049
18. Nahor, b c 2052, 2003
19. Terah, b c 2122, 2083, Amtheta
20. Abraham, b c 1992, 1817, Sarah

248

21. Isaac, b c 1896, 1716, Rebekah
22. Jacob, b c 1837, 1690, Leah
23. Judah, b c 1753, Tamar
24, Hezron
25. Aram
26. Aminadab
27. Naashon
28. Salmon
29. Boaz, b c 1312, Ruth
30. Obed
31. Jesse

KINGS OF ISRAEL

32. K David, b c 1085, 1015, Bathsheba
33. K Solomon, b c 1003, 975 Naamah
34. K Rehoboam, b c 1016, d 958, Maacah
35. K Abijam, b c 958, 955
36. K Asa, b c 955, 914, Azubah
37. K Jehosaphat, b c 914, 889
38. K Jehoram, b c 889, 885, Athaliah
39. K Ahaziah, b c 906, 884; Zibiah
40. K Joash, b c 885, 839, Jehoaddan
41. K Amaziah, b c 864, d 810, Jecholiah
42. K Uzziah, b c 826, d 758, Jerushah
43. K Jotham, b c 783, d 742
44. K Ahaz, b c 787, d 726, Abi
45. K Hezekiah, b c 751, d 698, Hephzibah
46. K Manasseh, b c 710, d 643, Meshullemeth
47. K Amos, b c 621, d 641, Jedidah
48. K Josiah, b c 649, d 610, Hamutah
49. K Zedekiah, b c 578, 599

KINGS OF IRELAND

50. K Heremon, b b c 580, Tea Tephi
51. K Irail, Foidh reigned 10 years
52. K Ethraill, reigned 20 years
53. Follain
54. K Tighermas, reigned 50 years
55. Eanbotha

56. Smiorguil
57. K Fiachadh Labhraine, reigned 24 years
58. K Aongus Ollmuchaidh, reigned 21 years
59. Maoin
60. K Rogheachta, reigned 25 years
61. Dein
62. K Siorna Saoghalach, reigned 21 years
63. Oholla Olchaoin
64. K Giallchadh, reigned 9 years
65. K Aodhain Glas, reigned 22 years
66. K Simeon Breac, reigned 6 years
67. K Muireadach Bolgrach, reigned 4 years
68. K Fiachadh Tolgrach, reigned 7 years
69. K Duach Laidrach, reigned 10 years
70. Eochaidh Buaigllorg
71. K Ugaine More the Great, reigned 30 years
72. K Cobhthach Coalbreag, reigned 30 years
73. Meilage
74. K Jaran Gleofathach, reigned 7 years
75. K Coula Cruaidh Cealgach, reigned 4 years
76. K Oiliolla Caisfhiachach, reigned 25 years
77. K Eochaidh Foltleathan, reigned 11 years
78. K Aongus Tuirmheach Teamharch, reigned 30 years
79. K Eana Aighneach, reigned 28 years
80. Labhra Suire
81. Blathucta
82. Eassamhuin Eamhua
83. Roighnein Ruadh
84. Finlogha
85. Fian
86. K Eodchaidh Feidhlioch, reigned 12 years
87. Fineamhuas
88. Lughaidh Raidhdearg
89. K Criomthan Niadhnar, reigned 16 years
90. Fearaidhach Fion-Feachtnuigh
91. K Fiachadh Fionoluidh, reigned 20 years
92. K Tuathal Teachtmar, reigned 30 years
93. K Coun Ceadchathach, reigned 20 years
94. K Arb Aonflier, reigned 30 years
95. K Cormae Usada, reigned 40 years
96. K Caibre Liffeachair, reigned 27 years

97. K Fiachadh Sreabthuine, reigned 30 years
98. K Muireadhach Tireach, reigned 30 years
99. K Eoachaidh Moigmeodhin, reigned 7 years
100. K Niall of the Nine Hostages
101. Eogan
102. K Muireadhach
103. Earca

KINGS OF ARGYLESHIRE

104. K Feargus More, a d 437
105. K Dongard, d 457
106. K Conran, d 535
107. K Aidan, d 604
108. K Eugene IV, d 622
109. K Donald IV, d 650
110. Dongard
111. K Eugene V., d 692
112. Findan
113. K Eugene VII, d a d 721, Spondau
114. K Etfinus, d a d 761, Fergina
115. K Achaius, d a d 819, Fergusia

SOVEREIGNS OF SCOTLAND

116. K Alpin, d 834
117. K Kenneth II., d 854
118. K Constantin II., d 874
119. K Donald VI, d 903
120. K Malcolm I., d 958
121. K Kenneth III, d 994
122. K Malcolm II, d 1033
123. Beatrix m. Thane Albanach
124. K Duncan I., d 1040
125. K Malcolm III Canmore, d 1055, 1093, Margaret of England
126. K David I, d 1153, Maud of Northumberland
127. Prince Henry, d 1153, Adama of Surry
128. Earl David, d 1219, Maud of Chester
129. Isabel m Robert Bruce III
130. Robert Bruce IV m Isabel of Gloucester

251

131. Robert Bruce V m Martha of Carriok
132. K Robert I. Bruce, d 1306, 1329, Mary of Burke
133. Margary Bruce m Walter Stewart III
134. K Robert II, d 1390, Euphonia of Ross, d 1376
135. K Robert II, d 1460, Arabella Drummond, d 1401
136. K James I, d 1424, 1437, Joan Beaufort
137. K James I, d 1406, Margaret of Gueldres, d 1463
138. K James III, d 1488, Margaret of Denmark, d 1484
139. K James IV, d 1543, Margaret of England, d 1539
140. K James V, d 1542, Mary of Lorraine, d 1560
141. Q Mary, d 1587, Lord Henry Darnley

SOVEREIGNS OF GREAT BRITAIN

142. K James VI and I, d 1603, 1625, Ann of Denmark
143. Princess Elizabeth, 1596, 1613, K Frederick of Bohemia
144. Princess Sophia m Duke Ernest of Brunswick
145. K George I., 1698, 1727, Sophia Dorothea Zelle,
     1667, 1726
146. K George II., 1727, 1760, Princell Caroline of Auspach,
     1683, 1737
147. Prince Frederick of Wales, 1707, 1751, Princess Augusta
     of Saxe-Gotha, 1744, 1818
148. K George III., 1760, 1820, Princess Sophia of
     Mecklenberg Strelitz
149. Duke Edward of Kent, 1767, 1820, Princess Victoria
     of Leinengen
150. Queen Victoria, b 1819, cr 1838, Prince Albert
     of Saxe-Coburg

"From this royal princess, we obtain, then, a direct and unbroken line of ancestry to King Fergus, who went from Ireland to reign as king of Scotland; and from King Fergus I. Of Scotland we get the same unbroken line to the time of King James of Scotland, who himself became king of England; and from King James we get the same unbroken line to our beloved Queen, she being, then, the seed royal to King David's house, and therefore the royal seed of King David; she is, and must be, the ruling monarch over the Ten Lost Tribes of Israel.

The Rev. Joseph Wild, D.D., says the old Irish histories say when Jeremiah landed in Ireland with Princess Tea Tephi, he took with him a stone which stone was known to have been in the temple at Jerusalem.

On this very stone all the monarchs in Ireland were crowned, until Fergus I., king of Scotland, who caused the same stone to be taken from Ireland to Scotland, and so were all the monarchs in Scotland crowned upon it, from Fergus to King James, after which it was brought to England; and so all the monarchs in England, from King James to our beloved Queen, have been crowned upon it, she being the last crowned upon this wonderful stone: so that for 2,450 years monarchs have been crowned upon this wonderful stone, which stone may be seen this very day under the coronation chair in Westminster Abbey, London. It received the names, Wonderful, the Precious Stone, Jacob's Stone and is now called Jacob's Stone. The Lord said Jacob's stone should be a pillar of witness that He would fulfill His promises to Israel. The stone was kept in the temple at Jerusalem as a witness, and from there was removed to Ireland, and then to Scotland, and now we have it as a witness in England. 'Joshua (xxiv, 27) said unto all the people, behold, 'this stone' shall be a witness unto us, for it hath heard all the words of the Lord, which he spake unto us; it shall be, therefore a witness unto you, lest ye deny your God.' I ask, why does this enlightened nation keep such a stone so many generations if there is no meaning in it? Why, because it must continue with the royal seed to be a witness that our Queen is the seed royal to King David's house, and her subjects are the Ten Lost Tribes of Israel.

Queen Victoria's peaceful, prosperous, successful reign for well nigh three-score years, has been almost phenomenal. Who next? Possibly the Prince of Wales for a turbulent time during the final war with Esau, and then possibly "A child shall lead them," since the next heir is a baby now. And then J*esus, who was born to this end.* "Thus saith the Lord God, Behold, I will take the children of Israel from among the heathen, whither they be gone, and will gather them on every side, and bring them into their *own land*; and I will make them one nation in the land upon the mountains of Israel; and ONE KING shall be king to them all, and *they shall be no more* TWO NATIONS, neither shall they be *divided into two kingdoms* any more at all."
". . . this is that which was spoken by the prophet Joel; And it shall come to pass in the last days, saith God, I will pour out of my Spirit upon all flesh: and your sons and your daughters shall prophesy, and your young men shall see visions, and your old men shall dream dreams: And on my servants and on my handmaidens I will pour out in those days of my Spirit; and they shall prophesy: . . ."
-- Acts of the Apostles 2:16-18

WHO GOD'S ANCIENT PEOPLE ISRAEL ARE

Frank Weston Sandford
1862-1948
Author, Publisher, Pastor, Evangelist, Bible School Founder
and Missions Visionary

Introduction
By Charles A. Jennings

As any honest student of Scripture would observe when considering the various aspects of the Kingdom God, throughout history God in His sovereignty has divinely hand-picked servants for strategic tasks in order to fulfill His plan at any given place and time. The same has been true throughout the history of the modern Christian church. Each of the Lord's servants has filled a specific need and performed his own particular service in the furtherance of revealed truth. One such servant of God was Frank Weston Sandford.

Sandford was born on October 2, 1862 in Bowdoinham, Maine and received his primary education at Nichols Latin School. On February 29, 1880, he had a genuine spiritual new birth experience through the transforming power of Jesus Christ. In 1886, he graduated from Bates College and then received one year of seminary training in Cobb Divinity School. With an intense spiritual hunger, he accepted the pastorate of the Free Baptist Church in Topham, Maine.

While pastoring in Grand Falls, New Hampshire in 1890, he accepted the Holiness teaching of Sanctification while attending a Methodist Campmeeting held in Old Orchard, Maine. Not long after that, he embraced the belief in divine healing through his contacts with the Christian Alliance. It was here that he became friends with A.B. Simpson and his associate, Dr. George B. Peck, a prominent physician who assisted Simpson in praying for the sick and who believed in the Anglo-Israel Message. He also attended summer schools led by Dwight L. Moody in Northfield, Maine. As a result, he became a member of Moody's *Student Volunteer Movement*. He soon became intensely interested in world missions. During the years 1893-1899, Sandford founded the *Holy Ghost and Us* Bible School, held evangelistic crusades, sought greater understanding concerning divine healing and produced a publication called *Tongues of Fire*. As part of a faith financed project he built a large Victorian structure and named it *Shiloh*. By 1904, there were some 600 residents in this new community.

Through his ministry, Sandford was instrumental in the training of many Holiness preachers who later became Pentecostal leaders, among whom were Charles F. Parham and A. J. Tomlinson. Parham was pivotal in the early days of the Pentecostal movement and Tomlinson was the central figure in the establishment of the large present day *Church of God* denomination of Cleveland , Tennessee in January 1906.

Sandford was a man of intense spiritual fervor for his Savior, Jesus Christ. In the fall of 1888 while in Niagara Falls he wrote his life long commitment to the work of the Gospel in order to rescue the souls of men for Christ, he said:

"Oh God, help me to do my part in keeping a poor lost world from the terrible rapids of sin, and that terrible fall which breaks over the edge of time and plunges the sinner into eternity. To this end I solemnly consecrate my every voluntary thought, word and deed. This one thing will I do, subject everything to one all-absorbing purpose – this world for Christ during my lifetime."

In studying the disciplined life and devoted ministerial work, rooted in his deep spiritual commitment to his Lord, it is evident that Frank Sandford was determined to follow the leading of the Holy Ghost. This he did in spite of misunderstanding from fellow Christians and even open opposition. He was committed in obedience to the teaching of the Holy Ghost even when 'revealed truth' was not popular or widely accepted. This was true in regard to his acceptance and teaching of the Anglo-Israel message of the Bible. While in the Holy Land for two weeks in

1898, after much prayer and fasting, Sandford was thoroughly convinced by the Holy Ghost of God's faithfulness in His promises to His Anglo-Israel people.

"The Kingdom" headquarters known as Shiloh

The following is a quote from Frank W. Sandford's biographer, Frank S. Murray's two books, *The Sublimity of Faith* and *All Israel Restored.*

"The mystery of what happened to the ten lost tribes of Israel had been engrossing the minds of Bible scholars for the last half century or more. When agnostics like Thomas Paine and Robert Ingersoll had turned against the Bible because God's promises to Israel manifestly had failed of fulfillment in the Jews, men of God had bestirred themselves to look around and find out why. Two schools of thought had arisen. The first and most prevalent had adopted the easy explanation that all the promises of material wealth and power had been spiritualized and fulfilled in the Christian Church. The other school, recognizing that such an answer left out a good part of the promises, had surmised that either they must have been fulfilled literally or else allowed to go by default.

"True children of God knew that even 'if we are faithless, He abideth faithful'; His promises simply could not be defaulted. Arguing from the integrity of God, they assumed that somewhere on earth a people had received not merely spiritual salvation, but material prosperity and power commensurate with the promises of Abraham, Isaac and Jacob. Since the greatest of such benefits had been predicted for the sons of Joseph, and since their tribes were among the ten lost to history, the next step was to ask what had happened to them. A complete Bible study and scrutiny of history such as this subject calls for is not possible here; suffice it to say that during the last half of the nineteenth century one Bible scholar after another came to the joyful conclusion that the lost ten tribes were to be found in the Anglo-Saxon people of the present, principally in England and America.

"Like most 'fundamentalists' of his time, Mr. Sandford in his Free Baptist days had scouted this idea as the rankest heresy. Once he stepped out from behind the protective shield of what some great 'doctor' has to say, however, and began to study the whole Bible for himself, he saw that Tom Paine was right. Either latter-day Israel would have to be a powerful 'nation and company of nations,' capable of 'pushing the peoples to the end of the earth' and 'possessing the gates of their enemies,' or the Bible - especially the Old Testament - was shot through with error.

"Sometime during the 1890's Mr. Sandford had come across the published studies of Professor Totten, a member of the Yale College faculty. This extraordinary genius had been in his youth a confirmed infidel, but on probing through the Bible, Ingersoll-fashion, seeking proof for his unbelief, he found himself thoroughly absorbed by the inspired record. Possibly he was affected also by earlier scholarship; nevertheless, he became convinced of the Anglo-Israel identity and saw that it cast light on hundreds of Bible statements that otherwise were hopelessly obscure. From that time on he devoted himself more and more to Bible study, until at last he retired from the Yale faculty to make the Word of God his full-time occupation. The *Putnam* (Connecticut) *Patriot* called him "the world's foremost authority on Scripture chronology"; he published a five foot shelf of books and pamphlets.

"In Mr. Sandford's view professor Totten was to Bible study what Galileo was to astronomy; the theologians who clung blindly to the old school, spiritualizing God's every promise of material prosperity to Israel were to him like the astronomers who insisted Ptolemy was right. The fantastic "cycles and epicycles" such men had to invent in order to maintain their position were far more of a strain to simple faith than the bold assertion that God meant exactly what He said. Mr. Sandford saw that Professor Totten's theories championed God's veracity, whereas the 'accepted' Old Testament interpretation did not. To be branded a heretic even as Galileo had been mattered little to him so long as he was on the track of truth.

"He was not alone in his conviction. Scores of eminent Bible students and thousands of spiritual Christians likewise were becoming convinced that the lost ten tribes of Israel were to be found in Britain, America, and a number of other smaller nations. The 'evidences' of this identity were far too numerous to be written off as coincidence. For these reasons, as we have noted, the 'Anglo-Israel truth' was standard fare for the Bible School from 1896 on.

"Their trip to Jerusalem made it doubly real to the two pilgrims. Audiences in Liverpool and in Charlton-cum-Hardy had received the teaching with gladness. Contacts with Britain's imperial might in her homeland, in Gibraltar, at Malta, and in Alexandria had inspired both men with the spiritual certainty of the Anglo-Israel truth. Whereas on his earlier visit to Jerusalem Mr. Sandford had written of himself as a Gentile, this time they were 'two Israelites' coming back to the land of their fathers.

"What could they do to spread this truth more widely? How could they protect their brethren from the slurs of sharp-minded infidels?

During their visit to Malta a Christian worker among the sailors had told them his experience of coming to the Anglo-Israel truth. One day an atheist had said to him with a sneer, 'You've got a great God! He never keeps His promises' - meaning those made to Israel. This apparently justifiable approach had set the Malta missionary to thinking, with the result that soon he rejoiced in the conviction that God's mighty promises to ancient Israel have not failed but been fulfill in England and America.

"Mr. Sandford and Mr. Gleason spent the eighteenth of July, 1898, fasting and praying in Jerusalem. As they were to separate the next day, they prolonged their fast through the night. The hours of darkness were occupied largely in writing a long public statement designed for the enlightenment of all who honored the Holy Ghost. The article that followed was 9,000 words long and must have taken far more than that one night to complete.

"What stands out most about this manifesto is its tone of authority. Where other men had been content to raise a question, Mr. Sandford pronounced an answer. The long array of Scriptures that he quoted were convincing indeed to any unprejudiced reader, but it was his own assurance that left no room whatever for doubt. He long ago had promised God not to preach on any subject that dealt in speculation; now he felt that the time for speculation about Anglo-Israel had come to an end. No longer was it a 'theory'; it was a 'truth.'

"Having examined the Old Testament predictions as to the latter day greatness of the ten tribes, and having proved that in no nations other than the Anglo-Saxon could these predictions be said to find fulfillment, [*Sandford wrote the following*, ed.]

WHO GOD'S ANCIENT PEOPLE ISRAEL ARE
By F. W. Sandford

Suppose a man should lose a horse in a certain field, and send out a person in search of the lost animal, with full description of the same; and suppose he found many horses which partly answered the description but none that perfectly did so, till finally he discovered one that answered the description in every respect. Would he not be warranted in declaring, "I have found him at last," and ending the search?

Before we answer this question as to who God's ancient people are, let us search the Scriptures to ascertain what God said they were to be. Confining ourselves principally to the Book of Genesis we shall find a full description of Israel "in the last days."

SEVEN-FOLD DESCRIPTION OF WHAT
ISRAEL IS TO BE IN SEVEN STRIKING DETAILS

1. Israel when found must be a great nation.
2. Israel was to be exceedingly multitudinous.
3. Israel as described in the Scriptures was to be irresistible in power.
4. Israel must be a royal nation among the nations.
5. Israel must be princely in character as well as regal in power and influence.
6. Israel in the last days was to possess God's special favor and blessing in every respect.
7. Israel was to be thus signally blessed in population, power, nobility of character, etc., for the one express purpose of acting for the Almighty as a world- wide herald of the Gospel.

The nation that we are looking for then must be great, multitudinous, powerful, predominant among the nations, princely in character, specially blessed of God, and a world-wide herald of the Gospel.

There is but one race on the face of the globe bearing all the above characteristics, and thus answering the required description. There is one race of people which in every respect meets the Scriptural requirements.

The blessing promised by the Almighty to Abraham passed to Isaac, thence to Jacob, thence to spiritual Israel, and being forfeited by the Jews passed to the ten tribes, and was especially to be wrought out through the tribe of Joseph, the dominant tribe among the ten tribes. Joseph, having received the double portion of the firstborn, became two tribes, Ephraim and Manasseh, proving the fulfillment of God's promise to Abraham, Isaac and Jacob that their descendants should be two-fold: one a great nation and the other a company of nations.

God said to His friend, "I will make of thee a great nation... and I will make nations of thee." And of Joseph's sons it was prophesied, "He (Manasseh) shall become a people, and he also shall be great, but his younger brother shall be greater than he. His seed shall become a multitude of nations."

The "great nation" and the "nations" promised to Abraham, then, found its fulfillment in Manasseh, who was to be "a great people," and his brother Ephraim, who was to be a "multitude of nations."

Now as you glance over the face of the earth what people comes to your mind as fulfilling the description that we have given? What people is great, ruling over a multitude of nationalities, unconquerable, feared and respected by other nations, dominant in influence among the great

260

nations of the earth, representing justice in law and high civilization, specially blessed temporally and spiritually, sending out missionaries to the ends of the earth, entering upon world-wide enterprises for the proclamation of the Gospel, holding the military strongholds of the earth, ruling over the sea, and owning colonies around the entire globe, thus "pushing the people together to the ends of the earth"?

What race do you think of as you read? Especially what two nations are the same blood? (For Ephraim and Manasseh were brothers.) The people we are seeking for must be two nations, yet one race. This requirement thrusts aside every nation on the European and Asiatic continents.

The United States of America is a "great" nation. England is a "greater" nation, ruling sixty colonies and three hundred fifty millions of people - a great and dominant power among the nations of this earth. These two, the "great" and "greater" nations are of the same blood, and in every particular meet the seven-fold description of the text.

NO OTHER TWO NATIONS ON THE GLOBE MEET THE DESCRIPTION. THESE TWO DO. OUR SEARCH IS ENDED. THE LOST IS FOUND.

Mr. Murray continues, "In the years that followed, Mr. Sandford and the movement he headed witnessed the spiritual power of this teaching. He had little patience with fundamentalist critics who tried to find fault with it. ' Oh, the blindness of the people who don't see we are Israel!' he cried a few years after his public declaration. "What are they going to do with the Scriptures?"

"That was just the point of issue. He knew that most critics of Anglo-Israel could not be honest with the plain statement of material prosperity promised to Israel in "the latter days." He saw that a careful scrutiny of the Bible combined with an attitude that refused to twist it by unnatural interpretation, left no choice but that of Anglo-Israel. Moreover, he was aware of the glorious warmth and vigor that flowed through all the prophetic writings for the student who understood this truth and could think, "They were talking to my own ancestors!" Through the Spanish American War, the Boer War, and both World Wars, Mr. Sandford would point to that otherwise impenetrable passage in Jeremiah where God says to Israel, "Thou art my battle-axe and weapons of war: and with thee will I break in pieces the nations..." (Jeremiah 51:20). He saw what so few Christians seem able to see, that God is not at all averse to showing His Hand in behalf of Abraham's blood descendants, even before the nations they comprise have been wholly converted.

"At the same time he recognized that there was not a case of Divine favoritism. It was not that Israel was superior, but simply that she had been chosen for special training. He applied to Britain and America the same adjective God used of Israel -"stiffnecked" - and considered people of all other races emphatically their equals as far as the Gospel is concerned.   In his opinion God had selected these nations not because they are necessarily any better, but because someone has to take responsibility and be trained to do so. "Mark my words," he would say, "it will be Israel first, then the Gentiles: it will be the hundred and forty-four thousand first, and then the countless multitude. That is the way God has chosen to work, and we had better work with God." And while he believed in foreign missions with all his heart, he also believed it of critical importance that Britons and Americans should realize who they were as they went to the mission field." (End of quote)

**This flag represented the twelve tribes of Israel
and the nations of the Gentiles**

BEHOLD HE COMETH
By Miss Sue Paine (1901)

These are days of restoration,
As the glorious time draws nigh,
When, "Behold! Behold, He cometh!"
Shall re-echo through the sky:
Now His herald is proclaiming
In prophetic tones and strong,
"Oh, prepare ye! Be ye ready!
For the King shall come 'ere long."

We have waited for the dawning,
Often peering through the gloom
Of this night of sin and darkness -
But 'tis breaking very soon;
And our hearts are taking courage
As His message now we hear;
"Oh prepare ye! 'Room for Jesus!'
He, the King, shall soon appear."

PASTORS ACCORDING TO MINE HEART

INTRODUCTION
By Charles A. Jennings

There have been many servants of the Lord throughout the history of the Christian Church who have made great contributions to the Lord's work, but are seemingly soon forgotten. As soon as twenty years after their passing from this mortal life, their ministry and deeds soon fade into oblivion. Every present day saint of God owes a debt of gratitude to those tireless saints of the past who labored to perpetuate the Gospel so that succeeding generations may hear the good news.

Many such men of God labored for the Gospel of Christ under severe adverse conditions. Some of them such as F. F. Bosworth suffered a physical beating to the extent he feared for his life. Others such as Luke Rader, built the big Gospel Tabernacle during hard economic times which necessitated him doing a large part of the physical labor himself. Throughout his ministry he took a firm stand against organized crime in his city which prompted the local crime boss to hire a hit man who fired a gun at Rader while he was preaching in his church one Sunday evening. Rader, along with many other well-known and unknown ministers of their day took an adamant public stand against the religious liberalism which was invading the ranks of the church. Their evangelistic efforts resulted in tens of thousands of genuine converts to Jesus Christ and the establishment of scores of local churches and mission works throughout the world. There have been many more such sincere servants of the Lord that could be mentioned that deserve rightful recognition. Yet it is doubtful if one in every thousand present day Christians have even heard the mention of their name. How soon we forget!

Due to the extreme popularity of certain religious beliefs of today, many Christians do not realize that these pet beliefs were not always accepted. Neither do they realize that some Biblical truths that today are widely rejected as heresy, were commonly accepted by many prominent ministers and thousands of Christian laymen of yesteryear.

One of the Biblical prophetic perspectives of yesteryear, yet rarely mentioned today is '*Historicism.*' Historicism sets forth the idea that the Book of Revelation, especially the events involving the judgment of the

265

seals, trumpets and vials, predicts events relating to the church, occurring from the First Century down to the present time. This has been the historic Protestant interpretation which was taught by the notable Protestant Reformers of the past. This viewpoint stands in sharp contrast to the modern day prophetic fallacy of *Futurism*.

Another Biblical, historical and prophetic viewpoint which is misunderstood, unstudied and widely rejected by the largely Biblically illiterate Christian public is the Anglo-Israel truth. This viewpoint sets forth the historical fact of the true identification of the Old Testament Israelites from the time of the Assyrian captivities (745-721 BC) in their migrations across Europe to their present day home in the Western World. These people are presently known as the Anglo-Saxon, Scandinavian and Germanic families which comprise the modern House of Israel. This Biblical perspective stands in sharp contrast to the fallacious belief that the modern Jewish people comprise the totality of all the twelve sons of Jacob. This Jewish-Israel theory has not always been accepted by all ministers, scholars and laymen of the past.

The ministers mentioned in this booklet and the other booklets of this series did not accept the Jewish-Israel theory. Even in their possible doctrinal differences, they all believed and taught the Anglo-Israel message of the Bible. This wonderful truth is hidden from the eyes of most Christians today, but as Frank Murray has said,; "Remember it is the glory of God to conceal a thing, especially when that thing is threatened by the god of this world."

In Frank Murray's book *"All Israel Restored,"* he shares a profound observation by J.B. Harriman. In Harriman's book *"Israel and The World Crisis"* he says, "We can conceive nothing more futile than to attempt to understand prophecy apart from the central theme of the Bible: the Israelite truth. The church has not taken Israel's place. The Jews are not the tribe of Joseph, with his birthright blessings and destiny. Those who reject the Anglo-Israel doctrine because it seems 'fanciful' are obliged to invent far more fanciful theories to explain how the church or the Jews can possibly inherit the promises made to the ten tribes."

Frank W. Sanford once wrote, "Oh, the blindness of those who don't see that we [the Anglo-Saxon people] are Israel. What are they going to do with the Scriptures?"

AARON MERRITT HILLS 1848-1935

Dr. A.M. Hills was one of the few spiritual giants of the holiness movement in the late nineteenth and early twentieth centuries. He was not only a spiritual leader, but an educational leader that led the movement in establishing its educational institutions that still exist today. He was born on February 4, 1848 in a log house built by his father in the Dowagiac settlement of southwest Michigan.  He descended from a long line of devout and committed Christians dating back to his ancestral family of Kent, England.

During those days while living in that rural community there were many physical hardships to endure. When only three years old, A.M. Hills' mother came down with malaria and suffered for six months with uncertainty of life. When his mother was certain she was dying, wrote a letter to her small son, sealed it in an envelope, to be opened when he was ten years old. This letter revealed how his Godly mother had dedicated her son to Jesus Christ and to preach His Gospel. His mother did recover and lived to the age of seventy-eight years.

A.M., as he later was known, accepted the challenge of his mother for a reward of one dollar, read the Bible through between his seventh and eighth birthdays. As a small boy, when the family attended a Baptist revival, he was converted to Christ along with two of his siblings. He had three opportunities given him by his mother's brothers to enter a career with very lucrative businesses. Each time, he was providentially kept from being side-tracked from the divine call of ministry that was on his life. In 1867, after completing high school, he entered Oberlin College. It was there where he received much that would prepare him for years as a minister, educator and author. While at Oberlin College, A.M. was further influenced toward Arminian theology and away from the Calvinism of his father's family and the Congregational Church of his earlier years.

Charles G. Finney was in his last year as president of the college when A.M. arrived. Finney and several other professors had a profound influence on A.M. The themes of holiness, soul-winning and the revivalistic atmosphere helped determine the direction and emphasis of A.M.'s life-long ministry. While at Oberlin College he met Altha A. Ford whom he married after a three year engagement. At the age of twenty two, while still at the college, one evening in turmoil of soul,

A.M. knelt and cried out to God to settle all doubts about his life's calling. Finally he said; "Woe is me if I preach not the Gospel."

A.M. graduated with a B.A. degree from Oberlin College in 1871 and that same summer enrolled in Yale University Divinity School. His choice of Yale rather than Harvard was because the "current of unbelief was altogether too strong there" [at Harvard]. His years at Yale are where he met and encountered new ideas and minds which broadened his understanding of both religious and educational principles. He studied under professors who affirmed the great truths of the authenticity of Scripture and the deity of Jesus Christ. This greatly strengthened his faith against the waves of destructive higher criticism that he was soon to encounter in public ministry. His Greek professor was none other than Timothy Dwight, the grandson of the former Yale president of the same name. Dwight's spiritual and scholarly influence on A.M. was so profound that he often reflected on that experience throughout his life.

Another professor that greatly influenced the life of A.M. was Dr. Samuel Harris, who filled the chair of systematic theology. A.M. fondly referred to him as a "noble man who filled the position most worthily. . .not trifling with the great foundations and essential doctrines of Christianity. [He] taught day by day for three blessed years practical truths of the Gospel that we could incorporate into our lives and preach to others . . . to me, his very name is precious."

While in divinity school, A.M. had numerous opportunities to preach. As a licensed Congregational minister, he began to hold revival meetings and served as a supply pastor during his summer vacations. After graduating from Yale in May 1874 he immediately began a ten year pastorate at the Ravenna, Ohio Congregational Church. While there he preached the ordination sermon for his Yale classmate R. A. Torrey. He served as secretary of the Ohio Association of Churches and a speaker for the Women's Christian Temperance Union. He would later serve congregations in Allegheny, Pennsylvania; Olivet, Michigan and Springfield, Missouri.

He helped sponsor a revival campaign with D.L.Moody and evangelized for several years in churches and camp meetings. With the help of Reader Harris and Dr. George Sharpe, Dr. Hills was instrumental in the spread of the holiness message in Great Britain and the founding of a church in Paisley, Scotland in 1908 and 1909. His ministry was in demand among the holiness movement in Great Britain and therefore he made subsequent return trips.

Dr. Hills was instrumental in the founding of and held teaching positions in seven holiness colleges located in Bethany, OK; Hutchinson,

KS; Nashville, TN; Quincy, MA; Pasadena, CA; Wheaton, IL and Nampa, ID. During this time Dr. Hills found himself with less in common with his Congregational affiliates and a more compatible place in ministry among the Church of the Nazarene. In 1898, he served as professor of Bible and Theology at Asbury College in Wilmore, Kentucky.

In 1899, the Texas Holiness University was established in Peniel, Texas and was associated with the Texas Pentecostal Church of the Nazarene. The trustees chose Dr. A.M. Hills as its first president, which he held for seven years. This college later merged with Southern Nazarene University in Bethany, OK where Dr. Hills served as Professor of Theology and Dean of the School of Religion in 1911-1912. After returning from another preaching tour of Great Britain, he taught religion courses at Pasadena University from 1916-1932.

Dr. Hills was a prolific writer. In addition to writing college textbooks, over thirty volumes of *Defense of the Christian Faith*, he wrote tracts, booklets, papers and articles which were printed in many holiness publications in the United States and Great Britain. J.B. Chapman's *Herald of Holiness* magazine published Dr. Hills' articles for years.

On September 11, 1935 at his Pasadena home, Dr. A.M. Hills passed away due to a cerebral hemorrhage. The editor of the Pasadena College *Clarion* wrote; "The only cloud upon the horizon was the passing of our dearly beloved Dr. A.M. Hills whose name will go down as one of the great holiness pioneer leaders. . ."

One of the most interesting facts about Dr. Hills was his knowledge and belief in the Anglo-Israel message of Scripture. Dating back to his student years at Yale, along with his beloved professor Dr. Samuel Harris, they both firmly advocated that Anglo-civilization was the resurgence of ancient Israel. One of the many books written by Dr. Hills was entitled *"Christian Education and Anglo-Israel,"* published by *The Christian Witness Co.*, 1906. It was composed of two lectures. The first lecture was *"The Importance of More Thorough Christian Education"* given in June 1906 at the Central Holiness University in Oskaloosa, Iowa. The second lecture was *"Israel Disguised and Lost"* which was first given upon request before the Ministerial Association of Springfield, Missouri in 1895. Dr. Hills employed "arguments from Scripture and from an impressive array of ancient and modern scholars to prove the identity of the Anglo-Saxon race with the ten lost tribes of Israel. Although not the most enduring acceptable of his writings to scholars, as a lecture it aroused great interest in the South and West whenever he gave it. As a main feature of the Texas Holiness University commencement events in 1906, the lecture made a profound impression, adding to the reputation of the departing president."

All of the above information and quotes were taken from: *Waves Against Gibraltar - A Memoir of Dr. A.M. Hills*, by L. Paul Gresham, published by Southern Nazarene University Press, 1992.

In his book, *Yale and the Ministry*, Roland H. Bainton says of Professor Samuel Harris' belief concerning the materialization of the Kingdom of God in America, "Harris also found that God had a plan for the ages. With [Jonathan] Edwards and [Lyman] Beecher he found the locus for the realization of the future holy commonwealth in these United States. 'God has always acted' said he 'by chosen peoples. To the English speaking people more than to any other the world is now indebted for the propagation of Christian ideas and Christian civilization. It is a remarkable fact in this day that the thinking of the world is done by Christian nations; that the enterprise and energy of the world are mainly theirs. They alone are colonizing, and by their commerce and enterprise pushing their influence throughout the world. So also the political condition of the protestant nations is that of constitutional government, popular education and a growing regard for the rights and welfare of the people."

The following quotes are from Dr. A.M. Hills' lecture entitled *"Israel Disguised and Lost."* They were given as concluding remarks to lengthy arguments previously presented in his lecture in favor of the Anglo-Israel truth.

"If the Scripture is to be accepted as authority, it is evident that the training to which the Hebrew nation was subjected was chiefly designed to prepare a people to spread the light of God's truth over the earth, to be the greatest of human instruments in spreading the kingdom of God. And today it is manifest to all eyes that the Anglo-Saxons are of all peoples that ever lived, the best fitted and circumstanced to spread the gospel and are now above all others being used to evangelize the world. How can we account for it, if they were not trained for it, and avowedly set apart as were no other people? By these long years of preparation God showed that he considered a training necessary in order to form fit instruments wherewith to work. But if the people who have been used for the work are not the people who underwent a training for it, how was it that they ever acquired the great faculties and genius and spiritual trend, which so well fit them to accomplish it? If the Anglo-Saxons did not derive their fitness for their great mission from forefathers who underwent a training for it in the land of Canaan, we know not how else

270

to account for it. For in that case no training was necessary and the very supposition charges God himself with folly." pp. 64-65

"Now we come to the real and final argument. If this theory is true that the Lost Tribes were to ultimately become so great as the English people now are, would the Bible be silent about it? Would no voice have come from patriarchs and prophets, and no promise from God himself to lead them to cherish so glorious a hope of future greatness?

"Right here the advocates of Anglo-Israel appear at their best and their argument is most reverent and wonderfully varied and literal to a surprising degree. They find the Holy Word literally full of their theme. They tell us that we have misread the Scripture, spiritualizing all the promises and prophecies concerning Israel and seeing them answered spiritually in Christ instead of literally in Israel, until we have well-nigh submerged the whole continent of inspiration. They tell us further that we gave hopelessly confused the prophecies concerning Israel and Judah, applying all of them to the Jews and so making the Bible a jumbled mass of hopeless contradictions." p. 71

"All that is asked for this theory by its advocates is unprejudiced painstaking, prayerful study. If the final verdict is that we are indeed in a special and literal sense the chosen people of God and heirs of the Covenants of God, will the TRUTH be of no value?

"Will it have no bearing upon scoffing infidelity, and especially the ignorant infidelity that surrenders the Word because the promises and prophecies SEEM not to have been fulfilled?

"Would it not rescue our Bible from the vandal hands of the Ishmaelites of criticism, and save it to reverent faith? Would it not explain the marvelous career of our race to itself, and show to its newly opened eyes the Hand of God in its history? Would it not arouse our people to a new consciousness of their heaven-appointed mission to evangelize the world and give a new impulse to missions, such as it has never yet received?

"Would it not point out to statesmen the manifest destiny of the nations and point out the only true and lasting settlement of the Eastern question? Would it not give inspiration to the statesmanship itself, and lift it from the low plain of selfishness to an exalted effort to further the plans and eternal purposes of the infinite God? p.87

"An editorial in one of our great secular papers reaches this sage conclusion, "The subject of the identity of the Anglo-Saxon race with the Ten Lost Tribes of Israel, has thus at last passed its probationary stage, and it is now high time to call a truce to mere ridicule, and to admit the hearing into the sober atmosphere of calm and deliberate investigation.

Let us change the venue, therefore, and have no more sneers upon this matter; but if any man has facts which can be arrayed against the claims set up by this certainly growing school of genuine students, let him duly produce his case in the same dignified manner, or let him sit in the audience and hold his peace. Henceforth this question is to dominate the most earnest and searching study from the ablest truth-seekers of the day. Give this full grown school of original thinkers a chance to state their case before a race which is deeply concerned in the issue. Frank Leslie's Weekly, Feb. 7, 1901." pp. 89-90

ADAM THOMPSON McKEOWN

If ever there was a life destined for service and ministry in the vineyard of the Lord, it was Adam McKeown. He was born on May 6, 1909 in Coatbridge, Scotland. He was the sixth child in a family of nine children. When just a small child, his family moved to the county of Antrim, Northern Ireland.

Adam's father, William McKeown was brought up as a strict Presbyterian and had a profound Godly influence upon his children. In the early days of the Pentecostal movement in Great Britain, Adam's parents were among the first to receive the Baptism of the Holy Spirit. The McKeown home was open every Saturday night as a place where many people gathered to hear the good news of the Gospel and experience the gift of Salvation. It was during those days that Adam and his family became familiar with great men of God like George Jeffreys and Smith Wigglesworth. It was in this spiritual atmosphere that young Adam was nurtured and raised. The McKeowns and the neighboring Harris home became the two main points of contact whereby the surrounding area experienced a time of divine visitation.

Through the influence of ungodly companions and a feeling of restlessness, Adam tried to find a sense of inward peace in a life of worldliness and rebellion. Having suffered from respiratory problems since childhood, then at the age of twenty-one he had a severe case of congestion of the lungs that lasted for four months. During the Christmas season of 1930, Adam was almost killed in an automobile accident while traveling with some friends to a dance. He then developed a severe case of pneumonia and was not expected to live. As his brother-in-law ministered to him, the Spirit of God convicted his

272

heart, changed his life and he became a new creature in Christ. He then began to attend the meetings conducted by his father in the "Upper Room" located in their home. There he received the Baptism of the Holy Spirit.

Soon after this experience, the Lord began to deal with Adam concerning his life calling as a minister of the Gospel. He began to assist very powerful and successful evangelists in meetings in Northern Ireland. In one such meeting he met Ann Williamson, to whom he was married in December 1934. He was ordained to permanent ministry with the Apostolic Church on April 10, 1944. In August 1945 Adam with his brother James and his family, set sail from Liverpool, England for Ghana, West Africa to serve the Lord on the mission field. On board ship the first night the Lord miraculously healed him of his respiratory trouble that he had suffered with since childhood.

While serving as a missionary in Africa, the Lord greatly blessed his ministry in establishing many churches throughout Ghana. He and his brother James were invited into the prison to minister to the eight men who were convicted of killing the local chief. All eight men eventually confessed Jesus Christ as their Savior. As a result of this incident, Adam was invited to conduct regular church services in Ussher Fort Prison with the blessings of the superintendent of prisons. While in Africa, under the ministry of Adam and his brother James, the church experienced great growth in both numbers and spirit. Many were blessed and miraculously healed of physical maladies.

In May 1948 the missionary board of the Apostolic Church sent Adam and his family to assist the Apostolic work in America. In July 1950 Pastor Fred Poole introduced Adam to the Latter Rain Revival movement. In this area of ministry he would meet Pastor Harry Hodges, Dr. Earl Lee, Dr. Thomas Wyatt and other prominent men of that era. He and his ministry team held tent revivals in several states of the northeast. In January 1953, he joined Dr. Wyatt on a missionary trip to Africa. There they saw the Lord confirm His Word by many signs and wonders. He also returned to his native Ireland and held several very successful meetings where the presence of God was very evident in miraculous power. He also held a pastorate for many years, but always remained in ministry with other churches in many places at home and abroad.

Throughout his Christian walk, Adam McKeown endeavored to follow the leading of the Holy Spirit, both in ministry and doctrinal belief. Therefore he became a strong believer in the Anglo-Israel message as it was revealed to him in the Word of God and by the Holy

Spirit. The following is his personal testimony of belief as recorded in his memoirs, *A Man Called Adam.*

"It has been said that God is not discovered, but rather, revealed and that by the Holy spirit. Truth is not discovered by simply reading books or by someone preaching it, truth is revealed to the hungry searching heart, by the Holy Spirit (John 16:13), and made a part of you by an operation of God by the Spirit. When that happens, truth becomes personified, the Word becomes flesh, and not just a doctrine we can discard at a moment's notice!

"I found myself leaving the Futuristic teaching of the prophetic Scriptures and accepting the Historicist viewpoint. I was also awakened to the identity of the real Israel of God, not as taught by most ministers and Churches, that the Jews were God's chosen people! At the time when God was dealing with me regarding these truths, two books came to my attention, 'Judah's Sceptre and Joseph's Birthright', by Bishop Allen, and, 'One Man's Destiny', by C.R. Dickey.

"I began to read the Old Testament in a new light, seeing the difference between the 'House of Israel' and the 'House of Judah'! That the house of Israel divorced and sent into captivity, had not in any way altered Jehovah's original plan, nor had He ever called a 'Chosen Church' as a substitute for a 'Chosen nation'. The House of Israel though put away for her sins, served the full penalty of the 'seven time' (2,520 years). But one has to rejoice with the Prophets who speak so glowingly of Israel's Redemption and Restoration to a greater glory than ever before, to fulfil her destiny. All this provides an interesting and exciting study to the spiritual and open-minded person. How the wandering tribes, divinely guided (Isaiah 42:16), moving ever westward, leaving the unmistakable marks of their true identity in the isles of the west, spoken of by the Prophet Isaiah; (The British Isles). The continuity of the Throne of David, his House and his Kingdom (2 Sam 7). The discovery of America, and the fulfillment of the prophecy of Jacob over his grandsons, Manasseh becoming a great people, while Ephraim (England) would be a company, or Commonwealth of Nations (Genesis 48)."

WILLIAM CATHCART 1893-1988

The life of William Cathcart can surely be described as proof of God's sovereignty, divine protection, supernatural interposition, faith, revelation and total surrender to his Savior and Lord.  He was born of Scottish parentage whose forefathers were in the Protestant Reformation in the days of the great reformer, John Knox. Later on his ancestral family was able to escape by a small boat by crossing the rough North Channel and arrived safely in Donegal, Ireland.

William was born in 1893 in County Antrim, Northern Ireland, the youngest of six children. His mother suddenly died when he was only three years old and he was raised by a very strict Presbyterian aunt. In reaction to this early life of strict discipline and religious drudgery, he became bitter and rebellious. He met the wrong crowd and had his first drink of liquor at the age of ten years. In spite of his rebellion, young William had his first supernatural experience at the age of seven while playing in his favorite tree. He was immersed in a strong power like electricity and it seemed to flow in and out and all over him as if it was liquid fire. He began to weep, pray and cry aloud and could not stop for about ten minutes or more.

His second supernatural experience at the age of sixteen came while passing by a street meeting on his way to meet his friends one Saturday night. The words of the preacher seemed to become the voice of God Himself as he heard *"For the wages of sin is death, but the gift of God is eternal life through Jesus Christ our Lord."* It was there that the Holy Spirit began to deal with him on his three mile walk home in the dark on a country road. Rising early the next morning with the consciousness that a divine change had taken place within him, he set out to find the people that held the street meeting the night before. Thus began his lifelong association with the people of God, which first included the "Faith Mission" and the "Plymouth Brethren" of Scotland.

On September 6, 1914, William answered his country's call by joining the British Army and served for the duration of World War I. Serving in France in the heat of battle, he experienced the brutality of war with all its ravaging and devastating results. There he was by the side of his brother John as he died from mustard gas poisoning. William was injured and suffered from loss of hearing and sight, severe dizziness, extreme weakness and confusion of mind. While confined to his hospital bed a lady came and gave him a New Testament. While holding his new gift, the Lord spoke to him and said, "Take that book, open it and hold it in your hands. You are coming back to me. I am going to heal you. I will give you a shepherd's heart and you will go to the uttermost parts of the earth for me." Not long after that the Lord gave him a mighty vision, healed and filled him with the Holy Spirit. He was introduced to the "Burning Bush" Church in Glasgow and Pastor Andrew Turnbull where he experienced many miraculous events and began to minister in the power of the Spirit with signs following.

William Cathcart was ordained to charismatic ministry in February 1920 in Edinburgh, Scotland under the auspices of the Apostolic Church, headquartered in Wales. This church was a direct outcome of the Welsh Revival of 1904-05. Under the prophetic direction of the Apostolic Church, he and his family moved to Australia where the Lord blessed his ministry resulting in the establishment of dozens of churches. Thousands of people were converted to Christ and hundreds were physically healed by an outward demonstration of the power of our risen Savior, Jesus Christ. He ministered with such men as William Phillips, and the Welsh revivalists John H. Hewitt and his brother Isaac. This Apostolic revival ministry expanded over into New Zealand where the same miraculous results happened.

William Cathcart served the Lord for over fifty-five years in Apostolic ministry which was marked with pioneering and miracle faith, prophetic utterance and divine revelation of truth. One of these truths which he so strongly believed and taught was the Anglo-Israel message of God's Word. It was this message of the Gospel of the Kingdom that he proclaimed along with the message of Salvation, healing and the Baptism of the Holy Spirit. The last several years of his life he spent in ministry in the United States where he wrote his autobiography *"From Gloom to Glory"* and his book *"The Glory of Christ Revealed in Charismatic Ministry."*

FREDERICK W.C. NESER

The life of F.W.C. Neser was one that was destined for ministerial service in the vineyard of the Lord and to be a recipient of divine revelation. Above the desire for ecclesiastical acceptance was his heartfelt passion to understand the plan of God concerning His people Israel. This desire for divine revelation over acceptance cost him a dear price throughout his

276

ministerial career.

Frederick Wilhelm Cornelius Neser was born on April 23, 1918 in Fauresmith, South Africa. His primary education took place at a farm school which consisted of one classroom. Pastor Neser, whose nickname was Frikkie, grew up with a genuine appreciation for God's creation, but unfortunately it was not possible for him to attend Sunday School until he was in high school. Growing up on a farm with plenty of work and very little time for idle play, Frikkie spent much of his free time reading the old Dutch Bible until he obtained his first copy of the Afrikaans Bible at the age of 17 years old.

In 1936 Frikke passed his mathematics and chemistry exams, then pursued his study of civil engineering at the University of Cape Town in 1937. In 1939, he obtained a Bachelor of Science degree in math and physics at the University of Stellenbosch. Not long after the outbreak of World War II, he acquired a position with the Met Office in 1940 under the command of the Air Force. As an officer he was a teacher of meteorology at the Royal Air Force Base in Nakura, Kenya. He then served active duty with the South African Air Force under the command of the 8th British Army joining with the 5th American Army in military conflicts in Tripoli and Tunisia. With the rank of Captain, he returned to the Met Office in Pretoria in 1944.

As a long time member of the Dutch Reformed Church, Frikkie was searching for a deeper understanding of the truth of God's Word. At one point he considered membership in the Moral Re-armament movement, but then declined. By divine providence in 1944 he was given a tract published by the British Israel World Federation which showed that the historical people of the nations of the western world are the descendants of ancient Israel. It was to these people to whom God gave His laws and with whom He had made an everlasting covenant. After much discussion and investigation of this new found truth, Frikkie realized that the identification marks which applied to Biblical Israel also applied to the Afrikaner people. Later he became a member and chairman of the Pretoria branch of the BIWF.

In 1945, Frikkie and Louie Kirsten were joined in holy matrimony in the Methodist Church in Johannesburg. Their marriage was blessed with three children. In 1946 he joined the department of Agriculture in technical support to the farming community. Continuing his search for Biblical truth, he came in contact with Pastor L. Shaw Butler, the South Africa secretary of the BIWF. In 1951 the Nesers met Pastor Brooke of the United Apostolic Faith Church and started attending his Bible classes. Pastor Brooke was a minister of the Pentecostal persuasion who also taught the Anglo-Israel truth. Being convinced of these truths, the Nesers became members of the U.A.F.C. and even opened their home for Bible studies. It was during this time in 1954 when Frikkie was clearly convinced of God's divine call upon his life for Christian ministry. The decision was made in 1956 to resign from his secular job and enter full time ministry. That same year he accepted the pastorate of a congregation in Vereeniging with only five families. Beginning in a rented hall with both English and Afrikaan speaking people, they were able to construct their own building the next year.

In Pastor Neser's remaining years, he established the Ecclesia Evangelistic Group in 1963 and a congregation in Pretoria in 1976. He retired from full time pastoring in 1989, yet remained in active ministry until his passing.

One of the divine truths that Pastor Neser boldly proclaimed was the true identification of God's people Israel. In his book *The Origin, History and Destiny of the White Race,* he wrote; "The history of the true Israel is the history of the white race as is found in the Anglo-Saxon, Celtic and kindred peoples and their descendants of whom the white people in Southern Africa form a part . . . The promises God made to Abraham were unconditional, everlasting and irrevocable. They were confirmed to Isaac and later to Jacob. The name of Jacob was later changed by God to Israel, meaning "a prince with God", or "ruling with God." It is through the true Israel that God will yet fill the world again with His image and establish His kingdom here on earth." He also wrote commentaries on the books of Daniel, Revelation, Isaiah and Romans which are a part of his 28 works of Biblical exposition. One of his most important works was a series of books entitled, *The 'Lost' Ten Tribes of Israel.* In book four he wrote; "It will be evident by now from what we have discovered thus far, why the nations from the west and the northwest European nations have descended, are called the Caucasian Race; it is because they entered Europe from Media through the Caucasian Mountains. They were none other than the so-called "lost" ten tribes of Israel."

Starting in 1968 Pastor Neser published a quarterly newsletter in Afrikaans entitled, *World Affairs* which continued until shortly before his passing. Pastor Neser was faithful to his Lord and to his calling in a Spirit-filled Pentecostal ministry for over fifty years. He chose to be faithful to divinely revealed truth rather than ministerial success and popularity. Someday he shall hear the voice of his Lord say; "Well done, thou good and faithful servant: Thou hast been faithful over a few things,

I will make thee ruler over many things: enter thou into the joy of thy Lord" (Mtt. 25:21).

Biographical source: *F. W. C. Neser -A Biography* by R. Searle, 2002

EPILOGUE

It is obvious from reading the accounts of the lives and ministries of the men in this brochure, that they willingly surrendered themselves to serve the Lord and others. They lived busy lives, endured hardships, served people joyfully and sacrificed personal ambitions while conducting intense and passionate ministries. One outstanding quality is that they had a very high regard for revelation truth when taught by the Holy Spirit. Each one placed a high priority on the Word of God and spent a lifetime of in- depth study. These among many others who believed and proclaimed the Gospel of the Kingdom were 'men of God'. Some were apostles, prophets, pastors, evangelists and missionaries, both at home and abroad. These ministers served in mainstream Christian denominations, worked with many well-known ministries and were very prominent among their peers. The Lord honored their labors with a bountiful harvest of souls.

The Gospel of the Kingdom (Mtt. 3:1; 4:17) is an extremely pertinent message for today's world because it includes the national message of the Bible. The Lord Jesus said, *"And this gospel of the kingdom shall be preached in all the world for a witness unto all nations; and then shall the end come"* (Mtt. 24:14). The national message is a call for the covenant nations to repent of their iniquities, but first these nations need to be identified. Here is where the Anglo-Israel message serves in identifying the people as the lineal descendants of the Old Testament covenant people of God, known as Israel.

Anglo-Israel Christian believers are a non-denominational fellowship that possesses and promotes no "sacred" book other than the Bible. We accept the five fold ministry of Ephesians. 4:11, with Jesus Christ being the chief cornerstone (Eph. 2:20). We teach that salvation is by grace through faith alone as a gift of God through the substitutionary death of Jesus Christ (Eph. 2:8). With the inspired Word of God as our guide and accepting all born again believers as part of the body of Christ, we have been and presently are a part of traditional Christianity.

279

JOSEPH IS YET ALIVE

Give ear, O Shepherd of Israel, Thou that leadeth Joseph like a flock..."   Psalm 80:1

Charles O. Benham

INTRODUCTION
by Charles A. Jennings

During the first half of the twentieth century, it was by divine providence that there appeared many spiritual giants on the American religious scene. One such man that God divinely called, anointed and sent forth to proclaim His Word was Evangelist Charles Orville Benham. He was born on March 4, 1891 in Green County, Indiana. As a young lad of only nine years old, C.O. Benham experienced the saving power of Jesus Christ during a Methodist revival near his home. It is reported that he was the only convert in that country church revival, but from there his Godly influence would touch the lives of multiplied thousands of people throughout his lifetime. Not long after his conversion, he felt the call of God into full-time Christian ministry. In 1914 he attended Moody Bible Institute in order to further his education in the Scriptures. One of his fellow students that same year was Dr. Bob Jones, Sr.

As a young man, Benham was active in evangelistic work with some of the early Pentecostal pioneers of the twentieth century. Early on, he learned to play the cornet and banjo which he used throughout his evangelistic career. He also wrote several gospel songs. With his musical

281

ability coupled with his spiritual zeal he was a real asset to prominent evangelists of his day. For a while he served as an assistant to Fred F. Bosworth in his evangelistic crusades and was for a time the song leader and music director for the famous evangelist Billy Sunday. In 1919, Benham attended an historic meeting of Assemblies of God leaders at the Stone Church in Chicago, Illinois. Among such well-known leaders attending were Stanley Frodsham, E.N. Bell, and J. Roswell Flower with whom he remained friends for many years. In 1924, while engaged in evangelistic crusades in the Northwest he met and married a young eighteen year old church soloist, Helen Mason. From this union God honored them with ten children.

The people of Eugene, Oregon were blessed with the preaching and faith-filled ministry of Dr. Charles S. Price during the years of 1923-1924. Also during 1924, Evangelist Benham set up a large Gospel tent and proclaimed Jesus Christ as both Savior and Healer. His 1200 seat capacity tent was filled each evening as the people crowed in to hear this young anointed preacher. He was still then associated with the Assemblies of God and was supported by a Christian and Missionary Alliance group of young musicians and workers from Seattle, Washington.

During those early twentieth century days when God's healing power was so prevalent in the land, many miraculous events took place. It was not uncommon for the healing power of Jesus Christ to be manifested in a tangible and visible way in the ministry of many pastors and evangelists. This was also true in the ministry of Evangelist Benham. Many miracles of healing took place in that 1924 Eugene, Oregon revival meeting. Fortunately, one of those testimonies of divine healing is recorded for us in Robert B. Mitchell's book, "*Heritage and Horizons–The History of Open Bible Standard Churches.*" On pages 62 and 63 he records the following account.

"One of the outstanding healings in the Eugene campaign was that of a young woman, Alice Goddard, whose family belonged to the 7th and Pearl Street Chapel. She had been injured by a fall on the slippery floor of the Eugene Cannery where she was employed. One hip was dislocated and the other injured so that she was unable to control either limb and had to walk with two crutches, dragging and swinging her legs along. Fourteen doctors engaged by the State Compensation Commission had examined her and pronounced her permanently disabled for life. For about two years many people had been praying for her healing. She was healed on a Friday night in July 1924. Attorney Alta B. King, who later became Lane County District Attorney, 1929-1933, was present at the

time because he had a part in handling legal details for her compensation and was also interested in the meetings. His wife, Eva C. King... gives the details of the miracle excerpted here:

That thin little slip of a young man, Evangelist C. Orville Benham, found that crippled girl painfully making her way up to the platform and into the healing line, standing until her turn came...My husband walked to the edge of the platform to be near her when the evangelist would anoint her with oil, lay his hands on her and pray the prayer of faith for her complete recovery...He stood by and saw her prayed for and saw her yield to the power of God; saw her body shake and shake until it was uncanny. They laid her prostrate on the floor of the platform, covered her with a blanket for warmth and went on praying for others in the line. The after-meeting went for an hour or more. When this young woman arose, she walked away on her own two good legs. Her crutches were hung on a centerpost in the front of the tent to testify to all who came to see, that God had come forth in the midst of His people and "made the lame to walk."   "A week later **The Eugene Morning Register** noted: There was a lively Friday evening when a young woman who had discarded her crutches gave her testimony. The local attorneys substantiated her statements, as also did her mother, her grandmother, a trained nurse and others who knew the case.

"In a telephone interview over fifty-six years later, Alice said, "Brother Benham looked at me in the choir and said, 'Alice, this is your night, come!" Many people were saved and others healed as a result of this revival."

Evangelist Benham went on to conduct many successful revival meetings in the Northwest. He was associated with many prominent ministers including Charles F. Parham. In 1926, Benham started producing a publication called "*The Overcomer.*" This was the beginning of his Gospel publications which lasted throughout most of his life. Later, he was responsible for publishing the "*National Forecast*" and the "*National Revivalist*" as monthly publications. In these papers he dealt with many issues, such as; the Cold War and the Communist threat to America, Bible prophecy, American racial tensions and many other sensitive subjects. He also authored many books during his ministerial career such as; "*101 Evidences Proving the Divine Origin and Destiny of the English-Speaking Peoples*", "*101 Signs of Christ's Coming–X-Raying Today's Chaos*" and "*101 Proofs that the Bible is True.*"

During his lifetime, Charles O. Benham was a personal friend with and sometimes ministered with the most prominent and well-known religious leaders of the twentieth century. His friends included Aimee S.

McPherson, Billy Sunday, F. F. Bosworth, T.L. Osborne, William M. Branham and several prominent Assemblies of God leaders. In recognition of his outstanding contribution, Benham was awarded an honorary Doctorate of Divinity degree from Oberlin College in Ohio. After a long and successful career of ministry for his Master, Charles O. Benham entered the presence of His Lord while residing in Topton, North Carolina in October of 1974.

The following article written in 1958 is excerpts of his edited and expanded commentary which Benham wrote on a sermon given by his friend, F. F. Bosworth. He entitled his commentary "*Joseph Is Yet Alive*" in which he affirms his long time belief in the Christian Anglo-Israel message of the Bible.

JOSEPH IS YET ALIVE

Israel Was to Become Christian and Evangelize The World

Rev. Joseph Wild, D.D., in his splendid book, **The Ten Lost Tribes,** published in 1879, emphatically states: "Nine-tenths of the Old Testament is a material history about one people, and that through them God's special providence was to flow to all other nations: and the New Testament plants the life and prosperity of the Gentile world upon the course and progress of Israel. God said to Abraham, *"In thee shall all the families of the earth be blessed";* and more, *"and in thy seed shall all the nations of the earth be blessed."*

Israel, being scattered and cast off, became a blessing to the world. They gave to the surrounding nations the only true idea of God, for in their lowest condition they preserved the name and knowledge of Jehovah, and Christ sent His disciples after them through one of their own tribe - namely Benjamin - telling them not to go into the way of the Gentiles, *'but go rather to the lost sheep of the House of Israel.'*

To these sheep Christ declares He was sent. Where were these sheep? They were scattered about in Central Asia and Europe ... From these very regions came the Saxons and kindred races; from here they spread North and West, being the most Christian of any people on the face of the earth then, as well as now. Their reception of the Gospel gave them power over the surrounding nations, to whom they were – as it had been foretold – witnesses of Jesus Christ...

God's Purpose Fulfilled

It is well always to remember that God is not dependent upon the harmonious co-operation of His creatures for the accomplishment of His purposes. He can gain His ends through our hate or love, resistance or co-operation. When the Jews had crucified Christ, they naturally thought that they had destroyed His career and cut off His influence, for so it would appear by all human reasoning. Even His close disciples did not see how He could be the *Messiah* and also the *Deliverer of Israel*, when He allowed Himself to be crucified.

The hope of Israel was buried with the dead Christ. They had hoped that it had been HE who should have redeemed Israel; but this hope was then dead. However, by His *resurrection* they saw through the secret of Providence, and they saw that God was faithful in devising a way to escape, and able to bring to pass His own glorious purpose. So Peter voices their experience when he says, *"Blessed be the God and Father of our Lord Jesus Christ, which according to His abundant mercy, hath begotten us again into a lively hope by the resurrection of Jesus Christ from the dead."*

The Jews soon found out that they had made a mistake in crucifying Jesus, for the risen Christ was mightier than the teaching Jesus. They had crushed a seed to the earth which sprang forth in renewed beauty and grace; whose death was life and whose loss was gain. They had been outwitted. They slew a *man* and he rose a *God*. They in wrath offered a sacrifice once and for all, even for the very sin in which they were indulging. They unknowingly *abolished death, and brought life and immortality to light.*

"Joseph is Yet Alive"

Now if Jesus Christ accomplished that work of salvation, where is Israel today? We must look for Israel, holding in our hands *the record* of her identity. For if He came to save them from their national as well as their individual sins in order that they might continue to fulfill their national functions in the earth, surely then Israel must be identified in these latter days when catastrophe threatens Christian civilization. If not, the work of Christ has failed, and Israel cannot be saved. But, on the other hand, if we identify Israel as a *national entity* functioning today, the English-speaking nations being the Joseph nations, it becomes unnecessary to question the veracity of the Holy Bible or to doubt the efficacy of the atoning work of our Lord in fulfilling His appointed task in coming to the earth.

Proper interpretation of the Prophetic Scriptures puts the skeptic on the spot and leaves him no place from Genesis to Revelation to cast suspicion on the truth of the Bible.

During the height of the battle of Britain in 1940, at a time when in the eyes of the world the destiny of that nation seemed at stake, a Belgian doctor who had taken refuge there exclaimed: "Why are you people so certain that you will not be defeated when all the evidence is to the contrary?" There was but one answer. Previous to World War II that people – including Sir Winston Churchill – had been strongly evangelized with the message of their identity as descendants of the Ten Lost Tribes of Israel, then when deep national affliction came, their faith strengthened for the ordeal and the adversary in all his fury could not beat it down.

Our faith, as inheritors of the Israel Covenants, is made rational and reinforced by Bible Prophecy and is fulfillment which demonstrates that as the prophecies of God regarding the past have been literally fulfilled, we can now look with assurance to the fulfillment of His promises for the future.

The transfer of the geographical center of Israel from Palestine to the West, for the furtherance of this destiny, is also confirmed in Holy Writ: *"Moreover, I will appoint a PLACE for My people Israel, and will plant them, that they may dwell in a place of their own, and move no more; neither shall the children of wickedness afflict them anymore, as before time."* II Samuel 7:10

That the fact of Israel's deportation into Assyria, and her emergence later under a new name after the migrations across Europe, would not retard but hasten the progress of the Divine Plan, is demonstrated in the New Covenant made with the House of Israel "forever", which proclaims the perpetuity of the nation Israel in the following dramatic words.

"Thus saith the Lord, which giveth the sun for a light by day, and the ordinances of the moon, and of the stars for a light by night, which divideth the sea when the waves thereof roar; the Lord of Hosts is His name: if those ordinances depart from before Me, saith the Lord, then the seed of Israel also shall cease from being a NATION before Me forever. Thus saith the Lord: if heaven above can be measured, and the foundations of the earth searched out beneath, I will also cast off all the seed of Israel for all that they have done, saith the Lord." Jeremiah 31:35-37

As we pass to the New Testament we find our Lord confronting the Jews, who at that time were the only official remnant of God's people left in Palestine. He told them plainly:

"The Kingdom of God shall be taken from you, and given to a NATION bringing forth the fruits thereof. And whosoever shall fall on this stone shall be broken: but upon whomsoever it shall fall, it will grind him to powder." Matthew 21:43-44

Here we come to an important parting of the ways inasmuch as the Jews rejected Jesus Christ as their Savior, while the cast-off Israel people accepted Him and became Christian. This was a fulfillment of the prophecy of Hosea:

"Yet the number of the Children of Israel shall be as the sand of the sea, which cannot be measured nor numbered; and it shall come to pass, that in the place where it was said unto them, Ye are not My people. there it shall be said unto them, Ye are the sons of the living God." Hosea 1:10

Herein lies the explanation of the fact that the light of Christianity has spread throughout the world from western Europe and North America, and that today all the free world looks to the English-speaking and kindred nations as the nations bringing forth *"the fruit"* of the Kingdom of God. This does not mean that they are perfect nations, but it does mean that under the guiding hand of God this group of Israel nations will press on toward that goal. The international idealist and the small independent nations of our day which are quaking with fear of losing their freedom as the Russian steam roller approaches, are sound in their instinct when they look to America for deliverance and guidance in this the world's day of peril. It must be remembered that when famine came *Joseph alone had bread.* As all the world then looked to God's Joseph, so all the world now looks to God's Joseph nations.

Our Identity is Important

There is every indication that in our own generation some of the crowning prophecies of all time are to be fulfilled – prophecies which tell of occurrences so momentous in their import, that the life of every person in the world will be affected. The greatest events ever witnessed by mortal man are now almost at hand! What are these events? The Bible has the answer; and the key fact to be remembered in the study thereof is the proper identification of Israel.

The people of Moses' day cried out for deliverance and God started His program through Moses by first challenging the orthodoxy of a

287

situation which was keeping God's people 'hide-bound." His first task was to prove to these enslaved millions their own identity and the great heritage that was theirs though faith in the Divine Covenant made with their fathers, which their identity substantiated. These were the very things that the Egyptian hierarchy wanted to suppress. It was to their interest to keep God's Israel working for them, which made their world conquest worth while and guaranteed its permanency.

Never in all history was the knowledge given by the prophets so needed as today. This is true because we are the people of that generation to whom the prophets addressed their message, and the scenes about us are those they so clearly described. It is plainly revealed that a free government is the agency of the teachings of Christ, the basis of the Christian civilization which created Great Britain and the United States of America. Only as the processes of government actually are infused with the Christianity upon which their tenets are based, can our nation overcome the Pagan "New Order" now threatening the world. Little progress can be made in the present struggle until this great truth is embraced by our leaders. Not until then could God consistently come to our rescue in a supernatural way. Such a matter as God *"blowing with His winds"* and upsetting the *"invincible"* Spanish Armada in 1588 A.D. would prove comparatively trifling compared with what God would then be willing to do.

Moses had to begin by challenging the obstinate narrow minded orthodoxy of his own brethren whom he loved and yearned to liberate. John the Baptist was such a man. Wycliff, Huss, Luther, Wesley and Finney were all such men. God's heroes usually run contrary to the conventionalities of their day. God's message for the hour is seldom orthodox and this Israel message is no exception.

God's Word Does Not Fail Us

Why should so many people be surprised that the old Book actually contains the vitally needed enlightenment for human happiness and welfare and carries within its sacred pages the authoritative solution for every problem we now face as a nation?

The continued existence of Israel, as a nation, is absolutely essential to the whole structure of the plainly outlined purpose of God. If Israel is not in existence today as a *"nation and a company of nations"* and a people as numerous as *"the stars"* and *"the sand"*, then the veracity of Jehovah God, is open to question. His own plan is a failure. And we know that if Genesis fails the whole Bible breaks down. *If Israel cannot be identified as foretold, then we have no hope for the consummation of God's plan.*

Study Zacharias' statement upon the occasion of the presentation of John the Baptist in the temple (Luke 1:67-79). Let us stand in the house of Joseph and Mary when the Angelic Visitor announces: *"Thou shalt call His name Jesus for He shall save His people from their sins"* (Matthew1:21). If He came to save "*His people*" (Israel) from their sins, why THAT people? Why Israel? They were not better than other people. Yet, for His own sake and for the sake of the whole world, God must save them. They were to be His instrument to carry out His plan for all mankind. We see here that Old Testament Israel is the key to His ministry. The honor of the Almighty depended upon the existence of and development of Israel. And this continuance of Israel was fully dependent upon the act of God through GRACE, because sin had disqualified them for continued existence as God's Chosen.

"When the fulness of time was come, God sent forth His son, born of a woman, born under the law, to redeem them that were under the law." (Galatians 4:4).

Now, of all the people in the world, none can be designated as "under the law", other than Israel. Their redemption was therefore necessary, for they had broken the law and incurred the penalties of disobedience. So Jesus came to *"save His people (Israel) from their sins"* because their salvation was imperative to the fulfillment of His purposes in the earth.

"O house of Jacob, come ye, and let us walk in the light of the Lord." (Isaiah 2:5). It is imperative, therefore, that the need for a *national* return to God and His Word be proclaimed throughout the land.

God's Holy Spirit is careful to reiterate the fact many times that Christ died not only as Savior of the world but as *"the Redeemer of His people Israel."*

"This shall be the Covenant that I will make with the House of Israel: After those days, saith the Lord, I will put My Law in their inward parts, and write it in their hearts; and will be their God, and they shall be My people." (Jeremiah 31:31)

So by the power of His Sacrifice we are a redeemed nation, a people soon to be brought back into full Covenant relationship with God. Prophecy makes plain that America is soon to nationally repent and awake to its great responsibilities. At present we are, as a nation, unrepentant and blind to our identity, but our triumphant destiny will be fulfilled and we shall acknowledge ourselves to be the servant nation of God on earth. *"Men shall call you the Ministers of our God."* (Isaiah 61:6)

Joseph's Mission will be Fulfilled

Emerging after all these centuries of obscurity, we discern the hidden **House of Joseph** engaged upon the secret purpose of the Almighty, in leading the final fight against the Anti-Christ, and it is coming in our generation. We are now witnessing precisely those phenomena which Prophecy identifies with the end of the age. The Apostle Paul tells us that the revealing of Israel would be life from the dead:

"For if the casting way of them be the reconciling of the world, what shall the receiving of them be, but life from the dead" (Romans 11:15).

Only by the work of the Spirit can Israel's blindness be removed, and the people know of their God-given origin and destiny.

"So will I make my holy Name known in the midst of My people Israel...and I will set My glory among the heathen, and all the heathen shall see My judgment that I have executed, and My hand that I have laid upon them. So the House of Israel shall know that I am the Lord their God from that day and forward...Neither will I hide My face any more from them: for I have poured out My Spirit upon the House of Israel, saith the Lord God." (Ezekiel 39:7, 21, 22, 29).

~~~~~~

THE BLESSING OF JOSEPH

"And of Joseph, he said, Blessed of the LORD be his land, for the precious things of heaven, for the dew, and for the deep that coucheth beneath, And for the precious fruits brought forth by the sun, and for the precious things put forth by the moon, And for the chief things of the ancient mountains, and for the precious things of the lasting hills, And for the precious things of the earth and fulness thereof, and for the good will of him that dwelt in the bush: Let the blessing come upon the head of Joseph, and upon the top of the head of him that was separated from his brethren. His glory is like the firstling of his bullock, and his horns are like the horns of unicorns: with them he shall push the people together to the ends of the earth: and they are the ten thousands of Ephraim, and they are the thousands of Manasseh."Deut. 33:13-17

"Joseph is a fruitful bough, even a fruitful bough by a well; whose branches run over the wall...Even by the God of thy father, who shall

help thee; and by the Almighty, who shall bless thee with blessings of heaven above, blessings of the deep that lieth under, blessings of the breast and of the womb:"
Genesis 49:22, 25

"For Judah prevailed above his brethren, and of him came the chief ruler; but the birthright was Joseph's:"
I Chronicles 5:2

REVIVAL INSIGHTS
An Overview of the Welsh Revival of 1904-1905
By Robert Phillips

Evan Roberts
The Welsh Revivalist

INTRODUCTION
By Robert Phillips

The **REVIVAL** of 1904-5 resulted in over 150,000 people converted and added to churches and chapels in Wales. Lives were **TRANSFORMED**! Lifestyles were **CHANGED**! Homes and families were HEALED! Churches were packed and on **FIRE** with fervour and zeal!

All this happened when young people began to experience the reality of God's divine power, and teams of young people, such as the one led by the most noted of the revivalist, **EVAN ROBERTS** and his revival party, travelled the country revolutionising the churches.

Just after eleven o'clock on a Wednesday evening a hundred years ago, a solo voice rang out with the beautiful Welsh hymn "Here Is Love Vast As The Ocean". Maybe a thousand people were in the Chapel at the time, leaning over the galleries, packing every pew and squeezing into every spare corner. They'd been here for more than four hours, in a service of intense emotion.

Meetings like it were taking place across Wales night after night, with fervent prayer and passionate singing - and similar disregard for the clock. They both excited and appalled left many puzzled and some frightened, but it was reckoned that in less than a year, over a hundred and fifty thousand people had made a new commitment to Jesus Christ. Whole communities changed, as men and women found themselves drawn into a powerful experience of God; and sparks from their awakening were soon to ignite fires in more than a dozen other countries. And the hymn that soloist struck up spontaneously, about "love vast as the ocean", was heard so often that it became known as "the love song of the revival".

Pentecostal Revival

The Welsh Revival of 1904 is generally considered as something quite distinct from other spiritual movements that developed before or after it. In fact, that is not the case, as we shall see.

The emphasis of the Revival was without doubt the baptism and fullness of the Holy Spirit, and, as we shall discover, it was not a phenomenon which happened and died out, but it has to be seen in the light of the Pentecostal Outpouring of the Holy Spirit in the early 20th century.

The Welsh Revival
was a Pentecostal Outpouring

The Welsh Revival of 1904 is generally considered as something quite distinct from other spiritual movements that developed before or after it. In fact, there is much evidence that the Revival was part of the Pentecostal Outpouring of the Holy Spirit in the early 20th century.

The emphasis of the Welsh Revival of 1904 was without doubt the baptism and fullness of the Holy Spirit. The early beginnings of the Revival were influenced by Reader Harris, founder of the Pentecostal League of Prayer, who preached a sermon in Carmarthen in January 1904 stating that the Church was to see another Pentecost.

The Pentecostal Connection

The Pentecostal nature of the Revival of 1904 is undeniable. Evan Roberts himself often exercised the gift of a word of knowledge during the meetings. His emphasis was constantly on the baptism in the Spirit. The form of the services remind us strongly of the pattern of those described in the New Testament letters. It is small wonder then that a large percentage of the 150,000 saved in Wales became dissatisfied with

the traditional churches and joined the newly formed Apostolic and Pentecostal Fellowships.

The Apostolic Faith Church

One minister dramatically influenced by the Welsh Revival was Pastor W.O. Hutchinson of Bournemouth, England. After being Baptised with the Holy Spirit, he founded the Apostolic Faith Church, which was the first Pentecostal movement to be established in Britain. The Apostolic Faith Church gave birth to many Churches and ministries throughout Great Britain and overseas.

The Apostolic Church

Under the ministry of the Apostolic Faith Church, converts of the Welsh Revival, Daniel Williams (affectionately known as "Pastor Dan") and his brother Jones were ordained as an apostle, and prophet respectively.

Called as an Apostle to Wales, "Pastor Dan", with the support of his brother Jones, pioneered the work under the name of the Apostolic Church. From the village of Penygroes in South Wales, it rapidly spread throughout Wales, England, Scotland, Ireland and overseas.

Elim & Bible Pattern Churches

Also notable amongst the converts of the Revival are George and Stephen Jeffreys, founders of Elim Foursquare Gospel Alliance. Their international Evangelistic and Healing Campaigns resulted in multiplied thousands who were saved and healed through the Lord Jesus Christ. George Jeffreys also founded the Bible Pattern Church Fellowship, and held an annual Convention in London's Royal Albert Hall.

The Israel Connection

The Bible says in Joel 2 vs. 28-29 :-
"And it shall come to pass afterward, that I will pour out my spirit upon all flesh; and your sons and your daughters shall prophesy, your old men shall dream dreams, your young men shall see visions: And also upon the servants and upon the handmaids in those days will I pour out my spirit".

This prophecy had an undoubted fulfillment during the Welsh Revival of 1904 as perhaps experienced nowhere else in quite this manner and scale, underlining the belief of many, that Wales is an Israel nation, part of the "lost" tribes of the House of Israel. Indeed, there are many who believe that the high proportion of ministers, both political and spiritual, produced in Wales, together with its identification as the "Land of Revival and Song" are a sure indication that a significant portion of the priestly tribe of Levi, including the descendants of Asaph - the appointed singers of Israel - are to be found in Wales!

Although there is no direct evidence that Evan Roberts specifically taught the message of Israel identity, it is evident that the prayers, and many of the messages preached both prior to, and during the Revival, were based on the promises God had made to His people Israel.

Reader Harris

In fact, one of the main inspirations of the Revival, was a sermon preached by the noted Judge, Reader Harris Q.C., founder of the Pentecostal League of Prayer, in Carmarthen in January 1904. An ardent believer in Britain's Israel identity, Harris based his belief that Wales and Britain were to experience a Pentecostal Outpouring, on God's promises to Israel.

W. O. Hutchinson

The Apostolic Faith Church, led by Pastor W.O. Hutchinson of Bournemouth, also influenced by the Welsh Revival, was the first Pentecostal movement to be established in Britain, and believed in, and preached, Britain's identity with the "lost" tribes of Israel.

Daniel and Jones Williams

Daniel and Jones Williams of South Wales, converts of the Revival, were ordained by Pastor W.O. Hutchinson, under auspices of the Apostolic Faith Church.

The work in Wales, renamed the "Apostolic Church", flourished in the ongoing Spirit of the Revival, throughout the British Isles and overseas. "Pastor Dan" Williams, with the support of his brother Jones, pioneered the work, from their home village of Penygroes, in South Wales.

The movement rapidly spread throughout Wales, England, Scotland, Ireland and overseas. Although the Apostolic Church no longer preaches the "Israel" identity, there is evidence that its founders, and many of its earlier leaders, believed in Britain's Israel identity.

George and Stephen Jeffreys

Undoubtedly George and Stephen Jeffreys were the most noted of the ministers to be produced by the Welsh Revival. Their international Evangelistic and Healing Campaigns resulted in multiplied thousands who were saved and healed through the Lord Jesus Christ.

Ardent believers in the "Israel" identity of the British and related peoples, when the Elim movement founded by him suppressed the message, George Jeffreys launched the Bible Pattern Church, which propagated this "Israel" truth. George Jeffreys also held a Convention, annually, with a packed house, in the Royal Albert Hall in London.

~~~~~~~~~~~~~~~~~~~~~~~~~~~~~~~

The purpose of the New Testament *Feast of Pentecost* is to empower the message of the *Feast of Passover*.

The proclamation of the *Feast of Trumpets* combined with the power of Pentecost is to call the Israel nations to repentance at the *Feast of Atonement*.

The *Feast of Atonement* is to prepare the hearts of the people of Israel for the coronation of their King, the Lord Jesus Christ at the *Feast of Tabernacles*.

Instead, modern Pentecostalism has built shrines to the past, playgrounds for the present and an escape route for the future. It refuses to sound the silver trumpets of salvation heralding the coming of King Jesus to His Kingdom, to sit upon the throne of His father David.

Charles A. Jennings

297

THREE SCHOOLS OF THOUGHT ON THE ISRAEL QUESTION

Evangelist George Jeffreys
1889-1962

George Jeffreys is recognized as one of Great Britain's greatest
evangelists since John Wesley

INTRODUCTION
By Charles A. Jennings

Throughout the history of the church, the Lord has been faithful in
visiting His people with times of spiritual refreshing and demonstrations
of His saving and healing power. During the early 20th century, Great
Britain experienced a 'Book of Acts' type of revival through the ministry
of Evangelists George and Stephen Jeffreys.

The sixth of eight sons, George Jeffreys was born in Wales in 1889.
He was raised in the Welsh Independent (Congregational) Church. He
and his older brother Stephen (1876-1943) were converted during the
Welsh revival on November 20, 1904. George had very ill health and
suffered from a speech impediment and facial paralysis. The same day in
April 1911 in which he was baptized in water, he was baptized in the
Holy Spirit and miraculously healed. Soon afterward he entered the
evangelistic ministry and in 1915 formed the Elim Pentecostal Alliance.

In 1924 both George and Stephen spent five months holding
evangelistic meetings in the United States and Canada.

George continued to hold revival crusades for many years not only in Great Britain, but in Sweden, Switzerland and other European cities. In each meeting, there were huge crowds, scores of healings and thousands converted.

In July 1914, while Stephen Jeffreys was pastor of the Island Place Mission, a vision occurred while he was preaching. On the wall of the church appeared the face of a lamb and then changed to the face of the "Man of Sorrows," which was witnessed up to six hours by hundreds of people. Until 1935 Stephen traveled and preached in the United States, New Zealand, Australia and South Africa which resulted in thousands of converts.

In his book *"With Signs Following,"* Stanley H. Frodsham reported that "from Wales God raised up two brothers who have been more or less leaders in the Pentecostal work in the British Isles." He continued by saying;

"The campaigns held by George Jeffreys have packed some of the largest halls in the British Isles, including the historic hall of St. Andrews, Glasgow, with its seating capacity of 4,500; the Guild Hall of Plymouth, which accommodates nearly 4,000; the Dome of Brighton, formerly the property of King George IV, with seating capacity of 300; and the Royal Albert Hall of London which accommodates 10,000. Over 1200 were swept into the Kingdom in the campaign held in Brighton, and 300 gave testimony to the Lord's healing power." One who attended this meeting writes, "Hundreds of people have testified in the meeting to having been healed. People who only a few weeks ago were bedridden, or wheeled about in chairs, are today walking and praising God for His kindness in healing them. Lame ones, who moved only by the aid of crutches, are able to dispense with these. Deaf ones have been made to hear, blind ones to see, fourteen testified to having been cured of cancer, tuberculosis or tumor."

Rev. Albert W. Edsor, in his book, *"George Jeffreys-Man of God"* states:

Principal George Jeffreys, founder of the Elim Movement in 1915 and later of the Bible-Pattern Church Fellowship, was undoubtedly one of this century's greatest evangelists and Bible teachers. As one has written: "...Beginning in obscurity, he was not only unsponsored by the religious denominations of his day but opposed by them. Yet he pioneered with the utmost courage the full New Testament message until the largest auditoriums of this and other lands were crowded to capacity with men and women who were being moved Godward by his powerful ministry."

Both George and Stephen Jeffreys were strong believers in the Christian Anglo-Israel message of the Bible. The following is an article written by George Jeffreys which both clarifies and confirms his belief in this great Biblical truth of the Christian Anglo-Israel message.

THE ISRAEL QUESTION
By GEORGE JEFFREYS

There are different Schools of Thought on the Israel question, just as there are on other questions and there are sincere teachers in all. How can it be otherwise if all are to contend earnestly for the whole Counsel of God! The purpose of differences of opinion in the churches is emphasized by Weymouth's translation of I Corinthians 11:19;
"For there must of necessity be difference of opinion among you, in order that it may be plainly seen who are the men of sterling worth among you."

We should, therefore, encourage the examination of various schools of thought, for by this means the mind is enriched, truth is revealed and the character tested.   Ever since my early pioneering days of the Pentecostal truth, with signs following the preaching of the Scriptures, opposers have known that the message could be hindered by cutting out discussion about it, whereas open discussion helped to spread it. We have not been ignorant of these devices and, following the example of the Apostle Paul, have gone on *"...disputing and persuading the things concerning the Kingdom of God"* (Acts 19:8).

The devices to hinder the Israel truth are exactly the same as those used to hinder the Pentecostal truth. The undercurrent of misrepresentation of the Israel truth confuses the mind and hides the truth, whereas free discussion opens up the understanding and spreads truth.

THE THREE SCHOOLS OF THOUGHT

The Jewish School

According to this School, Jews only are the lineal descendants of God's chosen people Israel and the prophecies and promises concerning Israel have either been, or yet will be fulfilled in the Jewish people.

I cannot accept the view of the Jewish school, because the Judah tribe is only a very small part of Israel. There are twelve heads of Israel tribes named in Genesis 49 and with Ephraim and Manasseh, the sons of

301

Joseph, of chapter 48, to whom the birthright came from Jacob/Israel through Joseph, there are thirteen in all.

Jacob/Israel's prophetic blessings to the descendants of Ephraim and Manasseh have not been fulfilled in the Judah tribe, neither can be, for the simple reason they were not promised to the descendants of Judah; "...he (Manasseh) also shall become a people, and he also shall be great: but truly his younger brother (Ephraim) shall be greater than he, and his seed shall become a fullness of nations" (Genesis 48:19 R.V. marg).

The descendants of the whole house of Israel are on earth today and will be revealed in the last days as one great nation, with Jehovah in the midst of them. That day, thank God, is very near!

"And I will make them one nation in the land upon the mountains of Israel; and one king shall be king to them all: and they shall be no more two nations, neither shall they be divided into two kingdoms any more at all" (Ezekiel 37:22).

"And ye shall know that I am in the midst of Israel, and that I am the Lord your God, and none else; and My people shall never be ashamed" (Joel 2:27).

The Church School

According to the Church School, the Church has taken the place of the Israel Nation and God's promises to Israel have to be spiritualized.

I cannot accept the view of the Church School because God has not substituted the Church of Christ for the Nation of Israel. God's promises to the earthly Nation have never been – and never can be – fulfilled in the spiritual Body of Christ.

Israel, the elect company of servant nations, with the members of the Church of Christ in her midst, has been and is being made a blessing to the whole world, as foretold in the prophetic Scriptures. Missionaries have been sent forth in the fullness of the blessing of the Gospel of Christ to the ends of the earth; the Scriptures are being distributed throughout the world; heavy burdens of other nations are being borne; the oppressed are being set free and bread is being dealt to the hungry. The Scriptural marks of Israel and its spiritual remnant can be seen by all who have eyes to see.

"I say then, Hath God cast away His people? God forbid. For I also am an Israelite, of the seed of Abraham, of the tribe of Benjamin. God hath not cast away His people which He foreknew ...For if the casting away of them be the reconciling of the world, what shall the receiving of them be, but life from the dead?" (Romans 11:1,2 & 15)

302

Israel Is An Election Of Race

"But thou, Israel, art My servant, Jacob whom I have chosen, the seed of Abraham My friend. Thou whom I have taken from the ends of the earth, and called thee from the chief men thereof, and said unto thee, Thou art My servant; I have chosen thee, and not cast thee away" (Isaiah 41:8-9).

The Church Is An Election of Grace

"Put on therefore, as the elect of God, holy and beloved, bowels of mercies, kindness, humbleness of mind, meekness, long suffering...And whatsoever ye do in word or deed, do all in the name of the Lord Jesus, giving thanks to God and the Father by Him" (Colossians 3:12 & 17).

The Israel School

According to the Israel School, a large part of the British Commonwealth of Nations, the Americans and other Celto-Anglo-Saxon peoples are the lineal descendants of Israel. But like the lineal descendants of Gentiles, each Israelite must be born again to enter the Church of Christ.

I accepted the view of the Israel School in the early days of my Elim ministry. That eminent barrister-at-law, Mr. John Leech, MA.,LL.B., K.C., introduced me to this School nearly 40 years ago (about 1920); and I have remained in it ever since.

The indisputable fact that, although some Jews are Israelites, all Israelites are not Jews, gave me the right premises that led to right conclusions. The truth is demonstrated in my own experience; all Welshmen are British, but all British are not Welshmen.

Should a person be so foolish as to teach that the Welsh people constitute the whole of the British Commonwealth of Nations, he would rightly be considered a fanatic of the first order. Yet some can teach that the Jewish people are the whole of the Israel Company of Nations and regard themselves as being wise!

Furthermore, those who teach that Israel and the Church are the same should be consistent and teach that the natural birth into the Israel Nation is the same as the spiritual birth into the Church of Christ.

It is evident that those who do not distinguish between the Jews, Israelites and the members of Christ's body have not paid much heed to Paul's message to Timothy:

"Study to shew thyself approved unto God, a workman that needeth not to be ashamed, rightly dividing the Word of truth" (II Timothy 2:15).

1.   Some Jewish people form the smaller number of the lineal descendants of the whole house of Israel. The larger number (partially blind to their destiny in Christ) are in the British Commonwealth of Nations, in America and in the Celto-Anglo-Saxon Nations.
". . .blindness in part is happened to Israel, until the fulness of the Gentiles be come in" (Romans 11:25).
2.   The promises made to Israel could not be applied to the Body of Christ, the Church. They were to have their fulfillment in families, nations, kings and land.
"And God appeared unto Jacob again, when he came out of Padanaram, and blessed him. And God said unto him, Thy name is Jacob; thy name shall not be called any more Jacob, but Israel shall be thy name; and He called his name Israel. And God said unto him, I am God Almighty: be fruitful and multiply; a nation and a company of nations shall be of thee, and kings shall come out of thy loins: And the land which I gave Abraham and Isaac, to thee I will give it, and to thy seed after thee will I give the land" (Genesis 35:9-12).
3.   After Abraham had offered up Isaac God gave him an unconditional promise concerning his seed. This has never been fulfilled in any one tribe, but it has been fulfilled in the peoples mentioned in The Israel School.
"And the Lord called unto Abraham out of heaven the second time, and said, By Myself have I sworn, saith the Lord, for because thou hast done this thing, and hast not withheld thy son, thine only son; that in blessing I will bless thee, and in multiplying I will multiply thy seed as the stars of heaven, and as the sand which is upon the sea shore; and thy seed shall possess the gate of his enemies; and in thy seed shall all the nations of the earth be blessed; because thou hast heard my voice" (Genesis 22:15-18).
4.   The Israel Nation was destined to be in existence as long as the sun, moon and stars are in existence. This was a promise concerning the whole House of Israel and not just one tribe.
"Thus saith the Lord, which giveth the sun for a light by day, and the ordinances of the moon and of the stars for a light by night, which divideth the sea when the waves thereof roar; The Lord of hosts is His name: if these ordinances depart from before Me, saith the LORD, then the seed of Israel also shall cease from being a nation before Me forever" (Jeremiah 31:35-36).
5.   Israelites and Gentiles must be born again before they can become members of the Body of Christ, the Church.

"That which is born of the flesh is flesh; and that which is born of the Spirit is spirit. Marvel not that I said unto thee, Ye must be born again" (John 3:6-7).

ALBION C. GAUNT

One of the converts under the ministry of George Jeffreys in the revival meeting held in Hull, England in 1922 was Albion C. Gaunt. He was later affiliated with Principal George Jeffreys in ministry and pastored a church with the Bible Pattern Church Fellowship.

In the publication; *These Bible Days '83* of November 1983 Pastor Gaunt related in a personal testimony his conversion to Jesus Christ and belief in the Anglo-Israel message.

A PERSONAL TESTIMONY
By Albion Gaunt

It was a joy to read about the revival days of the early part of this generation which were so graphically described by Pastor Albert W. Edsor in his article which appeared in the July issue of the 'National Message' and for which we have been given kind permission to reproduce in this edition of "These Bible Days, '83'.

As a grateful convert of those revival days, I feel inspired afresh to testify to the effect that that revival had on me regarding my conversion and subsequent call to the ministry.

Modern evangelistic ventures doubtless spring from a sincere sense of need. Crusades are arranged for specific areas and are prayerfully and well prepared by local churches over a period of months in advance of the proposed campaign. The visiting evangelist is, therefore, usually assured of an encouraging start from the word 'go'. However, in those early days, George Jeffreys and his brother Stephen, would come to a city to find no such welcome, local churches being often dubious of 'strange phenomena' associated with the meetings, howbeit, often by sheer hearsay. Some of the initial meetings in a city were often exceedingly small, but under the obvious blessing of God and anointing of the Holy Spirit, numbers mushroomed until the largest halls had to be requisitioned to accommodate eager crowds seeking true spiritual satisfaction.

305

Such a visitation took place in my home city of Hull in May 1922 when the evangelists came for a series of meetings following a God-honoured campaign at Grimsby. It was the news of outstanding revival scenes which had filtered through to Hull along with an advertisement in the local newspapers which brought together the first nucleus of people to an initial meeting in the Jubilee Methodist Church schoolroom where my father and mother were caretakers. Within the week, however, the large Metropole Ball room had to be hired and was packed to capacity with crowds outside not able to find even standing room.

I had been brought up in 'the fear of the Lord' by godly parents. My mother, in particular, had an implicit faith in the absolute infallibility of the Bible and its prophetic word concerning climatic world affairs and their pointing to the coming again of Jesus Christ to set up His kingdom on earth. Because of their teaching and daily conducting of evening prayers and Bible reading, I came to look upon my personal reading of the Bible and saying prayers as a solemn duty. Later, in the absence of my father who had volunteered to join the armed forces in World War I, mother continued faithfully to teach her children the way of the Lord. I remember well her faith in Psalm 91 and the way she used to commit us to the safe keeping of the Most High during the zeppelin raids on Hull. Nevertheless, in spite of her teaching and prayers, I found 'religion' only in an outward fashion which failed to give me peace of mind when confronted with continual failure to live up to all she had taught us. I was sorely conscious of sinful ways, and the learning of the 'Ten Commandments' at school only served to strike fear into my soul. The thought of one day giving an account of my life to God troubled me. Mother's comforting anticipation of the second coming of the Lord brought no such comfort to me. Would He come sometime and catch my parents away and leave me behind?

One day, mother asked me to take her to the revival meetings now transferred to the city centre. By the reports filtering through from Grimsby, I had conjured up in my mind that the visiting evangelists must be very holy men because, when they laid their hands on the sick unmistakable miracles of healing had taken place. The instantaneous raising up of a neighbor of ours who was a complete helpless and hopeless spinal case greatly impressed me for, I had never witnessed such a miracle before.

As the evangelist preached it became evident that there was something more than a mere outward form of 'religion'. I realised I must know Jesus Christ in a personal way. Jesus was not just a historical figure but is alive now and in my heart I recognised His voice. I became aware that night that I had sinned because I was a sinner by NATURE. As the meeting progressed, it became quite clear to me that I needed two vital releases; the BLOTTING OUT of my past personal sins and a CHANGE of heart which was the reason for my sinning. I learned, moreover, that the Son of God became flesh and lived amongst men and as such He voluntarily took upon Himself the PENALTY of sin and the breaking of the POWER of our sinful disposition in His great work of atonement on the cross in our room and stead. It suddenly dawned upon me what Jesus really meant when He said to Nicodemus, *"Ye must be born again"*, that is, to receive a NEW SPIRITUAL NATURE. The way was now open for me to accept the facts and enter into their benefits – pardon, peace and to be a *"partaker of the divine nature"* of Christ. For, the Bible declares, *"As many as RECEIVED Him, to them gave He power to become the sons of God"*. "Upon a life I did not live; upon a death I did not die; another's life, another's death, I stake my whole eternity". Tremblingly and yet assuredly I responded there and then to the call and accepted Jesus Christ as my Saviour. Not a shadow of doubt has crossed my mind from that day to this and the passage of time has only served to deepen that assurance.

My mother's faith in God and His prophetic word certainly laid a foundation in my life, a foundation I was not aware of at first but began to feel the reality of it when I came to know God for myself through my newly found salvation. Therefore, there was a ready response in my heart as George Jeffreys expounded in succeeding meetings, different aspects of the prophetic Word of God. Thus the Holy Spirit was graciously preparing me for further teaching which was to come later from Mr. George Aiers, the secretary of my first pastorate in Hornsey, N. London. Through his saintly care I came through to the baptism of the Holy Spirit and simultaneously to understand the wider issues of Israel's identity with that of the Anglo-Celtic-Saxon peoples as distinct from true Jewry and their plaice in the all-comprehensive plan of God as it is being translated into history. It is the strong conviction that the Lord has graciously given to me a particular emphasis relevant to these days which has always been and continues to be the driving force of my life.

" BRITAIN IS ISRAEL "

DECLARES FAMOUS REVIVALIST

WILL NOT BE CONQUERED

Speaking at the Albert Hall, Nottingham, on Thursday, Principal George Jeffreys, the famous revivalist, dealt with marvels of Bible prophecy.

Two-thirds of the Bible was prophecy, he said. When Jerusalem was delivered in 1917, a prophecy made 2,520 years before was fulfilled. It had been prophesied that the Lord would deliver the land "as birds flying." A bomber squadron flew over the city and the Turks fled, so fulfilling the prophecy.

"I do not believe for a moment that Britain is to be conquered," he asserted, "for the simple reason that she is Israel. To Israel the promise was made 'Thou shalt be a company of nations.' The only company of nations in the world to-day is the British Empire, so she must be Israel. Israel was to become a great family. The British Empire has 500,000,000 subjects. Israel was to possess the gates of her enemies. The British Empire possesses those gates at Gibraltar, Suez, Malta, Aden, the Straits of Dover, &c."

There were signs of Christ's second coming on every hand, he declared—the return of the Jews to Palestine, signs in the astronomical realm, and signs in the religious world.

"God will protect and deliver us," he said, "but the deliverance will come the sooner if the nation will repent and turn to God."

Principal Jeffreys' statements above were made on October 17, 1940. The article was published in the *Spalding Free Press* on October 21, 1940

308

LIFE BEGINS AT 47!

A Personal Testimony
and
THE STORY OF ISRAEL

John A. Lovell D.D.
1907-1974
Pastor, Evangelist, Author, Publisher
affirms his belief in the Gospel of the Kingdom

Introduction
By Charles A. Jennings

Among some of the most tireless and tenacious workers in the vineyard of the Lord, in spite of physical difficulties and opposing forces was Dr. John. A. Lovell. As a young man John Lovell was converted to a living faith in Jesus Christ. He received his B.A. degree from Harden-Simmons University in Abilene, Texas. In his burning desire to work for the Lord and to serve His people, in addition to his obligations while attending University, he would drive to various small churches to minister on the week-ends. He founded and/or served several Baptist churches during the late 1920's through the 1930's.

As a young man in his mid twenties, John Lovell began to reap the physical consequences of his ceaseless activities and tireless labor of love. He developed a serious throat condition and was advised to take a period of prolonged rest. In 1934 he traveled to Miami, Florida in hopes of finding a comfortable environment in order to recover. Even in his weakened condition, while in Miami he became involved in Christian ministry and in-depth study of the Holy Scriptures. While sincerely seeking the Lord through His Word and prayer, the Holy Spirit began to reveal to him the profound truth of the Christian Israel Kingdom Covenant message of Scripture and its fulfillment in the Western European people of today.

After leaving Miami he pastored churches in Texas and had a radio program out of Dublin, Texas, and later broadcast on more than one hundred radio stations. He pastored *Trinity Baptist Church* in Abilene, Texas and also churches in the Los Angeles area and finally established *First Covenant Church* and the *Kingdom Digest,* a Christian family magazine in Dallas, Texas.

In 1954, after years of seeking the Lord for a deeper walk in Him, Pastor John Lovell received the experience known as the Baptism of the Holy Ghost. He received this life changing experience during a revival service at the Hemphill Heights Assembly of God Church of Ft. Worth, Texas. His testimony was later printed in *The Pentecostal Evangel*, *Weekly Voice of the Assemblies of God* magazine of March 13, 1955 in an article entitled "Life Begins at 47."

Below is a copy of Dr. John Lovell's personal testimony in his own words.

*From **The Pentecostal Evangel,** March 13, 1955*

LIFE BEGINS AT 47!

Dr. J.A. Lovell of Fort Worth, Texas
Tells How a New Life Began For Him When He was
Baptized With the Holy Spirit.

"It has been my pleasure to be in the ministry nearly thirty years serving the Lord as faithfully as I knew how. During this time, having held several pastorates in Texas, California and Florida, having traveled over one million and a half miles and now editing one monthly and two weekly publications, being engaged in broadcasting and many other phases of Christian work, and pastoring the First Covenant Church in Dallas, I can truly testify that the Lord has led me along the way, protecting and blessing me wonderfully.

Yet, I can honestly say that the thing I am about to relate – that is, the experience I had last year – has brought more peace, happiness, power and blessings than any other experience I have had in my spiritual life.

During my entire ministry, despite the blessings I have had and the wonderful way in which God has blessed my work, I have often felt that there was something which some others had which I did not have. I always passed off the feeling by simply thinking that perhaps I was mistaken, that everything was all right, that I had all that God had to offer. It wasn't until recently that I became deeply concerned about a lack in my life and ministry – a lack of power, an emptiness that should certainly be filled before I could be the minister I wanted to be in shepherding the sheep the Lord had placed under my care.

It took some heartbreaking experiences, loss of appetite, inability to sleep, and many other trials to cause me to finally stop and begin seriously to inquire what was wrong in my life and ministry, and to remedy the situation, if possible. In fact, the condition finally became so acute that I lost nearly ten pounds over a three week period. I became depressed, discouraged, and weary, not knowing exactly what I was seeking after, not knowing exactly what was wrong, but knowing, at least, that something was sorely needed in my life and ministry.

I finally, in utter desperation, asked the Lord for some signs, some evidences, some concrete happenings which would show me what was wrong, what I needed and what steps I should take. One night after I had retired, a Baptist lady, who was a member of my congregation in Abilene, Texas, many years ago, called me on the phone. She awakened me out of a sound sleep to tell me that I had been put on her heart and she was praying that I would receive the baptism of the Holy Spirit. I believe she was a messenger of God. I began to consider that perhaps this was the thing that I should seek after in trying to solve my problem.

In the office two or three days later I asked the Lord to give me a verse of Scripture, and as I opened the Bible my eyes fell on this verse. *"Then laid they their hands on them, and they received the Holy Ghost."* That was the second sign I received. They were both definite leads that the Lord wanted me to seek the baptism of the Holy Spirit, a gift which He had freely offered, not only to me, but to all others who would qualify, who would humble themselves, cast aside their prejudices and pride, and yield themselves fully to God.

Another sign came –a letter from one of my good friends and contributors, telling me that she was sorry she had written me a letter saying that she didn't believe in the baptism of the Holy Spirit. She told me of her pastor, a Baptist minister, receiving the baptism of the Holy Spirit. She said that she too had received this precious gift and she now believed that it was a blessing every child of God should seek and receive.

Later I received word that several of my other friends (including Baptist, Presbyterians and Methodists, some of whom were ministers, others teachers) had begun to seek the baptism of the Holy Spirit as a solution to their spiritual problems.

I decided these were all the "signs" I needed. I knew it was the baptism of the Holy Spirit I should seek after. I felt the need of humbling myself, putting aside any misunderstanding, surrendering myself completely to the Lord and giving up anything and everything that might keep me from receiving this precious gift of the Holy Spirit. This I did, preparing my heart and mind for nearly two weeks, sleeping and eating very little, praying and meditating much.

Finally, one night, I visited Hemphill Heights Assembly of God in Fort Worth, Texas (E.R. Anderson, Pastor). I went for the purpose of going to the altar and seeking the blessing of the baptism of the Holy Spirit. Upon entering the building, I noticed a smell of fresh paint, which was quite strong. Having been allergic to it, such smell making me sick quickly, I thought I would enjoy the song service and then leave. A friend began to pray that I would be blessed, and that I would not be affected by the paint. I can honestly say the paint did not bother me that night, and it didn't bother me afterwards. (My own church has been painted also, and for three Sundays I have had to endure the strong smell of paint, yet it still hasn't bothered me – a miracle from God!)

Evangelist Paul McGechie delivered an earnest, Spirit-filled message from the Word of God, and then invited people to come to the altar who wanted to be filled with the Holy Spirit. I immediately went to the front, and there I knelt, humbly, at the old-fashioned altar. I began to ask the Lord to keep His promise. Having already made the preparation necessary, I asked Him to fill me with His Holy Spirit, to give me the gift that He has offered so freely to anyone who would qualify. Tender, understanding, sympathetic altar workers suggested that I lift my hands toward Heaven, and simply begin to praise the Lord for the gift He was going to give me that night. That I did, and after a few moments the blessing came. Having yielded myself completely to the Holy Spirit and having put out of my life everything that would hinder, I received the precious gift which I was seeking–the baptism of the Holy Spirit. The Lord gave the evidence by performing a miracle and making it possible for me to speak to Him in another language! Praise the Lord! This was His evidence that He had baptized me with the Holy Spirit! It was a glorious moment, a sacred hour–one that I shall never forget.

As I got up from my knees, I felt as if I weighed no more than a feather! I felt emptied of everything in me that should not be in a child of God. I was given a spirit of humility, a greater spirit of love, and a forgiving spirit, such as I never had. I was joyous. My mind was tranquil. I was happy in the Lord. My appetite returned. That night I had the first sound sleep in several weeks!

I had had a fear of going through certain downtown sections late at night, lest the "chain gangers" attack me. That night it was late when I drove through those sections of the city, but I was praising the Lord and enjoying my Christian experience, wholly unconscious of any fear whatsoever!

I can truthfully say that the baptism of the Holy Spirit has made a great difference in my spiritual life. It has made my home life richer, sweeter, and more complete. Our office is now heaven on earth. Our ten o'clock devotionals each morning with our staff are nothing short of an old-fashioned revival meeting! At our church in Dallas, which I have pastored for more than eight years, I told the congregation about my experience and eighty-one people, most of whom were adults, came forward showing their willingness to seek the baptism of the Holy Spirit. The next night I saw forty-three of these people on their knees before God, praying for the same blessing their pastor had received.

The Bible class I am teaching has been rejuvenated and revived. We have seen many souls saved. We are having the greatest revival in our church we have ever had. People are coming to my office to seek God. Some are seeking His Spirit; others come for healing. It is simply marvelous what a difference the baptism of the Holy Spirit makes in one's life.

I beg you, if you have not received the fullness of His Spirit, to seek this gift of God, this blessed baptism at once. God's Spirit being the life of God and the power of God, you will need this power, this divine life, this precious experience in the days that lie ahead. Prepare yourself. Wait upon the Lord! Praise Him until you have received the gift of the Holy Spirit and until your life is saturated, baptized, immersed and filled with this precious life and power of God – His Holy Spirit. You will be fortified and equipped for a closer walk with God and you will be able to touch and help more lives!

(Since I am now 47 years of age, and life means so much more to me than ever before in my Christian experience, it was suggested to me, as I prayed, that I make the title of this article, "Life Begins at 47!)" The following article entitled, *The Story of Israel*, is Dr. Lovell's firm affirmation in the Gospel of the Kingdom and how God in His great plan of mercy has chosen the Anglo-Saxon nations to be His servant people and the recipients of the covenants of the Bible.

313

The Story of Israel
By J. A. Lovell, D.D.

(Reprinted from the *Kingdom Digest*)

Our belief in the origin of the Anglo-Israel people and their lineal descent from the tribes of Israel does not take one iota from the weightier matters of salvation, which rest – as they must always do – on the precious sacrifice of Jesus Christ our Lord, who died that sinful men might live, and whose vicarious atonement alone can avail to rescue the sinner from the consequences of the fall, whether he be an Israelite of the kingdom of Ephraim, Manasseh, a Jew, or a non-Israelite Gentile.

Why we so persistently urge the fact of our descent from Israel upon the notice of our fellow men is because, if the facts be true and our deductions from them sound, they are to the glory of God and the comfort, consolation and safety of our nation temporally and spiritually, and evidence to all men throughout the world that there is a God who takes an interest in the affairs of men.

Our teaching, therefore, overthrows the arguments of the atheist and leaves the infidel confounded. Many professed atheists and agnostics have testified to their conversion to Christianity as the result of the teachings of the Kingdom Message.

We have one textbook – the Bible. The Bible is the most significant Book of all times. It contains the answer to all of the problems, which are troubling the world today, but it must be read with understanding. Such understanding we believe can only come as a result of the study of God's Word in the light of Kingdom teaching.

The Bible is an extraordinary book, or, rather, set of books. Writers of vastly different types compiled it over at least two thousand years. Critics and scoffers throughout the ages have assailed it, yet it is still the world's bestseller. It is misquoted, misunderstood and misrepresented, yet it is the priceless possession of the world's leading nations and the guide and comforter of kings, statesmen and humble peasants alike. Moreover, it purports to be "the Word of the Living God" yet, to most people, it is an appalling jigsaw puzzle. To assist and guide you – if you are willing to understand a little of its sublime picture – is my humble desire.

The picture presented by the Bible is like an ancient masterpiece over which, in the course of time, would-be students – as well as its severest critics – have painted their own ideas of what the picture should have been. The result is deep overlays of man-made opinions and ideas, which have to be removed little by little, or even chiseled off.

314

The story of the Bible begins with eternity and ends with eternity, but it is chiefly taken up with the events of a period of six thousand years, commencing 4000 B.C. (?), when Adam appeared on the scene.

For a moment, let us look at the first chapter of the book of Genesis, commonly called – even by many who should know better – "The Genesis Myth." The Bible purports to be accurate, and it opens with an extremely concise account of the creation of the universe and the formation of our solar system. Now science states that the five fundamental and basic elements are: time, force, space, matter and motion. Is it not wonderful that in the Bible – in the first book – in the first chapter – and in the first two verses – we find these words? *"In the beginning* (time) *God* (force) *created the heaven* (space) *and the earth* (matter), *and the spirit of God moved* (motion) *upon the face of the waters."*

And the marvelous scientific accuracy of this chapter and the other related passages does not stop there.

Just here I should like to give you what is to me a very beautiful tribute to the Bible:

Many years ago, with the Holy Spirit as my guide, I entered the wonderful temple of Christianity. I entered the portico of Genesis, walked down through the Old Testament art galleries where pictures of Noah, Abraham, Moses, Joseph, Isaac, Jacob and Daniel hung on the walls.

I passed into the music room of Psalms where the Spirit swept the keyboard of nature until it seemed that every pipe in God's great organ responded to the tuneful harps of David, the sweet singer of Israel.

I entered the chamber of Ecclesiastes, where the voice of the preacher was heard, and into the conservatory of Sharon and the lily of the valley's sweet-scented spices filled and perfumed my life.

I entered the business office of Proverbs, and then into the observatory room of the prophets, where I saw telescopes of various sizes pointing to far-off events, but all concentrated on the bright and morning star.

I entered the audience room of the King of kings and caught a vision of his glory from the standpoint of Matthew, Mark, Luke and John, and passed into the Acts of the Apostles where the Holy Spirit was doing His work in the formation of the infant church.

Then into the correspondence room, where sat Paul and Peter, James and John, penning their epistles. I stepped in the throne room of Revelation where towered the glittering peaks, and caught a vision of the King upon the throne in all His glory, and I cried:

315

"All hail the power of Jesus' Name:
Let angels prostrate fall,
Bring forth the royal diadem
And crown Him Lord of all."

Following quickly the story of creation, we are presented to Adam who came on the scene 4000 B.C.

As history shows, rapidly and continually, man went astray from God and His divine law, but some in every generation walked with God and strove to keep His commandments.

An extremely condensed history embodied in about a dozen chapters covers a period of more than two thousand years, which brings us to the call of Abraham about 1900 B.C. (Gen. 12:2,3), where we find the Lord saying to Abraham: *"And I will make of thee a great nation, and I will bless thee, and make thy name great; and thou shalt be a blessing: And I will bless them that bless thee, and curse him that curseth thee: and in thee shall all families of the earth be blessed."*

In due time Isaac was born – and to Isaac, Jacob was born. The blessings promised to Abraham and his seed were repeated to Isaac and his seed, and again to Jacob and his seed. These blessings were amplified, or rather, were given in greater detail on each successive occasion.

Jacob's name was changed to Israel – which means "ruling with God." Jacob begat twelve sons who became patriarchs, and from them sprang the twelve tribes of Israel known as the Israelites.

The Israelites, while few in number, went down into Egypt in the time when Jacob-Israel's son Joseph was what might be termed a prime minister there.

During the next several hundred years the Israelites increased and their Egyptian masters put them into bondage from which they were delivered about 1500 B.C. From Egypt they escaped as a rabble, a host of slaves who had just obtained their freedom. For forty years in the desert of Sinai they had to undergo a severe training to fit them for the work that lay ahead.

And the Lord said unto them, *"Now therefore, if ye will obey my voice indeed, and keep my covenant, then ye shall be a peculiar treasure unto me above all people: for all the earth is mine: And ye shall be unto me a kingdom of priests, and an holy nation. These are the words which thou shalt speak unto the children of Israel"* (Exodus 19:5,6).

God Himself was the King of Israel, and Israel was His people. He gave them laws both secular and religious, and by His servant Moses

316

trained them into an orderly community. He fed and watered them miraculously, and preserved them while disciplining them.

Then they were sent into the land of their forefathers, Abraham, Isaac and Jacob, to possess it. In the land of Palestine they were ruled over by Judges until they clamored for an earthly king in the time of Samuel, who reproved them saying: *"And when ye saw that Nahash the king of the children of Ammon came against you, ye said unto me, Nay; but a king shall reign over us: when the LORD your God was your king"* (I Samuel 12:12).

God allowed the Israelites to have an earthly king in the person of Saul. But Saul was not a success, and David was later chosen to replace him. Regarding David, it was promised (Jer. 33:17, 20, 26) that he should never lack an heir to reign *"upon the throne of the house of Israel."* David was followed by his son Solomon. Solomon's reign was a time of great expansion and prosperity, but also of very hard work; and at his death Rehoboam, his son, came to the throne.

The leaders of ten tribes came to Rehoboam and brought a mitigation of the strenuous labor conditions, which had been experienced under Solomon, but Rehoboam not only refused to grant their request but also threatened to greatly increase their burdens. So the ten tribes then revolted and formed themselves into the Northern Kingdom of Israel under Jeroboam the son of Nebat, leaving Rehoboam – Judah and Benjamin. The kingdom of Israel during most of its history had its seat of government at Samaria, while that of the kingdom of Judah was at Jerusalem. This division took place about 1000 B.C.

The Bible gives a resume of the history of these two kingdoms under their separate rulers. The histories are very short but very much to the point, and are to be found in II Kings 15:1-7. It is most explicitly pointed out that according as the people and their rulers kept the laws, which God had given them, were they blessed or punished.

During their period the power of Assyria had arisen in the area of the upper reaches of the Tigris and Euphrates with its capital at Nineveh. Assyria under Shalmaneser, attacked the Northern Kingdom of Israel, and finally his successor – King Sargon – took it into captivity and exile in 721 B.C. in the sixth year of Hezekiah, king of Judah, which was the ninth year of Hosea, king of Israel. And this fact is very important. In the fourteenth year of Hezekiah – eight years later – Sennacherib, king of Assyria, came up again against all the fenced cities of Judah and took them (II Kings 17:6,23; 18:1-13). Sennacherib – in an inscription – claimed to have sent 200,150 men of Judah to join the Israelitish captives near the Caspian.

From this exile these Israelites never returned. They, together with their Assyrian captors, have become lost to history. But the southern two-tribed kingdom of Judah continued its existence until about 120 years later, when it was invaded by the Babylonian forces under Nebuchadnezzar, and the first captives – including Daniel the prophet – were sent as exiles to Babylon in 604 B.C. The kingdom of Judah was subjected to attacks by Babylon for the next twenty years, until, after a siege, Jerusalem fell in 584 B.C. and King Zedekiah and his sons were captured. The Babylonians slew King Zedekiah's sons in his presence, put out his eyes, bound him with fetters and carried him away to Babylon. Jerusalem, the kings palace, the temple and all the houses were set on fire and destroyed, and the walls of the city were broken down. The vast bulk of the people were taken away to Babylon and only the poor of the land were left to be vinedressers and husbandmen.

This captivity – the Babylonian captivity – lasted seventy (lunar) years (Dan. 9:2), until Babylon was attacked and overthrown by the Persians under Cyrus in 536 B.C. In that year God moved Cyrus to issue a proclamation to the captives of Judah in Babylon (Ezra 1), authorizing them to return to their own land and to rebuild the temple.

You must keep in mind that during the intervening seventy years most of the original captives would have died. Others, deported as young children, were now very old men and women. Many had been born in Babylon and knew no other environment, so it is not surprising that less than fifty thousand elected to return to the land of their fathers (Ezra 2:64). These returned exiles were nicknamed Jews, and have never been lost to history.

Babylon fell, and as a world power, was succeeded by Medo-Persia, then by Greece and later by Rome. With Babylon disappeared the captive Israelites of the kingdom of Judah who did not elect to return to Palestine. These have been lost to history. So now ten tribes, plus the greater portion of the two-tribed kingdom of Judah, have disappeared from the pages of history.

The Jews continued in their own land until the time of the Romans. In 70 A.D., as a result of rebellion against their overlords, the Romans besieged Jerusalem, and after a terrible siege the city was taken and sacked, and the Jews were dispersed to become wanderers among the nations, without a country. (Jer. 24:9)

Between the years 700 and 500 B.C., a number of prophets – Isaiah, Jeremiah, Ezekiel, Daniel and others – prophesied the troublous times ahead, but all also spoke of a marvelous and blessed ending, for Israel, ultimately. Since 500 B.C., the greater part of the Israelites have been lost to history (though we all know where they are), and since 70 A.D. the Jews have been without a country of their own till recently – a despised race, downtrodden, their very name a by-word. So closed the Old Testament record..

Many people try to separate the Old from the New Testament entirely and thereby make for themselves unnecessary difficulties. The first book of the New Testament; the first chapter and the first verse reads: *"The book of the generation of Jesus Christ, the son of David, the son of Abraham,"* and proceeds to give a genealogy from Abraham onwards. Thereafter, there are constant references to the Old Testament prophecies and their fulfillment in – at that time – current events.

Christ Himself said that He came not to destroy, but to fulfill, and He was never tired of quoting the Old Testament. I am afraid that if you have not read and do not have a working knowledge of the Old Testament, you will not be able to fully understand the New.

From Matthew to Revelation, the New Testament is full of references to Israel and the old prophets. Much of the language is, of course, cryptic. Christ taught in parables, and when questioned by His disciples as to why He spoke in parables, He replied, *"He answered and said unto them, Because it is given unto you to know the mysteries of the kingdom of heaven, but to them it is not given. Therefore speak I to them in parables: because they seeing see not; and hearing they hear not, neither do they understand."* (Matt. 13:11,13). An effort has been made to understand, and those who will not make the effort are left in ignorance.

Christ came to His people at the time appointed and preached to them His message. Some believed, but the majority rejected Him and called down on themselves and their children that awful curse *"His blood be on us and on our children"* (Matt. 27:25).

Within forty years of His crucifixion, Jerusalem was destroyed, the temple – which was the center of this puppet theocratic state – was demolished, its services stopped, and the Jews dispersed as wanderers without a country until now. Where, then, is the wonderful future for which the seed of Abraham was raised, and which was the theme of the prophets? Yet Christ called His twelve disciples and commanded them, saying: *"...Go not into the way of the Gentiles, and into any city of the Samaritans enter ye not: But go rather to the lost sheep of the house of Israel"* (Matt. 10:5-6).

In Romans 11:1, Paul in his Epistle to the Romans writes, *"Hath God cast away his people? God forbid."* James (1:1) addresses his epistle *"to the twelve tribes which are scattered abroad."* And so we find

319

continuous evidence that ten-tribed Israel, though lost, were known to be in existence at the time of the early Christians.

Then we come to the last book of the Bible. *"The Revelation of Jesus Christ which God gave unto him,"* and which was communicated to John. In the Revelation are portrayed most vividly, often in a terrifying manner, events which, at that time, were still in the future. Throughout the Revelation constant references are made to Israel by word or by suggestion until the appearance of the New Jerusalem (Rev. 21:12), which *"had a wall great and high, and had twelve gates, and at the gates twelve angels, and names written thereon, which are the names of the twelve tribes of the children of Israel."*

So the story carries us on until the kingdoms of this world are become the kingdoms of our Lord and His Christ. Such is the basic theme of the Bible, the skeleton structure, as it were, on which the flesh and sinews are built, the whole body being given life by the Spirit of God – and dealing with one great theme – the story of Israel.

But the question arises, **"Where is Israel?"** Most of them were lost more than 2500 years ago – 500 years before Christ lived upon the earth. We – who know the Kingdom Message – can answer the question as to where Israel is. They are found today, largely among the Anglo-Saxon, Celtic, Scandinavian and Judah peoples. What a fascinating tale – The Story of Israel!

WHO HATH BELIEVED OUR REPORT?

FOREWORD
Pastor Ronald A. Poch

Isaiah begins the masterpiece of biblical prophecy in the 53rd chapter of the book that bears his name with this question, "Who hath believed our report?" Every sincere student of the Bible in the pursuit of truth must of necessity ask questions in order to be fully persuaded that the pathway they are on will not lead them into error, tragic detour, or spiritual confusion. All of God's people desire to have the Holy Spirit remove scales from their eyes to truly see God's marvelous plan and purpose unfold before them both personally and nationally. That has truly been my desire.

There have been doctrines, dogmas, and theological positions that I have held that were passed on to me because of what my denomination or my family believed. These can become strongholds to keep a person from progressing on in Divine revelation. I am not talking about lofty, ethereal, esoteric revelations, but that which is functional and extremely practical. What I mean is; God has a plan that will work; God has a Kingdom that will win.

What I now share with you changed my life in the early 1970's. I had pastored a Baptist church in a college town in northwest Pennsylvania from 1966-1968. Because of a sovereign move of the Holy Spirit I was asked to leave and subsequently invited to become a pastor in the Assemblies of God, the largest Pentecostal denomination in America. It was late 1971 that God sent two men into my life that would alter the course and direction that I would take and never again be the same. These choice vessels were Frank Daire and Edward Marks. Frank Daire was director of a ministry called *Word Emphasis Crusade* and Ed Marks pastored a church in East Lansing, Michigan called *Life Tabernacle*. Both of these men had been influenced by what was called the "Latter Rain" movement.

The "Latter Rain" movement was birthed in the late 1940's and early 1950's and one of the emphases was the restoration of the five-fold ministry of apostle, prophet, evangelist, pastor, and teacher according to Ephesians 4:11-14. Both Frank and Ed functioned in an apostolic and prophetic anointing. Much like Isaiah of old, the question they brought to my inquiring mind was the same as Isaiah's "Who hath believed our report?"

When these men crossed my path they didn't know the level of my desperation. I wanted more of God. I didn't need another good book or another tape to listen to. I didn't need another sermon to "wow" the people. These men touched my life, not with psychology, but with the "Spirit of the Living God." They didn't come to me with spiritual arrogance, a know-it-all attitude, or pompous pride. They came to harmonize the Word of God in my life. They showed me how to embrace the Scriptures and verify the truth and in doing so, deepen my commitment to Jesus Christ. I am so very grateful.

My, oh my, did changes ever come my way. You see, the Bible, God's Word, the Holy Scriptures are the foundation for change. If a sermon only reaches your feelings, your emotions, your thoughts, your mind and intellect, there will be no permanent change. This book that is now before you must touch your will. When the Holy Spirit moves in there will be permanent change. Also remember this; The Holy Spirit really doesn't care about the comfort of your flesh or your carnal nature. In this world there's nothing more dangerous than someone with nothing to lose...pride doesn't mean a thing.

Frank Daire and Ed Marks questioned me in two main areas of my belief system and as I look back with 20/20 hindsight, I see the providential hand of the Mighty God of Abraham, Isaac, and Jacob in what they declared to me.

The first question dealt with the interior part of me and the second question dealt with exterior issues, which affect us nationally to this very day. As a matter of fact these two doctrines that I came to embrace and cherish could be likened unto twin redheaded step-children left outside the door of the church...unloved and unwanted...with the leadership's strong rebuke --just go away!

The first issue they brought to me was about the Godhead and its correlation to water baptism. They encouraged me to look at Matthew 28:19, 20 and then find in the New Testament record where the apostles ever used the Trinitarian formula of Father, Son, and Holy Ghost. It can't be found! Believe me, I tried and tried. Searched and searched. It's just not there! This I found out later was the big issue in the early days of the "Pentecostal" Movement. In his book, *"People of the Spirit,"* Gary B. McGee gives a brief description of the magnitude of this issue in the early days of the Assemblies of God. "Interest had been growing since 1913 in restoring what some Pentecostals believed to be another apostolic pattern, one that required water baptism in the name of Jesus Christ only (Acts 2:38). But the matter involved much more than just an option from baptizing in the name of the Father, Son, and Holy Spirit as commanded by Jesus in Matthew 28:19. It represented a serious departure from biblical teachings and historic Christian doctrine. Called the "New Issue," it eventually led to a major division in the General Council in 1916. After the adoption of a strongly worded Trinitarian creedal declaration, those members who embraced "Jesus Name" or "Oneness" teachings walked out of the meeting. Ultimately, 25 percent of the ministers withdrew over the doctrine."

I must tell you that the revelation of the Name of the Lord Jesus Christ touched the very heart of me and I submitted in obedience to that Name and I was re-baptized according to Acts 2:36-38 and have never been the same and never regretted it, although it cost me my credentials with that denomination. I was disapproved by the organization but certainly hold no resentment or animosity toward them. It was an adventuresome time of life...and still is!

May I share with you this personal illustration? I recall with humor and laughter a time long ago when my wife asked me to feed our son John who was "graduating" from the small size jar of Gerber strained baby food to the larger "junior" size jar. Of course, the junior size was coarser and had lumps in it that the finely strained jar didn't have. I placed my boy in the high chair, tied the bib around his sweet face; spread the plastic tablecloth on the floor and armed myself with a plastic baby spoon. Was I ever in for a big surprise.

Number one mistake: I should have tied the bib on me. Why? Well, when I put the spoonful of the new coarser food in his mouth, it had a new and different texture to it that he didn't like. Not because it didn't taste good. Not because it didn't have nutritional value. Not because it was too hot or too cold. Simply because it was different than what he was used to. What do you think happened?

He scrunched up his face, puffed up his cheeks, shook his face from side to side, and drawing breath from inside those little lungs, his tongue shot out in rapid motion with spitting food in all directions, letting me know he didn't like the change of diet. I coaxed him, pleaded with him, and begged him with the game of "open your mouth, Johnny, here comes the choo-choo train into the tunnel." Did it work? No, he was addicted to the familiar. He was demonstrating a truth - "I don't like change."

Are you aware that God's people in the modern day church do the same thing? Why sure. If the minister of an average congregation sees a new truth or a deepening revelation and shares it with his people, what can he expect their reaction to be? Eyes widen, countenances change, heads shake from side to side, muscles tighten, arms fold in defiance against the preacher and just like my infant son John, spiritual food is spit in all directions with the unspoken thought of "false doctrine." The sad thing is; it's not false, just different from what they've been used to for years. Maturity is moving on in truth.

The second issue that Frank Daire and Ed Marks shared with me is what I call the "exterior" issue. This "exterior" issue is not a salvation issue but it surely will affect your world view. It will determine your prophetic outlook. This is what the church world refuses to deal with. This is what a popular preacher considers an anathema. Sort of "spiritual arsenic." It will most certainly create division, ostracism, or what I call "spiritual exile." Get out!!

That issue is..."Israel." Christians who perceive "Israel" to be nothing more than a few unbelieving Jews returning to the Middle East as the fulfillment of end-time prophecy are closing their minds to one of the most important truths in these last days. The Apostle Paul addressed this ever important question by asking; *"Hath God cast away His people?"* Paul's emphatic answer was; ***"God forbid."***

Others substitute the church for "Israel" and try to tell us that God has changed His mind, altered His eternal purpose, and broke His covenant with Abraham and now we are "spiritual" Israel. They thus hope that what God failed to do with Israel He will accomplish with the church. A lot of popular television preachers erroneously tell us that Israel is the Jew and the Jew only. This only leads to confusion, consternation, and controversy.

Where else can we look? How about the Christian nations of today? How do we explain that the greatest nation in the world today, America, has 6% of the world's population and possesses 50% of the world's wealth? Could it be that we are the "lost sheep" of the House of Israel? Why are we called Saxons? Why in the world are we called "Caucasians"? It's because our Israelite ancestors crossed the Caucasus Mountains in southeastern Europe in their migrations westward toward northwestern Europe and the British Isles. How is it that we send out most of the world's missionaries and print the majority of Bibles and Gospel literature? Surely, we are Abraham's seed that fulfills God's promise; *"and in thy seed shall all the nations of the earth be blessed"* Genesis 22:18. Let the voices of the past contained in this book be a witness to you and pray that the Holy Spirit will guide you into all truth.

THE GLORY AND THE VOICE
By Charles A. Jennings

Throughout the record of the Scriptures, it is very obvious that each time there was a visible manifestation of God's glory, the voice of God was heard to make known the progressive revelation of truth. The experience of Moses at the burning bush is a vivid example of God's glory being manifested in visible form that captured Moses' full attention. *"And Moses said, I will now turn aside, and see this great sight, why the bush is not burnt"* Ex. 3:3. After getting Moses' attention, *"God called unto him out of the midst of the bush"* Ex. 3:4. It was here that the Lord identified Himself as the covenantal God saying, *"I am the God of thy father, the God of Abraham, the God of Isaac, and the God of Jacob"* Ex. 3:6. He also revealed the very essence of His divine nature by telling Moses, *"I am that I am"* Ex. 3:14. The ultimate purpose of this supernatural phenomenon of the burning bush not being consumed, was to arrest the listening ear of Moses so that God could reveal to him His divine name and nature and the purpose for Moses' life work.

The first Pentecost as recorded in Exodus chapters 19-24, began with a visible and audible manifestation of God's majestic power and glory. Moses records that there was thunder, lightning, a thick cloud and the voice of the trumpet. In this first Pentecost Feast the Lord established a marital relationship with His people Israel. In Exodus 24:1-18 is recorded the wedding ceremony that would obligate national Israel to this very day to obey her vows made to her husband or suffer the consequences of her disobedience. Israel's binding promise was; *"All the words which the Lord hath said will be do"* Ex. 24:3. The first Pentecost was not just for the purpose so that people could enjoy the visible and audible display of God's power and glory upon Mt. Sinai. The voice of God trumpeted from Mt. Sinai and made known the calling of Israel as a national entity to be *"unto me a kingdom of priests, and a holy nation"* Ex. 19:6. There Israel received the Law whereby to live and govern its personal and national affairs as a faithful wife unto the Lord.

The antitype of the Old Testament Pentecost found in Acts 2 and following was for the same purpose, but under better terms of the New Covenant. The Lord manifest Himself in visible *"cloven tongues like as of fire,"* an audible *"sound from heaven as of a rushing mighty wind,"* and then the people *"were all filled with the Holy Ghost, and began to speak with other tongues"* Acts. 2:1-4. Is the gift of *"tongues"* the voice of God to Israel to reveal unto us her calling as *"a kingdom of priests, and a holy nation"* unto God, to place the law into the hearts of the Israelites (Heb. 8:8-13) and to reaffirm her marital relationship with her husband? Referring to Israel, the prophet Isaiah said *"with stammering lips and another tongue will he speak to this people"* Isa. 28:11. Paul the Apostle applies this prophecy to the gift of tongues in I Corinthians 14:21-22. The prophet Isaiah goes on to say that *"the word of the Lord was unto them precept upon precept, precept upon precept; line upon line, line upon line; here a little, and there a little"* Isa. 28:13. This clearly shows that through the Pentecostal gift of the Holy Spirit would be the means of the progressive revelation of truth to National Israel (the drunkards of Ephraim referred to Northern Israel, Isa. 28:1).

The Holy Spirit was definitely poured out as promised (Joel 2:28-29) upon the House of Israel in the early 1900's in Topeka, Kansas and Los Angeles, CA, which was only a down payment of which followed for the next fifty plus years. Has the modern Pentecostal movement, as a whole, seen the cloven tongues, felt the rushing wind, enjoyed the manifestation of God's power in miracles, yet never heard the real voice of God? What revelation of profound truth has proceeded from the experience of the Spirit's outpouring in the 20th Century? Has the Pentecostal movement received yet consumed the Baptism of the Holy Spirit upon its own lust and 'used' it for selfish reasons? Has the Holy Spirit and the gifts thereof been 'used' by men to further their ministerial reputations, build denominations and to distinguish one group of saints as being 'advanced' above all other saints, yet at the same time being deaf and sometimes despising the voice of God in the progressive revelation of truth?

In the Old Testament the Feast of Trumpets followed the Feast of Pentecost, but the modern Pentecostal movement refuses to move to the Feast of Trumpets so that it can hear the voice of God in unveiling of truth. Among the various reasons for the outpouring of the Holy Spirit, it was to; 1) *"let all the house of Israel know"* Acts 2:36. This was a reaffirmation of the covenantal and marital relationship with National Israel for; *"God hath not cast away his people which he foreknew"* Rom. 11:1-2. Another reason was to proclaim that 2) *"God hath made that same Jesus . . . both Lord and Christ"* Acts. 2:36. Through the power of anointed preaching by men with hearing ears tuned to the voice of God, the Holy Spirit makes known who Jesus really is. The purpose is to reveal that Jesus is "all in all" and that *"in Him dwelleth all the fulness of the Godhead* [deity] *bodily"* Col. 2:19. Jesus promised that when the Comforter was given to His followers *"he shall testify of me"* John 15:26.

To the spiritually keen observer it's blatantly clear that during the second half of the 20th century the modern Pentecostal movement was hijacked by religious alien interests. It is now being 'used' by the Zionist lobby, religious show business celebrities, prosperity seekers, prophets for profit, Hollywood-minded social competitors and the jet-set politically correct cultural reformers. Instead of progressing in truth the movement as a whole is regressing. The Bible standards that the Pentecostal preachers of yesteryear advocated, the present-day preachers now disdain. Sin that was once condemned is now condoned. Within the ranks of modern 'Pentecost' and Christendom at large it is now necessary to Christianize Christians.

- Apostolic Christianity started in Jerusalem as an **experience** with God. It resulted in a Divine relationship.
- It became an idea and philosophy in Greek culture for **debate.**
- Then it became an organization in Rome for **control.**
- It now appears to have become a financial enterprise in America for **gain.**

Has the modern Pentecostal movement grieved the Spirit of Grace whereby it was once sealed? Has it prostituted the gifts of God that were once the earmark of a genuine spiritual outpouring? Would the awful possibility spoken by our Lord Jesus apply to modern 'Pentecost'? He said; *"If therefore the light that is in thee be darkness, how great is that darkness"* Matt. 6:23. Modern 'Pentecost' needs a revival of **Spirit** and **Truth**. It needs to heed the many truths that men of God have been proclaiming for over a hundred years. One truth is the correct identification of the House of Israel and the House of Judah as being the Anglo-Saxon Germanic and related peoples. It needs to accept the Biblical fact of true Israel's marital and covenantal relationship with her Husband/Redeemer Jesus Christ and to recognize the moral and judicial law of God as the governmental constitution of the Kingdom that the Holy Spirit came to restore. The true Christian Israel nations as the offspring of Abraham (Gen. 12:1-2) has been a blessing to all the families of the earth, yet fails to recognize their calling. In their ignorance, most 'spirit-filled' Christians instead deny their covenantal relationship with their genealogical Israelite ancestors and give it away to an unbelieving Christ-rejecting people.

Within the very heart of the traditional Pentecostal movement the Lord has sent many anointed messengers proclaiming the Gospel of the Kingdom, yet most of them have been misunderstood, rejected and even excommunicated from fellowship. Some have been well-known, others less known and some unknown, but they continued to cry out as a voice in the wilderness of religious confusion. The ministers listed in this brochure all believed, proclaimed and received the Baptism of the Holy Spirit and opened their ears to the understanding of the Anglo-Israel truth that would transform not only Christendom, but western civilization, yet their message goes unheeded by the church at large. Among these were great men of faith, soul-winners, pastors, missionaries, apostles, prophets, Bible scholars, all having made a great contribution to the Body of Christ. Many of them had very unusual conversion experiences to Christ and received supernatural confirmations in their acceptance of the truth of the Anglo-Israel message of Scripture. The ministries of these men of God impacted multiplied tens of thousands of people for Jesus Christ and Biblical truth. The Pentecostal ministers listed here by no means include all those that believed and taught the Gospel of the Kingdom. If the truth be known there were hundreds who believed, but left no written record of any of their doctrinal beliefs.

If there is one group among the Body of Christ that should understand, appreciate and accept their Biblical heritage, it should be the Pentecostals. They are the ones who have seen the visible manifestation of God's power for over one hundred years. Instead, the gift of the Holy Spirit has been institutionalized and the people forced to strictly conform to religious protocol, thus restricting the saints from receiving any fresh truth by divine revelation. There are promises in God's Word concerning the outpouring of the Holy Spirit which definitely applies to and in turn identifies the recipients thereof as being the true House of Israel. Isa. 28:11-12; I Cor. 14:21-22; Isa. 44:1-3; Isa. 59:20-21; Joel 2:28-29

The Baptism of the Holy Spirit is an experience available today to every Christian believer according to Acts 2:38-39. I personally affirm my belief due to my own experience when only 17 years old.

Does not history record that spiritual revivals have primarily began among the western European people and they in turn took the message to other people, thus fulfilling one of the identifying marks of the children of Abraham? The Lord said unto Abram, *"and in thee shall all families of the earth be blessed."* Again, *"and in thy seed shall all the nations of the earth be blessed"* Gen. 12:13; 22:18. Our Lord has been faithful to His promises. Our Redeemer, the Lord Jesus Christ has come to Zion, sent unto us the Holy Spirit, placed His law in our hearts and His Word in our mouths. Praise the Lord, the lost sheep of Israel have been found.

CHARLES FOX PARHAM

Whenever the history of the latter-day spiritual outpouring is studied, Charles F. Parham is most likely always considered as being the father of the modern Pentecostal movement.

Charles Parham was born in Muscatine, Iowa on June 4, 1879, into a family of prominent English ancestry. When he was twelve years old his mother died while the family was living in Cheney, Kansas. As his mother was dying and saying her goodbyes to the family, she turned to him and said, "Charlie, be good." There in the presence of God and his dying mother, he vowed that he would meet her in heaven. Ever since the age of nine years old he had felt a divine call to the ministry and a strong attraction to Christian evangelism.

At the age of six months, Parham was taken with a fever that left him an invalid. He suffered for five years with dreadful spasms and enlargement of the forehead. As a young teenager, he was converted to Christ in a Congregational Church and enrolled in Southwestern Kansas College at sixteen. After a time of spiritual laxity, backsliding and then rebellion against entering the ministry, he was stricken with rheumatic fever. He was given up to die by his friends and physician. For several months he suffered while the words kept ringing in his ears; "Will you preach?" Finally, he began to repent and pray in desperation. Then every joint in his body loosened and every organ in his body was healed except his ankles. After renewing his vow to God to preach the Gospel, Parham experienced total healing. He records; "Then one night, while praying, under a tree, to which I had crawled on the old college campus, God instantly sent the virtue of healing like a mighty electric current through my body and my ankles were made whole, like the man at the beautiful gate in the Temple." Parham pastored a Methodist church for two years from 1893-1895 before joining the Holiness movement and opening the Bethel Healing Home in Topeka, Kansas in 1898. He began to publish his bi-monthly Holiness paper, ***The Apostolic Faith.***

After some time of further research into the Holiness movement and earnestly seeking for a greater personal manifestation of spiritual power, Parham returned to Topeka in September 1900. Here he opened a Bible school in an old mansion, where he encouraged the students to seek for a greater spiritual experience as recorded in the Book of Acts. One of the students, Agnes Ozman received the expected blessing and spoke in 'tongues' as a sign of its reception. This greatly encouraged Parham and the rest of the student body and within a few days he and about half of the students testified as to receiving the "Baptism of the Holy Spirit." A similar revival experience occurred in Galena, Kansas in 1903. From there, Parham went to Houston, Texas and held a ten-week training session which fanned the flames of the Pentecostal message throughout Texas. Soon afterward, the outpouring in Los Angeles, California occurred and quickly spread throughout the country. Among all the early leaders of the modern Pentecostal movement, Charles F. Parham is credited with formulating classical Pentecostal theology and is recognized as being its principle pioneer and founder.

As early as 1899 or before, Parham had recognized and was teaching the truth of the Christian Anglo-Israel message of the Bible. He earnestly contended for this truth until his death on January 29, 1929.

The following entries are excerpts or references to articles from various issues of *The Apostolic Faith*, which was edited by Charles Parham for over thirty years. In each article, written by him or another author, shows his commitment to the truth that the Anglo-Saxon and related peoples are the descendants of the ancient people of God, known as Israel.

THE KAISER'S LONG PEDIGREE

[London Chronicle] "Among the curiosities of the New Palace, Potsdam, which has been the scene of a fire, is a genealogical tree showing the name of King David engrossed at the root of it, with that of the Kaiser at the top, the descent being traced through his mother's family.

According to this genealogy the reigning house of Great Britain is descended from David through the eldest daughter of Zedekiah, who fled to Ireland in charge of the Prophet Jeremiah, and eventually married Heremon, King of Ulster."   ·   *The Apostolic Faith June 1913*

LOST TRIBES OF ISRAEL FOUND IN BRITAIN

"At the last session of the British Israel Association in this city, quotations were made from an address by the Hon. H.H. Stevens, and M.P. before the Forum of the First Congregational Church in Vancouver. Mr. Stevens said in part:

Christianity was brought to the Britains from Rome, but to the contrary, the Romans owed everything to the early Britains who established Christianity in their midst. The earliest Christian church outside of Jerusalem was established at Glastonbury, Somersetshire, England. And from there the new religion spread all over Europe.

Christianity was brought to the early Britains direct from Jerusalem by apostles of Christ shortly after the passion, and as early as 165 A.D. had become the National religion of the country. The general impression that Christianity had first been introduced into Britain by Augustine about 595 to 610 A.D. was entirely erroneous, as three British Bishops attended the Council of Arles A.D. 314."

The Emperor Constantine, who first supplanted the Crescent with the Cross at the head of his armies, was the son of a Roman General who had married a British Princess, and it was from his mother he learned Christianity. When King Caradoo, the ruling Sovereign of all the British tribes, was defeated after forty pitched battles and taken prisoner to Rome, his daughter Claudius accompanied him and established the first Christian church in Rome. Her brother Linus (both of whom are mentioned by Paul in II Timothy 4 and 21) was appointed the first Bishop of Rome by the Apostle Paul." *Charles F. Parham, October 1925*

A PLEASURABLE MEETING

While in California we had the great pleasure of meeting Bishop J.H. Allen in his home in Pasadena. We had known him for 35 years and from him many years ago had obtained the foundation truths of many things we are preaching today. Especially the wonderful message of Anglo-Israel. And any one wishing to get the most profound works on that subject printed today should write him for his book *Judah's Scepter and Israel's Birthright*, a book of over 300 pages, costing only $3.00. Though very aged and not fully recovered from a dislocated hip, he gave us some wonderful things relating to his visit to the world's Anglo-Israel Congress held in London last year as he was one of the leading speakers and the day he preached several of the Royal Family were present, then he told of a day spent in the Royal Library of the Kings Palace and while there said to the Librarian, "I understand that you have here a copy of the Kings pedigree back to Adam, Dr. Anderson and W.H. Milner, World renown genealogists attest as authentic and genuine and indisputably correct and that my friend Chas. F. Parham in America obtained a copy of it from the Librarian under the reign of Queen Victoria." He said, "yes, but we do not show it to very many." Then Brother Allen said that from a drawer well secreted by many papers covering it they drew a massive scroll 17 feet long and 5 feet across, bound in Gold and Scarlet and there my friend and daughter poured over the sacred document that means so much to all who believe that we are the true descendants of the

331

lost tribes of Israel and that the Kings of the earth today are the blood descendants of David, King of the Jews [Judahites].

Then he told us of the visit to Westminster Abbey where he was allowed to lay his hand on the stone of Scone under the Coronation Chair. The stone that is said to have been the one Joshua said this stone has heard all the words of our covenant with the Lord and which Jeremiah brought to Ireland and on which all the Kings of Judah were crowned and all the Kings of Scotland and all the Kings of England since James brought the stone from Scotland. God be praised for the long life of usefulness of our dear Bishop. *Charles F. Parham,   April 1926*

THE TRIBE OF JUDAH

It is very strange indeed that scholars who recorded the Aryan immigration into Western Europe never put two and two together and discovered that the cradle of the Aryan race was the exact country where previously the ten lost tribes of Israel were colonized.   While passing through Northern Greece, historians of that day frequently wrote of them, noted their peculiarities.   It was said by one historian that they believed in the immortality of the soul and one God, which the Greeks did not; also that in primitive times they had received their law and regulations from one Ike Moxes (Moses) who spent many days in the mountains and returned with the same.   Pushing their way westward into what is now Germany, many were captured and sold on the slave market of Rome. When Caesar inquired who these beautiful creatures were when they told him, he said, "They should be called angels;" a term which has ever followed them.

During their migration, they were known by different names, according to the country through which they were passing.   Such terms as Isuki, Sacae, Sacea, Suncea, Saxones, and many others, until it terminated in Saxons: their land was called Saxony.   Thus coupled with Caesar's title, they became Anglo-Saxons!   The word Saxon being a derivation of ISAAC'S SONS; fulfilling the prophecy. *"In Isaac shall thy seed be called."* (Gen. 21:12).   The Saxon conquest of Great Britain (and today coupled with the United States) of nearly all the world proves the Scriptures; they were to be the *"head and not the tail of nation."*

England is called the Lion because she possesses the sceptre of David and her ruling power is seed royal of Judah.   The Lion is a figure of kingship, Christ, the King, is often referred to as the Lion of the tribe of Judah.

Ephraim to be a company of nations, England.   Manasseh was to be the gathering of nations, United States.

Now, if the reader will carefully read Jacob's blessing upon his children, for the last days, and all the prophecies concerning Israel in the Old Testament, realizing they pertain to the above named nations, the Old Testament will become a new book to you of vital import and interest.   *Charles F. Parham,   Sept. 1926*

WHAT WE SAW AT WINDSOR CASTLE

The author of this article, Bishop J .H. Allen, relates the account of his visit to London in 1920 to address "The First World Congress of Believers in the Identity of the Saxons and Anglo-Saxons with the one time lost or unidentified House of Israel. . ." He goes on to describe what he saw at Windsor Castle. He saw the genealogical chart of the Royal Family of Great Britain, once owned by Queen Victoria, which proves their literal descent from King David.   *November 1926*

JUDAH'S SCEPTER AND JOSEPH'S BIRTHRIGHT

In the May 1927 issue of *The Apostolic Faith* there appeared a promotional ad for Bishop J. H. Allen's book *"Judah's Sceptre and Joseph's Birthright."* It was made available from the author at Pasadena, California address for the price of $2.00 postpaid.

WATCH THE 153 GREAT FISHES

This was another article by Bishop J. H. Allen concerning the British Royal Family as being descended from the House of David. It appeared in the May 1927 issue of *The Apostolic Faith*.

Another article printed in *The Apostolic Faith* magazine of March 22, 1899 was entitled "Queen Victoria's Descent from Adam." This article showed the genealogical Family to the royal dynasty of King David.

GEORGE WILLIAM SOUTHWICK
George Southwick was born on December 1, 1918 in Lakeland, Florida. When only a small boy, he and his family moved to Burbank, California where he was raised and graduated from Burbank High School in 1936. He then attended L.I.F.E. Bible School which was founded and

directed by the famous Aimee Semple McPherson. While there, he not only was taught by Sister McPherson, but also heard other well-known ministers and Bible teachers such as Frank C. Thompson of the Thompson Chain Reference Bible, Luke Rader of the Minneapolis River Lake Gospel Tabernacle, Adolph P. Gouthey and many more. Not long after graduation he received ministerial ordination with the International Church of the Foursquare Gospel. He was later ordained in the Assemblies of God, the Apostolic Holiness and the Whosoever Will Fellowship.

After George Southwick's marriage to Leona Rasmussen on March 1, 1942, he held pastorates in the Upper Michigan District and Adams, Wisconsin. While pastoring in Michigan during an evening service, the Lord manifested Himself in a visible ball of fire that rolled across the floor.

This was one of many miraculous visitations in his spiritual walk with the Lord that brought him from "Glory to Glory" throughout his ministerial life of service to the body of Christ. He later held pastorates in Oregon and California. Convinced that a life of learning is not lost and a love of books, he possessed a personal library of over 12,000 volumes. In February 1999 Logos Theological Seminary of Jacksonville, Florida conferred upon him an Honorary Doctorate of Divinity degree.

During his life of eighty-seven years, Pastor Southwick had the privilege of considering among his friends such men of God as: Fred Vogel, William Booth-Clibborn, Dr. Claud Phileo, A.E. Mitchell, Gordon Lindsay and Thomas A. Lindsay.

When just a small boy it was evident that the hand of the Lord was upon young George's life. He was converted to Christ at an early age and soon recognized a spiritual call upon his heart for a life of service in the vineyard of the Lord. He was greatly stirred in his spirit when at the age of ten his mother took him to hear the great Welsh Revivalist, Stephen Jeffreys. There he heard the first hand report of the story of the miraculous vision of the face of the "Man of Sorrows" on the wall of the Island Place Mission in 1914 in Llanelly, Wales. According to his frequent testimony, he related that early in his life many visitors would stop by the home of his parents. Often the topic of conversation would be the identity and location of the 'Ten Lost Tribes of Israel.' Not understanding the significance of this information, he pondered this subject and hid it away in his heart for many years.

Later on as a pastor, he began to earnestly seek the Lord concerning this subject. He diligently sought the Lord through prayer and study of the Scriptures for ten years before making a public mention of this subject. He became thoroughly convinced of the validity of this truth yet was hesitant to teach it for fear of the consequences from his fellow ministers. That fear was suddenly removed one day by a supernatural experience that he had while sharing this truth with another couple. He and his wife were sitting in the front seat of their car sharing the Anglo-Israel message with the couple in the back seat, when suddenly he felt the finger of God come through the top of the car and touch him on the top of his head. He felt the Spirit of God go throughout his body removing his fear to preach this message and confirming the validity of the Anglo-Israel truth. From then on he boldly proclaimed this great Gospel of the Kingdom throughout the nation in conferences and by means of a tape ministry. In 1975, Pastor Southwick and his wife founded *The Bible Educator Ministry*, through which he produced a publication called *The Kingdom Treasure* and hundreds of sermon tapes. He was a favorite conference speaker and was well loved by all who knew him. He passed away on January 21, 2006.

Frederick John Gabler (1917- 2010)

Frederick John Gabler was born into a home of German ancestry to Frederick Henry and Julia (Deschner) Gabler on August 8, 1917 in Flanagan, Illinois. Due to early childhood illnesses of the children, the local doctor recommended that the family move to a more humid climate. The family soon relocated to the German community of Fryberg, Texas. His grandfather, Adolph Gabler who lived a life of a rough cowboy was converted during a Methodist camp meeting in the German Methodist Church at Fryberg. It was at this camp  meeting that Adolph road up on his horse to observe the religious service when he was convicted by the Holy Spirit and subsequently delivered from whiskey and tobacco. It was there he was gloriously converted to Christ which had a profound impact upon the whole family. The spiritual influence of his conversion was felt throughout the community for many years.

His mother's brothers were Methodist ministers ordained with the Gold Star Methodist Conference located in Missouri. Being raised in a Methodist environment, Fred and his brother Martin were exposed to a religious home life and were christened at an early age in the Methodist Episcopal Church. Fred's mother told him many times that she had dedicated him to the Lord and Christian ministry even before his birth.

One tremendous experience that changed the course of the religious life of the Gabler family was the miraculous healing of his father's sister, Ida Hertel, who was suffering from a tumor on the jugular vein. Hearing of the great things that were happening in the ministry of E.N. (Eli Noble) Richey of Houston, Texas, the family decided to call him for prayer. In 1923, E.N. Richey and his son-in-law, E.G. Gerhardt came to the Gabler home. After prayer, his aunt was miraculously healed and therefore changed the course of the religious affiliation of the whole Gabler family. While at the home, E.N. Richey laid his hand upon six year old little Freddie's head and blessed him by asking the Lord to anoint and separate him for divine service. As a young man, Fred also experienced a miraculous healing of a severe stomach ailment.

In 1929 the family started attending Evangelistic Temple pastored by E. N. Richey (Dad Richey). It was there that Fred and his brother Martin witnessed scores of miracles that took place under the ministry of Dad Richey and his son Raymond T. Richey. While sitting in the balcony they observed the miracle of many deaf children being healed. Later on in the late 1940's, in this same tabernacle under the ministry of William Branham, Fred recalls witnessing visible and miraculous healings. Both he and his brother were saved at an early age and he later received the Baptism of the Holy Ghost at the age of 21 years old, at a young men's prayer meeting at an Assemblies of God Church pastored by Albert Lee Samford. As a young man, Fred attended a local Vo-tech school in Houston and earned a degree in automobile mechanics and was later hired at the local Ford dealership. During World War II he served his country as an airplane mechanic at Ellington Field military air base.

In 1945, after receiving a call from the Lord for full time ministry, Fred was licensed with the Assemblies of God of South Texas. Fred's older brother, Martin Philip, was ordained with the Assemblies of God and later became a Sectional Presbyter in the South Texas District. Fred later pastored the Full Gospel Church in Timpson, Texas. His marriage union was blessed with two children, with the first child being born in 1949 and the second in 1951.

On January 1st, 1946, Fred Gabler was ordained through the laying on of hands by Harry Hodge and Mordecai F. Ham at Trinity Tabernacle in downtown Houston.   In the early 1950's he experienced the Latter Rain outpouring at Garland Pemberton's Tabernacle in Orange, Texas.   During this early stage of his ministry he was seeking the Lord for further understanding and truth as found in the Word of God.   He began listening to Dr. John A. Lovell on the radio who was teaching the message of the Anglo-Israel truth.   He wrote for literature intending to criticize both the preacher and his teaching, but was convinced by the Holy Spirit and the prophetic words of Joel 2:28 that this message was true.   In his search for truth the Holy Spirit began to unfold the national message of Scripture in identifying the true House of Israel and the House of Judah.   It was here where the understanding of the Abrahamic Covenant and the birthright blessing given to the House of Joseph became clear.   This truth also brought to light the New Testament doctrine of the reconciliation of the House of Israel back to God under the terms of the New Covenant.   From this truth the Holy Spirit began to make known the revelation of the Sonship message.   During this phase of Fred Gabler's ministry, the person and work of Jesus Christ came into clearer focus in the Scriptural portrayal of Jesus as the fulness of God as manifested in the flesh and glorified in the Spirit.

In 1955, he and his family moved to Tulsa, Oklahoma to assume the position of associate pastor at Rays of Faith Tabernacle. There he had a Gospel radio program which served in expanding his ministry in the Tulsa area.   In 1956 he accepted the pastorate of Rose Hill Covenant Church and served as senior pastor for over 54 years. During the course of his ministry, the Holy Spirit had inspired Pastor Gabler in writing over 70 songs and choruses of praise and worship. He passed from this mortal life on July 13, 2010. One of his last statements to his visiting friends were; "I'll meet you in glory."

THOMAS A. LINDSAY   Even as a youth Thomas Lindsay was spiritually inclined and had a heart toward God.   He experienced a real Christian conversion at the age of twenty-two and never wavered in his faith from that time on.   In about 1905 he moved to Zion City, Illinois after hearing of the success of Dr. John Alexander Dowie.   There he met his wife, Effie Munn and started raising his family. While living in Zion, the Lindsays acquired a genuine lasting faith in the promises of God when seeing the  healing power of the Lord manifested in the ministry of Dr. Dowie.   As a former resident of Zion City, who learned much from Dr. Dowie, it is no

337

surprise that Thomas A. Lindsay, the father of well-known Gordon Lindsay was a believer in the Anglo-Israel message. In fact he was an executive member of the Anglo-Saxon Federation of Oregon after leaving Illinois. While living in Portland, the Lindsay's attended the church of Pastor John G. Lake.

In their senior years, Thomas Lindsay and his wife spent time in Dallas, Texas with their son Gordon. I was told that while there they often visited First Covenant Church to enjoy the sermons on the Anglo-Israel message given by Dr. John A. Lovell. Mrs. Lindsay passed away early in 1957 while Thomas Lindsay passed away at the age of 88 years old in late 1961.

****

"Unless the Prophets faithless be – and the Seer's words be vain Wher'er is found Jehovah's throne – Prince David's line shall reign"

****

GORDON LINDSAY   One of the 'household names' of the traditional Pentecostal and Charismatic movements is Gordon Lindsay. He was born in 1906 while his parents were living in Zion City, Illinois. His parents had moved there to attend the Christian Catholic Church and be participants in the Christian community founded by John Alexander Dowie. Dowie was also a strong believer in the Anglo-Israel message. (See our brochure # 58.) Later his family  moved to Portland, Oregon. At the age of eighteen, Gordon was converted to Christ under the ministry of Charles F. Parham (see our brochure # 54) while attending a church pastored by John G. Lake, a former resident of Zion city, Illinois. Before marriage to his wife, Freda, he joined the evangelistic ministry of Brother Lake, traveling throughout California and the southern United States. Lindsay began his pastoral ministry in small churches in California and Ashland, Oregon.

In 1947, Lindsay joined the ministry of William Branham to function as the campaign manager to promote and report on the meetings. This was when he first published his well known *Voice of Healing* Magazine. He later published   *World Wide Revival* and *Christ for the Nations* magazines. He became one of the most prominent men involved in the divine healing movement of the 1940's and 50's, organizing conventions of healing evangelists, serving as counsel for many of them and reporting the results of their meetings. His death in 1973 was a big loss to not only his family and friends, but to all the Pentecostal & Charismatic church world.

It is very obvious that Gordon Lindsay at one time was an advocate of the Anglo-Israel message. In 1940, his articles on the study of Biblical Chronological Timelines were printed in *The Anglo-Saxon World* published in Vancouver, British Columbia, Canada.   The printed purpose of the magazine was stated as: *"The contents of the magazine are dedicated to the more rapid teaching of the Anglo-Saxon identity with Israel and the bringing in of the Kingdom of God on earth."* (Feb. 1, 1940).   In the body of his article entitled, *"The Wonders of Bible Chronology"* Lindsay wrote:

"In connection with the subject about to be discussed, it will no doubt be of interest to the reader to understand that while the writer has long been convinced of the truth of the British Israel Identity, it was not until the amazing system of cycles of Bible chronology was discovered, that he was able to realize the tremendous importance this fact played in the Divine Scheme of the destiny of the nations. About two years after the completion of this chronology, its further consideration brought amazement to the writer when he discovered, that interwoven into the chronology was an astounding system of cycles, the mathematical ingenuity of which, was almost beyond belief. But more astonishing still, was the fact that these cycles were so ordered that they show every event of Bible and world history has been timed. Thus the significance of these events can be understood in their relation to one another. These cycles also point unmistakably to the fact that the identity of Britain and the United States of America is to be found in Israel."

In his March 1940 article entitled, *"The Thirteen Cycles of the United States"* Lindsay writes the following: "Let us for a moment briefly consider the nation of the United States, as it appears in prophecy. The fact that Israel was to develop into great and independent nations in the last days, is clear from the study of Genesis 48:16-19, and 49:1. In these Scriptures Jacob foretells her destiny in the descendants of Ephraim and Manasseh.

And let them grow into a multitude in the midst of the earth. . .He (Manasseh) also shall be great: but truly his younger brother shall be greater than he, and his seed shall become a multitude of nations.

"That such a destiny has never been fulfilled in the dispersed Jews is obvious. That it has been fulfilled in Britain and in America as Ephraim and Manasseh is just as apparent. Both have grown to be a *"great people"* in the *"midst of the earth."* America has become a great nation. The British Empire has become a Company of Nations. The lack of space in Britain made it necessary for the ever increasing population to migrate and colonize other lands. The breaking away of the first colonies (the original thirteen states of America) was foreseen by the prophet in Isaiah 49:20.

The children which thou shalt have, after thou hast lost the other, shall say again in thine ears, the place is too straight for me; give place to me that I may dwell.

"Britain lost the United States, in the Revolutionary War. This, as we have seen, as in the Divine plan."

In the April 1940 article entitled, *Cycles of the "Sign Woman" Israel*, Lindsay writes in the author's introductory note: "The writer has suspended, for the present, his active ministry, that he might give his entire attention to the preparation for publication of the amazing series of discoveries that prove beyond contradiction, the identity of Israel as the Anglo-Saxon nations." In the body of the article he wrote the following under the subtitle;

Israel-the Sun Clothed Woman

"In our article this month, we shall consider the prophecy of the sun-clothed woman of Rev. 12. As the chapter heading in the Scofield Reference Bible shows, there is general unanimity among prophetic scholars that this woman is a symbol of Israel. We shall not take space therefore, to prove this prophetic truth, which ordinarily is accepted, except that we might call attention to the fact that the symbols used are strongly Israelitish, and that the Man Child who evidently represents Christ, came of the seed of Israel.

"Bible scholars in interpreting this prophecy, concur in the teaching thus:

The Sign Woman is Israel, and the Man Child to whom she gave birth, is the Messiah, Jesus Christ. After fulfilling His earthly Ministry, Sufferings, and Death, the Man Child ascended to heaven. Satan, balked in his malevolent schemes to present the fulfillment of God's redemptive Plan in Christ, turned in frustrated fury upon Israel with the avowed purpose of affecting her destruction. But, as the prophecy reveals, the Lord protected the Woman and appointed to her a place of refuge, which is spoken of as "the wilderness." There she is preserved for a period of 1260 days, or a "time and times and half a time." At this point prophetic interpretation diverges; those who fail to see the British-Israel identity, are forced to the conclusion that this Flight of the Woman, refers to the Jews escaping from Palestine during the final troublous times of this age. There are a number of obvious reasons why such an interpretation cannot be true. One of these is the plain statement of Rev. 12:17, which declares that the Woman and at least a "Remnant of her seed–keep the commandments of God, and have the testimony of Jesus Christ." How could such a description refer to the Jews, who to this day as a people, stubbornly reject the Messiahship of Christ?

We must look, for the fulfillment of this prophecy, to a nation of which at least a portion of the people believes in the Lord Jesus Christ.

"British-Israel believers identify the Flight of the Woman to be that of the Lost Tribes of Israel, who, escaping Gentile domination, migrated to Britain the "Appointed Place." (2 Sam. 7:10.) There, surrounded by seas and protected from Continental attack, they renew their strength and finally achieve their destiny as a mighty nation."

It was after his rise to prominence in the healing revival movement that Lindsay abandoned his earlier belief in the Anglo-Israel message. In my twenty-five plus years of friendship with Pastor Southwick, he related the following story to me several times. When Pastor Southwick was living in Portland, Oregon, his friend Tom Lindsay would come by the pear packing plant where he was a manager and they would have long and pleasant visits together. Tom clearly said: "George, my son Gordon knows the Anglo-Israel message, but he refuses to preach it."

JOHN GRAHAM LAKE   As a young man, John G. Lake (born 1870) was converted to Christ and was ordained into the ministry at the age of twenty-one by the Methodist Church. In 1898, his wife, sister, son and a friend were miraculously healed under the ministry of John A. Dowie. Lake later became a deacon in Dr. Dowie's church in Zion City, Illinois. He was a very progressive and successful businessman, working in newspaper publishing, real estate and the insurance industry. Feeling a personal call to the ministry, Lake began to hold meetings in the evenings, while seeking for the Pentecostal experience of the infilling of the Holy Spirit. After receiving this experience in 1907, he felt a missionary call to South Africa. The Lord honored Lake's ministry while in Africa with hundreds of verifiable miracles of healing and divine provision for his family.

After the death of his wife in 1908, he continued his African ministry, but returned to the states in 1912. He settled in Spokane, Washington where he opened a "healing home" and thousands gave testimony of physical healing by the power of God. Concerning Lake's commitment to the Anglo-Israel truth, Herb Frizzell, in the draft of his unpublished book, records the following. "From personal sources I am told that Rev. John G. Lake became a believer in the [Christian Israel] message in the latter part of his ministry. Mrs. Ione E. Eaton . . . asserted to me personally that Dr. Lake definitely believed the message. This was ascertained after talking to various people who knew him personally. Ione Eaton told me that Dr. Lake use to come to their house and bounce her on his knee when she was a child. She says that Lake was a wonderful man of God, and he even baptized her when she was a child. Some derided him for believing in the message and, in fact, their memory of this was burned into their minds by the fact that they thought that dear old Dr. Lake has "gotten off the rails into error" and should have been corrected.

ALEXANDER SCHIFFNER   After pastoring in the city of Spokane, Washington for over forty years, he was known as the senior pastor of the city. Alexander Schiffner was born on March 24, 1900 in Walla Walla, Washington to German immigrant parents who arrived in the United States two years before his birth. His parents had agreed that if the first child born to them in this country was a boy they would dedicate him to the Lord for the work of the ministry. As an infant he was baptized in the Lutheran Church and was confirmed at the age of twelve in the German Congregational Church.

After completing his public education in Umapine, Oregon, he first worked on a ranch, then joined in partnership in a dry-cleaning and laundry plant. In 1917 he married Wadie Opal Alexander and soon moved to Los Angeles, California. There he worked in the dry-cleaning business and even purchased his own plants in Los Angeles and Hollywood. He became a very successful businessman even during the depression, living a life of ease yet extremely unhappy.

His younger brother Adolph was earnestly praying for Alexander's conversion to Christ and kept asking him to attend a Bible College. One day Alexander took the Bible his father had given him as a wedding gift and threw it on the floor and said to his wife and brother, "I'm going to prove that there is nothing to this Bible, it's a book of fairy tales written for the superstitious and for children." On their first day of attendance at a Baptist Bible College in Los Angeles on September 19, 1933, the Spirit of God began to deal with his heart. As their instructor, Rev. A.E.

Mitchell asked the class, "Why are you here?" Alexander's heart was gripped with conviction. With class dismissed, the instructor asked each student to kneel at their seat and pray. Dr. Schiffner later recorded; "It seemed as if a big ball of fire hit me on the top of the head and went down through my body to the soles of my feet, and I started to cry. I was a successful businessman who was unsentimental and unemotional and hadn't cried since my childhood. I heard some chains drop with a clank to the cement floor below. I don't know how long I was on my knees, but after I rose from praying, I rubbed my eyes in order to see more clearly, for it seemed as if I was walking in a great light. I asked Adolph, 'who dropped those chains while I was praying?"

Not long after his conversion while giving his testimony in a street meeting, he was introduced to a group of "Full Gospel" or "Pentecostal" saints. After a three day and two night season of fasting and prayer, he was alone when the Holy Spirit came upon him. He worshiped in tongues for more than two hours and finally heard the clear voice of God saying, "preach, preach, preach." While in a vision he saw a sea of hands reaching out of the pit beseeching for help. Not long afterwards he enrolled in L.I.F.E. Bible School founded by Aimee Semple McPherson. In September 1935, he, his wife and two children moved to Spokane and started a church affiliated with the Foursquare Gospel denomination.

While returning home on the train to Spokane from a convention, he experienced a supernatural visitation from an angel of the Lord. The angel said, "Fear not, my son, I have come to minister unto thee. I have poured my grace and my truth into your lips. Go forth and speak my word without fear or favor." On April 25, 1942, while in Bible study preparing for Sunday service, the Lord revealed to Dr. Schiffner the Anglo-Israel message from the 48th and 49th chapters of Genesis. Two months after he received this revelation he went to Portland to visit the Foursquare leadership. Dr. Schiffner writes, "He informed me that the Founder-President of the organization and other pastors, including himself, had studied the message of the Israel Identity but that the board and the headquarters officials had ruled that although the doctrine of Anglo-Israelism had Scriptural verification, they decided by majority vote that it was not yet time for the message to be proclaimed."

In time, Dr. Schiffner bought the old wooden tabernacle from the widow of John G. Lake which had been built for the Billy Sunday crusades. From this humble beginning *Bethel Temple* was built with both radio and television outreach Ministries. The monthly magazine *Prophetic Herald* was published for over forty years dealing with religious, economic and political issues. In over 44 years of ministry, Dr.

343

Schiffner wrote scores of brochures and booklets and was active in the Lord's work until the day of his death.

FRANK M. MAULDEN   Among the few details known about the early life of Frank Maulden is that he was born on August 7, 1897 and spent his early years in West Texas. As a young man he was converted to Christ and grew up under the influence of a Godly grandmother. A childhood experience where the Lord protected his grandmother from a crazy man greatly strengthened his faith in the reality of the power of God. An extremely mad man threatened to kill his grandmother with a gun. She said; "you can't harm me because I serve the Lord Jesus." When the man tried to pull the trigger his hand froze and then he suddenly fled.

In his early ministry Frank Maulden preached for the Assemblies of God in West Texas. Soon he met his wife Alma to whom he was married for sixty years. She passed away in 1986. After moving to the Northwest, he was affiliated with a Oneness Pentecostal Church and served as a district official in Yakima, Washington. In the 1930's, he and his wife moved to Idaho and pastored a 'Oneness' Church in twin falls and founded a church in Meridian which he pastored from 1953 to 1980. Frank Maulden remained faithful to the divine revelation of the Anglo-Israel truth in spite of his dismissal from the denomination. Pastor Maulden was highly respected and loved by his fellow ministers and laymen and remained faithful to his Lord until the day of his death on January 22, 1988 at the age of ninety-one years.

MAXIE A.X. CLARK   It is believed that Max Clark was born around 1892 and most likely in the western part of the United States. Not much is known of his early life, but it is suspected that he attended some of the meetings at the Azusa street outpouring between 1906 and 1911. Max Clark was definitely Pentecostal in his theology, experience and fellowship as clearly evident in his publication articles and his book entitled *The Pentecostal Movement-Forty Years of Power, Probation and Progress*. In 1913 he was ordained with the *Pentecostal Assemblies of the World* in Portland, Oregon. He was later ordained with the Assemblies of God in 1920, but his credentials were dropped in December 1924. Most likely from this point on he remained as an independent in his religious affiliations.

For many years he was the editor of *The National Christian Journal* and *The Pentecostal Journal* which dealt with issues of prophecy, history, theology, homiletics and current events. Articles in these magazines included prominent Pentecostal authors such as Evangelist Zelma Argue and M. Leslie Crosson of the Sixth Street Assembly of God Church in Sacramento, California. The sponsorship for these magazines was widespread according to the long list of commercial ads. The readership of these journals must have been very high and widespread throughout the Pentecostal, Fundamental and evangelical world as indicated by the letters to the editor. The responses were from Bible Schools, civil government officials, denominational officials such as J. Roswell Flower of the Assemblies of God and Howard A. Goss of the United Pentecostal Church. Among his many friends and subscribers were prominent Anglo-Israel pastors such as John A. Lovell and Dr. Alexander Schiffner.

Max Clark was a strong believer in the Anglo-Israel message of Scripture as proven by the many articles in his magazines. The article *The Five Sons of Judah* by Schiffner and Clark's article *Abraham's Posterity – A study in Racial Origins* shows the Anglo-Saxon people as fulfilling the promises that were prophesied as belonging to the sons of Joseph. These fulfillments have been and are primarily taking place in Great Britain and the United States. It is believed that he passed away sometime in the 1960's.

THEODORE FITCH   Little is known of the early life of Theodore Fitch, but one thing is certain and that was his life-time commitment to the Gospel of Jesus Christ. He was born on December 1, 1893 in northern Iowa and he made his home for many years in Council Bluffs.

As a young man he owned the Iowa Paint Factory. He was financially successful in this business, especially during the Great Depression due to large government purchases for their WPA projects. After he was converted to Christ, possibly in the Foursquare Church, he opened a city Union Mission for the homeless and derelicts. He would feed 150 men twice a day sponsored by his paint factory.

Theodore Fitch had a tremendous and glorious conversion to Jesus Christ somewhere around 1930. He then began to seek the Lord for a Pentecostal infilling of the Spirit and during this time he experienced a vision of Jesus in full life-like color. In this vision he heard a voice saying to him, "Jesus is God." After this supernatural vision, he then began to fellowship with the 'Oneness' churches. With this spiritual zeal he entered the ministry, doing evangelistic work in churches and on the radio and remained active for over sixty years until his death on December 21, 1991. He was a strong believer in the Pentecostal message and experience which is evident by his many books on the Baptism of the Holy Spirit and related subjects.

During his ministry he had many friends and associates and was known to accommodate in his home many ministers for weeks and even months in addition to his family of ten children. After the vision experience, Theodore Fitch accepted Jesus as the Great Physician for himself and his family. He believed in living a life of faith. When his son Jimmy was nine years old, he contracted a sleeping sickness with double pneumonia. A doctor visited the home and offered his services free of charge, but Fitch refused saying Jesus was the healer. After being asleep for three weeks and given up to die, a friend was impressed to visit the Fitch Family. He prayed for the boy and he was instantly healed. The boy woke up and said that he was hungry.

Theodore Fitch established *Bible Truths Restored* ministry with a mailing list of 50,000 names and published seventy-five different books with a worldwide outreach. Based upon the many books that he wrote upon the subject it is evident that he was a strong advocate of the Anglo-Israel message of Scripture. He was always a happy and vivacious person and expressed the joy of the Lord in his life and preaching. Just before he died he told his son that it was time for him to go. After his normal breakfast he went back to bed, simply closed his eyes and peacefully died.

<u>**GORDON MAGEE**</u>   Very little is known of the early life of Gordon Magee except that he was born in Plymouth, England on May 19, 1920. He was converted to Christ and called into the ministry as a young man and found ministry opportunities in Belfast, Northern Ireland. After receiving the Baptism of the Holy Spirit, his ministry was particularly fruitful in pioneering the revelation message of the Oneness of the Godhead. He was  also instrumental in establishing with other ministers the ***Churches of God*** in Ireland and their official magazine, *Standard of Truth*. Under his anointed ministry thousands were brought to the knowledge that the Anglo-Saxon people were the literal descendants of ancient Israel. By 1952 Gordon Magee was living and ministering in Toronto, Canada. He later moved to the United States and after extensive ministry established a church in Houston, Texas. During his long ministry of many years he

wrote and published articles and booklets including his widely circulated treatise, *Is Jesus in the Godhead or is the Godhead in Jesus?*

WILLIAM OLIVER HUTCHINSON

W. O. Hutchinson was one of the founders of the *Apostolic Faith Church,* which was the First Pentecostal movement in Great Britain. He also established Emmanuel Mission Hall in Winton, Bournemouth, England. After receiving the Baptism in the Spirit in the Church of England Vicarage at Sunderland in 1908, Stanley H. Frodsham assisted Hutchinson in the founding of Mission Hall. Frodsham later emigrated to the United States and became editor for 28 years of the Assemblies of God official organ, *The Pentecostal Evangel.* Hutchinson first published *Showers of Blessings* periodical in January 1910, which increased to a circulation of 10,000. This publication contained the teaching and reports of the activities of the many Pentecostal congregations in Great Britain connected with the Apostolic Faith Church. It is believed that Hutchinson adopted the name of his movement from Charles F. Parham's paper, *Apostolic Faith.*

During the early years of the Pentecostal movement in Great Britain, Hutchinson ministered with many men such as Smith Wigglesworth and Cecil H. Polhill, who later became very prominent in the Pentecostal movement. Hutchinson was the first minister in the modern Pentecostal movement to be publicly recognized as *Chief Apostle,* which position he held until his death. In his book *"The Origins of the Apostolic Church in Great Britain*, James E. Worsfold gives the following account of the life and ministry of W.O. Hutchinson.

"The first Pentecostal church building in Great Britain, Emmanuel Mission Hall, was opened on 5 November 1909. It owed its origins to the ministry of William Oliver Hutchinson. By 1909, Hutchinson's influence was already such that one of the guest speakers at the opening services was no less a person than Cecil Polhill, one of the famed Cambridge Seven.

"In this writer's view, Hutchinson is most definitely the father of the twentieth century apostolic-type of Pentecostal movements in Great Britain. The Apostolic Faith Church, Bournemouth, the Apostolic Church, Penygroes, and the United Apostolic Faith Church, London all owe their introduction to the apostolic ministry to this valiant pioneer preacher who believed that God would restore the New Testament ministries and offices of apostle and prophet.

"Hutchinson was born of Primitive Methodist parents at Blackhill, County Durham, on 11 January 1864. His father was a merchant tailor and local preacher. He began his working life as a shepherd and, while terrified during a violent thunderstorm high up in the hills, he vowed to serve God faithfully if He would only spare his life. Later, after receiving what he felt was Divine guidance, Hutchinson enlisted and became a Grenadier Guardsman, rising to the rank of sergeant. When evangelists Dwight Moody and Ira Sankey held services in London, young Hutchinson was greatly blessed as he witnessed scenes of revival. In mid 1888, while listening to the celebrated preacher, Charles H. Spurgeon, in the London Metropolitan Tabernacle, he heard the Holy Spirit speaking to him when the preacher said" "Awake, thou that sleepest – you! Sitting behind that pillar" (as Hutchinson actually was). This was a great moment of awakening in Hutchinson's life and he was fully determined to confess Christ before his fellow soldiers. This he did kneeling in prayer at his bedside in the barracks at Aldershot. That very night his outright testimony was such that not a few soldiers were ultimately converted to Christ. In December that year he married Miss Ada Cooper. Theirs was to be a strong and loving union for forty years.

"In March 1900 Hutchinson was sent to South Africa to fight in the Boer War where he was twice preserved from death. When his health broke down he was invalided home to spend a period in the Netley Military Hospital, returning to civilian life in 1903. He was then employed as an inspector for the London Society for the Prevention of Cruelty to Children, under the direction of Benjamin Waugh. During evenings and weekends he continued his evangelistic ministry, which bore much fruit, as a Methodist lay preacher. It was at this time that he accepted that the Biblical authority to baptize was a command to immerse. He responded, was duly baptized in water and thereafter supported the Baptist Church.

"Reader Harris, QC, of the Pentecostal League, was conducting meetings in Bournemouth at the time and through his teaching Hutchinson entered into the experience known as a "clean heart" before God. He mistook this encounter with God for the baptism of the Holy Spirit. Later, he came to see that the baptism of the Spirit should be accompanied by "speaking with other tongues". He declined an offer made by the local Baptist Church to be an assistant pastor with a weekly stipend, preferring to wait for the time when he would step out into the ministry and live by faith, believing that God would meet his financial needs by freewill offerings.

"In 1906 Hutchinson visited South Wales and was deeply stirred by the continuing revival scenes. He received a spiritual vision of three balls of fire, one above the other, increasing in size upwards over his head. The Holy Spirit spoke within him, saying that the first ball was about the gift of tongues. Hutchinson now began to seek God for a baptism of fire like the disciples received on the day of Pentecost.

"In 1908, responding to an invitation, he attended the first international Pentecostal convention called by Alexander Boddy at Whitsuntide in Sunderland. During one of these services, while kneeling before the Lord, Hutchinson was baptized in the Holy Spirit, speaking in tongues as the Spirit gave him utterance. Some ten years later Kent White gave more detail to this event. He states that Hutchinson was "pleading the Blood" for over two hours. Then, after hands were laid on him, he received the remarkable Baptism of the Spirit. Returning to Bournemouth, Hutchinson held a prayer meeting at his home where like-minded believers began seeking God. The first person he laid his hands on received the baptism of the Spirit and spoke in tongues. Several others had a similar experience.

"Hutchinson now sensed that God was at work in a special way and that he could no longer fully serve Him in the Baptist Church. He accepted the challenge to step out and commenced to conduct public meetings, preaching the Pentecostal message. Signs began to follow his ministry with many brought to Christ, baptized in water and in the Holy Spirit. Others received miraculous healings. Hutchinson's faith increased and in his heart was born a desire for a building where the work of God could be consolidated and a centre established from which the ministry could extend to other places."

W. O. Hutchinson was a strong believer in the Covenantal promises given to ancient Israel as being fulfilled in the Anglo-Saxon people of today. In the June 1922 issue of "*What We Believe and Teach*" he wrote the following statement::

> *"That God's Kingdom coming on earth has to do with the revealing of His chosen people Israel and that the blessing of Ephraim (Gen. 48:19) rest upon the British Empire and its throne through whom all nations shall be blessed. That America carries Manasseh's blessing."*

In his book, Worsfold gives the following account which reinforces the idea of the Anglo-Israel belief among the many members of the *Apostolic Faith Church*.

"At the fourteenth International Convention of the Apostolic Faith Church, Bournemouth, 1922, the newspapers reported that the following speakers were present: W.O. Hutchinson, Chief Overseer, J. Hutchinson-Dennis, Deputy, A. Murdoch, Chief Overseer (Scotland), W. P. Roberts and T. Bowen (Wales), James Brooke, Chief Overseer (South Africa and Rhodesia), George Dennis, Chief Overseer (East African Territory), J. Jack (Canada), J.G. Hutchinson, Assistant and J. Hume (Scotland) and W. Bovett, (England).

The reports went on to say:
'The Union Jack hangs from the rostrum, national anthems such as "God Save the King' and 'God Bless the Prince of Wales' were sung heartily. The Apostolic Faith Church claims the throne of Britain has a Divine setting and that the Empire is the company of nations with Ephraim which will, with America, secure the peace of the world. Pastor Hutchinson declared that King George was the King of Israel and that the Prince of Wales was the Prince in Israel... "

Worsfold gives the following statement of Hutchinson's death and the eulogy which was given at his funeral service.

"During the mid-1920 as a result of the strenuous life he maintained as leader of the Apostolic Faith Church, Hutchinson suffered a break-down in health. At the end of February 1928, at his residence, "Beulah", Hutchinson passed on to his eternal reward. He was sixty-four years old. The funeral service on 2 March at the church was presided over by a colleague, J.A. Jones, a minister from Southall, London. A large congregation attended, deeply-felt tributes were given, and many floral gifts were telegraphed from all over Great Britain, and from as far away as South Africa. In his eulogy, Jones said that William Hutchinson ". . . was a member of the British Israel World Federation and was a confident believer that the Anglo-Saxon races were the inheritors of the promises given through the prophets in the Bible to God's people, Israel, and some few years ago under the auspices of the above-named body addressed a large representative gathering in the Central Hall, Westminster, London."

P. JAMES BROOKE   The life and ministry of Pastor James Brooke is another mighty witness to the Pentecostal experience and the restoration of the Apostolic gifts to the body of Christ in the twentieth century. Born in the early 1880's, he was converted to Christ at an early age and held fellowship with the Baptist church. In 1905 he and Edith Hopkins were married and shared fifty years together until his passing in 1960. James Brooke became an elder and lay-preacher with the Baptist Chapel

in North East London and also served with the London City Mission. In 1910, he became the pastor of the Baptist Church, Cardigan Road, Bournemouth, England.

In his personal testimony contained in his book (c. 1943), *"Light On the Baptism of the Holy Spirit"*, he gave the following account. "Thirty-two years ago, while ministering at a Baptist Church in South of England, a yearning came into my soul for a closer walk with God. I longed for a fuller knowledge of His Word and a deeper experience of the power of God. Much prayer for this soul-hunger to be satisfied was made on my part to God our heavenly Father.

"During a vacation spent in London, I saw a notice of a meeting to be held. The subject of the address was to be *"The Baptism of the Holy Spirit."* With a friend I attended this meeting, and after the address, in response to the invitation, we went forward and knelt at the penitent form, desiring to have the wonderful experience of being baptized with the Holy Spirit.

"I went out after the meeting closed, telling the Lord that on His Word I believed that I had received. But the yearning remained; yes, an hunger of soul that could not be told was still mine. It seemed as though my soul would be torn asunder in the battle that raged within me.

"After three weeks of battling in the heavenlies, that is, in the spiritual realm, I realized there was a breaking down of the powers of darkness that hindered my receiving the Pentecostal blessing . . .One day, after having spent two hours in prayer, I said to a friend who was praying with me, "I cannot pray any longer, there is no more strength in me." "Just five minutes more," he replied.

"Those 'five minutes more' lengthened out into over two hours. But it was in the first five minutes of that time that the Holy Spirit came flooding into my soul with glory, and speaking through me in 'other tongues' as the Spirit gave utterance. Such praise in song, both in the language of the 'new tongue' and in mine own, broke forth from my lips, and in such beauty and power that I had never had nor thought could have been possible for me to utter."

Within a few weeks his wife had received the same glorious experience. Before long Pastor Brooke's ministry in the Baptist Church was terminated. He then moved his family to Swansea, South Wales in 1911 where he became the pastor of Bellvue Chapel. In Mrs. Brooke's account of their year or so stay there she said, "Tremendous days, I've

351

never seen the like of it. Every meeting was like a convention meeting. Crowds packed the church, and miracles and healings were taking place all the time."

One day while praying in his study, the Lord spoke to him and said, *"Prepare thyself for distant shores."* In February 1912, Pastor Brooke and his family set sail for South Africa where they labored for ten years in pastoral and missionary work. After returning to England in 1922, he built a church in the coastal town of Westcliff-On-Sea, Essex in obedience to the voice of the Lord. Up to this time, he had been one of the senior ministers of the Apostolic Faith Church. At this point Pastor Brooke with other ministers founded the **United Apostolic Faith Church** with headquarters in London. They would serve churches and missionary works in the United Kingdom, Canada, South Africa and elsewhere. Not long before his passing, he resigned as pastor of the local assembly at Tower Hall and Gospel Centre in London. He retained his responsibilities as General Overseer of the U.A.F.C. and editor of the **Pentecostal Times** monthly publication.

In his many years as General Overseer of the U.A.F.C. he traveled to South Africa to help establish churches and strengthen gospel mission centers. In 1946 and 1948, he went to Canada to help establish a church in the Toronto area. During his fifty years of ministry he wrote at least four small books, *"Light on the Baptism of the Holy Spirit," Light on Speaking in Other Tongues," The Prophetical Voice"* and *"Israel in the Last Days."* In his description of the latter named book he wrote, *"Great Britain and the U.S.A. identified as modern Israel. A much-discussed subject. The author describes how he came to a knowledge of this truth."*

He held to the Anglo-Israel point of view for the vast majority of his ministerial years. After his passing, his elder son Percy became the editor of the **Pentecostal Times** publication. In the Sept/Oct 1986 edition, Editor Percy J. Brooke re-affirmed the Anglo-Israel belief of the U.A.F.C. following Holiness preacher Maynard G. James' article *"Are the Jews all Israel?"* James was a staunch believer in this prophetic point of view as recorded in his biography, *"A Man on Fire"* by his son Paul James.

H.A. MAXWELL WHYTE   When recounting the rich history of the Canadian branch of the United Apostolic Faith Church, the life and ministry of Maxwell Whyte is most prominent. He was associated with the U.A.F.C. for many years of his ministry. In May 1978, he resigned from a 31 year pastorate of the church located at Scarborough, Ontario.

He was succeeded by his son, Stephen Whyte. While pastoring in Scarborough, a suburb of Toronto, he fellowshipped various Pentecostal brethren, who also attended his resignation celebration. It was held on the premises of the Christian Full Gospel television program, *100 Huntley Street*. After retiring from the Scarborough Assembly, Pastor and Mrs. Whyte went on an evangelistic tour of Southern Africa. He was greatly used of the Lord in the ministry of divine healing and deliverance from demonic oppression. While at Bethel Bible College in Johannesburg, the Lord confirmed His Word when a five year old girl took off her leg brace and ran to her astonished mother. The local pastor's wife who was suffering from severe back complications was healed and was able to remove her brace. Maxwell Whyte ministered in Pretoria, Verceniging, Boksburg, Durban and other cities including Cape Town where many were saved, baptized in the Holy Spirit and divinely healed. One outstanding meeting was held in the Assemblies of God Church in Pietermaritzburg in cooperation with other pastors where much was accomplished for the Lord's work in this united effort.

In his life and ministry Maxwell Whyte was a strong believer in the power of the blood of Jesus as the Christian's authority over all the power of the enemy. He wrote several books on the blood of Jesus and deliverance from demonic power which are still available through Whitaker House Publishers. They include *Demons and Deliverance, The Kiss of Satan, Dominion Over Demons, A Manual of Exorcism* and *The Power of the Blood.*

Maxwell Whyte also wrote a book entitled, *"Spiritual Aspects of the Kingdom of God,"* in which he clearly sets forth his commitment to the truth of the Anglo-Israel message of Scripture. The following quote is from the first chapter entitled, *The Bride of the Lamb.*

"It is the purpose of this article to SHOW FROM THE SCRIPTURES and the real identity of the Bride of Christ, for if we take the Word of God to mean exactly what it says - - and we do not spiritualize its obvious meaning, especially in its historical setting- -surely we shall arrive at the truth.

In the 19th chapter of Exodus, we have recorded the marriage of Jehovah to His bride, the Israel peoples whom He created to be His help-meet on earth, even as He had created a help-meet for Adam by taking one of his ribs from which He created Eve. From out of mankind, God took Abraham and from him He formed the nation of Israel - - HIS WIFE.

353

It is not our purpose now to study the sorry behavior of this FAITHLESS wife. But we do know that this Kingdom of God became split into the northern and southern houses of Israel, each with its own king. Sometimes, they even engaged in fratricidal wars, and in spite of the warnings of the prophets, they went further and further away into spiritual adultery until Jehovah was forced to cast them off and write them A BILL OF DIVORCE (Isaiah 50:1). From 741 to 580 B.C. the northern house was taken captive into Assyria and the southern house into Babylon.

Many assume that because God cast off His people so utterly, that this was the end of the story, and that the RELATIONSHIP BETWEEN THE LORD AND HIS WIFE WAS FINISHED. We feel sure that the following Scriptures will show how false this assumption is.

The first ten verses, of the 54th chapter of Isaiah deal with the restoration of God's people. They are especially addressed to northern Israel, who at the time of this prophecy were in dispersion (712 B.C.), while Judah was still in Palestine.

Thus, in verse 1, we read that northern Israel is counseled to sing because of her promised restoration, FOR MORE ARE THE CHILDREN OF THE DESOLATE (northern Israel) THAN THE CHILDREN OF THE MARRIED WIFE. (Judah still not cast off.)

She was to be encouraged to enlarge her tents or dwelling places, so that her seed might inherit the Gentiles. She was to fear, because the shame of her youth and the reproach of her widowhood would be forgotten.

Northern Israel fulfilled this by becoming the nation and company of nations (Great Britain and Dominions) and a great people (U.S.A.) as promised to Jacob (Genesis 35:11 and 48:19). Jehovah reassured her by saying, "For thy maker is thy Husband, the Lord of hosts is His Name, and thy Redeemer the Holy One of Israel; the God of the whole earth shall He be called "(Verse 5).Now, in Luke 1:68, we read that Jesus Christ is the Redeemer of Israel, and, in Isaiah 53:8, the prophet foretold that Jesus died for the transgressions of HIS PEOPLE ISRAEL. So, we see Jehovah, THE HUSBAND OF ISRAEL, is none other than Jesus Christ, the Redeemer of Israel!"

The Ministry of Maxwell Whyte was not limited to his church in Scarborough, but extended to various churches throughout North America. As a guest, he ministered at the Lake Hamilton Bible Camp in Arkansas, directed by Pastor Glen Miller. Pastor Miller was affiliated with the *Full Gospel Business Men's Fellowship International* from its inception and was a personal friend with its founder, Demos Shakarian.

Pastor Miller is also a believer in the Anglo-Israel truth. His testimony is found in a recent Campground publication, *"Voices From His Excellent Glory."* In the article *"That's Truth! That's Truth! That's Truth!* He tells how the Anglo-Israel truth was divinely revealed to him by the voice of God while standing in Westminster Abbey in London. In this article, which is subtitled, *"The So-Called Lost Ten Tribes of Israel-Thirteen"*, he gives the account of this supernatural revelation. He writes:

"I have always from my youth, heard about the ten (10) lost tribes and I have heard some say that they are the gypsies.

"However, an unusual happening in Westminster Abbey in London, England, when I was with the Full Gospel Business Men's airlift of some 750 men, that has since launched me to study the facts. In November of 1965, while a tour guide was telling us the history of the coronation chair and the stone under it which is Jacob's pillar or the stone of Scone, GOD spoke to me audibly. He said, "THAT'S TRUTH - THAT'S TRUTH - THAT'S TRUTH', three times over my left shoulder, in a very loud voice, which no one else seemed to hear. It felt like all the hair on my body was standing on end.

"This caused me to ponder, and begin studying what, "THAT'S TRUTH" is."

__EDWARD OASTLER STEWARD__   Edward Oastler Steward was born in Soham, a small rural town of Cambridgeshire, England in 1903 to Jane Oastler and Thomas William Steward. He was raised with his five sisters and three brothers (he was born sixth) in the village of Exning (near Newmarket, West Suffolk). Later in 1915 the family relocated to Swaythling, Southampton, where they continued in the Protestant faith, but as *Plymouth Brethren*.

At the age of 18, he began evangelical preaching. In 1926 at the age of 23 he joined the *Elim Foursquare Gospel Church*, which grew out of Principal George Jeffrey's Revival Campaign in Southampton. From then Steward took numerous preaching engagements and then married in 1928. In 1929 and 1930 he studied and graduated from Elim Bible College in London and was ordained a minister and for the next 20 years was a minister of various churches and saw numerous souls converted and many people miraculously healed.

In 1940, after deep research, personal study and soul-searching, he became firmly convinced of the Christian-Israel message. During the war he served as an Honorary Chaplain, Captain of a Fire-fighting Unit, and Shelter Warden. He also served on the board of Governors of the Paletine Schools (Blackpool) for two years.

In 1945 he was the founder-member with George Jeffreys (and others) of the Bible Pattern Church Fellowship; he was appointed a member of the first Advisory Council and for several years he was a member of the Coordinating Council. In 1946 he held evangelistic meetings in churches in France, which experienced many conversions and healings (especially in Nice). He also arranged and participated in George Jeffrey's Revival Campaign in Nice. In 1947 he attended the first World Conference of Pentecostal Churches in Zurich, Switzerland. In 1948 he spent seven weeks in Stockholm, Sweden and preached at many churches, preaching to over 3,000 people at the Filadelphia Church alone.

In 1950 he became a full-time lecturer for the *British-Israel World Federation*. He traveled over 300,000 miles delivering over 2,800 messages throughout Great Britain, Ireland, and the Channel Islands before retiring in 1969.

The foregoing testimonies of these Pentecostal Spirit filled men of God are further evidence of the widespread belief and acceptance of the Anglo-Israel message. By the simple fact that a pastor, evangelist or minister believed a certain truth and was widely accepted, clearly indicates that multiplied hundreds or thousands of laymen also believed that same truth in their areas of fellowship.

* * * * * * * *

THE WORDS OF OUR LORD
By Charles A. Jennings

The first recorded sermons ever preached by John the Baptist and Jesus were exactly the same. *"Repent, for the Kingdom of heaven is at hand."* Matt. 3:1; 4:17. All the parables spoken by our Lord in Matthew 13 are concerning the restoration of the mighty Kingdom of Israel that had once existed in Old Testament times. This Kingdom had consisted of a people that were the physical descendants of the family of Abraham, Isaac and Jacob/Israel.

During the times of the dispersions and captivities as recorded in the Old Testament, this family/kingdom was scattered, ruined and 'lost'! The New Testament word *'lost'* as used by our Lord in Matthew 10:6; 15:24; 18:11 does not mean 'no longer in existence' or 'impossible to be found,' but 'put away in punishment until the time of restoration.' Jesus stated that His mission was to go to the *'lost sheep of the house of Israel.'* This statement gave purpose and direction for the earthly ministry of our Lord and the continuing ministry of His disciples.

After following the Lord for over three years and hearing Him teach, His disciples knew well what He taught concerning the restoration of the Kingdom. One burning question which must be answered before their Master departed from them was: ***"Lord, wilt thou at this time restore again the Kingdom to Israel?"*** Acts 1:6. The disciples knew that this was one of the reasons for Israel's Husband/Redeemer coming to Zion. Even the Apostle James referred to this restoration in Acts 15:16 when he said, *"After this I will return, and will build again the tabernacle of David which is fallen down; and I will build again the ruins thereof, and I will set it up:"*

This restoration was and is to take place through the coming and work of the Holy Spirit. For the last one hundred years the Holy Spirit through many chosen vessels has identified the true family of Jacob/Israel and proclaimed the national message of the Kingdom, yet God's people have refused to hear. They have even despised the messengers.

It is time for the 'seventh angel company' to proclaim; *"The kingdoms of this world are become the kingdoms of our Lord, and of His Christ; and He shall reign for ever and ever"* Rev. 11:15. **Jesus is coming again** to sit upon *"the throne of His father David: and to reign over the house of Jacob forever; and of His kingdom there shall be no end"* Luke 1:32-33.

We believers today, in witness to the great men of God of yesteryear ask the burning question once asked by Isaiah the prophet: *"Who hath believed our report?"* We declare this grand message to Israel, those *"to whom the arm of the Lord has been revealed"* (Isa. 53:1).

MY TESTIMONY
By Charles A. Jennings

As further witness to the saving grace of God and the truthfulness of His Word, I add my testimony to the list of saints that have gone on before us. Along with my seven older siblings, I was fortunate to be born into a family ancestry which had been highly favored by Divine grace. My parents, Clarence G. and Mamie E. Jennings both gloriously experienced the life changing grace of Jesus Christ as young people in the 1920's while attending the Church of God. My mother's father, George Price was an early minister with the Church of God (Cleveland,

TN) and helped to blaze the Pentecostal message in the Carolina Piedmont area.

Our family has been blessed in knowing the reality of the healing power of God. In 1947, my father was instantly healed of a severe heart condition under the ministry of William Branham. As one among many in a fast moving prayer line under the tent, Brother Branham shook hands with my father and said; "God bless my brother." My father was healed and lived to be over 96 years old. In 1952, one of my sisters was instantly healed after being told by the doctors that she only had three days to live following twenty-eight months of serious illness. This miracle took place in the living room of our family home after a short season of prayer.

Being raised in a Godly home, a consciousness of Christian piety and reverence for sacred things prevailed throughout our family life. I experienced a salvation experience at the age of nine years old on a Sunday morning at the Revival Tabernacle Assembly of God Church in Miami, Florida, which our family was attending at the time. Spiritually maturing in a Pentecostal religious environment, I experienced the Baptism of the Holy Ghost at the age of seventeen.

My older teenage years were blessed with many wonderful Divine visitations in which the Lord was teaching me spiritual truth. One such visitation at the age of seventeen was a vision of a pipe which reached all the way to heaven through which the voice of God asked me the question; "Wonder if the United States is Israel?" It was immediately revealed to me the meaning and the answer to this question. In vision form I could see the godly Pilgrims and Puritans coming from Britain to establish this nation in righteousness. Somehow I had the reality of knowing that the people of Western European descent were the true House of Israel.

At the time, with little knowledge of the subject, I hid this truth in my heart for several years, including my time of ministerial training in an Assemblies of God college, when taught that this belief was a cult and a false doctrine. Yet in my inner man, I had the witness of the Spirit that the Anglo-Israel message was true.

In their ignorance, this message of the literal promises of the Abrahamic Covenant being fulfilled among the Anglo-Saxon and related people has been ridiculed by many Christian ministers and professors. In spite of Israel's blindness to her identity, the revelation of the New Covenant being made with the House of Israel and the House of Judah shall some day become a startling reality to the body of Christ and then to all the world.

When understood from a Biblical and historicist perspective, the Anglo-Israel message fits with all the great verities of Christianity. It offers answers that no other perspective gives and removes the blindness that has been cast over the eyes of all people.

Throughout Scripture, God's people Israel are known as sheep (Psa. 95:7;100:3; Matt.10:6;15:24). When Jesus, the blessed Savior came, He said; *"My sheep hear my voice, and I know them, and they follow me:"* (John 10:27).

BIBLICAL TRUTH -- NOT A CULT

Too often, Christian people accuse other Christian groups of being a cult without having a proper understanding of what a cult really is. Generally, they consider someone else of being cultish, but never themselves guilty of exhibiting any cult like traits. Intellectually dishonest persons consider other groups of being a cult who are simply different in belief and practice or believing something that the accuser does not understand. They often base their opinion on the unfounded prejudice of others and ignorantly use this accusation in an effort to discredit those they do not like in order to reaffirm their own doctrinal position.

Contrary to the mistaken accusation, the Anglo-Israel truth does not fit the description of a cult in any form or fashion. Some of the distinguishing marks of a cult are the following:

- A cult possesses and promotes a "sacred" book other than the Bible produced by its founder or followers. The Anglo-Israel truth has no "sacred" book other than the Bible, upon which its belief and practices are founded.

- A cult has an elevated earthly leader, even though they acknowledge the Lord Jesus Christ. This leader, whether dead or alive, demands obedience and allegiance and is usually the last word on any issue of doctrine or practice. This wonderful Kingdom truth has no Mary Baker Eddy or Joseph Smith.

- A cult always has an additional doctrine that must be believed or followed in word or practice in order to receive salvation. Usually this is simply salvation by works as opposed to the Biblical principle of salvation by Grace. Paul said, *"For by grace are ye saved through faith; and that not of yourselves: it is the gift of God: Not of works, lest any man should boast"* Eph. 2:8-9.

- A cult demands utter allegiance to its cause, its history, its leadership and fellow members. Usually this allegiance and obedience is in the area of inordinate control concerning the time, money and devotion of its members.

- A cult as a collective group and its members as individuals usually exude an attitude of spiritual elitism. They feel that they are in possession of secret or superior knowledge that non cult members do not have. Through the possession of this special knowledge they have been elevated to a higher plane of relationship with God and are therefore worthy of a greater reward in the afterlife.

- A cult may possess and practice secret oaths for membership initiation which puts its adherents under spiritual and psychological bondage to the group. Even secret passwords, pieces of clothing or a prescribed form of greeting among members may be practiced.

The truth of the Anglo-Israel message, the ministers and laity that believe this Biblical perspective do not meet any of the above descriptions of a cult. The thousands of people of the past and present that believe this Gospel of the Kingdom have been members of a wide range of Christian, Protestant denominations and groups. Many prominent true men of God have believed this wonderful truth and have incorporated it into their prophetic perspective of Scripture. They have been true Biblical scholars that have kept the proper focus of Christ in their message and have been instrumental in leading thousands of people to a personal knowledge of salvation by grace through faith. The major doctrinal difference between those who adhere to the Anglo-Israel perspective and other evangelicals is in the areas of history and prophecy. The correct identification of the historical people of Israel determines the correct identification of those same people in modern day fulfillment of prophecy. Being that Anglo-Israel believers have much in common with other evangelicals in the areas of salvation, divine healing, the ministry of the Holy Spirit and many other Biblical doctrines, we have been compatible in fellowship and ministry without contention. We seek the good of the whole Body of Christ.